Peirce and Contemporary Thought

**MARY AND JOHN GRAY LIBRARY
LAMAR UNIVERSITY**

Purchased
with the
Student Library Use Fee

PEIRCE
and
Contemporary Thought

PHILOSOPHICAL INQUIRIES

edited by

KENNETH LAINE KETNER

Fordham University Press

New York

1995

Copyright © 1995 by Fordham University Press
All rights reserved.
LC 94-38634
ISBN 0-8232-1553-9
ISSN 1073-2764

American Philosophy Series, no. 1
Vincent M. Colapietro, Editor
Vincent G. Potter (1929-1994), Founding Editor

Library of Congress Cataloging-in-Publication Data

Peirce and contemporary thought : philosophical inquiries / edited by Kenneth Laine Ketner.
    p.   cm. — (American philosophy series : no. 1)
    ISBN 0-8232-1553-9 : $35.00
    1. Peirce, Charles S. (Charles Sanders), 1839-1914.   I. Ketner, Kenneth Laine.   II. Series.
    B945.P44P44   1995
    191—dc20   dc20   94-38634
                                              CIP

Printed in the United States of America

To
Vincent G. Potter

Individual action is a means not our end. Individual pleasure is not our end; we are all putting our shoulders to the wheel for an end that none of us can catch more than a glimpse at—that which the generations are working out.

CONTENTS

Abbreviations	ix
Preface	xi

I PEIRCE AND LOGIC

1. Peirce's Continuum *Hilary Putnam*	1
2. Peirce's Logic *W. V. Quine*	23

3. Peirce's Underestimated Place in the History of Logic:
   A Response to Quine
   Randall R. Dipert
	32

4. Induction According to Peirce *Isaac Levi*	59
5. On Peirce on Induction: A Response to Levi *Joseph S. Ullian*	94

II PEIRCE AND SCIENCE

6. Peirce on the Validation of Science *Nicholas Rescher*	103
7. Peirce on the Reliability of Science: A Response to Rescher *Cornelius J. Delaney*	113
8. Charles S. Peirce, Mathematician *Carolyn Eisele*	120

9. Peirce at the Intersection of Mathematics and Philosophy:
   A Response to Eisele
   Helena M. Pycior
	132

10. Peirce and History of Science *Joseph W. Dauben*	146
11. Discussion: Peirce and the History of Science *Peter Skagestad*	196

III PEIRCE AND SEMEIOSIS

12. Unlimited Semeiosis and Drift: Pragmaticism vs. *"Pragmatism"* 205
    Umberto Eco

13. Indexicality 222
    Thomas A. Sebeok

14. Peirce and Communication 243
    Jürgen Habermas

15. A Response to Habermas 267
    Klaus Oehler

16. Peirce on Language and Reference 272
    Risto Hilpinen

17. History as Theory: One Linguist's View 304
    Michael Shapiro

IV PEIRCE AND METAPHYSICS

18. Peirce and Idealism 315
    David Savan

19. A Response to Savan 329
    Demetra Sfendoni-Mentzou

20. Peirce and Religion: Between Two Forms of Religious Belief 339
    Charles Hartshorne

21. A Response to Hartshorne 356
    Vincent G. Potter

22. Transcendental Semeiotic and Hypothetical Metaphysics of Evolution: A Peircean or Quasi-Peircean Answer to a Recurrent Problem of Post-Kantian Philosophy 366
    Karl-Otto Apel

23. Metaphysics, Science, and Self-Control A Response to Apel 398
    Christopher Hookway

Bibliography 417

List of Contributors 439

ABBREVIATIONS

Throughout this volume standard editions of Peirce's works will be referenced according to the following abbreviation scheme.

CB   A Comprehensive Bibliography of the Published Works of Charles Sanders Peirce. Ed. Kenneth Laine Ketner, et al. 2nd rev. ed. Bowling Green: Philosophy Documentation Center, 1986.

CP   Collected Papers of Charles Sanders Peirce. Edd. C. Hartshorne, P. Weiss, and A. Burks. 8 vols. Cambridge: Harvard University Press, 1935, 1958. References will be cited by volume and paragraph number: "CP 5.119" would refer to volume 5, paragraph 119.

HP   Historical Perspectives on Peirce's Logic of Science. Ed. Carolyn Eisele. 2 vols. The Hague: Mouton, 1985. References are to HP followed by numbers for volume and page.

MF   The Published Works of Charles Sanders Peirce. Bowling Green: Philosophy Documentation Center, 1986. a large microfiche edition of all of Peirce's lifetime publications, cataloged in A Comprehensive Bibliography of the Published Works of Charles Sanders Peirce, see CB.

MS   The Charles S. Peirce Papers, microfilm edition, Cambridge: Harvard University Library, Photographic Service, 1966. References to this film set of Peirce's unpublished papers held in the Houghton Library at Harvard will employ the numbering system for manuscripts developed by R. S. Robin in his Annotated Catalogue of the Papers of Charles S. Peirce. Amherst: University of Massachusetts Press, 1967, as emended by Robin in "The Peirce Papers: A Supplementary Catalogue," Transactions of the Charles S. Peirce Society, 7 (1971), 37-57. For example, "MS 325, 3" indicates Robin's catalogue manuscript number 325, page 3.

N   Charles S. Peirce: Contributions to The Nation. Edd. K. L. Ketner and J. E. Cook, 4 vols. Lubbock: Texas Tech University Press, 1975-1987. References are given as N followed by numbers for volume and page number.

NEM   The New Elements of Mathematics by Charles S. Peirce. Ed. Carolyn Eisele, 4 vols. in five. The Hague: Mouton, 1976. References are abbreviated as NEM followed by volume and page numbers.

PW   Semiotic and Significs: The Correspondence Between Charles S. Peirce and Victoria Lady Welby. Ed. C. S. Hardwick, Bloomington: Indiana University Press, 1977.

RLT   Reasoning and the Logic of Things. Ed. Kenneth Laine Ketner. Cambridge: Harvard University Press, 1992.

W   Writings of Charles S. Peirce: A Chronological Edition. Edd. Max H. Fisch et al. 4 vols. to date. Bloomington: Indiana University Press, 1982—. Citations will be given as W followed by numbers for volume and page number.

PREFACE

Often a length of time is required after the passing of a master thinker before civilization acknowledges him or her as someone of permanent importance. This process is now occurring in regard to Charles Sanders Peirce eighty years after his death in 1914. This book, with twenty-three essays by distinguished scholars of our day, is strong support for that truth, as is the entire international congress from which these presentations arose and those of other scholars in attendance. Furthermore, this volume (and others like it from the 1989 Congress now appearing[1]) forms a bulwark against a number of previously popular but erroneous opinions about Peirce and his work.

Perhaps the most unfortunate of these is what in 1976 (at the first international Peirce Congress) I called the doctrine of Peirce's interesting failure.[2] Briefly stated, this is the view that Peirce's work was a regrettable failure, but that there are a few nuggets within it which can be brought out of the mud and shined up to some purpose. It might be an interesting exercise to compare the state of Peirce studies in 1976 with conditions today. A closely related notion sometimes advanced is the slogan that "we must go beyond Peirce, who after all was but a mere precursor." While the ideas of honoring pioneers and of seeking further progress surely appeal to all scientific intelligences, it is poor economy of research to dash ahead without being fully aware of the progress made by one's ancestors. That is to say, how can we go beyond Peirce if we have not yet caught up to the waypoints he reached? That Peirce was ahead of his time, and in some respects is still ahead of our time, is a theme one finds recurring in serious Peirce scholarship.

Yes, there have been and still are barriers in the way of our access to Peirce. In past decades only those persons who made the effort to work with Peirce's manuscripts could really appreciate the full greatness of his accomplishments. It is pleasing to survey nowadays the continually growing numbers of editions of his previously generally inaccessible work, based upon the steady and persistent work of careful scholars. As this process comes to its inevitable fruition, yet another myth will fall into disreputability: the almost ritual chant that he published only one book, that being his *Photometric Researches*, which was, after all, merely a work within science and not philosophy, and an outdated work in science in the bargain. But such a claim can no longer be sustained.[3]

Another irony is connected with *Photometric Researches* and Peirce's other scientific publications. This interpretative approach has, I think, also had its day; it can be summarized as the view that Peirce was a philosopher who dabbled in science merely to earn a living. In other words, Peirce's activity in science was seen as merely something that took him away from his favored task of pursuing philosophy. This view is often associated with the failure thesis; that is, it is easy to see how he failed in philosophy since he could not devote enough time to it because he had to "waste" his efforts in science as an occupation. Such an approach is almost exactly upside down in relation to the truth of the matter. Max Fisch and Carolyn Eisele have carefully established that truth in their work over the years. Peirce's philosophy was a science in his eyes, which grew out of his general devotion to and pursuit of science as the way of life of a community of persons devoted to the ideals of scientific intelligence.[4] It is often debated whether Peirce had a system of philosophy. I think that is the wrong question. What he had was a system of science, in which mathematics, philosophy, value theory, logic/semeiotic,[5] metaphysics, and special sciences all had a place and a function.[6]

His work in science was carefully planned to develop his abilities as an original researcher in more than one field so he could pursue his real scientific speciality, the study of methods, with the benefit of diverse firsthand scientific experience. Once one realizes that his system was one of science focused upon methods, then the whole thing fits together about as well as any system ever could.

A literary device[7] that has sometimes been used as an interpretative guide for understanding Peirce's efforts is the image of a wasp in a bottle, imprisoned because its programmed and robotic responses continue to focus its efforts against unyielding walls while it is incapable of changing directions to escape through the open bottle mouth. Lee Auspitz has written a masterful review of recent Peirce scholarship which includes items arising from the 1989 Peirce Congress as well as from other sources.[8] There he argues with convincing evidence—to continue the literary device—that there was an organism in the bottle well enough. Yet instead of being a wasp, a poor robotic being, the creature so entombed was a non-robotic self-correcting organism of some kind which has recently emerged from the crystal enclosure *that was placed around it*. If we think this revised image through, we might agree that it represents but a corollary of a larger theorem that Peirce loved to quote: Truth forced to earth will rise again.

* * *

In acknowledging the many debts to persons who aided the 1989 Peirce Congress to come into being, it is fitting to begin by listing some dear colleagues who are no longer with us: Edward C. Moore, David Savan, and Vincent G. Potter.

Earlier versions of the essays in this volume were presented in the plenary sessions of The Charles S. Peirce Sesquicentennial International Congress which opened at Harvard University on September fifth, 1989, and concluded on the tenth, the one-hundred-fiftieth anniversary of Peirce's birthday. The Congress had been convened by the Charles S. Peirce Society, based on an idea by Michael Shapiro. The organizing institutions were Harvard University and Texas Tech University. The Congress was guided by an Organizing Committee consisting of the following persons: Hilary Putnam (President of the Congress), Kenneth Laine Ketner (Chairperson of the Organizing Committee), Hanna Buczynska-Garewicz (U.S.A. and Poland), Gerard Deledalle (France), Umberto Eco (Italy), Takashi Fujimoto (Japan), Susan Haack (United Kingdom), Jaako Hintikka (U.S.A. and Finland), Christian J. W. Kloesel (U.S.A.), Dan Nesher (Israel), Klaus Oehler (Federal Republic of Germany), Nicholas Rescher (U.S.A.), David Savan (Canada),

Israel Scheffler (U.S.A.), and Michael Shapiro (U.S.A.). Congress Administrative Assistant was Joyce Abbott (Division of Continuing Education) in Lubbock; in Cambridge, Alexandra Collins (Programs in Professional Education) was in charge of local arrangements. Congress headquarters was Sever Hall on Harvard Yard, formerly the site of the residence of Professor Benjamin Peirce Jr., where Charles grew to adulthood.

The Congress was supported by the following individuals and institutions: The Claude Ventry Bridges Memorial Fund (Texas Tech University), The National Endowment for the Humanities, The Charles S. Peirce Foundation, The Charles S. Peirce Society, The College of Arts and Sciences (Texas Tech University), Division of Continuing Education (Texas Tech University), Institute for Studies in Pragmaticism (Texas Tech University), The Library (Texas Tech University), Department of Philosophy (Harvard University), Programs in Professional Education (Harvard University), Mr. W. B. Rushing (Lubbock, Texas), The Mary Baker Rumsey Foundation (Lubbock, Texas), and the Society for the Advancement of American Philosophy. During the five days of its existence, the Congress was host to approximately 500 scholars from 26 different nations.

K.L.K.

NOTES

1. *Peirce and Law: Issues in Pragmatism, Legal Realism, and Semiotics*, ed. Roberta Kevelson (New York: Peter Lang, 1991); *Reasoning and the Logic of Things: The Cambridge Conferences Lectures of 1898 by Charles Sanders Peirce*, ed. Kenneth Laine Ketner (Cambridge, Mass.: Harvard University Press, 1992); *Charles S. Peirce and the Philosophy of Science—Papers from the Harvard Sesquicentennial Congress*, ed. Edward C. Moore (Tuscaloosa: University of Alabama Press, 1993); *From Time and Chance to Consciousness: Studies in the Metaphysics of Charles Peirce*, edd. Edward C. Moore and Richard S. Robin (Oxford: Berg, 1994); *Peirce and Value Theory: On Peircean Ethics and Aesthetics*, ed. Harman Parret (Amsterdam: John Benjamins, 1994); *Living Doubt: Essays Concerning the Epistemology of Charles S. Peirce*, ed. Guy DeBrock and Menno Hulswit (Dordrecht: Kluwer Academic, 1994); *Peirce's Doctrine of Signs: Theory, Applications, and*

Connections, ed. Vincent Colapietro and Thomas Olshewsky (Berlin: Mouton de Gruyter, to appear 1994); *Studies in the Logic of Charles Sanders Peirce*, edd. Nathan Hauser and Don D. Roberts (Bloomington: Indiana University Press, to appear 1995); *Religious Dimensions of Peirce's Thought*, ed. Arthur F. Stewart (Beaumont, Tex.: Lamar University Center for Philosophical Studies, to appear 1995/1996); *Contemporary Essays on Charles S. Peirce* (Beaumont, Tex.: Lamar University Center for Philosophical Studies, to appear 1995/1996).

2. Kenneth Laine Ketner, "Peirce as an Interesting Failure?" in *Proceedings of the C. S. Peirce Bicentennial International Congress*, ed. K. L. Ketner et al. (Lubbock: Texas Tech University Press, 1981), pp. 55-58.

I have often been asked why the Bicentennial Peirce Congress preceded the Sesquicentennial Peirce Congress. The 1976 Bicentennial was of the birth of the United States of America, not of Charles Peirce. The Congress of 1976 was held in Amsterdam under the auspices of the United States Ambassador to the Netherlands as his official Bicentennial event. It was appropriate to do so in view of the long friendship between The Netherlands and the United States, and in view of the well-known intellectual openness of Nederlanders.

3. See the preface to *A Comprehensive Bibliography* for an incomplete list of other books by Peirce published during his lifetime.

4. For a discussion of these matters in Peirce's own words, see the chapter on Peirce in *Classical American Philosophy*, ed. John J. Stuhr (New York: Oxford University Press, 1987).

5. In his mature efforts, Peirce identified logic with semeiotic. By the way, his preferred spelling for the name of this part of his work was not 'semiotics,' but 'Semeiotic' or 'semeiotic', a term which is pronounced in English rather like the related term in German, '*Semiotik*.' It has generally become customary among Peirce scholars, in accordance with the principles of his Ethics of Terminology, to refer to Peirce's relevant efforts as semeiotic (the study of semeiosis or sign action, as opposed to dynamic action), whereas the term 'semiotics' is often used to describe other ways of addressing a similar set of problems. And contrary to one form of the "interesting failure" thesis—namely that Peirce launched no enduring school of thought (another obvious counterexample of course is pragmaticism)—Peircean semeiotic is a lively and growing tradition today, one that was clearly founded by Peirce.

6. This thesis is eloquently defended by Frances Williams Scott in "C. S. Peirce's System of Science," Ph.D. diss. Texas Tech University, 1985, chaps. 1–4.

7. Literature was unfortunately not represented among the subjects directly addressed during the Congress. But there are some interesting recent works discussing Peirce's contributions even in this area: Michael

Cabot Haley, *The Semeiosis of Poetic Metaphor* (Bloomington: Indiana University Press, 1988); Joel Weinsheimer, "The Realism of C. S. Peirce, or How Homer and Nature Can Be the Same," *American Journal of Semiotics*, 2 (1983), 209-24 (this article is part of a special issue on Peirce); *A Thief of Peirce* (University Press of Jackson, Mississippi, to appear 1995).

8. Josiah Lee Auspitz, "The Wasp Leaves the Bottle," *The American Scholar* (Autumn 1994), 602-18.

I

Peirce and Logic

1
Peirce's Continuum

Hilary Putnam

IN THE EIGHT LECTURES that Peirce delivered near Harvard Square early in 1898, at 168 Brattle Street, entitled *Reasoning and the Logic of Things* (RLT), under the auspices of "The Cambridge Conferences," he said that he would like to call his metaphysics Synechism because "it rests on the study of continuity" (MS 948, 31).[1] Yet Peirce's own notion of continuity, or, rather, of the continuum, is not the one that became standard in the course of the nineteenth and twentieth centuries. Understanding Peirce's conception of the continuum is essential to understanding this metaphysical system, which he said he had spent the previous fifteen years in developing.[2] If this topic is more technical than one might expect, I have at least the excuse that Peirce himself, when he lectured to the Cambridge Conferences, would have liked to be much more technical than he was allowed to be. Writing to James, who persuaded him (no doubt wisely) not to make the lectures full of technical logic, Peirce complained:

"My dear William:

I accept all your conditions.
I have no doubt you gauge the capacity of your students rightly. It agrees with all I hear and the little I have seen of Cambridge, though the method of graphs has proved quite easy to New Yorkers, whose minds are stimulated by New York life. . . .
My philosophy, however, is not an 'idea' with which I 'brim over'; it is a serious research to which there is no royal road, and the part of it which is most closely connected with formal logic is by far the easiest and least intricate. People who cannot reason exactly (which alone *is* reasoning), simply cannot understand my philosophy,—neither the process, methods, nor results. The neglect of logic in Cambridge is plainly absolute. My philosophy,

and all philosophy worth attention, reposes entirely upon the theory of logic. It will, therefore, be impossible for me to give any idea of the nature either of my philosophy or of any other of any account . . ." [quoted in RLT 26].

I like to think, therefore, that I may be about to do the sort of thing that would have pleased Peirce himself. Peirce's "metaphysical speculations," as he called them, are characterized by enormous originality and profundity in conception combined with precision in technical detail, and they cannot be understood without reconstructing the detail. But I assume that most of my readers are not mathematicians, and since with some at least the mathematics learned in school may be "rusty," let me begin by very briefly recapitulating what one learns about the continuum—that is, about the *line*—in elementary mathematics.

The conception of the line which developed during the nineteenth century and became virtually the exclusive mathematical conception in the twentieth century, or at least the exclusive conception until the recent appearance of something called "Non-Standard Analysis," is that the line is isomorphic to the real numbers. So, let me recall what the real numbers are.

First of all, we must remember what the rational numbers are. A rational number is what in ordinary language we call a fraction, say 2/3 or –31/10. The negatives of the rational numbers are also rational, and so is zero. Real numbers are simply the rational numbers together with all the numbers that can be expressed as the limits of sequences of rational numbers.[3] The square root of two, for example, is the limit of the sequence 1, 1 + 4/10, 1 + 41/100, 1 + 414/1000, . . . and is thus a real number, as are all the numbers one can express in decimal notation, whether the number of digits after the decimal point be finite or infinite.

Descartes taught us to use letters of the alphabet such as x, y, z, etc., to stand for the lengths of line segments, whether those lengths be rational or not, and, perhaps as a result of this, the assumption gradually grew up that there is a complete isomorphism between the system of points on the line and the system of real numbers. Indeed, mathematicians often refer to the system of real numbers as "the real line." Peirce, however, decisively rejected the idea that the geometrical line, as I shall call it, is isomorphic with the system of real numbers. And it is Peirce's conception of the geometrical line that I shall be discussing, although the discussion will require us to take a look at Peirce's set theory and at his metaphysics of possibility as well.

Although I doubt that his view was the same as Peirce's, it may be useful to point out that a great philosopher-logician of our time expressed doubt about the isomorphism of the real numbers and the geometrical line. Kurt Gödel remarked (in a short unpublished note I was shown a number of years ago) that, at least intuitively, if you divide the geometrical line at a point, you would expect that the two halves of the line would be mirror images of each other. Yet, this is not the case if the geometrical line is isomorphic to the real numbers.

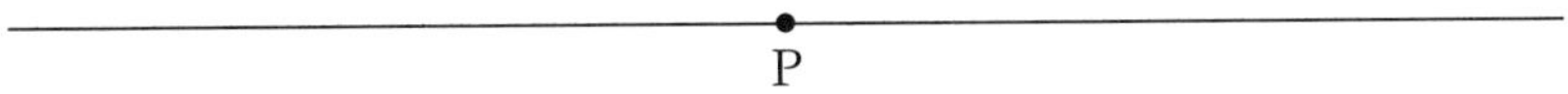

P

FIGURE 1

A division of the real numbers into two sections, say, a left section L and a right section R, is called a "Dedekind Cut."[4] The term is also applied to divisions of the rational numbers with the following four properties. Since it is supposed to correspond to a division of the line, it has the properties that

(1) L and R are not empty;
(2) if a number belongs to L, then so does every smaller number;
(3) if a number belongs to R, then so does every bigger number;
(4) every number belongs to exactly one of the two sections.

A theorem, which I shall call the Dedekind Cut Theorem, says that no matter how the Dedekind Cut is made, it is always the case that *either* the left section L has a greatest member *or* the right section R has a least member (but of course not both, since then neither section would contain the numbers between the greatest member of L and the least member of R). The two halves of a Dedekind Cut—an arbitrary "division" of the real numbers—are not mirror images of each other. For if they were mirror images, then if L has no greatest member, then R should have *no* least member (which is impossible by the Dedekind Cut Theorem), and if L does have a greatest member, then R should *also* have a least member (which is also impossible, as I just remarked). If the geometrical line *is* isomorphic to the real number system, then when we divide the line at P, we must either include the point P itself in the right half of the division (but not in the left half, since a "division" is an *exclusive* affair) or include the point P itself in the left half of the division (but not in the right half). Then one of the "half lines" created by the division will have an endpoint and the other will be an "open" half line— a half line with no endpoint—and the two half lines will not be mirror images.

But how could Gödel have thought that the geometrical line might fail to obey the Dedekind Cut Theorem? I cannot answer with confidence, but there is a very old view, which I am sure was known to Gödel, that was very likely the view he had in mind. This is the Aristotelian view that points are simply conceptual divisions of the line.

The Aristotelian Conception of the Line

At first blush, it does not seem that Peirce could have had an Aristotelian conception of the line, since he did speak in at least one place of the line as "a collection of points." Later on, I will argue that, apart from terminology, Peirce's view is broadly Aristotelian, although it has many elements that could not have been present in Aristotle's, and that what made it possible for Peirce to incorporate Aristotelian elements in his view is a certain conception that Peirce had of the nature of "collections." But that is getting ahead of my story. Let me stick for a moment with Aristotle. If we adopt his view, the line is an irreducible geometrical object, not a collection of more elementary objects. If I divide a line into two parts, that is what I do: I divide the line into two parts. And the two parts are mirror images of each other. But the question "To which half does the point of division belong?" makes no sense on the Aristotelian view.[5] For him, points do not *belong* to lines, although they *lie* on them; that is, they are divisions of them (and also terminations of them, in the case of line segments and curves with endpoints). To elaborate what I take to be Aristotle's view in a way that will facilitate comparison with Peirce's, consider not a line but a line interval (Figure 2A):

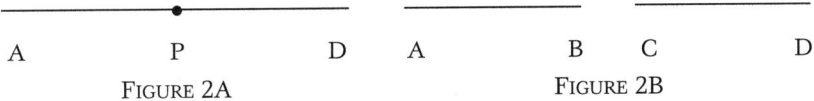

A   P   D   A   B   C   D
FIGURE 2A   FIGURE 2B

Suppose we divide the line interval at a point P and then separate the two broken halves by moving the right half a short distance to the right (Figure 2B). This moving of a line segment to the right must be thought of, not, as it is on the modern conception, as a one-one mapping of one collection of points onto another collection of points, of course, but as a primitive and irreducibly geometrical transformation, as it presumably was for Euclid. And in Figure 2A the endpoints A and D are to be regarded, not as *members* of the line segment AD, but simply as loci distinguished by the fact that an object we have constructed or considered *ends there*. What about Figure 2B? The left half of the original segment AD (which has not been moved) still has two endpoints. In the Aristotelian conception, there is no such thing as an "open" line interval; a line interval by the mere fact of existing as a line interval "defines," as it were, its endpoints. They are abstract properties of the line interval itself, and the notion of a line interval with no endpoints is senseless. Now, look at the right half of the original segment AD, which has become the right-hand segment CD. The endpoints of this segment are again abstract properties of the line segment itself, not "members" of the line. Where did C come from? Well, C was originally the point of division of the two halves of AD; that is to say, C was originally P. But B, the right-hand endpoint of the left half, is the original P. Dividing and separating the line segments has had the effect of dividing the point P into two points, or, if you like, performing this geometrical transformation has "mapped" the original point P onto two points: it is its own image under the transformation, but, equally, its image may be said to be C.

To use the language that Peirce used about such a construction in the third[6] of his lectures (RLT) (MS 439, 27), the point P has "become" the two points B,C.

Although what Peirce said about this sort of case makes sense on the Aristotelian view, there is another case that Peirce considered (MS 439, 27) which appears to make no sense on that view.[7] Imagine again that we start with a line interval, and instead of dividing the line in the middle, we simply take the right-hand endpoint and move it a short distance to the right, thus:

——————————————— •

FIGURE 3

This construction, which did make sense for Peirce, would seem not to make sense for an Aristotelian, for it treats the point not as an abstract property of the line but as a real geometrical part of the line. For Peirce this was also a case of one point's "becoming two points." But it is time to let Peirce speak for himself.

THE ODD BEHAVIOR OF PEIRCEAN POINTS

In MS 439 (the draft of the third Cambridge Conferences Lecture[8] on which I am relying), Peirce said a number of things that sound completely bizarre to today's mathematical sensibility, and then challenged anyone who might think he is crazy to show that he had actually contradicted himself. What is worse, it looks very easy to show that he did indeed contradict himself.

According to Peirce, if I reverse the transformation shown in Figure 2A–2B, then the two points B and C will become "one single point" again. Now, this much an Aristotelian will say too. But an Aristotelian would not say that B and C might *keep their order* after they have "become one single point" again. Peirce said (MS 439, 27-28) that one point

might burst into any discrete multitude of points whatever, and they would all have been one point before the explosion. Points might fly off, in multitude and order like all the real irrational quantities from 0 to 1; and they *might* all have had that order of succession in the line and yet all have been at one point in the line. Men will say this is self-contradictory. It is not so. If it be so prove it. The apparatus of the logic of relatives is a perfect means of demonstrating anything to be self-contradictory that really is so, but that apparatus not only refuses to pronounce this self-contradictory, but it demonstrates, on the contrary, that it is not so.

Well, suppose just two points fly off in the "explosion." Let B and C be the two points that were "one point before the explosion." This explosion might be imagined to happen, for example, by just the transformation depicted in Figure 2B, the case in which one point has "become two." The order of B and C after the explosion is that B is to the left of C and C is not to the left of B. Suppose B and C had "that order of succession in the line" before they flew apart (when they "have been at one point"). That is to suppose that B and C had that order even in Figure 2A, when B and C "have been at" the one point P. Then at that time the following was the case (read "xLy" as "x is to the left of y"):

$$BLC \ \& \ -CLB \ \& \ C = B$$

But in Predicate Calculus with Identity this *is* a contradiction, which is certainly a part of Peirce's Logic of Relatives. Had Peirce then simply lost his marbles in 1898?

First of all, we should be suspicious of the symbolization of the inference that if C and B were "at one point," then at that time it was the case that C = B. For consider the following statements: India is larger than Pakistan and Pakistan is not larger than India, and Pakistan and India stood in that relation when they were still one country. If I symbolize (what I take to be a consequence of) that statement in the following way (read i for India, p for Pakistan, and "xLy" as "x is larger than y"):

$$iLp \ \& \ -pLi \ \& \ i = p$$

then I have a contradiction in the Logic of Relatives. But, clearly, it was true in 1940 that what we now call India and Pakistan were one country, and that India was larger than Pakistan. What

"A and B are one country" means in such a sentence is that A and B are both parts of one country. This is an equivalence relation, but it is not the relation of identity. Once we see that "India and Pakistan were one country before 1940" does not (in such a use) mean that India and Pakistan were identical in 1940, then we see that the statements about India and Pakistan are consistent.

Similarly, if we suppose that what we ordinarily call a "point" can in some sense have *parts*—and I am going to argue that this is what Peirce believed—then the "contradiction" between Peirce's statements also disappears. B and C are separate *point parts* that have become separate points as the result of my moving the line segment CD. Before that line segment was moved, on the interpretation of Peirce's view which I am proposing, they were parts of what we ordinarily call one point but they had the order that B was to the left of C but not vice versa.[9]

How can I justify putting the notion of a "point part" into Peirce's mouth when he did not explicitly use any such notion?

Infinitesimals and Peirce

Although he did not make it explicit in RLT, we know from his mathematical writings that Peirce believed in the existence of infinitesimals. Indeed, he said things in a number of places in these Lectures[10] which directly imply the existence of infinitesimals, including geometric infinitesimals, that is to say, line intervals whose length is not zero but is less than any positive real length whatsoever.

Infinitesimals were indeed standard in mathematics, but their use gradually died out during the nineteenth century. As the result of the work of Abraham Robinson (1966) and others, it has been revised, and we now have a well-developed theory called Non-Standard Analysis which can be used to construct models for mathematics in which infinitesimals really do exist.

But let me explain what bearing the existence of infinitesimals has on what I have been discussing. Suppose that somewhere on the line there is an infinitesimal segment, that is, a segment with endpoints AB whose length is infinitesimal. Let P be any other point on the line. By the axioms of Euclidean geometry, it is possible to find two points, P' and P", such that P' is to the left of P and P" is to the right of P and the intervals P'P and PP" are congruent to the interval AB. In short, if there is even one infinitesimal segment on the line, then there are infinitesimal segments beginning/ending with any point whatsoever. The line has the same structure in all its parts. In Non-Standard Analysis we say that two points P and Q whose distance is infinitesimal are "identical modulo the infinitesimals," and we symbolize this by using a wiggly equals sign: P ≈ Q. If P is a point, the collection of all points Q such that P ≈ Q is called the *monad* of P. It can be shown that every point[11] has to lie in the monad of a "standard" point, that is, a point whose distance from the origin[12] is a (standard) real number.[13]

Now, I suggest the following interpretation of the supposedly contradictory passage I quoted from Peirce's Third Lecture. Suppose that Peirce's view there was that what we ordinarily call "points" are really monads. Although this does not account for everything that Peirce said there, it does remove the appearance of "self-contradiction" to which Peirce himself alluded. In accordance with my hypothesis about what Peirce meant there, in what follows I will often refer to the individual points on a line as "point parts," and I will refer to monads as "points." In this language, what Peirce was telling us is that within a single point one can find at least **c** different point parts, where **c** is the power of the set of real numbers. This is true, because if there is even one infinitesimal interval AB, then for every positive real number r, there is an infinitesimal interval whose length is r times the length of AB. (Proof of this requires certain geometric assumptions, of course.) It is easy to show that within one monad one can find a set of points (point parts) which is ordered exactly as the real numbers between 0 and 1 are ordered—and this, according to the interpretation advanced, is exactly what Peirce claimed!

What Peirce was doing, then, was first imagining a transformation as the result of which these point parts fly apart, without changing their relative order, that is, they are mapped onto distinct points (distinct monads) having the order type of the real numbers between 0 and 1; and Peirce was saying that even before the transformation, that is, even when the point parts were parts of a single line (were "at" a single point) they had that same order. On my proposed reconstruction, he was quite right in claiming that there is no contradiction in this point of view.

I return to the question: How do we know that Peirce really did believe in the existence of *geometric* infinitesimals? Well, the Third Lecture of his Cambridge Conferences Lectures clearly implies their existence, although Peirce did not draw the conclusion for his lay audience. For, in a part of the lecture not yet cited (MS 439, 28), Peirce insisted that the cardinal number of the points on the line is much greater than **c**; that is, he claimed that the points on the line are of a higher order of infinity than the real numbers. This implies the existence of non-standard points on the line, and hence of infinitesimals.

Peirce referred to the infinite cardinals of Georg Cantor. (He remarked that Cantor's work became generally known only after 1890.) Following Cantor, Peirce defined what it is for two collections to have the same cardinality, and he gave Cantor's proof that the set of all subsets of a given set is of a higher cardinality than the set itself. He introduced Cantor's term "denumerable" for an infinite collection that has the same cardinality as the set of all integers. It was also known from Cantor's work that the set of all real numbers is of the same cardinality as the set of all collections of integers, so by Cantor's proof the set of all real numbers is non-denumerable, or, as Peirce said, "abnumerable."

The set theory that Peirce informally presented in Lectures Three and Eight of his Cambridge Conferences Lectures has points of resemblance to both Zermelo's and von Neumann's. Like both of these, it seems to envisage[14] a universe of sets arranged in cumulative types (cumulative because, unlike Russell's types, each type—or "rank," to use von Neumann's term—in Zermelo-Frankel-von Neumann set theory includes all the lower ones). For the purpose of understanding Peirce's lectures, we might think of the individuals as the finite cardinal numbers (the "finite multitudes," in Peirce's terminology). Call the collection of all the finite multitudes N, and take N to be rank zero. Then the union of the set of all subsets of N—that is, the collection of all collections of finite multitudes—with N itself would be rank one; and for n greater than zero, the set of all subsets of rank n would be rank $n+1$. Rank zero is denumerable; rank one has the cardinal that I have called **c** and Cantor called $2^{aleph\text{-}null}$; and, in general, rank $n+1$ has the cardinal $2^{cardinal\ of\ rank\ n}$. Peirce's (informally presented) set theory resembles von Neumann's in that in addition to what I have called "sets" ("collections of discrete individuals," in Peirce's terminology), Peirce allowed collections of sets which do not themselves occur in the hierarchy of sets; for example, the union of all the ranks (call it **V**) is a collection, but not a "collection of discrete individuals." For von Neumann there would be many more ranks than there were for Peirce, because von Neumann extended the series rank zero, rank one, rank two, and so on, through the transfinite. But for von Neumann, as for Peirce, the union of all the ranks recognized by the set theory is a special kind of collection: von Neumann called it a "proper class." The proper classes are all the collections of sets which are not themselves sets, that is, which do not themselves belong to one of the ranks.

The cardinal number of *his* universe of collections of discrete individuals (which I have called **V**) was recognized by Peirce as a special kind of cardinal (call it Ω), a cardinal which is not a set, but only an ideal limit of the cardinals in **V**.

In his informally presented set theory Peirce said, in fact, that the multitude of the points on the line is not only greater than **c**, but greater than the cardinal number of any set. In fact, it is similar to the multitude of the whole universe of sets ("collections of discrete individuals"). If we call the cardinal of the universe of sets Ω, there are Ω points on the line!

Now, if there are more than **c** points on the line, then almost all the points on the line must be "non-standard." But, as I have already pointed out, every non-standard point has to lie in the "monad" of a standard point. Thus, at least provisionally, we may think of Peirce's continuum as consisting of the standard points together with all the non-standard points in their monads. In fact, in the monad of each standard point there must be Ω non-standard points!

Peirce's Aristotelianism

This reconstruction of Peirce's view of the continuum is still far from complete. To determine what Peirce's view was, we have to see how he could come so close to what at the beginning I called the "Aristotelian" view. First, a couple of corrections to what I have said so far: although I have used the terminology of contemporary Non-Standard Analysis to explain Peirce's conception of the line, that terminology is in a way extremely misleading. When one does Non-Standard Analysis, one starts by expanding the real number system by adding non-standard real numbers that are infinitesimally close to the standard real numbers (as well as infinite non-standard real numbers) and then one assumes that the non-standard geometric line is isomorphic to the non-standard real numbers. But this is not Peirce's view at all. Peirce did not propose to add non-standard numbers to the real number system. He simply proposed that there are non-standard points on the geometrical line. This means that the question "Which point in a given monad is *the* standard point?" would make no sense on Peirce's view. On his view (as I reconstructed it), what we mean when we ordinarily talk of points on a line are monads (and sometimes parts of monads, as when a point "becomes two points"), not points (which I called point parts) at all. The real numbers do, at a first pass, give us all the "points" on the line; or, more precisely, they give us all the points until we begin to divide those points and thereby to construct non-standard point parts.

But I am getting ahead of myself. For the moment, let me suggest the following: let us think of the line as consisting of monads that can be put into one-to-one correspondence with the real numbers, each of which contains Ω potential point parts. (What I mean by calling them *potential* point parts will become clear shortly.) Within a given monad, none of the point parts is any more "standard" than any other point part in that monad. This is a very large difference from Non-Standard Analysis as we have it today. The monad corresponding to $x =$ *the square root of 2* can be divided into Ω point parts, but none of those point parts is *the* point $x =$ *the square root of 2* or the standard point $x =$ *the square root of 2*.

In saying this I am not further interpreting Peirce. I am simply *subtracting* from the account that I gave certain extraneous elements that were introduced by my use of ideas from Non-Standard Analysis.

Now, let me go back to my Aristotelian examples in Figures 2A and 2B. To someone familiar with Non-Standard Analysis it would seem that introducing infinitesimals will not bring us any closer to the Aristotelian view. For present-day Non-Standard Analysis is constructed in such a way that a principle called the Transfer Principle holds. This principle says that all theorems of usual mathematics (with the usual conception of the continuum) which do not explicitly contain the words "standard" and "non-standard" continue to hold when we add the non-standard elements to the line or to the real number system. In other words, it makes no difference whether a mathematician proves a theorem using the methods of standard analysis or of Non-Standard Analysis; if a theorem can be proved using Non-Standard Analysis, then the theorem will still be valid even if one does not believe that there really are infinitesimals. But the Transfer Principle was not part of anything Peirce was committed to. The reason for mentioning the Transfer Principle is this: if the Transfer Principle is true, then the Dedekind Cut Theorem must hold for the non-standard line as well as for the standard line; that is, even if we add infinitesimals, it must remain the case that when we make a division in the line, the two halves will not be mirror images of each other. Now, Peirce did not explicitly say that he accepted the Aristotelian intuition, that the two halves are mirror images of each other, but I see no reason to *doubt* that he thought this, since he did think that (in Figure 2B) both AB and CD have two endpoints.

At this point, I think the following speculation is a reasonable one, given Peirce's views. Suppose that when we divide the line at a point P what we do is actually divide the monad of P into two halves. The points in the left half of the monad of P become the new "endpoint" of the left half of the line (become the point B in Figure 2B), and the points in the right half of the monad of P (or their images under the translation that moves that half of the line to the right) become the new "endpoint" of the right half of the line (become the point C). Then AB and CD will still have two endpoints, as Peirce asserted they do; and it is still possible (although incompatible with the Transfer Principle, to be sure) that AB and CD should be mirror images of each other.

Peirce's Metaphysics of Potentiality

Still, the problem remains: even if some divisions of the line produce halves that are mirror images of each other, how can *every* division of the line have this property? Why can I not divide the line by putting the monad of P in the right half of the division, together with every point that lies to the right of P by some *finite* amount, and putting all the other points (the points that lie to the left of P by some *finite* amount) in the left half of the division? It would seem that this would divide the line cleanly into two pieces in such a way that the left half of the division would contain no greatest "point," that is, it would contain no greatest monad. This would violate both the Aristotelian intuition and that much of it which, as we have seen, Peirce himself was definitely committed to: namely, that if we divide a line or a line interval and then separate the two segments, then the left half of the division will have a right-hand endpoint. I believe that I know the answer to this question, and, not surprisingly, it takes us deeper into Peirce's metaphysics than anything I have talked about so far, because what I have said so far does not really appeal to much of Peirce's metaphysics; it appeals only to his belief in the very large cardinality of the points on the line. In particular, we have not so far interpreted Peirce's mysterious idea that when a multitude becomes *that* large, its individuals *lose their distinct identities*.

Let me go back for the moment to the Aristotelian view. On the Aristotelian view, as well as on Peirce's view, I have said that we can understand the transformation shown in Figure 2A–2B as causing two points to arise from a single point. But let us consider the simpler case shown in Figure 1. Suppose we ask an Aristotelian whether the point P existed before the line was divided. The Aristotelian would, of course, say that there is an ambiguity in the notion of existence: P existed *in potentiality* before we divided the line, *in actuality* only when we made this particular construction. And Peirce's language is close to this (MS 439, 27): "The line is a mere conception. It is nothing but that which it can show; and therefore it follows that if there were no discontinuity, there would be no distinct point there . . . that is, no point absolutely distinct in its being from all others." This suggests that for Peirce, as for the Aristotelian, points are in some way the results of mathematical or conceptual operations, such as dividing a line or noting that a curve has an extremity. It is true that Peirce also spoke of a line as a collection of points (MS 439, 26). But in the same paragraph he said, "No point in this line has a distinct identity absolutely discriminated from every other." I provisionally interpreted this as meaning that what we ordinarily call points are really monads, or large aggregates of point parts. But what is a "large aggregate"?

In the Eighth of his Cambridge Conferences Lectures, Peirce repeatedly referred to infinite sets as *potential* aggregates: for instance, "We have a conception of the entire collection of whole numbers. It is a *potential* collection, indeterminate and yet determinable, and we see that the entire collection of whole numbers is more multitudinous than any whole number" (MS 948, 13). What this language suggests is that Peirce had in fact what I have called in other publications a *modal logical view of set theory* (Putnam 1983; see also Parson 1983). Peirce apparently did not think of sets (or "collections") as mathematical "objects." His language suggests that we *could*—not, of course, in the sense of physically or psychically "could," but in the sense of logical or "metaphysical" possibility—aggregate the natural numbers, and that when we consider the collection of natural numbers what we are contemplating is this possibility, not an object. In this respect, Peirce's picture is like Brouwer's, but with one all-important difference. Peirce thought of both points on the line and sets as the results of conceptual construction processes: one lists objects and forms an aggregate, or one divides a line or curve, or determines that a line segment or curve has an extremity and thereby determines a point. But the difference is this: for Brouwer, *our finiteness* is an omnipresent consideration. For Brouwer, it does not even make *mathematical* sense to imagine completing an infinite number of operations. Peirce had no such scruples. For Peirce, completed infinite processes are perfectly conceivable—or, rather, they are perfectly conceivable as long as the cardinal number of steps in the process is less than Peirce's ideal limiting cardinal (which I called Ω).

This is not as speculative, as an interpretation of Peirce, as it may seem. For Peirce himself said, following the sentence I just quoted, that:

> In like manner, the potential aggregate of all the abnumerable multitudes [Peirce was referring here, not to the set of all non-denumerable cardinals, but to the idea of "a collection of distinct individuals which is an aggregate of one collection of each of these multitudes"—that is, to a union consisting of sets of all the different non-denumerable cardinalities] is more multitudinous than any multitude. This potential aggregate cannot be a multitude of distinct individuals any more than the aggregate of all the whole numbers can be completely counted. But it is a distinct general conception for all that . . . a conception of a potentiality.

This language is strongly consistent with the idea that the collection of points on a line (which is of the same cardinality as the potential aggregate of the abnumerable multitudes) is, like the collection of the abnumerable multitudes, "the conception of a potentiality."

There is, then, a sense in which a line is a collection of points and a sense in which it is not. A line, taken in intension, is a perfectly definite relation; in fact, the ordering relation of the line *is* the line, taken in intension. For Peirce has told us (at MS 948, 14) that when there is a collection of the kind I have been discussing, a collection of cardinal Ω, then the members of that collection are never distinguished by the members of the collection each having its own individual *quality*. Peirce made it clear that the difference of the points on the line is entirely a relational difference; and, characteristically, he thought that the underlying relation was triadic (MS 948, 14–15). But the relation is not a relation that obtains between individuals that exist in any one possible world. The indeterminate relation between points on a line can be made partially determinate in a possible world by actually constructing *aleph-null* or **c** or $2^{\mathbf{c}}$ or . . . points on the line; but one can never construct *all possible* points on the line, because there is no possible world in which there are actually Ω "distinct individuals." The reason that the line is a collection of points that "lack distinct individuality" is that it is a collection of *possibilia*, and possibilia are not fully determinate objects for Peirce. To say that the line is a collection of possibilia is to say that one can construct things that stand in a certain triadic relation, the relation "Proceeding to the right from A you reach B before you reach C" (MS 948, 15). *What answers to our conception of a continuum is a possibility of repeated division which can never be exhausted in any possible world, not even in a possible world in which one can complete abnumerably infinite processes.* That is what I take Peirce's daring metaphysical hypothesis to be.

To complete this reconstruction of Peirce's view one thing remains, and that is to say what constructing an infinitesimal distance could be. But I do not think we have far to seek. The examples I began with are almost all that are needed. If I first perform the transformation represented by Figures 2A and 2B and then reverse the transformation, I have conceptually divided what was originally an indeterminate point P into two parts B and C which have to be an infinitesimal distance apart. This can be regarded as the construction of one infinitesimal interval. Are there point parts between B and C? As we have seen, there are *in potentiality*, which is the only way points exist until they are actually constructed. The midpoint of the infinitesimal segment BC (I am referring to C after the right-hand segment has been "moved back," of course) is itself between B and C. Once we have an infinitesimal interval, we can also subdivide that interval into n equal subintervals, for any natural number n. One should also regard *division* of the already constructed points as also a construction, one which always creates *both* a right-hand endpoint of the left half of the division *and* a left-hand endpoint of the right half of the division. And if we lived in a possible world in which we could complete infinite processes, all these constructions could be performed abnumerably many times. (For example, in **c** steps we could actually construct monads corresponding to all the real numbers.[15]

Concluding Remarks

There are still a few loose ends to tie up. I began by listing two difficulties with attributing an "Aristotelian" view to Peirce. One was that associated with a quotation in which Peirce said of a certain curve, "This line is a collection of points." But the sentence that follows glosses that remark: namely, "For if a particle occupying at any one instant a single point moves until it returns to its first position, it describes such a line, which consists only of the points that particle occupied during that time." But no Aristotelian would disagree with that gloss; and, as I have already indicated, Peirce added, "But no point in that line has any distinct identity absolutely discriminated from every other." The other difficulty was that Peirce accepted a construction that would not make sense to an Aristotelian, a construction in which we remove a point from the end of a line and move it. But if we accept my hypothesis that by a point Peirce meant a monad, then the point of this difficulty becomes somewhat different. The difficulty now is: if we move a whole monad from the end of a line, then how can what is left of the line still have an endpoint? This endpoint must, after all, belong to the very monad that we moved, since after all if we reverse the transformation, and return the point to the end of the line, the new endpoint of the line and the point "returned" will "keep their order" even though they will now be "at one point." The answer, I think, is this (and again, the spirit will be somewhat Brouwerian): when we move a monad, we must think of that as moving *the monad as so far constructed*. But by moving it (in effect, making a Dedekind Cut in the already constructed points) we extend the construction. The monad that is moved is not a "collection of distinct individuals" but a "notion of a possibility." When we move it, we act on it in a way that further determines that structure, and we determine it by specifying that some of the points in that monad (the ones previously constructed) are to be (mapped onto points) infinitesimally close to a point at the new location, while other points in that monad (one of which—namely, the new endpoint of the line segment—we have constructed by the transformation itself) all become point parts of the new endpoint of the line segment.

Now, suppose that someone tries to block this move by specifying that the monad to be moved is *the whole proper class* of points which *could ever be constructed* in the monad of the original point. I take it that Peirce's answer would have been that this is simply not a possible *construction*.

Peirce's view, if I have it right, is that moving a point away from the end of a line segment or curve always produces new points (point parts) distinct from the points that were moved, just as dividing a line or curve does. The metaphysical intuition that is behind all this is that we live in a world—since Peirce did think that there actually are continua in the real world—in which there are an enormous number of possibilities: *compatible* possibilities. Moreover, the reason that they cannot all be actualized is not that the realization of some of them logically precludes the realization of particular others, although that kind of case exists too. That is not what is involved in Peirce's statement that there cannot exist Ω distinct individuals. The Peircean picture is that the multitude of possibilities is so great that as soon as we have a possible world in which some of these possibilities are realized—say, a possible world in which some abnumerable multitude of the divisions are made—then we immediately see that there is a possible world in which still *more* divisions can be made, and hence there is no possible world in which all these *non-exclusive* possibilities are *all* actualized. We might summarize this by saying that the metaphysical picture is that possibility intrinsically outruns actuality, not just because of the finiteness of human powers, or the limitations imposed by physical laws.

My aim was not, of course, to expound the whole metaphysics of Peirce's Cambridge Conferences Lectures, but to reconstruct one key element, which, if it could not be shown to be consistent, would represent a fatal flaw in the whole edifice. And that, I believe, has been done.

Notes

1. When I refer to material as coming from the "Third Lecture" or the "Eighth Lecture" as the case may be, I am referring RLT.

2. See MS 951, 32 where Peirce spoke of "all the hard work I have done for the last fifteen years" in trying to "bring all the action [of the universe]

under a single principle." Interestingly enough, Peirce also described this work as "metaphysical speculations to which I had not before been inclined."

3. Quoted in Ketner's introduction to RLT.

4. Weierstrauss showed that we can explain what it is for a sequence of rational numbers to be convergent without using the notion of a real number; that is, that it is possible to define the notion of convergence in terms of the intrinsic properties of the sequence of rational numbers itself, so that instead of saying that the real numbers are the *limits* of convergent sequences of rational numbers, one can identify the real numbers with *equivalence classes* of convergent sequences of rational numbers under an appropriate equivalence relation, and this is what is done in formalized systems of mathematics such as *Principia Mathematica*.

5. The term is also applied to divisions of the rational numbers with the four properties listed in the text.

6. Here I am, of course, answering a modern question on Aristotle's behalf; Aristotle himself did not consider this question.

7. Peirce's example differs only in that he considered breaking a closed curve rather than a line segment.

8. Peirce considered a curved line rather than a straight one, but such "affine" properties as straightness are irrelevant to the present discussion.

9. This is the draft that was selected for use in RLT, although there Ketner remarks that it is not *certain* that it was this Lecture as delivered, but "it exhibits many of the features this lecture must have."

10. Notice, by the way, that in his formulation of the paradox, Peirce said that the points have been *at* one point, and that the symbolization " = " is not a natural one for *being at one point*, although it does sound natural for the other locution Peirce used, apparently interchangeably, of having "been one point." Another problem, of course, is that Peirce spoke as if things could be identical at one time but not at another, yet in the logic of relatives, as in present-day predicate calculus, identity is treated as a tenseless relation. If "being at one point" is not an identity relation, even for points, then this problem disappears.

11. For example, in the Fifth Lecture Peirce made it quite clear that he believed in infinitesimals. He had just said that the most common form a certain fallacy takes is treating every collection as if it were finite. Then he continued: "Somewhat more subtle forms of this fallacy are Euclid's assumption that every whole is greater than its part and that reasoning of the doctrine of limits which thinks it proves a quantity to be zero by saying let E be its value, and goes on to show that the value is less than E. What this does prove is that the value of the quantity is less than that of any quantity chosen as E has been chosen, generally as a finite quantity. This

proposition really proved is *less* than the truth, even though the proposition supposed to be proved is more than the truth" (MS 445, 21-22). The inference that Peirce just declared to be a fallacy is the inference from a proof that a quantity is less than any finite quantity to the conclusion that the quantity is zero; and the only way the inference *can* be fallacious is if there are quantities less than every finite quantity but not zero, that is, if there are infinitesimals.

12. Ignoring points at infinity, if there are any. Peirce in fact believed in points at infinity, but in the sense of Projective Geometry, not in the sense of contemporary Non-Standard Analysis. See Peirce's Eighth Lecture.

13. I am assuming that we have arbitrarily picked a point as the origin and a unit of length.

14. To see this, let P be any point on the line which is not a standard point. Divide the *standard* points into those that are to the left of P (L) and those that are to the right of P (R). By the Dedekind Cut Theorem, either L has a greatest member or R has a least member, and since L,R is a division of the *standard* points, this distinguished point is itself standard; call it P°. There is no standard point between P and P°; for if P° is the greatest member of L, then any standard point between P and P° would be a standard point to the left of P and greater than the greatest member of L, which is a contradiction, since every standard point to the left of P is in L (and similarly we get a contradiction if we suppose P is the least member of R and some standard point is between P and P°). But every interval of finite length contains standard points. So the interval PP° must be of less than finite length, that is, it is infinitesimal. Thus, if there are any non-standard points, they all lie in the monads of the standard points.

15. I say "seems to" because the presentation is so brief. What Peirce did was describe the series of cardinals aleph-null, the cardinal of the power set of aleph-null, the cardinal of the power set of the power set of aleph-null, ... These Peirce took to be all the infinite cardinals there are, apart from the cardinal I call Ω, which is the cardinal of what we would call a proper class but not a set. The fact that he did not believe that there are sets of cardinals other than these strongly suggests that his universe of sets is the one I describe here. It also indicates that he assumed the Generalized Continuum Hypothesis, almost certainly without recognizing that it *is* an independent assumption.

16. I speak here of "possible worlds." This could be regarded as a *façon de parler*; that is, "there is a possible world in which X is the case" could be regarded as merely a way of saying that "there *could* be a world in which *X* is the case"; however, the *façon de parler* is not wholly inappropriate, since at times Peirce did seem close to the David Lewis view in which other possible worlds really exist. At least in MS 498, 34 Peirce explicitly held that

possibility open, and he also said that the whole collection of possible worlds (which he called "a Platonic world," and—metaphorically—"the mind of God") is itself only one of a number of really existing systems; there are not only our logical space, but other whole logical spaces (MS 948, 34).

2
Peirce's Logic

W. V. Quine

WHEN I BEGAN to read mathematical logic in 1928, it was fashionable to date the inception of mathematical logic with George Boole's *Mathematical Analysis of Logic* (1847) or *Laws of Thought* (1854). Fashionable, yes; but fashion in mathematical logic was microfashion in 1928, if not now.

In 1939, when I was preparing historical inserts for my otherwise completed book *Mathematical Logic* (1940), I came to feel rather that mathematical logic properly so called came alive only with the proper logic of quantification, or predicate logic, and that Boole and his early followers were rather the last of the medievals, marking only the false dawn of mathematical logic. Quantification, clearly grasped and full blown, is what makes the difference.

If we conceive of time multi-dimensionally, and then limit our attention to a single strand of it, we can trace out a chain of development of logic from Boole up through De Morgan, Mitchell, Peirce, Schröder, Peano, Russell, and Whitehead, to logic in its modern estate. Where the inception of mathematical logic comes in this chain is in 1883, when quantification becomes clearly articulated by Charles Sanders Peirce. Even the terms 'quantifier' and 'quantification,' thus applied, are his.

Real time is linear, however. In real time, with the publication of Gottlob Frege's little monograph *Begriffsschrift* in 1879 the predicate calculus emerged, complete with quantification. It emerged full-grown from Frege's brow, four years before it was achieved by Peirce.

Frege scooped Peirce in quantification, he scooped Dedekind and Peirce in the theory of chains, and later he scooped Peano in class abstraction and Church in function abstraction. But the

Begriffsschrift was scarcely noticed except for an unappreciative review by Schröder. Frege's important *Grundlagen der Arithmetik* of 1884 and *Grundgesetze der Mathematik* of 1893 fared little better. The three logic volumes of Peirce's papers (in CP) contain no mention of Frege, to judge from the indices.

It is not until Whitehead and Russell's great *Principia Mathematica* (1910–1913) that Frege's influence perceptibly enters the mainstream. Even here there was less explicit borrowing than unwitting duplication of effort. Moreover, the austere and unwavering formalism that was characteristic already of the *Begriffsschrift*, and has proved indispensable nowadays in computer theory, proof theory, and the philosophy of mathematics, was not recaptured even in *Principia Mathematica*. It came back into its own only later, largely through Hilbert and his school.

It was in my historical probings in 1939 that I came fully to appreciate Frege's firsts. I could not find a copy of the *Begriffsschrift*, but some faithful notices by P. E. B. Jourdain were good secondary sources. I then proceeded to tout Frege as the father of modern logic.

But it remains instructive to trace the slightly subsequent and independent emergence of quantification through Peirce's writings. Frege affords no such genetic insight, since quantification is already full-fledged in his maiden publication. In an important sense, moreover, Peirce, not Frege, was indeed the founding father; for Peirce's influence was continuous through Schröder's work, with side channels into Peano, and culminating in *Principia Mathematica*. Frege had been a voice crying in the wilderness.

In 1867 (CP 3.20–41), to begin with, Peirce modified Boole's logical algebra into what we now call Boolean algebra. It was a needed rectification, but anticipated by Jevons in 1864. In 1870 Peirce followed up with a notable seventy-page monograph, "Description of a Notation for the Logic of Relatives, Resulting from an Amplification of the Conceptions of Boole's Calculus of Logic" (CP 3.45–149), in which he transformed De Morgan's relation logic, a haphazard affair, into something foreshadowing the smooth algebra of relations in *Principia Mathematica*. An unproductive preoccupation of Boole's continues to dominate much of this monograph: namely, the Procrustean forcing of analogies with themes and theorems of classical mathematics. But what is especially interesting in this monograph is Peirce's atomistic approach to relations as sums or aggregates of what he called simple relatives—what we may think of as ordered pairs (or triples or quadruples as the case may be). It was this feature that was destined to evolve into quantification through Peirce's writings of ten to thirteen years later.

He handled relations, or relatives, as sums or aggregates—I said—of simple relatives. "All right, which is it—sums or aggregates?" That is our natural response, but it is anachronistic. A relation, we say, is a class of ordered pairs (or triples, and so forth), and the question is whether to see Peirce's so-called simple relative as an ordered pair or as the unit class of an ordered pair. The question is anachronistic because the idea of a unit class seems not to have emerged until 1890 in a paper by Peano. It will not matter which way we think of Peirce's simple relatives.

Another distinction that calls for a passing gesture, if only of dismissal, is that between relations and relatives. We talk nowadays of relations as over against properties; Peirce, De Morgan, and their predecessors talked of relative terms—'father of'—as over against absolute terms such as 'house' or indeed 'father.' The relative term denoted not the pairs but the bearers of the relation, *as bearing* it. This 'as' is vague and unproductive. Nothing will be lost by taking the relatives as relations, classes of pairs.

Peirce went on to draw uninteresting distinctions galore, for he made a hobby early and late of taxonomic terminology. We have self-relatives, aliorelatives, cyclic relatives, equiparants, disquiparants, concurrents, opponents, and copulatives.

Peirce's atomistic approach to relations was evidently meant merely to facilitate the exposition and study of the operations of relation algebra, such as converse, relative product, and crossproduct, with no inkling that it would evolve into quantification. He rightly criticized a fumbling attempt by Boole to meet the needs of existence statements by weaving an indefinite singular term 'something' into the algebra of logic, but then he stooped to a similar attempt himself (CP 3.73).

In the last third (CP 3.214–251) of a long article "On the

Algebra of Logic" in the *American Journal of Mathematics* of 1880, Peirce got back to simple relatives, which he now called individual relatives. Confusingly, he now put his old term 'simple relative' to an opposite use: the complement of an individual relative. The pair of Abraham and Isaac is an individual relative; the sum or class of all pairs except that one he now called a simple relative.

He adopted the Greek capital letters 'Σ' and 'Π' from their familiar use in mathematics, where they express summation and productation over a class of numbers. Subscripts were appended, as usual, as indices of summation and productation. Peirce used the notation for logical sums and products of relatives. Any relation, say the father-son relation, is the logical sum or union of all its component individual relatives, and the logical product, or intersection, of all the corresponding simple relatives. In this adoption of 'Σ' and 'Π,' with appended indices, Peirce took another significant step toward quantification. For him at the time, still, it was just a further means of streamlining and generalizing his algebraic manipulation of relations.

The device recurred in a short paper of 1882, "Brief Description of the Logic of Relatives" (CP 3.306–322, see CP 220), privately printed. The paper is obscure, but comes no closer to quantification. A year later, however, in "The Logic of Relatives" (CP 3.328-358), quantification emerged. The paper appeared in a volume by Johns Hopkins philosophers (Peirce 1883).

Here we may think of all individuals as arbitrarily numbered, and we may think of l_{ij} as 1 or 0 according as person number i does or does not love person j. Then $\Sigma_j l_{ij}$ will be a number, a strictly arithmetical sum of ones and zeroes: a one for each person whom person number i loves. So $\Sigma_j l_{ij}$ is how many people person number i loves. So $\Sigma_j l_{ij} > 0$ if and only if person number i loves some people. Quantification dawns.

Now let us get 'Π,' productation, into the act. What of the product $\Pi_i \Sigma_j l_{ij}$? It will be $\Sigma_j l_{1j}$ times $\Sigma_j l_{2j}$ times $\Sigma_j l_{3j}$ times, and so on—hence, how many the first person loves times how many the second person loves times, and so on. The product of all these numbers will be large if there are no misanthropes, but a single misanthrope would reduce the whole product to 0. Conclusion: $\Pi_i \Sigma_j l_{ij} > 0$ if and only if everyone loves somebody or other. Quantification is running on both cylinders.

We can leave the '>0' tacit, Peirce observed (CP 3.351–354), and read '$\Pi_i \Sigma_j l_{ij}$' no longer as a number but simply as 'For all i, for some j, i loves j.' The variables cease to refer to numbers and come to refer directly, in this case, to persons. The 'Π' and 'Σ' come then no longer to express arithmetical product and sum of numbers, or even logical product and sum of classes, but direct quantification over, in this case, persons.

The example hinged on a two-place predicate, 'loves.' Predicates of one and many places fare similarly, and indeed open sentences generally, of whatever form and however many variables. This becomes explicit in a paper of 1885 (CP 3.359–403). Our full, familiar quantification is then at hand.

I see in the Peirce story a fascinating interplay of quest and serendipity. Already in 1870, in his criticism of Boole's treatment of 'something,' Peirce showed awareness of the inadequacy of logical theory in matters of 'some' and 'all.' But the successive innovations that led him at last to quantification were not laid out with that happy ending in mind. First he atomized relatives, next he imported 'Σ' and 'Π' to express logical sums and products, and finally he restored 'Σ' and 'Π' to their numerical use, reckoning up the numbers of loved ones. These two magic letters ended up as the signs of quantification, we see, and they continued in that use through the writings of Schröder and his followers, as a fossil record of its evolution. They have turned up as late as 1940, though superseded in most quarters by notations of Peano and *Principia Mathematica* and subsequent variants.

Actually, the two symbols are appropriate for quantification also apart from this erratic history. If in the Boolean tradition we think of the alternation of sentences as logical addition, and of conjunction as logical multiplication, then existential and universal quantification are indeed aptly rendered as logical summation and production, Σ and Π. Such could, one feels in retrospect, have even been the simple history of quantification, but it was not.

The state of the art at the time of Peirce's breakthrough— Frege apart—is instructively reflected in a paper by O. H. Mitchell in that same Johns Hopkins volume (Peirce 1883). Like Peirce as of that and previous years, Mitchell focuses on relatives, primarily dyadic ones, rather than on open sentences in general. He has quantifiers of a sort, universal and existential, but they enjoy no flexibility of scope. There consequently remains the crucial problem of distinguishing between everyone's loving somebody or other and there being someone loved by all. He copes with it lamely by adopting two kinds of existential quantifier, one of which implies identity of the object from case to case. His quantifiers submit poorly to any nesting.

Quantification as we know it goes fairly smoothly into ordinary language, scope and all. We say, on the one hand, that everybody loves somebody, and, on the other, that somebody is loved by everybody, and we are apt to feel—I do, anyway—that the mere order of these verbal quantifiers helps to settle the vital distinction of scope. Granted, we touch up our words to stress the contrast: 'Everybody loves somebody *or other*' vs. 'Somebody is loved by *all*.' But in the complacency of our hindsight we have trouble imagining how people—logicians, even—a scant century ago could fail to see that mere grammatical scope, at least hinted at by word order, is all it takes to make the difference. I draw two morals: that predicate logic is instructive, and that history is broadening.

Quantification made its way into the logic literature again after Peirce by another route, and I find it interesting to contrast the two lines of thought: Peirce's and Peano's. As I said, there is no tracing the evolution of quantification in Frege's mind; but we can trace it in Peano's.

Boolean algebra at its most primitive readily expresses the non-emptiness and the all-inclusiveness of a class α: thus $\alpha \neq \Lambda$ and $\alpha = V$. Invent class abstraction, then, '$\{x:Fx\}$,' and you have quantification.

$$\exists xFx \leftrightarrow \{x:Fx\} \neq \Lambda,$$
$$\forall xFx \leftrightarrow \{x:Fx\} = V.$$

This was how Peano came to quantification in 1888. It was a decade when quantification was breaking out all over. Peano's way into quantification was an obvious way, but it had not been open to Peirce, for Peirce did not have class abstraction. Frege did not have it either, when he achieved quantification by pure unimplemented thought in 1879. He introduced abstraction only in 1884, and Peano came out with it independently, it would seem, in 1888. Peano was meticulous with his references and credits, but there were none to Frege.

In later writings, Peano dropped '≠Λ' in favor of a second-order predicate '∃.' His notation for class abstraction was '$x∂Fx$,' so his existential quantification comes to look almost familiar: ∃xɜFx, meaning ∃(xɜFx). He abandoned universal quantification except as applied to conditionals and biconditionals, which, after all, is where it is usually needed. There he rendered it with a variable subscript—thus 'Fxɜ$_\chi Gx$' and '$Fx \equiv_\chi Gx$?

From Peano to *Principia Mathematica* we notice a grammatical shift in existential quantification. Peano had applied a second-order predicate '∃' to the term 'xɜFx.' Whitehead and Russell applied an operator '(∃x)' to the sentence 'Fx.' I sense an ontological motive: reluctance to posit an abstract class, xɜFx, in first-order logic. Actually, Peano drew no distinction between 'xɜFx' as a class name and as a mere predicate, a general term or relative clause. He verbalized it either way as suited his context. The paradoxes were still unknown which show that some relative clauses cannot determine classes.

Another alternative is open, however, better than the one chosen by Whitehead and Russell. Stick to Peano's grammatical grouping, but construe the abstraction expression steadfastly as a relative clause—a general term, or predicate. '∃' becomes an operator on relative clauses, 'such that' clauses. So does '∀.' The bound variable becomes strictly a variable for forming 'such that' clauses, and no longer has anything specifically to do with universal and existential sentences, or vice versa. The operators '∃' and '∀' become applicable to predicates generally—to simple predicates and to schematic predicate letters 'F' and 'G,' as well as to `such that' clauses. The great virtue of this attitude is that it isolates the essential business of the bound variable, which is purely combinatorial business—pure cross-reference and permutation—rather than anything to do with quantity. The variable comes to stand forth explicitly as the regimentation of the pronoun.

Other operators on predicates enter the picture on a par with '∃' and '∀.' One is '⅂' 'the one and only,' which goes back to Peano. Another candidate is a class-forming operator, say 'ℸ.' We have '∃F', 'there are F'; '∀F', 'all is F'; '⌐F', 'the F'; 'ʌF', 'the class of all Fs'. Bound variables serve all and none of them on an equal basis, simply by forming 'such that' clauses to play the role of 'F'.

We have seen two routes to quantification. One, Peirce's, was through the summation and productation operators of arithmetic. The other, Peano's, was through the 'such that' construction, or relative clause. This is the shorter route from ordinary language. It is remarkable that the key to it, the abstraction operator, made its way into mathematical logic only after both Frege and Peirce had arrived at quantification.

Such is my story of quantification. Of Peirce's lesser efforts in logic, one worth mentioning is his long-unpublished anticipation of Sheffer's stroke. He pointed out in a manuscript of about 1880 (CP 4.12) that all truth functions can be generated from 'neither-nor', and in 1902 he noted further (CP 4.264) that the function 'not both' would serve as well.

Another anticipation on Peirce's part, less widely known, was his anticipation of Claude Shannon's discovery in 1938 of a correspondence between truth functions and electric circuits (see Burks 1972). Thus, picture two terminals and two intervening switches. If the switches are connected in parallel, the current is on just in case the one switch *or* the other is closed. If they are connected in series, the current is on just in case the one *and* the other is closed. Such are the roles of alternation and conjunction. As for negation, it answers to the throwing of a switch. Thanks to the resulting correspondence between truth-functional formulas and complicated circuits, the logical techniques for reducing complicated truth-functional formulas to simplest equivalents afforded a cheap way of designing the simplest possible electric circuits for complicated purposes. Minimization of complex truth-functional formulas can itself prove more laborious than one could expect, but electrical engineers found it worthwhile to compile and publish the simplest equivalents of the 65,536 truth functions of four variables. All this happened pursuant to Shannon's discovery. Peirce's anticipation decades earlier had had little notice, for complex circuits had not as yet played a role in industry.

The logical enterprise to which Peirce devoted most attention and attached most importance in later years was his evolving system of "entitative" or "existential" graphs (see CP 1897, 1903). It is a complex and cumbersome apparatus. It seems anachronistic at so late a date, when Peano's transparent and efficient logical notation was already inspiring Whitehead and Russell to embark on *Principia Mathematica*, and Peirce's equally efficient notation of 'Σ' and 'Π' had long since inspired Schröder.

The conventions governing Peirce's graphs are somewhat as follows. All formulas written are affirmed, unless encircled by a closed loop. The loop denies that all the formulas within it are true; it affirms that there is a falsehood somewhere within it. So, an empty loop is itself a flat falsehood, professing as it does to encircle a falsehood when in fact it encircles nothing. Accordingly, a loop encircling an empty loop forms a logical truth. Attaching a dash or open curve to a predicate says something fulfills the predicate; hence, existential quantification. Attaching that existential curve to two predicates, or branching it to touch three or more, says that something fulfills them all. The curve thus figures as an existential quantifier and bound variable, and indeed, graphically, as the bond itself. By encircling, then, we can get negations of existential quantifications; hence, universal negative quantifications.

There is no way in this system of expressing an open sentence in isolation, since we have only the predicates and the existential curves. A consequence is that there is no way of negating an open sentence before existentially quantifying it. We must approach the existential negative rather as a negated universal, after getting the universal somehow from scratch. Peirce got it, and eventually the various complex nestings of universal and existential quantifiers, by sundry conventions governing the intersecting of the existential curves with the loops of negation.

His graphs do suffice in the end to depict any closed formula of first-order predicate logic, including identity. Peirce formulated rules of proof, some of which are far from obvious. It is interesting to think them through for validity, since the system diverges so substantially from our familiar patterns of formulation and proof. One does find them valid, and Don Roberts (1973) has gone on to a completeness proof.

3

Peirce's Underestimated Place in the History of Logic: A Response to Quine

Randall R. Dipert

CHARLES S. PEIRCE'S PLACE in the history of logic is difficult to describe. I think that in his *ability* (if one can so speak) he was in the very first rank of logicians, with Aristotle, Boole, and Frege. I also will argue that his influence on modern mathematical logic is far greater than usually acknowledged (including by Professor Quine) and actually exceeds that of Frege—although this bold assertion comes with a number of caveats. But whatever his true status in the history of logic, it would be inappropriate to such a critical thinker as Peirce simply to swoon and gush over his logical virtuosity. Consequently, I want to place my remarks about Peirce's logic in the framework of methodological and evaluative considerations in the history of logic.

There are at least three axes along which we might be justified in considering Peirce's logic today. First, we might see him as a *discoverer*, as the *first* in the history of logic to develop certain ideas. Second, we might be interested in the historical *influence* of Peirce's logic, the extent to which his work lay along the vast and complicated causal chain leading to our present logical world, and especially how he contributed to the great results in mathematical logic in the first half of this century. Third, we might be interested in Peirce's distinctive ideas in logic for their merit and utility today.

I

Many, including myself, have been especially interested in Peirce as logical discoverer, and strains of this motivation are evident in much work on Peirce, with a sometimes fevered attempt to establish his place in the pantheon of logical greats still dominated by Frege, Cantor, Russell, and others. One thus points to "firsts" such as: (1) Peirce's extensive development of a symbolic relational logic; (2) his use of the expression and concept of "quantification"; (3) his use of "indices" as variables, and of π and Σ as quantifiers binding them; (4) his independent use—natural to him as a chemist—of the notion of "saturation" (Frege's *Gesättigkeit*) to describe a completed predicate expression; (5) his development of numerous suggestive axiom-like formulations of logical theories; (6) hints of something like an awareness of the expressive capacities of propositional, class, and monadic predicate logics, on the one hand, and a full first-order predicate logic with multiply quantified relations, on the other (that is, shades of Church's Theorem), as well as correct descriptions of certain notions and techniques which became useful only many decades later, such as various prenex and normal forms, unusual propositional functions like what we now know as the Sheffer stroke function, models and independence results, and so on. There remain, I think, many more such gems in the vast and scattered Peircean corpus.

Yet I do not now see enormous benefits or value in this line of inquiry. It is true we perform an act of historical justice in unearthing Peirce's nuggets and maybe, as Aristotle suggests in the *Nicomachean Ethics* (1101A22f.), there is honor to be restored even beyond the grave. We also provide an inspiring logical fable of what an individual working virtually alone in an atmosphere of adversity and lack of intellectual sophistication can accomplish. Finally, we who are Americans still have, I would contend, an enormous desire to show the viability of our "frontier" intellectual life. Although in the twentieth century it is rather clear we Americans have developed a tradition in logic and philosophy for which we need not feel inadequate (even as its depth, applicability to traditional philosophical problems, and apprehension by the general citizenry remain problematic), the *roots* of modern logical life remain embarrassingly European. A century after Mark Twain and other knights of the Gilded Age waged a battle for American cultural independence, we still have ringing in our ears Clemenceau's savage comment that

America became an industrial and military power so quickly because it spared itself the time-consuming effort of developing a culture and intellectual life. Hence, my guess is that there are powerful cultural needs (which I shall seek to guard against) at work in attempts to legitimize American logical thought in American roots. These have led to the eager resuscitation of logical discoverers such as Peirce, the American Postulate theorists (Huntington and Veblen), and Royce.

More troubling I think, in the "Peirce was first" vein, is the lack of care with which I and others have occasionally hailed Peirce as the "discoverer" or pioneer of this or that. The well-founded assertion of a Peircean novelty would require a careful study of the nineteenth-century logical milieu, both to ascertain what was already there and to see what would have been obvious and was simply "in the air." Given Peirce's almost encyclopedic knowledge of the history of logic, this is already a tall order and would require at least as much familiarity especially with his nineteenth-century contemporaries as he himself had—if we are to praise him personally and not merely commend his era.

As an example, to hail Peirce as the discoverer of the logic of relations requires that we know the state of the logic of relations when Peirce began his work. This would require very careful study of De Morgan (which is really just now being undertaken, by Daniel Merrill and others), of the history of the theory of functions, and of the long and complex history of the "oblique syllogism" (as the phenomenon of relational inference in the late Middle Ages and Renaissance was called)—material that Peirce the worshiper of De Morgan and collector of medieval manuscripts knew very well. We should also give some hard thought to the difficult question of how much conceptual progress is made by symbolism and symbolic rigor alone. Although Frege and Peirce are largely beyond suspicion, it is rather clear that the recent history of logic has appeared to value any, and sometimes quite shallow and unenlightening, symbolisms and axiomatizations and tended to dismiss any non-symbolic, historical account (for example, those of Aristotle or Ockham) as so much empty verbiage. This trend begins definitively with Church's bibliography (1936) on the history of logic in the early issues of the *Journal of Symbolic Logic*, where a necessary condition for inclusion was the use of one or more symbol.[1] At root is a twentieth-century misconception of what it is for a logic to be "formal." Namely, it need not be symbolic; nor is symbolization a guarantee of a helpful formal analysis. The nineteenth-century logicians, beginning with De Morgan's *Formal Logic*, kept in mind better than we what it is to be usefully 'formal' (that is, in attending to logical *form*) rather than merely symbolic at all costs.

Now, I am not saying that Peirce was *not* the first great pioneer of the substantive (symbolic) *theory* of the logic of relations. He was, although De Morgan had partially lighted the path. I *am* saying that precisely and justifiedly asserting in *which* sense Peirce "discovered" *what* is far from easy. I make these claims as a repeatedly humbled historian of nineteenth-century logic who has toiled in fields populated by such arcane figures as Drobisch, Trendelenburg, and H. Grassmann, and who still does not know so much of the logical landscape as Peirce did.

As a further object lesson in the "discovery" game, it is sometimes suggested that Peirce (or O. H. Mitchell) was the first to use the English expression 'quantifier' in the modern sense, and that this is significant. But the use of this expression was, in the nineteenth-century context, extremely obvious, and Peirce, although himself extremely sensitive to nomenclature, attached virtually no significance to it. The expression 'quantification' was of course bandied about in the earlier nineteenth-century Hamiltonian debate over the "quantification of the predicate" (and quite possibly before, although *The Oxford English Dictionary* credits Hamilton). And various cognates of 'quantity' in many languages had been used for millennia in a logical sense; a non-numerical sense of quantity was also employed by numerous nineteenth-century algebraists (such as Grassmann and including Boole) to gesture in the direction of the non-numerical referents of algebraic terms.

The more interesting question of Peirce's co-discovery of a (symbolic) theory of quantifiers, and of his appreciation of variables and variable-binding operators in logic, is extremely complex. As Quine observes, Peirce's notation painstakingly evolved, and was at first bound up with notions of summation and productation on classes. Lamentable is the lack of effort Peirce made to describe rules for using quantifiers in the rigorous way we see in Frege.[2] Such an attitude toward rigor was clearly part of the logic as it had been, rather than of logic as it was to become. Peirce himself repeatedly deliberated whether his quantifiers and indices were "eliminable" in favor of purely algebraic expressions. Unlike Frege and many of his followers, Peirce, however, clearly posed this question, and was troubled by it. I will return to this important point.

My general point here is that even if we could ascribe a clear value to the activity, responsible attributions of priority, discovery, or originality require more subtlety in description, and more research, than almost anyone is willing to give. Peirce would almost certainly come out a "winner" in this picture of logical history as a race, but saying precisely what award he won would be a longer story than most are willing to tell.

II

To move on to the second methodological axis: our interest in the claim that Peirce influenced current conceptions of logic should bring us similar second thoughts. It presumes, perhaps quite logico-centrically, that where we are now in logical theory is an especially wonderful place to be, rather than where we could or should have been.

But I think in the theme of *influences* we have a more promising justification for closely examining Peirce's work than in the naïve praise of him as an unheralded pioneer. For one thing, by tracing whence we came, logically speaking, we can better understand important assumptions that may lie at the foundation of our present mode of doing logic, and that we now take for granted. We see decisions, or historical accidents, that committed us to views about what is true and what is false, about logical methodology and goals, and even about what a 'logic' is supposed to do. We may, of course, be impressed with the wisdom of these decisions and the luck of these turns of fate. Or we may be appalled at the capriciousness and even meanspiritedness with which our present logical world came to be.

I have already tipped my hand a bit about my view that the

central "paradigm shift" in symbolic logic in the 150 years, from an algebraic conception to ones employing various variable-binding operators à la Frege and Russell, was essentially a matter of caprice (of ignorance on the part of Frege and aesthetic taste on the part of Russell). The central question, were this shift rational and justified, should have been the expressibility of the algebraic theories.[3] Regardless of when the topic has recently been addressed, and how it has finally been resolved, my point is the historical one of what *should have been* the dominant question in the move from algebraic, variable-less systems to our present variable-strewn systems: Can an algebraic theory, or an otherwise modified traditional "logic of terms" in Fred Sommers's formulation, unambiguously represent, at least as well as first-order predicate logic,[4] those propositions we need for a fruitful life, for science and for mathematics? Or can it not? As far as I am aware, first Peirce, then Schröder, were the only ones from 1880 to 1920 who ever posed and were troubled by this question. Peirce arrived at no conclusions, but usually tilted toward the eliminability of variable-binding operators,[5] as did Schröder.[6] For Frege, the issue of expressive power never emerged in his ignorant raging in the early 1880s against all manner of Boolean logics, a reaction apparently precipitated by Schröder's review of the *Begriffsschrift*. In Russell's *Principles of Mathematics* the algebraic method, enriched with relations, is called simply "less convenient." Tarski muddied the waters in 1941 by simply claiming to have discovered formulas expressible in first-order predicate logic but not in some (unspecified) algebraic theory; he never produced the proof of why he thought so. In the end, due to observations originally made by Korselt, an algebraic theory of relations, formalized in the modern way, does not have the expressive power of the first-order predicate calculus. This should have been one of the most important questions in early modern logic, but never was. It is on the topic of quantification that I think Quine's remarks are especially deserving of attention. I think he is quite right in seeing Frege as having given the first account of what we know as quantifiers. Frege certainly, alone in the nineteenth century, gave sufficient and rigorous rules for using them. But what is packed into this description of "our quantifiers"—the universal quantifier alone, or the existential and universal quantifiers together? There had been variable binding and term-forming operators in logic and mathematics both before and after Frege. Some of these operators yield theories with the expressive power of quantifiers, such as Hilbert's ϵ-calculus, and the Peano-esque theory Quine himself hints at in the last part of his paper. In fact, Quine suggests that such a quantifier-less theory based on set abstraction might be preferable, and thus accidentally mutes his praise of Frege as the discoverer of those wonderful things, the quantifiers. Earlier work of Quine's is also devoted to developing variable-less logical systems (1966; cf. Kuhn 1983).

In fact, some such quantifier-less theories are actually preferable to the first-order logic we have inherited in yet other ways. As Quine remarks in his address, "the essential business of the bound variable . . . is purely combinatorial business—pure cross-reference and permutation—rather than anything to do with quantity." As the phenomenon of "branched quantifiers" shows (see Quine 1986), the linear way of writing quantifiers does not express this cross-reference and priority optimally, although branching is perhaps a marginal phenomenon. By speaking of variable-binding operators in mathematics before Frege I mean mainly those of the infinitesimal calculus (in Leibniz's notation; Newton's obscures it)—and it is probably no accident that the teaching duties and early research of both Peano and Frege hovered around the teaching of calculus. By term-forming operators, I have in mind the 'v' ([proper] subset-forming) operator of Lambert, Boole, Jevons, and so on. These lack the "cross-reference" capacity of variable-binding operators—in essence binding at most one variable—but probably inspired the later more useful operators, especially the notion of set abstraction we see in Peano.

But even after we mute our praise of Frege's quantifiers in this way, there are other aspects in which we must still further limit his honor. Although his theory was indeed the first with the expressive power of the first-order predicate calculus, there is a good sense in which Frege did not know what he had accomplished. He was unaware of its expressive power over previous logical theories. Its essential and clear technical superiority comes, I believe, in the introduction of multiply quantified relations. Without that, a calculus is typically but one more theory with the expressive power of propositional/Boolean/class/monadic-predicate logics. Totally lacking an historical picture of the difficulty with relations that would have come with a deeper knowledge of the history of logic, such as what Peirce had, and early attached to a metaphysics that makes *functions* primary—multiply quantified relational statements get short shrift in the *Begriffsschrift*. Probably also wounded by and offended at Boolean logicians and logics, Frege really had no good idea *why* his logical theory was superior on other than quite debatable philosophical and methodological issues (for example, the "superficial" similarities between algebraic and arithmetical operations in Boolean systems). His unpublished counter-attacks in the early 1880s against the Booleans are largely uninformed criticism of long-abandoned positions and shows no knowledge of De Morgan, Peirce, earlier work on relations, or Jevons.[7] My guess is that the question of quantificational *vs.* quantifier-less logic will return to haunt modern symbolic logic. It will do so on multiple fronts, but especially from research in cognitive science, artificial intelligence, and a more careful study of the "best" theory of representation for natural language and thought.

The central piece of mythology in modern logic that touches upon Peirce's influence is the thesis that modern symbolic logic sprang, *ex nihilo* and full-blown, from the brow of Frege. Quine aids and abets this myth. Frege had, we are told, glanced casually at previous logics, found them seriously wanting, and produced without reliance on any predecessor or contemporary almost all of what we needed to surge into the twentieth century. His notation was repaired a bit by Peano, Russell, and others, and his theory was later outfitted with a semantics, rules of formation, and so on. The usual suggestion seems to be that without him the twentieth century would have been a logical disaster.

If this story were true, a discussion of the influence Peirce had, and his causal connections with modern logic, would be very short. His work would be at the tragic conclusion of a dead-end path. His role would be just what Quine seems sometimes to ascribe to him—great American symbolic tinkerer and logical "also ran."

To wax sociological for just a moment: my guess is that this myth about Frege is as popular as it is because it would, if true, relieve us of any obligation to study the history of logic before 1879, and relieve us of the obligation to rethink some of the fateful decisions made in fin-de-siècle Britain, Germany, Italy, and France. Quine shows no such symptoms, but few prominent logicians in the twentieth century (Church, Bochenski, Mates, and Prior being the notable exceptions) have shown great curiosity in the history of logic, although the situation has markedly improved in the last twenty years. (It is just possible that this myth, however unjustified, has been therapeutic to the extent that it has lightened the educational burden of logicians and intensified their efforts on more technical and less historico-speculative endeavors.)

But the myth of Frege as Romantic hero and single godfather of our logical world is seriously mistaken on at least two counts. First, while not wanting to diminish Frege's monumental accomplishment, we have been altogether too gullible in accepting his own picture of himself as virtually uninfluenced by any source. Those who have written about Frege, especially in English, have typically known very little about the vast and complicated history of logic (and philosophy) in the nineteenth-century German-speaking world, very little about Frege's own educational history (to this day poorly understood), and of the possible interaction of his reading and lectures on the foundations of the calculus and on the emergent field of analysis with his logic.

There is in fact an extensive, now little-known tradition of what may be termed "Rationalist" approaches to logic that runs from Leibniz, through Lambert and Ploucquet, Maimon, touches Kant and neo-Kantian logicians, and is especially pronounced in works of "anti-Kantians" such as Drobisch, Trendelenburg, the Grassmanns, and others which we know Frege read but to which he never referred. Some of this logical work is symbolic, some suggests the approach to relations *via* functions (Lambert) which Frege actually took[8]—rather than through generic relations as we see in De Morgan and Peirce—and some suggests German penchants for graphical, conceptual notational systems with the same motivations we see in the *Begriffsschrift*. Although the details of his masterful handling of quantifiers seems to be uniquely Frege's accomplishment, there is a "big picture" in the philosophy of logic to be seen here which would put Frege's work in a more reasonable, if only slightly diminished, perspective. Such a larger perspective is suggested but only partly developed in Hans Sluga's fine book on Frege (1980; see also Thiel 1979, 755-70), but otherwise, the Frege mythology remains largely intact. Peirce, incidentally, knew this Rationalist work quite well, and referred to it often, even if his own formalisms are Boolean.

We, of course, see in Peirce a similar but far more sustained effort toward a "conceptual notation," in his philosophy of logic and theory of diagrams, and in the development of his existential graphs—which, like Frege's own notation, have proven abidingly repulsive to some logicians. The upshot of these reflections is that not only is the *ex nihilo* picture of Frege solidly mistaken, but the intellectual heritages and agenda of Frege and Peirce turn out to be, in some respects, remarkably similar.

But a second major logico-historical myth comes in thinking that the causal influences of modern logic narrow in the nineteenth century to Frege alone. In a paper and article, "Peirce the Logician," Hilary Putnam (1982) points out that the notation we now use is far closer to Peirce's earlier, non-graphical one than it is to Frege's. He furthermore says that the important results of Löwenheim (and Skolem and Bernays, I would add), which lie at the beginning of the great twentieth-century discoveries in logic, were presented in the Peirce-Schröder system, with no discernible influence of Frege, Russell, or even Peano.[9] The great tradition and results of Löwenheim and Skolem can thus be entirely traced to Schröder, and thence to Peirce—without mentioning Russell, Frege, or even Peano. The tradition of the *Principia Mathematica* is more myth-laden. I would argue that its notation and presentation (certainly in the early chapters), including its theory of quantification, are traceable to Peano with almost no discernible influence of Frege. This is confirmed when we see the enormous influence Peano had on Russell, deriving from their joint attendance at the 1900 International Congress of Philosophy; although Frege was present, it was Peano who made then the greater impact (Russell 1959, 265). There is even direct evidence that Russell knew Peirce's work on relations, admired it greatly, but seems to have forgotten it a few years later, when Peirce's logical contributions are mentioned again, but now unfavorably.

The evidence for this is quite clear. In a short article in 1901, "Recent Work on the Principles of Mathematics" (brought to my attention by K. L. Ketner), Russell wrote:

> Nevertheless, in each decade since 1850 more has been done to advance [the subject of logic] than in the whole period from Aristotle to Leibnitz. People have discovered how to make reasoning symbolic, as it is in Algebra, so that deductions are affected by mathematical rules. They have discovered many rules besides the syllogism, and a new branch of logic, called the Logic of Relatives [Footnote: "This subject is due in the main to Professor Peirce of Harvard."], has been invented to deal with topics that wholly surpassed the powers of the old logic, though they form the chief contents of mathematics" [85].

Later he complained that Peano had not yet taken up the logic of relations, and, in ignorance apparently of Leibniz, credits the goal of a "universal characteristic" to Peano (87). In the Foreword to Feibleman (1946/1969) Russell wrote:

> I am—I confess to my shame—an illustration of the undue neglect from which Peirce has suffered in Europe. I heard of him first from William James when I stayed with that eminent man in Harvard in 1896. But I read nothing of him until 1900, when I had become interested in extending symbolic logic to relations, and learnt from Schröder's "Algebra der Logik" that Peirce had treated of the subject.

Reading this passage carefully, it is not clear which works by Peirce Russell might have read, or even if he actually knew his work entirely through Schröder.

Furthermore, we in fact have a great deal more information about Peano's intellectual odyssey than Quine suggests, and the investigation brings us again to Peirce and Schröder, not to Frege. Peano had in fact studied, in the year before his 1888 *Calcolo geometrico*, the works of Boole, Peirce, Schröder and the Grassmanns.[10] The *Calcolo geometrico* contains specific references to both Peirce's 1880 "On the Algebra of Logic" and his 1885 article—in which quantifiers are treated in the "modern" way—of the same name (Peano 1957, 2:19). Except for class abstraction (very briefly discussed there, really) and elegant and thoughtful changes in notation that were to become the hallmark of Peano's work, the logical section of the *Calcolo geometrico* is squarely within the tradition of the algebra of logic, and Peano was quite conscious of this fact.

Peano's notation for class abstraction thus comes after he had been steeped in the works of Schröder and Peirce, and influenced only by them. We may nevertheless see it, as Quine does, as a significant advance, especially given the Booleans' often autonomous use of capital letters for both predicates and their extensions. Notational differences aside, it is clear that Peano's use in 1897 of universal and existential quantifiers derives from Schröder and thus ultimately, again, from Peirce. Peano's references to Schröder after 1888 are extensive, climaxing in his praise of Volume I of the *Vorlesungen* as "magisterial" and as "summarizing all that is to date known about this subject" (Kennedy 1980). His references to Frege are few, slight, and generally unappreciative.[11] Consequently, if we trace back *Principia mathematica* and regard it as primarily inspired by Peano's work, then we are led directly, or indirectly *via* Schröder, to Peirce—even if Russell and later logicians did not appreciate the connection.

In any case, I think Putnam's point is substantially correct, and Peirce's influence on the development of modern symbolic logic was massive, if usually indirect and unacknowledged. (The situation suggests a certain similarity with the debate over the discovery of the infinitesimal and differential calculus: in the English-speaking world, Newton was usually credited with the discovery, but it was Leibniz's notation we all used. There are also, I conjecture, deeper connections of the history of logic with the history of calculus in the theory of, and notation for, variable-binding operators.)

It is frequently pointed out that results using models and interpretations, and eventually a fully conscious semantic theory, arrived very slowly in the twentieth century. Again, Löwenheim's 1915 paper is frequently cited as a watershed. Yet we must be careful here. Results using interpretations of a formal calculus, even rather odd ones, occur repeatedly in Schröder's *Vorlesungen*. It is also clear from scattered notes and marginalia in Peirce's manuscripts that he also used non-standard interpretations to establish results (especially using various binary combinatoric tricks). On the other hand, Frege nowhere employs such techniques, and was rabidly against them since his quantifiers were to range over *everything*, period.[12] For one thing, Boolean logic was inspired from its inception by non-standard interpretations of numerals and quasi-numerical operations. (Additionally, the use of the formal Boolean calculus to cover both classes of "things" and classes of times or occasions as a propositional logic—exactly what so offended Frege—was perhaps one of the first clear uses of semantics in symbolic logic.)

We must also admit that multiply interpretable "abstract" algebras were appearing all over Europe in the first half of the nineteenth century. Furthermore, semi-independently of these results, Italian and German geometricians (probably first Beltrami, then Klein and others) were using semantic techniques to establish results in "formal geometry." Another, apparently independent formal tradition is to be found in Dedekind, in which he writes of "disregarding" the special nature of the elements treated by a theory (1888, 134). In short—to paraphrase Quine—semantics, like quantification, was "breaking out all over," although emphatically not in Frege's work!

Especially interesting along these lines is Quine's remark that Frege was the author of an "austere formalism" that later came back only with Hilbert. If we understand formalism as axiomatic-like rigor and ignore the hint that Frege alone inspired the return to formalism, this is certainly correct. Peirce, by contrast, was rather cavalier about stating clearly such formal systems, as I have already observed.[13] But if we understand 'formal' in the sense of a multiply interpretable ("uninterpreted") symbolic calculus, Frege would certainly have had nothing of that.[14] Nowhere is the dogmatic semantic attitude clearer than in Frege's correspondence with Hilbert over the foundations of geometry where he shows himself to be, in this sense, the great anti-formalist. Semantics would have withered away under

Frege's influence, but, as it was, blossomed in the less dogmatic climes of Boolean logic.[15]

Thus, neither in "formal" model theory nor in "formal" rigor did Frege appear to have any discernible influence. I am not sure what great importance these etiological ruminations have, except perhaps to show us that no single figure (such as Frege) is as important to the development of modern symbolic logic as we sometimes think, that it was in fact a broad movement, active in the United States, France (Coutourat), Germany, England, Italy, and Russia (Poretsky). We also see that Peirce's work lay upon *all* the most important causal chains leading to present-day logic; Frege's actual influence and historical importance was, I think we see, far smaller—at least until translations of his works began appearing in English, and the history of logic got rewritten.

III

I do not mean to suggest that I am totally contemptuous of the first two of the three approaches to the history of logic, Peirce as pioneer and our debt to Peirce, but I am more inclined to think that the real value of the Peircean *oeuvre* consists for us today in its probing and sometimes quite idiosyncratic views in the philosophies of logic and mathematics. These are, of course, part of a grand philosophy of mind, epistemology, metaphysics, and conception of the world whose sweeping breadth is found only in logicians such as Aristotle, Ockham, and Leibniz. Any probing discussion of "Peirce the logician" necessarily turns into a discussion of Peirce the philosopher, and Peirce the meta-mathematician. I would like to conclude my remarks by indicating several areas of logical work by Peirce that I think still remain of considerable interest and value.

1. *The expressive power of algebraic theories.* I have already indicated one such area: an investigation of the expressibility of various algebraic theories. By 'algebraic' I do not mean Boole's own meager class logic and its variants, which have expressive power only on the order of the propositional calculus, but rather a calculus without variable-binding operators that combines

propositional, class-inclusion, and relational operators. Peirce, Schröder, Peano, and Coutourat used such "mixed" formulas, but never formulated or exploited a full theory of them. (I sidestep the issue of twentieth-century algebraic and equational logics, since they have taken a different turn.) Related issues include the metaphysical commitments of such theories, and their utility in mathematical and scientific communication and discovery, as well as the question in cognitive science or semantics of which representation "best" captures thought or language. I am here hinting, with such recent authors as F. Sommers and P. Laird-Johnson, that some such theory might be better in multiple respects than first-order predicate logic and its allied set theories, which have not proven so wonderfully fecund for other-than-foundational mathematical and scientific research as pragmatists should demand, cottage industry though it may be for logic teachers.

2. *Logic as a part of mathematics*. A second area of research lies near to Peirce's perplexing claim that logic is part of mathematics, and not vice versa, which he uttered in response to the logicism of Frege and Russell. At first glance, this might appear to be nonsense. It could be taken merely as echoing Boole's remark that the "ultimate laws of logic are mathematical in form." And it duplicates, from a source taken to be more legitimate by some, Peano's repeated claims that logic was "a mathematical science."

But Peirce meant by 'mathematics' something more like the systematic and rigorous theory of diagrams and formal representations used in necessary reasoning. Mathematics would thus include not only the formulas, diagrams, graphs, and so on that mathematicians do employ, but also, for example, the grammar and transformation rules of natural languages. The operant slogan behind Peirce's seemingly perverse reverse-logicism is his view that all thought and all communication is "diagrammatic," and the question is then simply one of which diagrams are most "useful" in a robust sense. Logical and mathematical notation, Peirce came to believe, had been held captive by typography and, with that notation, our minds as well. Observe here the clear scents of a search for a Leibnizian *lingua philosophica*, and a *characteristica universalis*, which inspired Frege (through Trendelenburg, as Günther Patzig, I believe, first observed), Peano, and the later Schröder (1892), as well as Peirce.

Peirce's thesis of the desirability of other-than-linear and other-than-typographically-convenient notation has been partially borne out by such phenomena as branched quantifiers and the continuing pedagogical and higher-level use of non-linear representations in mathematics and logic. Recent theoretical work by Jon Barwise and John Etchemendy (with a computer program under development along the lines of their program "Tarski's World" demonstrating the theory) proposes a language of, and theory for, manipulating combined linear and non-linear diagrammatic information. Both for pedagogical purposes and for research in knowledge representation, in artificial intelligence, and in cognitive science, something like Peirce's theory of representation will surely be discovered or re-invented.

The particulars of the often clever existential graphs interest me less than their motivation. (Peirce wavered on the value of the existential graphs, at one point, in MS 513, arguing that the "cumbrous algebra, with all of its faults, seems preferable to the graphical.") But on behalf of the graphs, we might cite Frege's defense of his own, far less thoroughly two-dimensional notation.[16]

3. *Logic as a normative, not "foundational" science.* But the real difficulty for twentieth-century philosophers going to late nineteenth-century logic lies, I think, in the following problem. For Boole, and later more emphatically for Peirce, Peano, and Schröder, logic had a "normative" purpose: to improve, to facilitate our ability to reason about, and in, mathematics and other fields. Its goal was *not* to describe or serve as a foundation for our present language, natural or mathematical: in the sense first expressed clearly in Frege, but anachronistically applied to his predecessors and contemporaries, and some of his successors. The misunderstandings resulting from failing to appreciate the difference in purpose between what we might call the descriptive/foundational approach to logic that now predominates and the normative/therapeutic view that predominated in the nineteenth century have caused enormous mischief.

Consider one purpose we see in modern logic as "revealing the real, inner structure of utterances in a natural language." We see, of course, hints of this in Quine's remark that a certain formalism behaves like the pronoun in English. First De Morgan, then Peirce, regarded natural language as extremely weak in helping us to grasp and manipulate multiply quantified relational expressions. They would have sneered at setting as our goal merely to "describe" or analyze such a feeble tool of expression.[17]

The goal of De Morgan, Peirce, and sometimes even Frege, was to improve it: to devise notational systems that would most facilitate the grasping, and promote inferentially proper manipulation, of diagrams representing relationally complex thoughts. The difference in purpose between describing or analyzing how we *do* in fact speak and think—not, of course, understood in the sense of how we ordinarily speak and think, but logic as a foundation for a philosophy of language—and how we *should* write and think is very great, and marks the difference between twentieth-century and nineteenth-century goals and purposes for logic. The inspiration for the normative notational enterprise seems to have come from Leibniz. Peano devoted most of his life to it (and to the facilitation of international communication). It was a central feature of Peirce's grand schema for the sciences that logic was one of the three branches of the normative sciences, together with aesthetics and ethics.

It is alone in Peirce, however, that we see any sophisticated views about diagrams, representations, iconicity, and usefulness. Other authors, including Frege and Peano, simply plunged in, asserting that such and such a notation was "simpler" or "better." It is a pity that logicians and philosophers have ceded so much of Peirce's work on "diagrams" and their usefulness to the semioticians, with their quite different interests.[18]

4. *Semantics.* Two additional views of Peirce in the philosophy of logic are his view that propositional, predicate, and even meta-logic are formally to be treated by the same basic calculus (using his '$-\!\!\prec$'and his suggestion that domains of discourse may be composed of unusual items, such as *possibilia*, abstract and absurd entities, or even of non-discrete entities, that is, a continuum. Many major figures in the history of logic had regarded

propositional ("hypothetical") logic as a marginal phenomenon, and treated it as best reduced to relationships of classes or terms. Thus Boole and Schröder reduced propositional logic to relationships among classes of times, instants, or "occasions." It is perhaps one of the virtues of Frege's historical ignorance that he seems originally not to have heard about these attempts and, once he did find out, harshly condemned them. (His own view makes propositional logic, insofar as it can be considered a subject in its own right, a special case of 0-place predicates or fully saturated predicate-expressions.) Peirce rejected the crude reductionist efforts of his predecessors and contemporaries to turn propositional logic into class logic by their semantic trick of declaring the universe of discourse to be a class of times, instants, or occasions. His own view, however, was offensive—even incomprehensible—to most Booleans and likely to offend modern logicians as well. Namely, he saw propositional logic, class and relational logic, as well as meta-logical relationships such as that of logical consequence ("illation") as species of a more general "diagrammatic" genus. In the case of the material conditional, class inclusion, and logical consequence, respectively, this common relationship was designated by '—<,' and the three species were distinguished ("semantically") by the kinds of objects subsumed under the terms. The shared notion was a formal metaphysical relationship, or "representation," whose chief internally definable characteristic was transitivity, as well as having other "formal" laws governing its use. The frustratingly evasive semantics, crossing language, and meta-language, is distinctively Peircean. But seen from his dominant formal-algebraic and "diagrammatic" tendencies, this view is rather natural. There is a sense in which there are no distinctive propositional, class-, or relational logics in Peirce; one calculus, with different interpretations for the categorematic terms (and, in a sense, for the syncategorematic terms as well), expresses it all!

A related topic is Peirce's exploration of algebraic expressions that are interpreted in more than the universe of discourse, or in which the universe of discourse is non-standard—"continuous" universes or universes with abstract entities, containing properties, or (other?) non-existent objects. This semantic fleet-of-foot suggests later work with multi-sorted quantifiers, free variables, second-order logic, and the like. Although largely having the status of a mere suggestion, it is most highly developed in the work of Peirce's student, O. H. Mitchell, and was the crux of a controversy in the portion of Peirce's correspondence with Schröder that is extant.[19]

5. *Peircean set theory*. Peirce elaborately considered the views of Cantor and Dedekind, and discussed "foundational" issues in set theory in an extremely sophisticated way. His discussions of what we may call "philosophical" foundations of set theory are especially probing, and fill holes left wide open by Cantor and his successors (and on which Frege took aim). Twentieth-century logic has by and large contented itself with strictly implicit, formal descriptions of the notion of a set: a set is just what the axioms of the set theory in question say it is. Occasionally one still hears talk about THE notion of a set, and which theory best captures it, or hears phenomenological remarks about what it is to think of a set or of something as "belonging" to a set—having a brace-like aura around it, for example. But, basically, the substantive philosophical question of what a set is or should be has been undeveloped since Cantor's quite vague remarks, and with Cantor's own reflections on the subject sometimes dismissed as "theological."[20] In the schools of Brentano and Husserl, matters are a bit better, and one does now hear mutterings in the Anglo-American world about the unsatisfactoriness of the situation.

A study of Peirce's writing on this subject would return us to where earnest thought on the subject dropped off. It is probably true that had extensive discussions about the metaphysical nature of sets taken place first and at the expense of technical developments, progress would have been much slowed. But it is my guess that here too the piper must eventually be paid or, to give a post-logicist paraphrase of Dedekind, and in a different spirit: *Was sind und was sollen die Mengen?*

6. *Logic and all thought*. Finally, not only in its normative quality, but also in its breadth and focus, we find in Peirce a conception of 'logic' as the study of *all* ways in which thoughts succeed each other ('inference'). Peirce's conception of what falls under the umbrella of 'logic' does not have the warm, peculiar

fuzziness of Hegelian, and other Idealist, conceptions of that discipline, but Peirce does at least have a "big picture" of the place of deductive thinking in the scheme of all thought. This, again, is very unlike Frege and those who have followed him, who may well have been craftsmen of the theory of *deductive* logic, but who lacked larger conceptions of what they were doing—for example, of non-necessary modes of inference. Peirce saw, as we have already mentioned, logic as the study of positive value in thought, and, especially, in inference of all sorts. From his earliest important essays on the fixation of belief in the 1870s, this came to be a theory of the scientific method, and ultimately, his conception of it as consisting of abduction, deduction, and induction.[21]

CONCLUSION

My remarks have been less a stirring testimonial to Peirce's logic and more an attempt to give a sober, methodologically disciplined account of Peirce's logic in the context of late nineteenth-century logic. One might, more exuberantly and with some justification, say that Peirce was, or was on the verge of being, the greatest logician since Aristotle. Yet his logical works, even in the best editions, resemble a vast, tantalizing heap of rubble. (Here I echo Murray Murphey's similar description of Peirce's metaphysical system.) There was no major book or pamphlet, and no single article of monumental insight—unlike Leibniz, with whom he is frequently compared regarding the state of logical and philosophical writings, but who at least slapped together the *General Investigations*. The famous 1870 paper on "notation" was written just enough before the great surge of interest in symbolic logic on the continent—Schröder's *Operationskreis* (1877), Frege's *Begriffsschrift* (1879), and R. Grassmann's *Die Begriffslehre* (1872)—to escape attention altogether. The dull thud made by the extensive and sometimes quite interesting articles by Hugh MacColl and W. E. Johnson in the 1870s and 1880s, in such conspicuous places as the *Proceedings of the London Mathematical Society*, *Mind*, and elsewhere, shows, I think, just how little interest there was in logic in the English-speaking world at this crucial time, until it was reinvigorated by novel German and Italian symbolic approaches.

Both Peirce's 1870 article and his less expansive articles of the 1880s had the problem of placement in what were probably regarded as minor journals from the edge of the civilized world.[22] From a late-twentieth century perspective, we Americans might naïvely wonder why Peirce was not taken more seriously in the nineteenth-century international academic world. But from a nineteenth century European perspective, ours was a land of Indians, shoot-outs, and energetic, but unsophisticated, large cities that imported their culture from Europe; the chances of anything but homespun logic or philosophy coming from such a place must have seemed very remote indeed.

Even in the 1883 anthology *Studies in Logic*, Peirce missed a wonderful opportunity to write a major survey article on his work in deductive logic. The wrenching failure of his academic career had its most devastating effect on his logic, in which he had shown the most promise. Logic was a discipline semi-languishing for thousands of years and now finally poised for big things, and was the discipline closest to his conception of himself. Peirce thought of himself, first, as a logician.

Yet we cannot be too bitter at the American intellectual community for failing to nurture and treasure Peirce, or at logicians since for failing to extol his importance. Two "accidental" facts limited Peirce's influence and later audience. One was that for a place in the history of logic, nineteenth-century America was not the place to be. The second was that with the lack of a clear program like logicism, there is no rhyme or reason to the logical theorems one presents, or what counts as interesting ones. Although it is a "literary" point, nearly everyone who reads the works of Peirce and Schröder complains about the chaotic parade of apparently inconsequential theorems, observations, and notations. (Even Peirce complained about Schröder's *Vorlesungen!*) But in the last instance, Peirce, and Peirce alone, must be held responsible for his work habits and for his notorious, self-acknowledged "lack of control" in all manner of social and academic niceties. It was perhaps neither fate nor the failings of others that primarily determined his limited logical accomplishments and minimal fame. It is a sign of his greatness as a human being that, in his best moments, he realized this too. Maybe, however, we are allowed to shed just one tear and finally to praise him these long decades after the finish of his life.

Notes

1. And also manifests itself in Moore 1982, where Moore refuses to give Peirce credit for the first precise definition of an infinite class or set (in 1881, CP 3.288), apparently because Peirce expressed his formulation verbally.

2. The icons of 1885 we see in CP 3.359 ("On the Algebra of Logic . . .") are as much stratagems for manipulating quantifier expressions as they are "rules of inference." Consequently, there is no distinction made by Peirce (here following Boole and others) between the useful and the deductively essential. After introducing the idea of a universal quantifier in 1885, he wrote, characteristically, "The rules of the use of this notion are obvious." He does give some "icons"—roughly, axioms—for their manipulation, but leaves out two in his own numbering. His axioms or rules for quantifiers give the impression of not having been carefully considered, or been for him a top priority. He does not later modify them, or even refer to them in later work in any systematic way. His attitude toward axiomatization and rigor in 1870 was especially clear: "But these axioms are mere substitutes for definitions of the universal logical relations, and so far as these can be defined, all axioms may be dispensed with. The fundamental principles of formal logic are not properly axioms, but definitions and divisions . . ." (CP 3.149; W 2: 429).

3. For perhaps the most recent treatments of the subject—long overdue—see Hugly and Sayward 1984, 289-302, and the introduction to Tarski and Givant (1987) and their references (xiii-xvi) to work by Kwatinetz and others.

4. Named more revealingly by the German 'Quantorenlogik,' or the English 'quantificational logic' since it is variable-binding individual quantifiers, not 'predicates,' that are distinctive.

5. See MS 419 and the much earlier (ca. 1873) MS 383 where all reasoning is claimed to be reducible to syllogistic form and dependent on the transitivity of the copula.

6. Compare Löwenheim's 1915 statement (quoted and discussed in Goldfarb (1979, 355-57): "'Every theorem of mathematics . . . can be writ-

ten as a relative equation; the mathematical theorem then stands or falls according as the equation is satisfied or not. This transformation of arbitrary mathematical theorems into relative equations can be carried out, I believe, by anyone who knows the work of Whitehead and Russell.'"

As Goldfarb remarks, a similar comment occurs in Löwenheim's 1913 review of Padoa. Löwenheim escapes my general claim since he is not "troubled" by the question of the expressive power of the algebra of relatives; he thinks there is an obvious answer!

Goldfarb questions whether this could be done to the "higher-type sets in *Principia*"; but Goldfarb's remark ignores some unusual parts of Schröder's *Vorlesungen* (for example, the hierarchy of manifolds discussed in Church's "Schröder's Anticipation of the Simple Theory of Types" and in my dissertation; see Dipert 1978a) that Löwenheim might have had in mind. There are similar ideas in Peirce (or Peirce/Mitchell; for example, the idea of "dimensions" of universes of discourse) that could be invoked in a higher-order theory, although it is unlikely Löwenheim would have known about them. In any case, it is quite unclear what Löwenheim means when he speaks of "a" relative equation, or "the" algebra of relatives if it includes all of the *Vorlesungen*—hardly a single formal system in the modern sense.

7. Cf. Sluga 1987, 80–98, who, however, does not show a clear awareness of the state of Boolean, Grassmannian, and De Morganian logic in the 1870s and early 1880s. See also Thiel 1981, 21–23.

8. Lambert's work is virtually ignored in the Kneales' history of logic (1962) but is noted briefly in Styazhkin 1969, 124. Since it was in German, and widely available, I strongly suspect Frege had read some of Lambert's works. The equational logical system would not have impressed or influenced him, but the intensional approach and handling of functions and relations might have. Considerable work on late eighteenth- and early nineteenth-century German logic needs to be done before we are in much of a position even to guess where Frege might have gotten some of his ideas. I work with a methodology that one should not simply *assume*, because an author gives no references and may wish to portray himself as original, that the author was indeed completely original.

9. I in fact doubt if Skolem or Löwenheim had read carefully Peirce's papers, contrary to Putnam's claim. Nuances of their notation and a scrutiny of all of the citations in their earlier articles lead us to Schröder's *Vorlesungen über die Algebra der Logik*, which refers to Peirce often and generously, and whose notational system was first developed by Peirce. In the case of Löwenheim, this is clear from the notation and references in his "Über Möglichkeit im Relativkalkül" (1915, reprinted in van Heijenoort 1967b), and continued into his attempt to "Schröderize" all of what had

then become logic and the foundations of mathematics in his 1940 "Einkleidung der Mathematik in Schröderschen Relativkalkül." Compare also the notation and references in Heinrich Behmann's 1922 "Beiträge zur Algebra der Logik, insbesondere zum Entscheidungsproblem," Hilbert's famous address of 1900, and his Heidelberg address of 1904. For Skolem, see his "On the Structure of Groups in the Identity Calculus" (1913) which begins: "Studying the well-known treatise of Schröder on the algebra of logic my attention was drawn . . ." through to his 1928 "Über die mathematische Logik," which is still entirely expressed in the Peirce-Schröder system (Skolem 1970). For a discussion of similar issues, see Goldfarb 1979— which nevertheless makes a number of mistakes in writing about Schröder.

On the significance and influence of the Peirce-Schröder tradition, one might refer to the Bernays review of Volume I of the 1890 *Vorlesungen* of Schröder in the 1970(!) issue of the *Journal of Symbolic Logic*, and to numerous works of Tarski and McKinsey (for example, McKinsey 1940 and Tarski 1941).

10. Kennedy 1980, 21, although Peano mentions both Hermann and Richard Grassmann, not just one Grassmann, as Kennedy puts it.

11. He has a small footnote to Frege in 1889. In 1895 he published a review of Frege's *Grundgesetze*, in which he concentrates almost exclusively on the motivation for Frege's notational system going back to the *Begriffsschrift*: he compares it unfavorably to his own ideographic system, concluding "The book must have cost its author much labor; reading it is also quite tiring." The extant correspondence is polite, but indicates Peano's considerable irritation with Frege's notational system, Peano always asking Frege for translations of his formulas into Peano's before considering them. Peano throughout his writing never endorsed, and even rejected, Frege's goal of giving mathematics a "foundation"; instead he saw himself as giving mathematics a clarifying language—with logic itself always described as a "mathematical science." See Kennedy 1980 for references, and, especially, an extensive discussion of the relationship of Peano and Frege.

Whitehead, from his work in preparing the *Universal Algebra* (1898), clearly knew of Schröder's notation and handling of relations—even if he did not there adopt them, or even deal with relations. It is less clear how well he knew Peirce's papers.

12. But I do not think that the semantic techniques we see in Peirce and Schröder were original with them, either, even if they used them more extensively than earlier Booleans and perhaps directly inspired work like Löwenheim's (which did indeed lead to the later uses of, and the theory of, modern semantics). To quote Goldfarb again: "Löwenheim's paper of 1915

contains a number of ideas central to much subsequent work. He uses the notion of a universe of discourse susceptible to change, a notion coming from the Boole-Peirce-Schröder tradition" (in Herbrand 1971, 2).

13. Hilbert's penchant for formalism was already well established in his *Grundlagen der Geometrie* of 1899, and codified in his *Axiomatisches Denken* of 1918 (in which the influence of his work in geometry plays the larger role).

This tendency for rigor was already in full swing by the end of the nineteenth century, quite independently of Frege, and we see it in the work of Huntington and, in Boolean logic, in work by B. A. Bernstein (1914 and 1916). As for Hilbert and Ackermann's view of the history of logic, we see enormous emphasis placed on the influence of Peirce and Schröder, with Peano and Frege providing an "exact foundation [for mathematics]" and a "strict axiomatic treatment": "The first clear idea of a mathematical logic was formulated by Leibniz. The first results were obtained by A. De Morgan and G. Boole. The entire later development goes back to Boole. Among his successors, W. S. Jevons, and especially C. S. Peirce enriched the young science. Ernst Schröder systematically organized and supplemented the various results in his *Vorlesungen* . . . , which represents a certain completion of the series of developments proceeding from Boole" (1967, 1–2).

14. Quantifiers in his system must range over everything, and any attempt to play games with their domains would surely have brought his wrath as quickly as did the Boolean's flexible "universes of discourse."

15. Quine himself shares with Frege the view that logic is and should be a clear representation of one's metaphysics (for example, "To be is to be the value of a variable"); it is Frege's more extreme view that all and only existents are to be the range of quantifiers that is problematic—and idiosyncratic in the modern history of logic. Furthermore, the demand to be a clear and adequate representation of one's metaphysics may well impossibly add to the burdens placed upon the "purposes" of logic.

16. Cf. Kennedy (1980) and Frege's "Über die Begriffsschrift des Herrn Peano und meine eigene": "Eine Gruppe von Schriftzeichen kann wiederholt und auf verschiedenen Wegen vom Auge überblickt werden; so kann ihr Sinn mit allen darin enthaltenen Beziehungen der Teile zueinander dem Geiste mehrfach vorgeführt werden, und es gelingt leichter, das Ganze zu erfassen und gegenwärtig zu erhalten. Durch die zweifache Ausdehnung der Schreibfläche wird eine Mannigfaltigkeit von Stellungen der Schriftzeichen zueinander möglich, und das kann für die Zwecke des Gedankenausdrucks benutzt werden" (1896, 222).

17. See MS 573 on the faults of ordinary language as an instrument of logic; ordinary language is "pictorial," not "diagrammatic," serving well the

purposes of literature but not those of logic.

18. In the loss or rejection of the normative approach to logic, Frege is particularly the villain here. In his shrill attacks on Boolean "laws of thought" and related attacks on psychologism, he never seems to have considered the possibility that the "laws" in question might be normative/legislative rather than descriptive (as in "laws of nature"). For Kant and neo-Kantians, logical rules have a similarly mixed normative and descriptive function. There were probably few if any pure "descriptivists" in logic and mathematics in the nineteenth century—not even Mill—and so it is difficult to see what Frege was ranting about.

On the matter of ideography and ideal language, Frege seems to have understood Leibniz very poorly (if even at first hand), yet repeatedly and willfully pushed his Begriffsschrift with an agenda that could only have been interpreted by his better-read audience (for example, Peano and Schröder, and anyone aware of Trendelenburg) as Leibnizian. The term 'Begriffsschrift' was itself Trendelenburg's translation of Leibniz's project. See especially Frege's more sustained exploration of the Begriffsschrift, *calculus ratiocinator* and *lingua characteristica* in "Peanos Begriffsschrift . . ." (Frege 1967, 227). The problem his terminology caused seemed to have dawned on Frege only in 1919 (van Heijenoort 1967b, 1) when he wrote: "my Begriffsschrift differs from the similar creations of Leibniz and his successors, in spite of its name, which perhaps I did not choose very aptly." But then what is the justification for his notational system, since it is hardly clear that decomposed (*zerfällt*) thought should be two-dimensional? What is worse, he seems to have never appreciated that the goals of giving a foundation to existent mathematics—or, as moderns probably anachronistically read him, of natural language—and those of *improving* reasoning and communication might be at cross-purposes.

19. I have dealt with the Peirce-Schröder controversy in my dissertation (1978a) and with Mitchell's work on "dimensions" in an unpublished paper on Mitchell presented at a 1983 conference on nineteenth-century logic.

20. Here I echo views of Michael Hallett (1984) and others.

21. I was quite correctly reminded by Professor Demetra Sfendoni-Mentzou, after my original talk, of my failure to address anything but deductive logic in isolation, which was hardly true to Peirce's conception of logic. Her point required that I add at least this paragraph to remedy the situation.

22. There are substantial sociological and geographical considerations here as well. How obtainable in Jena, Turin, Karlsruhe, Stettin, and so on were the American journals in which Peirce published? How long did letters across the Atlantic take, at a time when intra-European contacts in logic and mathematics were extensive and accelerating? Was it possible for

anyone not at the 1900 international congresses of mathematics and of philosophy to have later been perceived as significant? Why *was* Peirce absent—in favor, for example, of the far weaker Creighton? Although Peirce's French was presumably quite good, why did Peirce always write to German logicians in English (Schröder, Cantor—apparently not even knowing how well the latter could read English), whereas Schröder, Peano, and even Russell, wrote—not just read—English, German, French, and Italian, as the need suited them. Did he ever submit articles to the British journals, or consider submitting any to the still more important German mathematical ones?

4

Induction According to Peirce

Isaac Levi

IN A LECTURE delivered at Harvard sometime in April or May 1865, Peirce invited his auditors to suppose that we know no more of Man than what is contained in the definition of Man as the rational animal (W 2:272–86; see also Lecture XI [W 2:286–302], the Lowell Lectures of 1866 [W 2:258–504] and "Upon Logical Comprehension and Extension" of 1867 [W 3:7086]). Relative to such an information base, men might come in two varieties: man risible and man non-risible.

In that setting, the connotation, intension, or comprehension of "man" is less than both "man risible" and "man non-risible." That is to say, given the available knowledge, that x is a risible man entails that x is a man, but not conversely. On the other hand, the extension of "man risible" is less than that of "man." It is known that all risible men are men, but not conversely.

Suppose that the information available to us is supplemented by the discovery that there are no non-risible men. Peirce commented on this eventuality as follows:

> Henceforward the idea of man and that of risible man are changed. The extension of risible man has become equal to that of 'man' and the comprehension of 'man' has become equal to that of 'risible man' (W 1:275).

According to Peirce, prior to the change in information, the claim that all men are risible was an informative thesis. After we find out that it is true, it no longer furnishes us with novel information. The comprehension of "man" has become equal to that of "risible man."

Peirce suggested that before we find out that all men are risible, the extension of "man" is greater than that of "risible man."

Peirce ought to have said that the extension of "man" is *judged* not to be less than that of "risible man" relative to that information or, better yet, that the available information implies that the extension of "man" is not less than the extension of "risible man." Relative to that information, that the two terms have the same extension is not ruled out even if, relative to that information, they have distinct intensions.¹

This infelicity in Peirce's discussion should not deter us from appreciating the fact that in the period from 1865 to 1867, Peirce relativized the intension, comprehension, or depth of a term to the total information available to the inquiring agent.² To utilize the expressions "informed depth" and "informed breadth" that Peirce himself introduced in his essay "Upon Logical Comprehension and Extension" of 1867 (W 3:70–86): two terms have the same informed depth relative to the available information K if and only if K entails that they have the same extension—that is, if and only if they have the same informed breadth relative to K.³

Peirce's discussions of informed depth and breadth appeared in the period from 1865 to 1867 first in the Harvard Lectures of 1865, then in the Lowell Lectures of 1866, and finally in "Upon Logical Comprehension and Extension" of 1867. This is a full decade before the inquiry-oriented problem-solving approach of "The Fixation of Belief" of 1877 (or views like it) were explicitly stated. Yet, both the Harvard and the Lowell Lectures took as one of their central aims to show that the syllogistic or, more generally, deductive inference is not the sole form of inference to be encompassed by an "unpsychologistic" logic. The subject matter of logic, according to Peirce, concerns the "forms of symbols" (W 1:165). Symbols have a denotation or extension and an intension or comprehension regulated by "principles" of their use (W 1:165). There are no symbols without background assumptions relative to which they have intensions or connotations determining their extensions. This is what distinguishes them from both signs and icons. The most general principles regulating the use of symbols are the province of logic. Peirce contended that both hypothetic and inductive inference proceed by formal principles regulating our use of symbols. Hence, hypothetic and inductive inference properly belong to the study of logic. In Lectures II, X, and XI of the Harvard Lectures of 1865, Peirce gave what he claimed to be an account of these formal principles not only for syllogistic reasoning but for inductive and hypothetic reasoning as well.

In the case of deduction, Peirce thought that identifying the forms of deductive arguments sufficed to furnish a criterion of the validity of these arguments. He denied that this is so for inductive or hypothetic inferences (W 1:437). But even though inductive inferences cannot be considered formally valid or invalid, considerations relevant to assessing the merits of inductive (hypothetic) inferences can be identified. Peirce made suggestions along these lines at the end of Lecture II (W 1:188–89), Lecture X (W 1:285), and Lecture XI (W 1: 286–94).

According to Peirce, the formal structure of an inductive inference is a permutation of the formal structure of a categorical syllogism. In particular, syllogisms in Barbara correspond to inductive inferences of the following form:

All S are P
All S are M
Therefore, all M are P.

Prior to reaching the inductive conclusion, the two premisses are in the body of available information. The inquiring agent faces a choice between adding the conclusion, which results from substituting "M" for "S" in "All S are P" to his body of assumptions or resting content with what he has. If the three terms are symbols, adding the conclusion to the body of information increases the informed depth or intension of M and the informed breadth or extension of P. This can happen, according to Peirce's account of informed breadth and depth, only if adding "All M are P" increases the informational value of the available information. As Peirce pointed out in 1865 (W 1:285) and in the 1867 lectures (W 2:85), the substitution of "M" for "S" in "All S are P" increases the informed depth of "M" by increasing the informational value it carries.

But because relative to the initial information, "M" has more informed breadth than "S" (that is, is judged to have at least as much extension), adopting the inductive conclusion incurs a risk of error. Whether one should accept the conclusion "All M are P" of the induction or rest content with "All S are P" involves a trade-off in which the inquirer needs to decide whether the increase in information (or "more truth," as Peirce wrote in 1865 anticipating James's misleading usage) obtained by choosing "All M are P" is worth the risk of error incurred. Peirce wrote:

> Which of the two theories to select in any case [that is, whether to draw the inductive conclusion or remain with the data] will depend on the motives which influence us. In a desperate practical case, if one's life depends upon taking the right one, he ought to select the one whose subject has the greatest connotation. In a cool speculation where safety is essential, the least extensive should be taken [W 1:285].

Thus, Peirce used his early theory of extension and intension relative to information in formulating a conception of evaluating inductive inferences in terms of the risks of error they incur and the increases in information which accrue.

In 1865, Peirce said that this analysis applies to deciding between two "theories"—that is, to deciding whether to rest content with "All S are P" or to add "All M are P" where "S," like "P" and "M," is a symbol carrying an intension as well as an extension. But Peirce thought that induction often proceeds "from fact to theory" where "S is a mere enumerative term and has no connotation at all"—that is, is a sign rather than a symbol (W 1:285). Peirce thought that induction of this sort is unavoidable. If "S" is a symbol and not merely a sign, Peirce contended that "All S are P" is itself the conclusion of an induction. He appears to have thought that some inductions must be cases where "S" is a mere sign while "M" is a symbol.

In such cases, substituting "M" for "S" increases connotation "absolutely" so that "All M are P" is to be preferred absolutely to "All S are P" (W 1:285). Peirce qualified this claim by requiring that there be "no question between this theory and some other and as long as it is not opposed by some other induction." But as long as this condition is met, Peirce seemed to think that the absolute preference for "All M are P" over "All S are P" derives from the fact that all genuine judgment involves symbols. Because "S" is not a symbol, "All S are P" does not assert a proposition. To make a judgment, "S" must be replaced by a symbol.

Peirce insisted in these early papers that symbols carrying

connotation must describe "real" properties. Disjunctive and negative terms do not always qualify. The domain of symbols is not closed under the ordinary Boolean operations.[4] But Peirce insisted:

> All thinking is a process of symbolization, for the conceptions of the understanding are symbols in the strict sense. Unless, therefore, we are to give up thinking altogether we must admit the validity of induction. But even to doubt is to think. So we cannot give up thinking and the validity of induction must be admitted [W 1:469].

There is something deeply and obviously wrong with this view. According to the young Peirce, if agent X judges that neat, sheep, swine, and deer are herbivorous, X is not properly judging at all, because the subject term is not a symbol. The agent X is not thinking until the inductive extrapolation is made to "All cloven-hoofed animals are herbivorous." But Peirce's essays of the period from 1865 to 1867 convey the clear impression that the permutations of syllogisms structuring inductive inferences are supposed to be formalizations of symbolic thinking and not merely transitions from the use of non-symbolic representations to symbolic ones.

Furthermore, Peirce nowhere explained why he rejected the closure of symbolic terms under Boolean operations. In the case of individual designators, he retreated in 1866 from the claim he made in 1865 that they can be non-symbolic. This suggests that he may have had qualms about the matter.

Peirce's account of induction in these early papers is badly flawed. Yet, elements of his discussion anticipate his later more important discussions. I believe that even in the period 1865–1867 Peirce was sensitive to a serious problem and sought to address it by restricting the Boolean closure condition on symbolic terms. The solution he proposed is, in my judgment, unacceptable; but the problem is genuine enough. Moreover, he did succeed by 1879 in proposing a much more interesting solution to the problem. Flawed though it may be, Peirce's discussion of induction in 1865–1867 introduces the problematic which he himself addressed more successfully in his later work. For this reason alone, it merits our attention.

In these early papers Peirce thought of induction as involving a trade-off between risk of error and new information, and favored the view that the trade-off is decisive in favor of incurring risk (*ceteris paribus*) when the new information enhances explanatory power. Moreover, it is clear that in "admitting the validity of induction" one does not presuppose that the conclusions of inductions are always true. In Lecture VII of the Lowell Series of 1866, Peirce asserted that of the "most rigid and careful" inductions only an "infinitesimal proportion are never found to be in any respect false" (W 1:470). Such inductions are good approximations, however, and Peirce asked why this should be so. His answer is, "there is a certain vague tendency for the whole to be like any of its parts taken at random because it is composed of its parts" (W 1:470–71). It is clear that Peirce regarded this "vague tendency" to be some stochastic process as is posited in the theory of errors. Finally, as he explicitly emphasized in Lecture VI of the 1866 series, "there is no valid inference from parts to whole if the parts have not been taken at random" (W 1:441).

Peirce offered little in the way of an explication of the notion of random selection. He wrote in 1866 that:

> When we say that neat, swine, sheep and deer are a sample taken at random of cloven-hoofed animals, we do not mean to say that the choice depended upon no other condition than that all should be cloven-hoofed; we can not know *that* and the presumption is the other way since there is a certain limitation of that class indicated by our having taken so few instances. What we mean, then, in saying that neat swine sheep and deer are taken at random from among cloven hoofed animals, is that being cloven hoofed is the only condition that consciously guided us in the selection of these animals [W 1:433].

Peirce seemed to be acutely aware of the inadequacies of this characterization and, in general, avoided giving a definition of random selection. Instead, he identified certain conditions which are axiomatic of random selection. Such a condition is stated in his 1867 review (W 2:98–102) of John Venn's *The Logic of Chance*. I do not know when Peirce first saw Venn's book (its date of publication is 1866), but it is not too far fetched to assume that the issues about Venn's book which preoccupied him in his review were on his mind when he discussed induction in his Harvard Lectures of 1865 and Lowell Lectures of 1866.

Peirce expressed his sympathy for the conception of probability found in Venn's *Logic of Chance* and his opposition to the "conceptualist" views of the followers of Laplace and De Morgan. According to the conceptualist view, probability is the degree of credence which ought to be placed in the occurrence of an event.

Peirce contended that unless the "ought" is a matter of morals, it alludes to the degree of credence one should assign a proposition in order to escape error:

> But propositions are either absolutely true or absolutely false. There is nothing *in the facts* which corresponds at all to a degree of credence, except that a genus of argument may yield a certain proportion of true conclusions from true premisses. Thus, the following form of argument would, in the long run, yield (from true premisses) a true conclusion two-thirds of the time:
>
> > A is taken at random from among the B's;
> > 2/3 of the B's are C;
> > Therefore, A is C [W 2:98–102].

Notice that Peirce required not merely that A be selected from the "reference class" of B's but also that it be taken at random. Whatever else might be meant by random selection, Peirce assumed that if A is randomly selected from the B's, the chance or statistical probability or long-run relative frequency of such random selections being C's is equal to the proportion of C's among the B's. This will obtain if a random selection from the B's is unbiased, in the sense that each element of the set of B's has the same chance of being selected as any other.

But what is to be meant by "chance" or "probability" here? As I understand him, Peirce granted to the conceptualist that the agent ought to assign a degree of credence to the proposition that A is C equal to 2/3. We should not be under any illusion that such a judgment is either true or false. On the other hand, it is grounded in the "facts" conveyed by the two premisses and the fact that two-thirds of arguments of the same form with true premisses yield true conclusions. Because of this grounding, it is all right to say that the investigator ought to assign a 2/3 degree of credence to the proposition. But in the absence of such grounding of judgments of degree of credence or subjective probability in knowledge of statistical probability, Peirce denied that we may say what the degree of credence should be. His quarrel with the conceptualists is that they think there are principles (like insufficient reason) for determining what degrees of credence should be even when no such grounding is available.

So, Peirce was not against assigning a degree of credence to the proposition that A is C. In this sense, he was not against "single case" probability any more than the arch-frequentist Reichenbach was.[5] What he was against is recommending that judgments of this sort should be made without grounding via an inference cast in the form of a probabilistic or statistical deduction from knowledge of statistical probabilities. This is the crux of Peirce's anti-conceptualist (that is, anti-Laplacian or anti-Bayesian) position—a position he took throughout his career.

Although Peirce endorsed Venn's opposition to what we now call Bayesianism, he devoted half his review to chastising Venn over his retention of what Peirce regarded as a "remnant" of conceptualism. The point is interesting, because it indicates what Peirce took to be serious problems about probabilistic reasoning. The question of what to conclude when a reliable witness attests to an incredible story vexed Venn and preoccupied Peirce throughout his life. In his second edition, Venn considered the following ancillary problem aimed at illustrating some aspects of the issue.

Suppose that 9/10 of the consumptives who visit Madeira survive the first year, whereas 1/10 of the Englishmen survive and the rest die. A consumptive Englishman applies for life insurance. What would be a fair rate of insurance for him? Venn argued that you could insure him based either on the 9/10 probability for survival or on the 1/10 probability as long as the company is in the practice of writing policies both on consumptives and on Englishmen. Peirce chastised Venn on the grounds that the statistical probability of a consumptive Englishman's surviving is unknown. Hence, there is no known fair rate of insurance. There is, in effect, no way to ground judgments of credence in knowledge of statistical probability. Venn's recommendations allowed the agent arbitrarily to assign a degree of credence without knowledge of statistical probabilities just as the conceptualists sometimes do.

The most important feature of Peirce's discussion is that his interest in a frequency interpretation of probability was not focused primarily on specifying truth conditions for probability statements but rather on characterizing the "validity" of what he called probabilistic or statistical deductions and what are also known as statistical syllogisms or direct inferences. To be sure, a statistical probability statement asserts, according to Peirce and Venn, what the limit of relative frequency would be with which a certain kind of event would occur in an infinite sequence of experiments of a given kind were such a sequence (normally counter-to-fact) implemented. In his later writing, Peirce was clear that the sense in which a fair coin would land heads with a relative frequency converging on 1/2 were it tossed an infinite number of times is quite compatible with claiming that in such an infinite sequence of tosses it could land heads every time. The probability of its landing heads on an infinite number of tosses with a relative frequency of 0.5 is itself 1, but this does not preclude an infinite sequence of nothing but tails. Thus, it is clear that Peirce did not succeed in specifying truth conditions for probability statements in terms of conditionals concerning relative frequencies in repeated trials. Probabilities were presupposed in the conditionals Peirce invoked, and Peirce knew it.

I myself have thought for a long time that those who, like Venn and Peirce, wished to provide for a notion of probability used in describing natural features of electrons, genes, gases, roulette wheels, and coins ought to follow the lead of Kolmogorov (1950), Cramer (1945), and Braithwaite (1953) in understanding statistical probability predicates to be theoretical primitives whose relevance to experimental behavior is best understood by invoking principles licensing judgments of personal probability on the basis of information about statistical probabilities and the experiment under scrutiny.[6] The kind of inference licensed is precisely the sort Peirce called a statistical or probabilistic deduction. It is often called "direct inference" nowadays. There are substantive disputes among those interested in the topic concerning the conditions under which such direct inferences are legitimate. What Kolmogorov, Cramer, and

Braithwaite recognized tacitly and what authors like Hacking (1965) insisted explicitly is that such inferences themselves are not justified because of the long-run frequency of success in using them. To be sure, one might predict a relative frequency of success in drawing correct conclusions from true premises, but such a prediction itself would be a direct inference utilizing a statistical syllogism. If its validity were in need of justification by looking at long-run success, the putative justification would initiate an infinite regress.

Following Kolmogorov et al., I am inclined to take a principle of direct inference to be a fundamental condition of rational subjective probability judgment which is not derivable from knowledge of long-run relative frequencies. The rationale for introducing it, so I argue, is that such a principle links a statistical probability attribution with predictions of test behavior in cases where one cannot invoke Carnapian reduction sentences to do the job.

This is not the place to elaborate on this line of thinking; but if it is right, the importance of Peirce's discussion of probability is found, not in his frequentism, which is at best unhelpful in clarifying the concept of statistical probability and at worst misleading, but in his discussion of statistical or probabilistic deduction—that is, direct inference. One can drop Peirce's frequentist predilections and still find something importantly insightful in what he had to say. Furthermore, even if it is undeniable that Peirce was some sort of frequentist, when seeking to explain his conception of statistical probability, he did not address the problems of characterizing a "collective" or showing how a limit of relative frequency interpretation can model the calculus of probability. Instead, he was concerned with the kinds of inferences that judgments of statistical probability warrant concerning test behavior. That is to say, he was interested in direct inference. The review of Venn's book offers striking evidence of this point. Moreover, the preoccupations of the review remain central to Peirce's thinking on probability throughout his career, whereas supplying a semantics for probability statements in terms of limits of relative frequency languished in relatively benign neglect.

I have emphasized the fact that early in his career Peirce was interested in the problem of direct inference and that this interest remained throughout his life. He stood in opposition to the view he identified in Venn for determining what probability judgment to make in a single case x known to be of type A and also of type B where the statistical probability of an A being a C is known to differ from the statistical probability of a B being a C. Both Venn and Peirce would have agreed that if one knew the statistical probability of an object which is both A and B being a C one should assign a credal probability to the proposition that x is a C equal to that statistical probability. But in the absence of such knowledge, Venn asserted that one could use personal judgment to assign a belief probability. Peirce resolutely resisted this whiff of conceptualism. Peirce was, therefore, on the side of those who insist that in direct inference one should appeal to the strongest information one has about the single case under study even if this prevents assigning numerically definite credal probabilities.

With this understanding, we can shed some light on Peirce's rather mysterious refusal to countenance disjunctive terms as symbols. In random selection of individuals from a population A, we will obtain information not only that an individual is selected from A but other information as well—for example, concerning the time and place it was selected. In random selection from cloven-hoofed animals, we find out that some of the individuals selected are neat, some are sheep, etc. This extra information can interfere with the randomness assumption in a manner similar to the one that worried Peirce in the Venn review. If we select names at random from the telephone book with the aim of identifying the ethnic composition of the community and obtain a person whose name begins with "Mc," the extra information may very well undermine the judgment that the probability of that person's being of Polish descent is equal to the percentage of individuals of Polish descent in the population sampled. The extra information in this latter example may very well be known to be statistically relevant. In other cases, it will not be known whether it is relevant or not. In the Venn review, Peirce insisted that in such cases one cannot proceed on the basis of the randomness assumption. Only if one knows that the extra information is irrelevant statistically can one do so.

Now, in induction by simple enumeration, extra information

is available. It is known that some of the cloven-hoofed animals selected are neat, some are sheep, etc. For the induction to be legitimate, we need to ensure that the extra information be irrelevant. What Peirce seems to have done is to guarantee that the extra information will be irrelevant by denying that it is genuine information at all. This is done by denying that disjunctive terms have connotation.

I certainly do not wish to defend Peirce's maneuver. It is blatantly ad hoc. It does not cohere well with his insistence that induction is a species of inference characterized by forms of symbolization. The premisses of the inference should, so one would have thought, been symbols carrying information—counter to this solution.

Nonetheless, Peirce ought to be credited with having recognized a problem that anyone who takes direct inference seriously must face—to wit, how one is to confront nuisance information that can interfere with assumptions of randomness, especially when direct inference (statistical deduction) is linked with induction as Peirce explicitly did in the 1870s and seems to have done in the 1860s as well. I believe that Peirce came up with a better answer to this question in the 1870s than he offered in the 1860s. Nonetheless, he recognized the problem in the 1860s and sought to address it with the aid of his conception of symbolic representation.

Furthermore, Peirce's Harvard Lectures of 1865 and Lowell Lectures of 1866 are testimony to the fact that his interest in a theory of representation was tied very closely to his interests in probabilistic reasoning as it applies to induction. A critical difference between the analytic traditions associated with Frege and Russell and the views of Peirce is that for Peirce, the importance of notions of denotation, connotation, and information resides in their use in characterizing values in inquiry. We risk error for the sake of new information, and it is only relative to a body of information that terms have denotation and connotation—that is, have the status of symbols. Neither Frege nor Russell thought of tailoring his semantic categories to fit the needs of an account of ampliative inference. Peirce's efforts to move in a different direction may not always have succeeded, but, in my judgment, his philosophical insight runs deeper than either Frege's or Russell's.

Peirce discussed quantitative induction in as much technical detail as he ever did in two papers: "The Probability of Induction" of 1878 (W 3:290–305) and "A Theory of Probable Inference" of 1883 (CP 2.694–754). In the notes for a "Minute Logic" of 1902, Peirce declared his intention to present his views on induction and abduction, both of which he had considered in the 1883 paper. His remarks are informative concerning what he thought of his earlier views:

> The discussion of probability naturally brings us to the interesting question of the validity of induction. I undertake to demonstrate mathematically that the validity of Induction, in the proper sense of the term, that is to say, experimental reasoning, follows from the lemmas of probabilities, from the rudiments of the doctrine of necessary consequences, without any assumption whatever about the future being like the past, or similar results following similar conditions, or the uniformity of nature, or any such vague principle. I shall set forth the reasoning in strict accuracy of form; and I defy anyone to find a flaw in it. The importance of the question for every man is tremendous. Having fully set forth my doctrine of induction, with the very strict rules to bind it down which are necessitated by the demonstration mentioned, I pass by for the present the consideration of all other theories, and proceed at once to the study of Abduction. Upon this subject, my doctrine has been immensely improved since my essay "A Theory of Probable Inference" was published in 1883. In what I said there about "Hypothetic Inference" I was an explorer upon untrodden ground. I committed, though I half corrected, a slight positive error, which is easily set right without essentially altering my position. But my capital error was a negative one, in not perceiving that, according to my own principles, the reasoning with which I was there dealing could not be the reasoning by which we are led to adopt a hypothesis, although I all but stated as much. But I was too much taken up in considering syllogistic forms and the doctrine of logical extension and comprehension, both of which I made more fundamental than they really are. As long as I held that opinion, my conceptions of Abduction necessarily confused two kinds of reasoning. When, after repeated attempts, I finally succeeded in clearing the matter up, the fact

shown out that probability proper had nothing to do with the validity of Abduction, unless in a doubly indirect manner [CP 1.102].

In this passage, Peirce admitted that his long-standing obsession with attempting to reduce the contrast in abduction, deduction, and induction to permutations of premisses and conclusions of categorical syllogisms was not so "fundamental" a project as he initially had thought. Indeed, he virtually gave up the project of assimilating the three kinds of reasoning to different permutations of the premisses and conclusions of a syllogism. Instead, he emphasized a distinction in terms of three kinds of tasks to be performed in inquiry rather than three ways of trying to prove some proposition and, as becomes clear, the "reasoning" involved in some of the categories does not sustain a relation of confirmation or proof between premisses and conclusion. Indeed, the kinds of reasoning he classified as abductive in the 1883 paper are no longer counted as such in later work but qualify as qualitative inductions instead.[7]

Essentially, then, Peirce's chief reservation with his 1883 paper concerned the way he understood abduction, not the way he treated induction or what he later called "quantitative induction," which is my main focus here. In addition, Peirce claimed that his account of the "validity of induction" does not depend upon "any assumption whatever about the future being like the past, or similar results following similar conditions, or the uniformity of nature, or any such vague principle." He did not deny that substantive assumptions are needed for the "validity" of inductions. Assumptions about the randomness of sampling procedures are needed, in particular. But assumptions about the randomness of a specific sampling procedure are assumptions about a specific category of experiments or sampling techniques far removed from "vague principles" like the uniformity of nature. Peirce denied any reliance on such presuppositions. And he displayed no interest in justifying the specific assumptions about randomness crucial to the validity of inductions, even though they are not the product of the testimony of the senses and the records of the memory. Peirce was not interested in Hume's problem of induction.[8]

Peirce's view of direct inference lies at the core of his characterization of the conditions under which induction is valid. Consider an urn containing 99 red balls and one white or one red ball and 99 white. The agent does not know which of these hypotheses is correct. He has an opportunity to observe one ball sampled at random from the urn and to note its color. Then he is to guess the composition of the urn.

Conceptualists like Bayes, Laplace, and De Morgan might proceed by first saying that in a state of ignorance each of the hypotheses has an equal probability. That is to say, in a state of ignorance, each hypothesis ought to be assigned a degree of credal probability of 0.5. Given this prior probability, Bayes theorem implies that the conditional probability that the urn contains 99 red balls given that the ball selected is a red one is 0.99. Conceptualists urge us to assign a degree of credence of 0.99 to the hypothesis that 99 balls in the urn are red via conditionalization on this observation and Bayes theorem.

At the close of "The Doctrine of Chances" of 1878 (W 3:289), Peirce promised to undermine the conceptualist analysis of this problem in his next essay in *Popular Science Monthly* and delivered on his promise in "The Probability of Induction" (W 3:290–305). He devoted sections II and III of this essay to an explanation of the conceptualist approach, its virtues and deficiencies, before turning to his own approach to the problem. So interesting did his discussion of the conceptualist approach turn out to be that he is credited by some contemporary Bayesians with insights that they as loyal Bayesians cherish (for example, Good 1983a, 1981, 1983b).[9] Thus, Peirce introduced a notion of balancing reasons (CP 7.164–167, 182) which has been embraced as a Bayesian account of the Keynesian conception of weight of argument.[10] But Peirce introduced this and other notions in an elaboration of conceptualism designed in the end to reduce it to absurdity. He did this in "The Probability of Induction" in 1878 and in the typescript "The Logic of Drawing History from Ancient Manuscripts" dated 1901.[11] Peirce was quite clear about this. He was no Bayesian. Indeed, Peirce's complaint was that prior probabilities based on insufficient reason are not grounded on knowledge of statistical probability via direct inference.

The relative probability of this or that arrangement of Nature is something we should have a right to talk about if universes were as plenty as blackberries, if we could put a quantity of them in a bag, shake them well up, draw out a sample, and examine them to see what proportion of them had one arrangement and what proportion another. But even in that case, a higher universe would contain us, in regard to whose arrangements the conception of probability could have no applicability [W 3:300–301].

Thus, from Peirce's point of view, it is illegitimate to derive a posterior probability from a prior probability and the data via Bayes theorem. There is, however, a way to employ the data to obtain a result. Prior to drawing the ball from the urn, we can say that the statistical probability of obtaining a red is 0.99 if the hypothesis that the urn contains 99 red balls is true, and that the statistical probability of a red is 0.01 if the urn contains 1 red ball. Let us say that the outcome of the draw from the urn is a winner if and only if either the ball drawn is red and there are 99 red balls in the urn or a white ball is drawn and there is 1 red ball in the urn. The outcome is a loser if and only if it is not a winner.

The statistical probability of obtaining a winner on a random selection is 0.99. Hence, prior to drawing a ball from the urn, the agent has a degree of credence of 0.99 that a winner will be drawn. This he can obtain via statistical deduction, that is, direct inference.

R. A. Fisher had the thought in the late 1920s that if one observes a red ball, one is still entitled to assign 0.99 degree of credence to the hypothesis that a winner will be drawn via direct inference. Since, in the light of the information that a red ball has been drawn, the claim that a winner is drawn is equivalent to the claim that 99 of the balls in the urn are red, Fisher argued that we could assign a credal probability to the hypothesis that 99 of the balls in the urn are red, appealing to knowledge of statistical probability and direct inference. Without being a "conceptualist" or Laplacian who invokes a principle of insufficient reason, one can obtain their conclusions after all. This, in the crudest terms, is the core idea behind Fisher's notorious "fiducial argument" (Fisher 1930, 533).[12]

Someone like Peirce would have objected to this. If, in addition to knowing that the chance of a winner on a random selection is 0.99 and that a ball has been selected at random, one knew that the ball selected is red, the random selection is now known to be one where the ball selected is red. To use direct inference here to obtain information about whether the ball selected is a winner, one would have to know the statistical probability of obtaining a winner on a random selection yielding a red. Although this statistical probability is given to be 1 if 99 of the balls in the urn are red and to be 0 if 1 of them is red, the agent does not know which of these statistical hypotheses is true. This predicament is quite parallel to the case of the English consumptive planning a trip to Madeira and similarly structured problems about the testimony of reliable witnesses to improbable events. In all these cases, the agent knows the precise probability of an event of kind R occurring on a trial of some kind S, knows that a trial of kind S and also of kind T will occur but does not know the probability of an R occurring on a trial of kind S&T. In the case before us, the statistical probability of a winner on a random selection which is also a selection of a red ball is either 0 or 1. No degree of credence can be mandated for the outcome of experiment. The statistical probability of a winner on a random selection yielding red is either 0 or 1. Consequently, direct inference fails to license any numerically definite degree of credence for the hypothesis that a winner is drawn or to the hypothesis that 99 of the balls in the urn are red.

Nonetheless, there is no doubt that Peirce did understand induction to involve an inference superficially like the fiducial argument. Before a ball is drawn from the urn, the experiment is known as a random selection of the ball from the urn. The inquiring agent knows nothing about the color of the ball to be drawn. As long as it is known that a sample is to be taken, direct inference does justify the degree of credibility of 0.99 to the hypothesis that a winner will be drawn. It is only after we find out the color of the ball obtained that we can no longer make this judgment.

Suppose that instead of looking for a winner, we were considering a rule for adopting answers to the question as to the contents of the urn. We might contemplate various functions for determining what answer to adopt depending on whether a red or a white ball is drawn. One such rule is to predict that the urn has 99 red if a red is drawn and to predict that the urn has 1 red if a white is drawn.

Such a rule is a program for making predictions we endorse before observing the outcome of sampling. On the assumption that we will follow the rule, we can determine a statistical probability of success on an application of it. That will be 0.99. By direct inference, we can, before the trial, assign credal probability 0.99 to the hypothesis that using the rule will yield a correct answer.

It would be a mistake, however, to assign a credal probability of 0.99 to the claim that the urn contains 99 red balls given the observation of a red ball. That would betray the principles of direct inference which Peirce gives every indication he endorsed in the review of Venn and in his discussions of reliable testimony to improbable events throughout his career.

The core of Peirce's theory of quantitative induction runs as follows: Before experimentation or sampling, devise a program for using data of observations as input where the output would be the adoption of some answer to a question and where the statistical probability of avoiding error can be assessed with reasonable definiteness relative to the information available before testing. Peirce explained his theory as it applies to estimation of binomial parameters and the means of normal distributions in sufficient detail to make it clear that he was proposing the Neyman-Pearson theory of confidence interval estimation a half a century before they did.

In particular, Peirce unequivocally and quite clearly understood that once one has observed the data and accepted them as evidence, one cannot use these data as evidence to justify assigning credal probabilities to the hypotheses being considered, as the Laplacians or advocates of Fisherian fiducial probability would do. In the example of the urn, Peirce would have said that having observed the red ball, we can say that either we have obtained the right answer or, if we were to repeat the experiment, the statistical probability of detecting our mistake would be 0.99. It is in just this sense that Peirce thought that induction is self-correcting.[13]

The role of the probability judgment is to indicate that if, for whatever reason, the issue is reopened, repeating the experiment will uncover whatever error may have been made in the original estimate with the given probability. Hence, even in 1883, Peirce understood that there was more to the transformation of the syllogism than the operations just described. Probability had to be understood quite differently in the direct inference and in the induction.

In my judgment, the critical distinction between Peirce's mature account of induction and his accounts in the papers of 1865–1866 derives from his recognition in his later work that the data of inductive inference are used as input and not as evidence. Thus, in planning beforehand to sample at random from the cloven-hoofed animals, one may obtain as a result all sorts of neat, sheep, swine, etc. But prior to obtaining the verdict that all cloven-hoofed are herbivorous, the inquirer is not supposed to find out any information concerning the data. It is not as though the term "is either a cow or a sheep or a swine or a deer" lacks an informed depth so that even though one finds out that all items to which this term is observed to apply are herbivorous and uses it as evidence, the new information does not interfere with the randomness of the sample. (That was the position Peirce took in 1865 and 1866.) Rather, it is that when the agent undertakes to follow a program for using data as input, the agent does not have any such information at all because the data function as input. Hence, as Peirce himself wrote in his retrospective description of his earlier work, the deployment of the notions of intension and extension in discussions of induction and hypothesis are not so fundamental as he thought they were. I contend that it is his recognition of the "forward look" or the possibility of using data as input rather than as evidence that led to this shift in attitude.

Whether one adopts Peirce's earlier approach to induction or his later one, however, inductions are not inferences from premisses to conclusions. According to his earlier view, they are not inferences because the so-called premisses are not propositions which must be symbols carrying information. According to the more mature view, inductions are not inferences because the inquirer commits himself in advance of collecting data to following a rule for using the data as input. This does not preclude regarding the data reports as reports of the truth of propositions carrying information. It does preclude using such reports as premisses of an argument to the inductive conclusion.

Peirce was no clearer in his later writings than in his earlier writings on this point. He called this approach "quantitative induction" and thought of it as a species of inference from premisses to conclusion. In doing so, he perpetuated one of the mistakes he made in his 1865–1867 papers. But then Neyman and Pearson were not terribly clear about the matter either. Neyman and Pearson called their approach a theory of "inductive behavior." I am inclined to think this view misleading. If by "behavior" one means engaging in some activity other than forming a new belief, then speaking of inductive behavior is too restrictive.

Induction, according to Peirce's conception, is the process whereby the conjectures proposed in virtue of abduction are subjected to testing and a conclusion is incorporated into the settled assumptions. Given the array of conjectures that represent potential answers to the question obtained via abduction, and given also substantive statistical assumptions about the experimental design being deployed, Peirce contended that no further assumptions about uniformity of nature and the like are required.

Philosophers worried about Hume's problem will no doubt wonder about the substantive statistical assumptions concerning the statistical design, including in many cases the claim that sampling is random. Advocate of the belief–doubt model of inquiry that he was, Peirce was not perturbed by this. Either these assumptions are settled for the moment, in which case they are not open to serious doubt, or they are conjectural. In the former case, the "validity" of the induction is not open to serious doubt. In the latter, the validity is conjectural and the implementation of the procedure is not validated.

Although Peirce was right, in my opinion, in turning his back on Hume's problem and other questions provoked by the Cartesian tradition, there is an aspect of his account of induction which seems to me to be doubtful. Suppose our inquiring agent X begins by taking for granted that either 99 of the balls in the urn are red or 99 of the balls in the urn are white. Suppose that he samples at random with replacement 10 times from the urn.

Suppose he obtains 5 red balls and 5 whites. Nothing here is inconsistent with X's initial assumptions. And one can devise an inductive rule to accommodate such outcomes. Such a result should provoke the response to remain in suspense between the rival hypotheses.

But X might feel that the result of experimentation ought to warrant reconsideration of his background assumptions. Either he should open up his mind to other hypotheses about the contents of the urn (for example, the hypothesis that 50 per cent are red and 50 per cent are white), or he should question the assumptions made about the design and conduct of the experiment, or both.

Of course, matters could be even worse. The experiment might have yielded a green ball and that would, indeed, be inconsistent with the background information. If X had committed himself in advance to endorsing the deliverances of experimentation, this result would leave him in difficulty.

Peirce, of course, explicitly acknowledged that the background assumptions of an inquiry may be subject to revision as the result of inquiry. However, he failed to attend to the reasoning involved in giving up settled assumptions with the same care he devoted to adding new assumptions to the background via induction. Nor is this merely an oversight. Although Peirce seemed to say that the output of an induction is not a conjecture or a guess in the sense in which the output of an abduction is, his view on this matter is not always clear. And there is good reason for this. Peirce's conception of the aims of inquiry and scientific progress are at odds with his advocacy of the belief–doubt model and critical common-sensism (Levi 1980a, 1980c, and 1984b).

According to these doctrines, in the context of any inquiry, the inquiring agent takes for granted a variety of assumptions relative to which he, at that time, judges truth—in Quine's phrase—"as earnestly and as seriously as can be." Peirce also advocated, as the ultimate aim of inquiry, contributing to an eventual consensus on the part of the "community" on the true complete story, and hoped that the methods on inquiry would, in the end of days, converge on that true complete story were the community of inquirers to keep up the pace for that long. From the perspective of Peirce's messianic realism, however, it would be counter-productive to give up any settled assumptions—at least, given the perspective of the inquiring agent who endorses these assumptions. To give them up incurs the risk that they will eventually be replaced with claims the agent is currently certain are false. To incur such a risk is to deliberately betray the ultimate goal. But to engage in quantitative induction or any technique of what I have called elsewhere "routine expansion," where new information is acquired by programs for using data as input, is to incur such a risk. The value of induction is thereby undermined.

It seems to me that to avoid this unpleasant result either Peirce's belief–doubt model, which suggests that truth is judged relative to the evolving doctrine, must be given up or his messianic realism abandoned. Peirce himself did not seem to want to do either of these things and as a result, in the face of the tension, took several inconsistent lines. Popper, who shared with Peirce a penchant for messianic realism, bypassed the problem by abandoning induction and with it the belief–doubt model. Dewey retained the belief–doubt model but abandoned Peirce's messianic realism. For Dewey, not only was the quest for the true complete story of the world not the ultimate aim for inquiry, but truth was not a value for inquiry at all as it seems to have been for both James and Peirce, albeit in different ways. I have gone on record as favoring Dewey's rejection of messianic realism while retaining the belief–doubt model. But I have sought to develop a view of truth and avoidance of error as a common feature of proximate aims of specific inquiries which retains avoidance of error as a value directing the conduct of inquiry and the development of its methods. Within the framework of such "myopic" or "secular" realism, it is possible to preserve an important place for Peirce's insights into the importance of using data as input as a means for obtaining new information and, in this sense, for his conception of induction. By way of contrast, Peirce's own insistence on a conception of scientific progress toward the truth, which he shares with so many others, creates problems for his own most original insights.[14]

Notes

1. Whether K entails that the extension of one term A is no less than that of another B or entails that it is greater, the informed depth of B is greater than that of A. The extension of A is judged to be no less than that of B in the first case and to be greater than that of B in the second. Peirce would say that the informed breadth of A is greater than that of B in both cases, but would then have said that the excess of the breadth of A over B in the first case is "uncertain" whereas it is "certain" in the second.

Peirce's approach could have been extended to yield an account of individual designators and identity statements. When it is taken for granted that the morning star is identical with the evening star, "the morning star = the evening star" provides us with no new information any more than "the morning star = the morning star" does. Relative to the information that the morning star is identical with the morning star, neither identity statement has any more cognitive worth that any other. Frege (1952, 56–57), of course, thought otherwise. Statements like "a = a" are analytic, whereas statements of the type "a = b" often contain valuable extensions to our knowledge. Frege appealed to this point in motivating his celebrated distinction between sense and reference.

From the point of view suggested by Peirce's 1865 Harvard Lectures and 1866 Lowell lectures, Frege's argument fails. For the agent who takes for granted that a = b, this judgment no more extends his or her knowledge than the claim that a = a.

Of course, if the inquiring agent does not as yet take for granted that the morning star is identical with the evening star, this claim carries novel information not carried by the claim that the morning star is identical with the morning star. "The morning star" and "the evening star" have different "informed depths" or, perhaps, "informed senses," even though, as far as the agent knows, they might refer to the same object. But, in the context, the agent is not supposing that the morning star is identical with the evening star as Frege invites him to do.

I suggest that Peirce ought to have taken this approach to this topic had he broached it. To my knowledge, he did not. Indeed, his remarks about individual designators in these early papers show some ambivalence as to how they should be treated.

In his Harvard Lectures of 1865, Peirce held that particulars are signs rather than symbols. They have breadth or denotation but lack depth or connotation, and their denotations are not relative to information. He took proper names to be signs of this sort. He acknowledged that there are singular terms which, in contrast to particulars, are symbols, and it is entertainable that he might have included definite descriptions among these, although I have no solid textual evidence to this effect.

In Lowell Lecture VI of 1866, however, Peirce seemed to deny that it was possible to have singular terms which are signs although they were considered to be conceivable. Proper names like "Daniel Webster" are symbols precisely because such names are replaceable by descriptions relative to background information (W 1:460–61). The 1866 view of individual designators is compatible with the extension of Peirce's epistemically relativized contrast between extension and intension to Frege's problem.

This view of individual designators ought to have been congenial to Peirce. When it is already settled and known that the morning star is identical with the evening star, there is no real and living doubt concerning the issue. Relative to that information, the identity claim is judged true with the same certainty as the claim that the morning star is identical with the morning star is. Whatever one may think of the distinction between the a priori and the posteriori or the analytic and the synthetic, these distinctions have little bearing on what does or does not have cognitive value to an inquiring agent. What is of cognitive value to the problem-solving inquirer is the acquisition of new, error-free information. If the truth of a proposition has already been settled, it makes no difference whether it is a priori or empirical, analytic or synthetic, as far as its cognitive worth is concerned.

Of course, when in ignorance, we may remain assured that the morning star is identical with the morning star while doubting that the morning star is identical with the evening star. In such a state of information, the latter identity has a cognitive value the former lacks. It represents possibly true new information. The inquirer may be interested in deciding whether it is true or false. Thus, an interesting distinction between sense and reference arises. "The morning star" and "the evening star" have different informed senses because the available information entails neither identity nor difference of their references.

2. Frege would object strenuously to the approach ascribed to Peirce in note 1. He insisted that the sense of a name ought not to be confused with ideas associated with it. Different persons may associate different ideas with the same name (Frege 1952, 59). Yet, they can communicate with one another by means of expressions containing the name. Frege supposed that there must be a common *Sinn* which differs from the idiosyncratic ideas to account for such interpretation. The information available to one agent is not, in general, the same as that available to another. States of information, states of belief or "interpretants" as Peirce sometimes called them, like ideas, are idiosyncratic. So, the informed depth or informed sense could not, for Frege, be serviceable for the purposes of accounting for communication any more than ideas could.

Frege's objection begs the question against views like Peirce's. Frege explicitly introduced the sense-reference contrast to account for the cognitive value of identity claims, not to account for the way agents communicate with one another. The Peircean response relativizes cognitive value to states of information or interpretants. Even if it were inadequate as a means for explaining communication, it does not follow that it is inadequate as an account of the cognitive value of identity claims.

In any case, the Peircean approach can handle the worry about communication as well. If X is in a cognitive state implying that the morning star is identical with the evening star and Y is in a cognitive state implying that they are different, they can still communicate with each other for the purpose of carrying on a joint investigation to settle the differences between them without begging questions. To do so, they must be able to supply truth conditions for "the morning star is identical with the evening star" relative to a potential belief state or state of information which leaves the truth value of the disputed claim unsettled. The cognitive state or "interpretant" as Peirce called it reflects the shared agreements between agents X and Y.

If X and Y were prepared (perhaps counter-to-fact) to undertake a joint inquiry to settle their disagreement, they should both come to doubt the truth of the claim that the morning star is identical with the evening star. From that perspective, they would avoid begging controversial issues.

Even if X and Y are prepared to go their separate ways without trying to resolve their dispute, they can at least understand each other's view in the sense that they can characterize truth conditions for each other's convictions relative to a set of assumptions that would represent the non-question-begging shared agreements they would endorse were they to engage in a joint inquiry.

If X doubts whether Y agrees or disagrees with him about the identity of the morning and the evening star, he is not obliged to follow Davidson's counsel of charity and deploy hermeneutical ingenuity to promote agreement. It would be more congruent with a Peircean perspective to obey the injunction to acknowledge disagreement only when a potential belief state can be found relative to which the issues under dispute can be adjudicated without question begging.

If Y's utterances suggest that Y believes that the morning star exists but is distinct from the morning star, it is difficult to see how X and Y can move to a system of shared agreements relative to which X and Y assign truth conditions to "the morning star = the morning star" without begging the question. The minimal requirements for doing so are undermined and, in this sense, communication is frustrated. In such cases, more radical hermeneutical surgery may be called for. Perhaps Y's verbal declaration "the morning star = the morning star" is reconstrued as "the morning star$_1$ = the morning star$_2$," so that X can identify a contraction of his current state of belief relative to which he is in doubt as to the truth of this sentence. "Morning star$_1$" might be said to refer to Venus and "morning star$_2$" to the star that rises in the morning.

Communication requires the satisfaction of conditions for identifying agreements and disagreements for the purpose of undertaking joint inquiries and deliberations. There is no reason to think that designators need to have associated with them context-independent senses in order to be useful in such communication.

3. Friends and foes of theories of "direct reference" may mistakenly think that I am attributing to Peirce and advocating myself a doctrine of direct reference. My approach is "Millian" in claiming that designators lack senses independent of states of information or belief. But this is true of every designator, not just logically proper names. On the other hand, my view is "descriptivist" in denying that any designator "d" is judged to have a reference relative to a body of information unless the body of information implies the identity of d with the one and only F where 'F' is some extralogical description. For example, if all I know is that Gödel proved the incompleteness theorem, then all I know is that someone proved the incompleteness theorem, not that only one person did. If I do not know that at most one person proved the incompleteness theorem, the expression "Gödel" is not judged to have a reference. To this extent, the view I favor resembles descriptivist views like Frege's. But neither Peirce's view nor mine is descriptivist any more than it is Millian.

4. In the Harvard Lectures of 1865, singular terms are said to lack connotation and, hence, the status of symbols. But as I noted in note 2, Peirce seemed to change his mind about singular terms in the Lowell Lectures of 1866. He continued, however, to resist the automatic recognition of disjunctive and negative terms as having connotation.

5. In Reichenbach 1938, sections 33 and 34, he obliquely acknowledges that degrees of credence (or "weights" as he calls them) can be probabilities assigned to "the single case." In spite of rhetorical pirouettes aimed at masking this concession to subjective interpretations of probability, neither Venn, nor Peirce, nor Reichenbach denied applicability of probability measures in representing degrees of belief used in assessing fair betting rates.

6. In Levi 1967 and 1980a and elsewhere, I take the position that statistical probability attributions resemble disposition predicates in being "placeholders" for descriptions acceptable in fundamental explanation relative to a research program. Relative to descriptions of test behavior, such

statistical attributions are "theoretical." The links with test behavior are specified by means of direct inference, however. These are rules of inference irreplaceable by truth-value–bearing bridge laws.

7. In a manuscript of 1905 (CP 2.755–760), Peirce classified inductions as crude, quantitative, and qualitative. A comparison with the discussion in "The Theory of Probable Inference" suggests that qualitative induction in 1905 is hypothetic inference or abduction in 1883. As he admitted in 1883, hypothetic inference may be viewed as "an induction respecting characters instead of respecting things" (CP 2.707). He also conceded that "characters" have to be weighed rather than counted. The terse description of CP 2.759 suggests that in 1905, he thought qualitative induction to be this type of reasoning. This interpretation is confirmed by Peirce's letter to Paul Carus in 1910. There he explicitly admitted that he used to "confound" qualitative induction with hypothesis or abduction (CP 8.233). Peirce muddied the water a bit in the next paragraph by suggesting that what he called "hypothesis" in 1883 "is so far from being that, that it is rather Quantitative than Qualitative Induction. At any rate, it is treated *mostly* as Quantitative. Hypothesis proper is in that paper only touched upon in the last section" (CP 8.234). I suspect that the allegation that what he called hypothetic inference in 1883 was more quantitative than qualitative induction derives from his greater confidence in 1883 than in 1905 or 1910 that the "weighing" of characters could be presented in quantitative form. If this is right, the crucial point remains. Insofar as Peirce's fiddling with syllogisms has any merit at all (whatever merit it has, seems to me, can be obtained more effectively with other means), it concerns the relation between statistical deduction and induction.

According to Peirce's twentieth-century view, the task of abduction is identifying potential answers to questions and evaluating them as interesting enough to test in subsequent inquiry. Induction is the procedure of reaching a conclusion as to the status of a potential answer on the basis of the data yielded by a test. Should it be subjected to further test? If not, should it be rejected, or should it be accepted as part of the settled background information? It is the task of induction to draw inferences of this sort. Peirce realized in later life that the reasonings appropriate to these differing tasks are not captured by formal structures corresponding to different permutations of syllogisms. As a consequence, Peirce also abandoned his earlier explicit statements grouping abduction and induction together as species of ampliative inference. Via induction one does acquire new information and, in this sense, induction is ampliative. Abduction does not yield new information but rather potential additions to information in the guise of conjectures meriting further scrutiny. The difference between the acquisition of new information to be taken as resources for subsequent inquiry and conjectures is not, according to Peirce's belief–doubt model of inquiry, a mere question of degree.

But he did not abandon the distinction between the two ways of permuting premisses of categorical syllogisms with their conclusions. To the contrary, he retained the distinction but now saw it as two distinct types of induction—quantitative and qualitative. The point is important; for, as Peirce saw it, his account of induction pivoted on the possibility of permutations of the premisses and conclusions of probabilistic or statistical deductions or syllogisms.

For an excellent discussion of Peirce's revisions of his ideas about the relationship between induction and abduction, see Fann (1970).

8. Although Peirce mentioned Hume in connection with topics like associationist psychology and testimony for improbable events, to my knowledge, his only reference to Hume in connection with induction appears in his 1865 lecture on Kant, the seventh in the Harvard series of 1865 (W 1:240). He read Hume as showing that "the principle of causality" cannot be learned from experience and as concluding from this that "the whole notion of cause is illusory." He did not dispute the claim that the principle of causalty cannot be learned from experience but sympathized with Kant that the concept of cause is not illusory. But at no point during this lecture or any other lecture in the 1865 series did Peirce undertake to refute Hume's skeptical arguments. Indeed, in his 1865 Harvard Lecture on Whewell, Mill, and Compte, Peirce took Mill to task for begging the question in justifying his uniformity principle by induction (W 1:219–23) and repeated the same complaint in his 1866 Lowell Lectures, Lecture IV. To my knowledge, in his subsequent discussions, he paid the topic no further attention. His subsequent criticisms of Mill's uniformity principle are chiefly addressed to the complaint that Mill neglected stochastic processes. Given that Peirce was not interested in Hume's problem, his account of the validity of induction cannot be construed as a vindicationist or pragmatic response to Hume's problem along the lines of Reichenbach, Feigl, and Salmon. These authors regarded Hume's problem as a legitimate problem and sought to address it by invoking appeals to the aims of inquiry and the idea that rational agents ought to avoid weakly dominated options. No such argument is to be found in Peirce. And it is a good thing too; for even if one were to take Hume's problem seriously, as Peirce does not do, vindicationist arguments are notoriously defective. They assume that in scientific inquiry we are indifferent between obtaining an erroneous informative answer and an error-free but uninformative answer. Thus, if we compare the instruction to predict that there is no limit to a series of experiments no

matter what the data with some so-called known-to-be-convergent rule, vindicationists would say that if there is no limit, the two options are equally bad. If there is a limit, the known-to-be-convergent rule is better. So, following a known-to-be-convergent rule weakly dominates the alternative. But surely, if there is no limit, anyone who predicted that would have been right, and that would seem to be better than being wrong by projecting a false and, indeed, non-existent limit (Levi 1965). Peirce never expressed such indifference to truth when he talked about aims of inquiry. So, not only is the worry that provokes vindicationist arguments not one that Peirce would take seriously, but had he taken it seriously, he could not have endorsed the value judgments on the basis of which vindicationist arguments are typically advanced. Peirce had no pragmatic justification of induction because he offered no justification of induction at all. He did offer an account of conditions under which he thought inductions, or at least quantitative inductions, are valid. But he never presented them as a response to Hume's problem, and rightly so; for they are not a relevant response to Hume's problem. Peirce's reaction to Hume's problem, if one can call it that, was to change the subject. He thought Kant was trying to do the same thing. Hence, his early admiration for Kant. I cannot say confidently whether Peirce was being overly charitable to Kant or not. In any case, Peirce surely changed the subject on Kant as well as Hume. Instead of asking how are synthetical a priori judgments possible, he asked how are synthetical judgments possible altogether?

9. Good originally charged Peirce with an error that Peirce did not make. Good's misreading of Peirce is twofold. He took a lengthy passage in Peirce which is part of an effort to develop implications of the "conceptualist"—that is, Laplacian or Bayesian—outlook which are unacceptable as representing a point of view Peirce endorsed. In addition, he failed to take into account Peirce's requirement that "concurrent" arguments be "independent." Under this assumption, the alleged technical mistake is no mistake at all. But Peirce uses the assumption of independence to derive an absurd result, which he supposes conceptualists must endorse (W 2:296). This assumption is one which Good would not accept and no Bayesian is obliged to accept. So, Peirce's argument is not so compelling, in this respect, as he thought it was. But see note 7 above.

10. In CP 7.176, Peirce clearly stated that the method balancing likelihoods is acceptable when the assumptions supporting it are in place. But he insisted as he did earlier that these assumptions are factual statistical assumptions and are not to be endorsed a priori. In the 1901 essay, Peirce took the method of balancing likelihoods to be a reconstruction of Hume's "excessively crude" account of the logic of testimony in his essay on mira-

cles (CP 7.165). He also credited De Morgan with the technique (CP 7.168), which may, perhaps, explain why he links it so tightly with the conceptualist view in his 1878 paper.

11. R. A. Fisher, 1930 especially p. 533. Fisher did not, strictly speaking, consider simple examples of the sort described in this paragraph. We should thank I. Hacking (1965) for introducing this kind of illustration into the discussion of fiducial reasoning. The example illustrates well the main thrust of Fisher's reasoning. See Levi 1980a, chaps. 14–16 and Seidenfeld 1979.

12. Fisher did not, strictly speaking, consider simple examples of the sort described in this paragraph. Hacking (1965) may be credited with introducing this kind of illustration into the discussion. See Levi 1980a, chaps.14–16, and Seidenfeld 1979.

13. In reflections on his 1878 "Doctrine of Chances" written in 1910 (CP 2.662), Peirce suggested that terms like "verisimilitude" or "likelihood" be used rather than "probability" in evaluating conclusions of inductive reasoning. An account of the Neyman–Pearson approach is offered in chap. 17 of Levi (1980a) and in Seidenfeld (1979).

14. These issues have an important bearing on the Peircean insistence that our knowledge is fallible. Three versions of fallibilism, though interrelated, ought to be isolated for critical scrutiny (see Levi 1980a, chaps. 1–3). Epistemic fallibilism is the view that some proposition h in X's body of knowledge K at time t is possibly false according to X's standards for serious possibility at t. Corrigibilism is the view that every item in K is possibly removable from K later on according to X's standard for serious possibility at t. Categorical fallibilism is the view that every logical possibility is a serious possibility according to X's standard for serious possibility at t.

Epistemic fallibilism is a thesis about the relationship between X's knowledge at t and his standard for serious possibility at t—that is, how X at t distinguishes between what is possibly true and not possibly true in the sense of "possible" in which doubting that h is true is judging it possible that h is false. Epistemic fallibilism denies that X's knowledge at t coincides with his standard for serious possibility.

I understand Peirce's belief–doubt model as claiming that if belief that h is settled for X at t, it is "indubitable" and that this means that according to X at t, there is no serious possibility that h is false. Furthermore, according to the belief–doubt model, X is not required to justify what is settled pending confrontation with good reasons for unsettling it. I have not been able to discern a dominant univocal use of the term "knowledge" in Peirce's writing. I suspect that sometimes knowledge or perfect knowledge is the opinion that is permanently settled according to the viewpoint of the "community" at the end of days. Such knowledge is incorrigible; but there is no serious possibility that it is false from the point of view of the community at the end of days. Hence, if X is the community at the end of days, epistemological infallibilism is satisfied. But it is violated for any other agent.

Knowledge in this sense, however, has little bearing on the belief–doubt model except insofar as Peirce hoped that fixing beliefs scientifically would, if pursued indefinitely, converge on the error-free incorrigible community opinion.

It is at least compatible with much of what Peirce says to equate knowledge that h with error-free and doubt-free belief that h. From X's point of view at t, if X is free of doubt that h is true, X is convinced that X knows that h. X's knowledge at t then coincides with X's standard for serious possibility.

Given this sense of "knowledge," the belief–doubt model implies rejection of epistemological fallibilism. It also implies rejection of characterizations of knowledge as true justified belief. From X's point of view at t, if X does not doubt that h is true at t, X knows that h at t even if he cannot offer a justification for his belief. Justification is required for revising one's point of view. Advocates of the view that knowledge is true justified belief confuse knowing that h with coming-to-know that h. From X's point of view prior to adding h to his settled convictions, X can say that he will come to know h if and only if (i) he comes to believe that h, (ii) h is true, and (iii) he is justified relative to what he currently knows in coming to believe that h (see Levi 1980a, chap. 1). From X's point of view prior to adding h, however, what he already knows is true. He has no doubt about this, and, hence, there is no serious possibility that it is false. There is no need to justify his conviction or his continued conviction in what is already settled.

I cannot claim that Peirce uses the term "knowledge" so that knowledge is equated with an agent's standard for serious possibility—that is, with what is free of doubt. But Peirce's belief–doubt model clearly does not require inquiring agents to justify beliefs which are free of doubt and, hence, in the standard for serious possibility. What may need justification are revisions of belief. But what is currently free of doubt is in no need of justification, and the inquiring agent X does not and should not be searching for such justification (see "The Fixation of Belief" of 1877 and "How to Make our Ideas Clear" of 1878 in CP 3.242–276 for early versions of this view; it is reiterated in "Issues of Pragmaticism" of 1905, CP.5.438–462). Hence, if X's knowledge at t is not equated with X's standard for serious possibility at t, the belief–doubt model suggests that in inquiry X is not concerned to come to know what is currently settled, whether what is currently settled is known or not.

I am not interested in engaging in senseless and tedious logomachies concerning the term "knowledge"; but for anyone who thinks that in inquiry we seek to add to our knowledge (that is, to come to know what is currently unknown), either the belief–doubt model or the distinction between knowledge and the standard for serious possibility is questionable. In this sense, the Peircean belief–doubt model equates X's corpus of knowledge at t with his standard of serious possibility at t. Hence, epistemic fallibilism is rejected.

But if knowledge is equated with the standard for serious possibility, Peirce was an epistemic corrigibilist. Because the standard for serious possibility is revisable and, indeed, legitimately so, it cannot be restricted to logical truths on all occasions and, hence, categorical fallibilism must also be rejected. (This too is apparent in the papers just cited.)

My contention is, therefore, that Peirce's advocacy of the belief–doubt model early in his career and his return to a variant of it in his discussion of critical common-sensism later in his career implies a distinction between corrigibility, on the one hand, and fallibility (both epistemic and categorical), on the other. Moreover, it implies that Peirce was *not* a fallibilist in either the epistemic or the categorical sense, although he was a corrigibilist.

In unpublished fragments from the 1890s, Peirce presented a point of view substantially at odds with this one. His conception of knowledge is, in his own words, "fallibilist," and by this he means not only what I call "corrigibilist" but also epistemically and categorically fallibilist. "But what is worse, from our point of view, they begin to look upon science as a guide to conduct, that is, no longer as pure science but as an instrument for a practical end. One result of this is that all probable reasoning is despised. If a proposition is to be applied to action, it has to be embraced or believed without reservation. There is no room for doubt, which can only paralyze action. But the scientific spirit requires a man at all times ready to dump his whole cartload of beliefs, the moment experience is against them. The desire to learn forbids him to be perfectly cocksure that he knows already. Besides positive science can only rest on experience; and experience can never result in absolute certainty, exactitude, necessity or universality. But it is precisely with the universal and necessary, that is, with Law, that conscience concerns itself. Thus the real character of science is destroyed as soon as it is made an adjunct to conduct; and especially all progress in the inductive sciences is brought to a standstill" (CP 1.55, from a manuscript on the History of Science, ca. 1896).

This passage and others like it clearly endorse epistemological fallibilism and, quite likely, categorical fallibilism as well. It seems to be at odds with his endorsements of the belief–doubt model and critical common-sensism early and late in his career. These expressions of Peirce's fallibilism appear in unpublished papers in the 1890s and may represent temporary and private waverings from the views he held during most of his career. It is also possible that they reflect different uses of epistemic terminology and are, after all, consistent with his other views.

However, I think there is more to the story. I have argued elsewhere (Levi 1980a, chaps. 1-3; 1984a, chap. 6; and 1984b) that Peirce's messianic realism is at odds with the belief-doubt model. According to messianic realism, the ultimate aim of scientific inquiry is to obtain a true complete story of the world. For Peirce, this is a community project which cannot be fully realized except in the infinite long run and then only with moral (not absolute) certainty even if the community of scientific inquirers were to continue forever. Messianic realism precludes revisions of the standard for serious possibility—counter to the requirements of the belief-doubt model. It may be the case that remarkable passages like the citation given above and others from the same period reflect one way Peirce sought to come to terms with the tension between the belief-doubt model and messianic realism.

Philosophers who attach importance to the a priori/a posteriori or to the analytic/synthetic distinction have tended to conflate corrigibility with fallibility as Peirce did in the 1890s. X is justified in placing maximum conviction in the a priori (analytic truth). There is no serious possibility that it is false, and it is immune from revision. These various properties fall apart if one distinguishes between corrigibility and fallibility as the belief-doubt model does.

According to the belief-doubt model, X at t does not distinguish between logical truths or mathematical truths and any other settled assumptions in his corpus with respect to the certainty of X's conviction as to their truth. X should assign them all belief or credal probability 1. According to X there is no serious possibility that any of them is false.

On the other hand, should there be any pressure to give some item of K up, some items of K are more open to being given up than others. To some degree, grades of vulnerability to revision of this sort are context-dependent, but some assumptions (such as logical or mathematical truths) may be maximally incorrigible or nearly so. Many of the assumptions that exhibit this property according to X are those that would widely be taken to be a priori. One might, therefore, contemplate replacing the concept of the a priori with the concept of the incorrigible. This will not quite do. Assumptions in X's corpus such as "X exists" are incorrigible for X though, of course, not for Y. Such "idiosyncratic incorrigibles" do not fit well into the surrogate for the category of the a priori. But, perhaps, the non-idiosyncratic incorrigibles do.

What about so-called analytic a priori truths? They are not incorrigible for anyone. Perhaps, claims like "all fathers are male" are highly resistant to removal from the evolving doctrine, but they lack the incorrigibility of "all fathers are fathers." So, even if logical truths and some of the truths of set theory and mathematics are a priori in the sense that they are non-idiosyncratic incorrigibles, so-called analytic truths do not qualify.

But theoretical assumptions entrenched in widely endorsed theories are often more resistant to being given up than "all fathers are male" is. Conservation of mass-energy is, I dare say, less vulnerable to revision than this paradigmatic analytic truth.

One might, of course, suggest that analytic truths are incorrigible as long as changes in meanings of terms representing settled assumptions are not made. But suppose at t, X has corpus K which implies that all fathers are male. Suppose, further, that it is alleged that this claim is conceptually incorrigible in the sense that it is immune to removal unless the meanings of terms are altered. Finally, assume that a hermaphrodite, John-Jackie, successfully impregnated a woman who gave birth to a child, and X finds this out. Hithertofore, X has taken for granted that if a human successfully impregnates a woman who gives birth, that human is the father of the child. X also was convinced hithertofore that no hermaphrodite does this. But X felt compelled to give this up and replace this view with the claim that the hermaphrodite John-Jackie successfully sired a child. In giving up the claim that no human hermaphrodite sired a child, X must also give up one of the claims "all fathers are male" or "all humans who successfully impregnate a woman who brings a baby to term are fathers." Now, I take it that friends of the analytic-synthetic distinction would agree that "no human hermaphrodite sired a child" is synthetic and, hence, that giving it up is not a conceptual change. I take it also that "all fathers are male" would count as analytic, and giving it up would qualify as a conceptual change. Would this alleged fact encourage one to give up "all humans who successfully impregnate a woman who brings a baby to term are fathers"? Would it deter one? I suspect that it would not count with us one way or the other. What would count, I suspect, is that the distinction between the roles of partners in human sexual reproduction would be assigned greater importance in both scientific and legal classifications of parents than classification of parents according to sex—at least in the contemporary world— so that "all fathers are male" would be given up and "all humans who successfully impregnate a woman who brings a baby to term are fathers" would be retained. Or, alternatively, there may be some desire to retain both classifications. This would mean introducing two terms "father$_1$" and "father$_2$" and claiming that all fathers$_2$ are male, whereas all humans who successfully impregnate a woman who brings a baby to term are fathers$_1$. Before confronting the case of John–Jackie, X was convinced that all fathers$_1$ are fathers$_2$, and conversely. There was no need for two terms. In his new predicament, however, X retains the converse but abandons the claim that all fathers$_1$ are fathers$_2$. There is a use for two terms. But it is idle to ask whether "father$_1$," or "father $_2$," preserves the meaning of "father." I do not mean to suggest that there is no useful notion of conceptual revision. The introduction of the distinction between fathers$_1$ and fathers$_2$ is a conceptual innovation that would have seemed unnecessary save for the advent of John–Jackie's offspring. The challenge is to identify a notion of conceptual change which is of importance for belief revision and is such that conceptual incorrigibility relative to it introduces an interesting conception of analyticity. To my knowledge, this challenge has not been met.

5

On Peirce on Induction: A Response to Levi

Joseph S. Ullian

PROFESSOR LEVI HAS PUT US in mind of many salient features of Peirce's thought on probability and induction, and has traced some of the ways that they changed over the years. Peirce's position did develop. Still, his central doctrines on these topics remained almost constant throughout his career: his frequentist construal of probability and his attendant distaste for conceptualism, his view of properly designed statistical inference as deductive and as rooted in the same principle as probable inference, and his picture of induction as a self-correcting procedure bound to serve us in the long run. Peirce extolled "the wonderful self-correcting nature of ampliative inference," adding "this is the marvel of it" (CP 2.729). Further,

> the true guarantee of the validity of induction is that it is a method of reaching conclusions which, if it be persisted in long enough, will assuredly correct any error concerning future experience into which it may temporarily lead us. . . . There is no possibility of a series of experiences so wanting in uniformity as to be beyond the reach of induction [CP 2.769].

Again, "the validity of an inductive argument consists . . . in the fact that it pursues a method which, if duly persisted in, must, in the very nature of things, lead to a result indefinitely approximating to the truth in the long run" (CP 2.781). And even, "That the rule of induction will hold good in the long run may be deduced from the principle that reality is the only object of the final opinion to which sufficient investigation would lead" (CP 2.693).

Now, in the light of these claims it is hard to agree with Levi's pronouncements that Peirce "was not interested in

Hume's problem of induction" (p. 72) and, from a footnote (no. 8), that "Peirce had no pragmatic justification of induction because he offered no justification of induction at all." Peirce indeed did not label anything as Hume's problem. He did not find necessary connections where Hume saw none, nor did he hold up induction by simple enumeration as a paradigm. (Rather, he inclined to disparage it as the weakest form of induction, though at least a form where if you are wrong you will find out definitively.) In fact, as Levi noted, Peirce did not see the validity of induction in terms of the validity of *forms* of arguments at all: "while there might be valid arguments in these forms, there might also be invalid arguments having the same forms. . . . in the case of induction and hypothesis, we find that each of these groups of arguments, comprises some which are good, and others which are bad" (W 1:437).

G. H. von Wright claimed that Peirce's argument to the effect that "our experiences are 'fair samples' from a larger totality," whence induction "is the best mode of reasoning about the unknown" was original with Peirce (1957, 160). He did object that Peirce had neglected to worry about whether there were limits for our experience to converge to, "that the proportion to which we generalize *exists*." Peirce had seen that his definition of random sample applied only to finite populations (CP 7.210); but he had also held that even "endless series must have some character" (CP 2.784), which perhaps lays him open to von Wright's criticism.

The Peircean position whereby we can embrace the results of samples, assuming their randomness, as to the proportion of some character in an entire population brings to mind the argument of my very first teacher on the subject of induction, Donald C. Williams. Williams's book *The Ground of Induction* (1947) purported to show induction valid by claiming that a population was as likely to resemble a sample as the sample was to resemble the population. But in Peirce we find

> The principle of statistical induction is that two proportions— namely, that of the Ps among the Ms and that of the Ps among the Ss [the Ms being the whole population and the Ss the sample] are probably and approximately equal. If, then, this principle justifies our inferring the value of the second proportion from the

known value of the first, it equally justifies our inferring the value of the first from that of the second [CP 2.702].

For Peirce, this was just the "convertibility" of equality (see CP 2.718).

Yet Williams's argument was not Peirce's. For Williams took a subjectivist view of probability, indeed one according to which "a probability inference is 'unbiased' unless its bias is known" (1947, 67). So, whereas for Peirce there was the immense practical burden of establishing randomness of sample, for Williams there was only the soft demand of having no inkling of any bias in it. Williams's arguments have been rejected by most and forgotten by many.

Nonetheless, one might have expected Williams to have saluted Peirce as the principal progenitor of his own argument. Instead, he identified Josiah Royce's position as the one closest to his, while noting that Royce had attributed his theory to Peirce (1947, 196).

Williams gave Peirce mixed reviews. He did call Peirce "a coruscating sun whose darkest spots are usually brighter than the orbs of other luminaries" (1947, 196). But he expressed exasperation over "how incessantly Peirce seemed to be asserting the right doctrine, the fertile one, concerning the roster of 'possible inferences', and how fatally his account always slewed around into the abysmally different and sterile frequency theory" (1947, 199).

In fact, Williams went yet further in responding to Peirce's long-run-ism and his position that "Logic is rooted in the social principle." He accused Peirce of indulging in "the metaphysics of communistic transcendentalism" (1966, 416)—a great phrase, at any rate.

Further underlining should be given to one of Peirce's contributions to the subject of probabilistic reasoning, the concept of *weight of evidence*. Carnap (1950), Popper (1959), and I. J. Good (1983a) are among those who mark Peirce as the first (by far) to introduce it. Even though we may have a continuing belief that the probability of a certain character's being present is 1/2, it may happen that as we accumulate data we have more and more reason to believe that this is the probability. We judge the chance as before, but that judgment itself is rendered more likely. As Peirce put it, the whole utility of probability is to insure us in the long run, and as that assurance depends, not only on the value of the chance, but also on the accuracy of the evaluation, to express the proper state of our belief, not one number but two are requisite, the first depending on the inferred probability, the second on the amount of knowledge on which that probability is based [CP 2.677].

In fact, as Peirce footnoted, "strictly we should need an infinite series of numbers, each depending on the probable error of the last"; but in practice, two normally suffice. "Our belief ought to be proportional to the weight of evidence" (CP 2.676), measured by taking the logarithm of an appropriate quantity and thus turning out to be essentially additive, as a notion called "weight" ought to be. Popper has argued that consideration of this concept and its role in belief serves to undermine the subjectivist conception of probability (1959, 406f.). This would, of course, have been entirely pleasing to Peirce.

Levi has pointed out some difficulties that arise on Peirce's view. Given his frequentist scruples, together with his insistence on choosing the reference, or genus class, in terms of the total data, cases like that of the 99 to 1 urn are problems for him. Given the draw of a red ball, he seems prevented from making the natural numerical assessment of the probability that the urn has 99 red balls. Of course, in many cases Peirce was entirely content to have no numerical assessment of probability; for there is not always a clear reference class, and even when there is, one often lacks information about it. Still, from his writing about "Uniformities," it seems clear that Peirce would at least be willing to *favor* the conclusion that the urn's balls are mostly red.

> If we know that among a certain people—say the Icelanders—an extreme uniformity prevails in regard to all their ideas, then, if we found that two or three individuals taken at random from among them have all any particular superstition, we shall be the more ready to infer that it belongs to the whole people from what we know of their uniformity [CP 2.741].

In the assumptions of our case we do know that the balls in the urn are very nearly uniform in color, so even one red draw should steer us right somewhat.

In another note (no. 5) Levi speaks of Peirce as performing "rhetorical pirouettes aimed at masking this concession to subjective interpretations of probability." Levi seems to want to repair Peirce by injecting some elements of subjectivism into his doctrine. It is not at all clear that Peirce would welcome the repairs. In some cases Peirce was able to fix the probability of a seeming single case by appeal to what Hacking called "the long run of human guessing" (1965, 47). But I agree with Levi that there is a problem for Peirce in the related issues of nuisance information and probabilities for isolated cases.

In some later writings Peirce resorted to the supposed existence of "would-bes" in order to explain statements of probability. "The probability, if a die be thrown from a dice box it will turn up a number divisible by three, is one-third *means*," Peirce wrote, "that the die has a certain 'would-be', where a would-be is a property, quite analogous to any habit a man might have" (CP 2.664). I find it hard to see this notion as providing any more clarification than Molière's "*virtus dormitiva.*"

Levi's own views come forth quite strongly at the end of his paper. He finds tension between Peirce's "messianic realism" and his "belief–doubt model"—a topic that he has developed at length elsewhere. Here Levi writes about the vices of fallibilism and the "virtues of myopia," to use a Levi-athan phrase. I do not see why a defender of Peirce's consistency can't simply invoke the Neurath figure of rebuilding the boat, plank by plank, standard by standard, while sailing toward our destination—no plank, no standard to be spared if its replacement looks advantageous. Peirce was, after all, a *pragmatist*.

And what philosopher do you suppose said this "The problem of how an accidental regularity can be distinguished from an essential one is precisely the problem of inductive logic"? If you said Nelson Goodman, you have probably read him on the subject of counterfactuals and the new riddle of induction (Goodman 1983); but the right answer is: Charles Peirce (CP 3.605). Peirce had just observed that "No collection of individuals, be it finite or infinite, can be arranged in succession without the succession's perfectly conforming to some law or regularity."

We know now that any theory of induction which purports to judge generalizations wholly on the basis of their form must fail to deal adequately with Goodman's new riddle. We observed that Peirce avoided that pitfall. Now, we might wonder further what in his writings suggests a way of responding to that riddle, or at least a way of distinguishing between "All emeralds are green" and "All emeralds are grue." To be sure, those are what Peirce might have called "crude inductions." Yet, if there were no Peircean ground for making this rudimentary distinction, there would be little hope of dealing with more sophisticated cases.

A first thought might be that "grue" is a disjunctive term, whereas Peirce disparaged such terms. (Levi offered an interesting thought as to why.) But this observation cannot get us to the root of the matter. For we have the usual Goodmanian symmetry: "green" is as disjunctive in terms of "grue" and "bleen" as "grue" is in terms of "green" and "blue." A next thought might regard randomness of sample. For all the emeralds in the sample have been examined prior to the pivotal time, and the time of examination is relevant here. But, again, this cuts no ice as between the two hypotheses, for time can be seen as no more relevant in the one case than in the other.

I submit that what *does* lead to a way of making the needed distinction is Peirce's doctrine of predesignation. It was in terms of predesignation that Peirce characterized induction: "The inference that a previously designated character has nearly the same frequency of occurrence in the whole of a class that it has in a sample drawn at random out of that class is induction" (CP 6.409). And he wrote "The great rule of predesignation, which must guide [the inductive method] is as much as to say that an induction to be valid must be prompted by a definite doubt or at least an interrogation" (CP 5.584). Coming from another direction, but to the same effect: "If we limit ourselves to such characters as have for us any importance, interest, or obviousness, then a synthetic conclusion may be drawn. . . . The induction has its full force when the character concerned has been designated before examining the sample" (CP 6.413). Now, to designate such a character is, nearly enough, to project it. The predesignated character, one that we see as important or of interest, is likely to be a veteran of projections and so a well-entrenched predicate. This is where I see a link between Peirce and Goodman, and the wherewithal, in Peirce, for dealing with Goodman's riddle.

II

Peirce and Science

6

Peirce on the Validation of Science

Nicholas Rescher

The Fundamental Question

WHY BELIEVE the teachings of natural science? Why should we endorse and accept the answers that science gives to the numerous questions that we have about how things work in the world?

This issue has two aspects, one easy to deal with and one not so easy. The easy aspect lies in the following formulation of the problem: "Why accept what science tells us, rather than rely on other sorts of procedures for getting answers to our questions?" After all, there are alternatives to relying on the methods of science for getting answers to our questions. Peirce himself considered three in particular:

1. the method of tenacity: to hold to what we already have on hand (because it is convenient or expedient or familiar);
2. the method of authority: to hold to what is well spoken for by authoritative advocates (by "experts" and people who are "supposed to know");
3. the method of plausibility: to hold to what seems reasonable on general principles, accepting what we have "an instinctive inclination to believe."

The reason why the method of science qualifies as superior to these available alternatives is simple: it has a better track record. The tenor of the course of available experience clearly indicates that natural science provides us with more reliable information than these alternatives do.

The difficult aspect of the matter lies in a somewhat different direction. It pivots, not on the question "Why should we accept what science tells us?" but on the question: "Why should we accept what science tells us today?" After all, we realize full well that science is constantly changing its mind. We know in our heart of hearts that the world-picture of natural science in the year 3,000 will differ from our present-day science no less radically than this itself differs from the science of Newton's day. The clearest lesson of the history of science is that science keeps changing its mind in various fundamental ways about the *modus operandi* of nature. So, why should we actually go ahead and believe what science tells us nowadays? (And this, of course, holds just as much for tomorrow as for today.)

THE METHODOLOGICAL TURN

In addressing this second, more difficult question, Peirce brought the full force of his ingenuity to bear by exploiting a distinction between two very different sides or aspects of science, science as a system and science as a process:

1. the doctrinal side: science as a body of assertions; a collection of claims: theses, theories, hypotheses; a propositional structure or system of knowledge
2. the methodological side: science as a family of methods; a collection of techniques, procedures, processes for testing and substantiating claims; a procedural organism or methodology of inquiry as an information-generative praxis.

On the basis of this distinction, what Peirce proposed to do was to validate the first of these via the mediation of the second. His strategy was not to authenticate the teachings of science directly as a body of assertions. Rather, his idea was that the legitimacy of science is fundamentally methodological. In the first instance, we are to validate the methods of science as methods for the fixation of belief, and only thereafter—only subsequent to the issue of method—do we authorize certain beliefs precisely because they are endorsed by these validated methods. As Peirce put it:

> Wherein lies the essential peculiarity of this [scientific] knowl-

edge? Some thinkers agree with the ancient Greeks in making it consist in the Method of knowing, the manner in which the truth is laid hold on. The majority of modern writers regard the Systematic character of the doctrine itself as more characteristic. Both marks of scientific knowledge are exceedingly important; but the former is deeper cut, and because it is at present less noticed, more needs to be emphasized [CP 7.49].

So, on this Peircean approach, the fundamental question becomes: What validates the methods of science? What speaks for their being superior to their rival processes of belief-authorization? What marks them as our best procedures for getting not necessarily at the truth, but as close to it as we can manage to get at this particular stage of the game?

From this standpoint, methodological assets and advantages emerge as the paramount considerations. And as Peirce saw it, the methods of science have some salient virtues in this regard. The first among them is self-correctiveness.

THE LEGITIMATING VIRTUES OF THE METHODS OF SCIENCE

(a) Self-correctiveness

Only at the most general and abstract level is the method of science something fixed (namely, alignment of belief with experience). The more concrete, subordinate methods for implementing such general objectives are plastic, changeable, and readjustable in the light of the experience we have with them. For not only can our substantive beliefs be changed in the light of new, additional information but so can our very methods of belief-substantiation. The method of science is self-corrective in this crucial sense: that the subordinate methods can be revised on the basis of their performance. The fundamental inductive principle of "alignment of belief with experience" also serves as a corrective to our methods of inquiry and confirmation. The history of science illustrates this phenomenon of methodological innovation and emendation time and again.

The cognitive methods and substantive procedures we deploy for structuring our view of reality evolve selectively by an historic, evolutionary process of "trial and error," analogous to the mutations affecting the bodily mechanisms by which we comport ourselves in the physical world. Our cognitive methods develop subject to revision in response to the element of "success and failure" in terms of the teleology of the practice of rational inquiry. The central issue is a matter of "survival of the fittest," with fitness assessed in terms of the practical objectives of the rational enterprise—particularly in the successful guidance of man's interactions with nature. Their evolutionary development proceeds by explicitly rational selection, rather than by some purpose-indifferent process analogous to the natural selection of the standard biological case.

It is not difficult to give examples of the operation of Darwinian processes in the cognitive domain. The intellectual landscape of human history is littered with the skeletal remains of the extinct dinosaurs of this sphere. Examples of such defunct methods for the acquisition and explanatory utilization of information include astrology, numerology, oracles, dream-interpretation, the reading of tea leaves or the entrails of birds, animism, the teleological physics of the Presocratics, and so on. There is nothing intrinsically absurd or contemptible about such unorthodox cognitive programs; even the most occult of them has a long and not wholly unsuccessful history. (Think, for example, of the prominent role of numerological explanation from Pythagoreanism, through Platonism, to the medieval Arabs, down to Kepler in the Renaissance.) Distinctly different scientific methodologies and programs have been mooted: for example, Ptolemaic "saving the phenomena" *vs.* the hypothetico-deductive method, or, again, Baconian collectionism *vs.* the post-Newtonian theory of experimental science. The crucial point is that the methods of science have been selected not on the basis of superior performance. The development of the means of inquiry and explanation invites a Darwinian account.

Admittedly, the scientific approach to factual inquiry is simply one option among others, and it does not have an unshakable basis in the very constitution of the human intellect. Rather, the basis of our historically developed and entrenched cognitive tools lies in their (presumably) having established themselves in open competition with various rival options. It has come to be shown before the tribunal of bitter experience—through the historical vagaries of an evolutionary process of selection—that the accepted methods work out most effectively in actual practical vis-à-vis other tried possibilities.

The new methods adopted in the later stages of methodological evolution are (*ex hypothesi*) capable of accomplishing the work of the old (where the old were successful) and improving on it (by succeeding in some respect in which the old did not). Progress in the development of inquiry procedures thus arises when the new methods can encompass (and account for) strengths of the old, and add new ones off their own bat: when it can dominate the old ones at their own work, so to speak.

(b) Hypothetical Effectiveness

There is—perhaps regrettably—no categorical assurance that science will ultimately get at the real truth of things. But what can be shown, Peirce maintained, is the next best thing: namely, the hypothetical assurance that IF any method of inquiry can lead us to the truth, THEN science can. The reasoning that demonstrates this hypothetical claim is relatively straightforward. For we can argue essentially as follows:

> That "the truth" about the world is conveyed by propositions adequate to the whole of experience in the theoretical long run. The inductive method of science is to adjust our claims optimally to our experience in the actually achieved run. But the constant readjustment in our body of achieved-run claims as experience grows larger and more complex is bound to reflect the long run if there is indeed convergence, that is, if there is a real truth in the matter at all.

As Pierce himself put it:

> The validity of induction is entirely different; for it is by no means certain that the conclusion actually drawn in any given case would turn out true in the majority of cases where precisely such a method was followed; but what is certain is that, in the majority of cases, the method would lead to some conclusion that was true, and that in the individual case in hand [lies in the fact that] if there is any error in the conclusion, that error will get corrected by simply persisting in the employment of the same method. The validity of an inductive argument consists, then, in the fact that it pursues a method which, if duly persisted in,

must, in the very nature of things, lead to a result indefinitely approximating to the truth in the long run [CP 2.781, 1902].

What we have at this stage is a deep vindication of science with reference to the very nature of truth. In the course of his many years of reflection on the issue, Peirce's theory of truth underwent considerable development and transformation. But it moved step by step closer to the idea that we humans have to understand empirical truth as follows: "The truth of a matter is what our inquiries would eventually reveal about it if sufficiently prolonged under sufficiently favorable conditions." On this basis, one arrives at the idea of truth as the ultimate consensus of the ideal community of rational inquirers. Where there is no ultimate settlement of opinion there is no truth of the matter.

How, after all, do rational inquiries proceed? By their very nature they proceed by aligning opinion with experience. But if ultimate experience *is* the truth, then the scientific method is ultimately bound to reach the truth if truth there is. Thus, scientific inquiry is demonstrably adequate to its intended function, its reason for being to get at the real truth of things. This factor of its hypothetical effectiveness is a second major virtue of the scientific method.

(c) Theoretical Comprehensiveness

But Peirce was (perhaps unfortunately) not content to let the matter end with the preceding point about the ultimate efficacy of science—the idea that long-run science yields the truth and nothing but the truth. In his more metaphysical moments he also went further to maintain the (clearly much more problematic) thesis that long-run science yields the whole truth: that in the end (in the eventual long run) whatever can be known will be known, that reality will eventually be known completely and exhaustively. Accordingly, Peirce held that the real is, in this sense, ultimately rational, that it contains no hidden reserve of truth that is impervious to inquiry, that there are no incognizables.

Let us inquire briefly into Peirce's grounds for maintaining this (obviously problematic) position. Basically, there are two possibilities here. If "the (ultimately) known" and "the real" are said to stand in strict correlation, the question remains open: Which is the dependent, and which is the independent, variable? On which side does the ultimate responsibility for this coordination lie? Does it obtain because cognition is so powerful in its grasp that reality cannot elude it or because reality is so restricted in its scope that inquiry cannot fail to exhaust it?

Peirce took the second line here. His reasons were rooted in metaphysical considerations—in his theory of reality. For Peirce, to be real is by definition to have a discernible effect, an effect which, in virtue of this discernibility, lies open to the inspection of mind. Reality is knowable reality. But Peirce's epistemic optimism entails that "to be knowable" is one and the same thing as "ultimately to be known." Thus, "to be real" and "to be (ultimately) knowable" are one and the same thing.

The Peircean tendency to equate the domain of inquiry (= nature as such) with the domain of experience goes back to Kant: "I do not by this argument at all profess to disprove void space, for it may exist where perceptions cannot reach, and where there is, therefore, no empirical knowledge of coexistence. But such a space is not for us an object of any possible experience [and so can have no objective reality for us]" (*Critique of Pure Reason*, A214 = B261). Peirce's thinking of himself as a follower of Kant was no idle fancy. For what Kant said here of the *spatial* domain is exactly what Peirce maintained with respect to the *ontological* domain of reality at large. As Peirce saw it, science is comprehensive. If something exists at all, it exists because science will eventually tell us about it.

Peirce's metaphysical theory of reality accordingly identifies reality as the domain of the knowable, and identifies knowability-in-principle with ultimate knowledge-in-(ultimate)-practice. This position is understandable and clear enough, but it is also clearly problematic. For where is the Moses who has come down from the mountain with the tablets that assure us humans that what is discernible must in the long run be discovered by us? This idea—central to Peirce's theory of the real and to his rejection of incognizables—is deeply problematic (as his own struggles with it over the years betoken). But the fortunate thing is that for present purposes it represents a work of supererogation: the thesis of the completability of science is, in the final analysis, dispensable as far as the *validation* of science is concerned.

THE VALIDATION OF SCIENCE

Returning now to our basic question, "Why believe what science says now?" we see that the basic term of Peirce's reply is twofold:

1. because science is the best available means of belief-fixation in the context of the pursuit of truth. It aligns belief with experience and this is simply the best we can do.
2. because by following this practice conscientiously we will eventually get it right. The tolerance of present error is the price we have to pay for the assurance of eventual access to the truth.

We cannot, of course, deny the imperfections of present science. One cannot sensibly maintain that in using the method of science to answer our present questions we will answer them correctly, or even that these particular answers are better (more accurate) than answers we might arrive at in other ways, or even in some objective sense of probability that they are more probably correct than others. But what we can argue is that (1) there is no reason to think that any other method, agent from science, holds superior powers, and that (2) by prevailing in a reliance on science we are fostering a good cause—the cause of eventually getting at the truth of things if this is indeed possible for us.

The ultimate crux of Peirce's position is that we should trust science because doing so is to our ultimate advantage insofar as present-day science has the virtue of being an indispensable way-station on the road to ultimate science, and ultimate science is, as Peirce saw it, the effective arbiter of truth.

THE LIMITED NATURE OF PEIRCE'S VALIDATION

Despite these extremely optimistic and ambitious claims on science's behalf, Peirce did not set science up as a be-all and end-all. For—as he saw it—science rests, in the final analysis, on an extra-scientific or pre-scientific foundation:

> Inquiry must proceed upon the virtual assumption of sundry logical and metaphysical beliefs; and it is rational to settle the validity of those before undertaking an operation that supposes their truth. Now whether the truth of them be explicitly laid down on critical grounds, or the doctrine of Common-Sense prevent our pretending to doubt it, along with all these other sound first principles will be admitted, and so the whole inquiry will be concluded before the first outward experiment is made. But this preliminary inquiry is long and arduous. . . . That is to say, they [common-sense beliefs] rest on experience—on the total everyday experience of many generations of multitudinous populations. . . . all science, without being aware of it, virtually supposes the truth of the vague results of uncontrolled thought upon such experiences cannot help doing so, and [science] would have to shut up shop if she should manage to escape accepting them. No "wisdom" could ever have discovered argon; yet within its proper sphere, which embraces objects of universal concern, the instinctive result of human experience ought to have so vastly more weight than any scientific result, that to make laboratory experiments to ascertain, for example, whether there be any uniformity in nature or no, would vie with adding a teaspoonful of saccharine to the ocean in order to sweeten it [CP 5.521–522].

Science is accordingly not final, not fundamental, not autonomous. It stands, not on its own feet, but on the feet of a broader "experience"—the non-systematic, pre-, or sub-scientific experience of everyday life. The ultimate reason why we should accept the teachings of science is not that they are somehow self-authenticating, but that they provide us with the optimal means of making thoroughgoing sense of our cognitively relevant experiences overall, in everyday life even as in science itself.

Moreover, as Peirce saw the matter, science is not our only or even our primary guide to life. For science is a special-purpose tool: a cognitive instrument for answering questions about the world—for what Peirce called the fixation of belief or what we might call the securing of information.

> For . . . [the scientist] man is nature's interpreter; and in spite of the crudity of some anticipations, the idea of science is, in his mind, inseparably bound up with that of a life devoted to single-minded inquiry. That is also the way in which every scientific man thinks of science. That is the sense in which the word is to be understood in this chapter. Science is to mean for us a mode of life whose single animating purpose is to find out the real truth . . . [CP 7.55].

But man does not live by information alone: information, however important, is not the whole of life. The process of leading a human life is one in whose complex overall course there are many desiderata.

The validity of science is bound up with its functional efficacy in the achievement of its characterizing mission: the fixation of belief. And this identity would be undermined by inflating the aim of science in a different direction—as a guiding instrumentality for the conduct of life at large. The fixation of belief is clearly only one of life's prime desiderata—pivotal though it be for a rational creature.

Peirce did not lose sight of these fundamental realities. He believed in science, but not in scientism. He regarded science as a special-purpose instrument, not as life's be-all and end-all. Science for Peirce is a fundamentally social process, but cognitive interactions are not the only sort of meaningful dealing we have with one another. Human affection counts for much, and "to love" is no less essential a human capacity than "to know" is. Even as war is too important to be left to the generals, so Peirce was prepared to see the management of human life as something that is too large and important for its management to be left entirely to the scientists. But, of course, to say this is not in any way to deny science's optimality at the discharge of its prime and characteristic mission: the fixation of rational belief.

7

Peirce on the Reliability of Science: A Response to Rescher

C. F. Delaney

AFTER MAKING THE FUNDAMENTAL POINT that for Peirce science is best conceived not as a body of doctrine but as a method, Professor Rescher portrays Peirce's view of scientific method as a set of interrelated features of a specific way of fixing belief or getting answers to our questions. As I read this portrayal, Peirce is presented as being committed to three things: first, that among the different ways of fixing belief there is a distinctive "scientific method"; second, that this method is "better than" other methods; and, third, that there are dimensions of our cognitive life outside the scope of this method. I want to raise some questions about Rescher's treatment of each of these three points.

1. *That there is a distinctive "scientific method."* That this is Peirce's view is uncontroversial; it seems to me, however, that Rescher makes several points in his construal that either compromise Peirce's position on this matter or at least call for further clarification. In discussing the self-correctiveness of science he makes the point that the method of science itself can be *revised* in the light of its successes and failures; and in his discussion of the dominance of science he makes the related point that science would just *co-opt* other methodologies that were more successful. My question grows out of this concern: Is the notion of "scientific method" simply a formal notion meaning "the best method," or is it distinguishable from other methods by some intrinsic characteristics? On the assumption that it is the latter (and it does seem clear to me that Peirce wanted a substantive principle of demarcation at the level of method), how much revisability or co-opting is possible?

We have to remember the context here. Peirce surely believed that science is the key to our understanding of the world, but he just as surely did not believe that the world really is exactly the way our present scientific theories depict it (although it must be said that he was much more optimistic about at least the basic structure of "present science" than we are inclined to be today). The final picture of the world might be quite different from our present sketches. What, then, gives content to his endorsement of science such that it is more than the vacuous claim that the world is the way it will be correctly depicted to be? Here Rescher correctly sees Peirce moving to the level of method such that the endorsement of science becomes "the world is the way in which investigators following *this* method will ultimately find it to be." But if this claim is to avoid the vacuity of the earlier one, there must be a certain material determinateness with regard to what is to count as scientific method as distinct from other methods of fixing belief.

Rescher reads Peirce as drawing a distinction between scientific method "at the general and abstract level" and scientific methods "at the concrete and subordinate level." The former is the constant that gives substantive content to the endorsement of science, while the latter are progressively malleable over time. It is not clear to me where precisely Peirce drew this distinction, but it does seem to me to be a perfectly sensible distinction and one that Peirce might well have drawn to sustain his view in the face of methodological innovation. I want to raise two questions: What exactly is this stable core of scientific method, and how would a defender of it respond to the basic Feyerabendian objections to the tyranny of method?

Rescher in two places gives us a clue as to how both he and Peirce would articulate this stable core. He speaks of the "alignment of belief with experience" and "the inductive readjustment of theory to observation." *But what is to count as an experience or an observation?* Can this question admit of a merely formal answer of the type "whatever plays the reporting role in future scientific investigation," or must it be answered materially in terms of some internal characterization along the lines of our present perceptual propositions involving a sensory core? It seems to me that Peirce's answer would be the second and that it is at least in part in terms of the monitoring role that such robustly characterized perceptual propositions play in science that he is able to demarcate science from other forms of inquiry. They are central to the claim that there is a substantively specifiable scientific method. This feature is not revisable; other methods that do not honor this cannot be co-opted.

If this is the case, then those in this tradition must have some line of response to Feyerabendian invectives "against method": namely, the dual claim that the history of science does not reveal a community that has shackled itself to a single method and that it would be bad for the scientific community to do so. That Peirce would undertake such a line of response, I have little doubt—because he felt that his normative views about scientific method were firmly grounded both in history and in logic.

2. *That scientific method is "better than" other methods.* The important question here is "Better for what?" In his most famous paper Peirce was quite clear about his answer to this question: namely, better for "the fixation of belief," where this is understood initially in psychological rather than epistemic terms. His claim is that it is the only method for fixing belief which is truly adaptive and has the resources to *stabilize* belief so as to render possible effective long-run cooperative interaction with an expanding community and a shrinking environment. In other words, it is the only method that, given the world we have to interact with, can fix belief effectively, where "effectiveness" is parsed in terms of stability. Rescher does not develop this pragmatic sense of "better than" but concentrates on the rather more contentious legitimations of science in terms of self-correctiveness, effectiveness, and comprehensiveness, where these are construed epistemically as bearing on the matter of truth. Let me look at each of these in turn.

That scientific method is self-corrective is one of the most discussed and contested of Peirce's views. The standard objection to Peirce here is that at most he established the self-correctiveness of quantitative induction, and, as he himself explained, this makes up only one small part of scientific method as a whole. Accordingly, the objection is that he fell far short of giving us any reason to think that scientific method as such is self-corrective. Rescher's reconstruction of Peirce's view in response to this line of criticism seems to me both historically accurate and philosophically defensible. He acknowledges that quantitative induction and scientific method are not identical but rather related as part to whole, and that the specific "proof" of self-correctiveness applies directly only to quantitative induction. But inasmuch as the specific role of quantitative induction is to monitor the adequacy of scientific procedure as a whole, Rescher goes on to make the point that its acknowledged self-correctiveness is communicated to the entire process. Scientific method is self-corrective in the broad sense because it can be effectively monitored by statistical techniques that are self-corrective in the narrow sense. This does seem to me to be the picture Peirce had in mind, and as such seems to be an adequate response to the standard objection as initially formulated. Whether or not it can stand up to a reformulated objection in terms of the ultimate adequacy of such statistical techniques for monitoring the progressive development of science is another question entirely.

That scientific method is effective is claimed to be its second legitimating virtue. After stipulating that what he means by "effective" is the ability to "get at the real truth of things," Rescher distinguishes between categorical and hypothetical effectiveness and attributes to Peirce only the claim that science is the latter. Rescher spells out the claim of hypothetical effectiveness as "IF any method of inquiry can lead us to the truth, THEN science can." I want to raise two points: first, is this what Peirce had in mind by hypothetical effectiveness; and, second, is hypothetical effectiveness all that Peirce claimed? When Peirce did talk in the hypothetical manner, it seems to me that he had a somewhat different antecedent condition in mind, a condition in fact that Rescher himself quotes. As I read Peirce, the condition he had in mind is "if there is any truth in a given domain, then science will enable us to grasp it" or "if there is any fact of the matter here, then science will ultimately ascertain it" (cf. CP 7.77, 7.87). These seem to me to be much stronger claims (because they specify a weaker condition) than the one Rescher attributes to Peirce: namely, "if any method can lead to the truth, scientific method can." Rescher's condition allows that there might be truths or facts that no *method* can get at, whereas the ones that I have attributed to Peirce do not. Second, Peirce was not always so circumspect as to restrict himself to the hypothetical claim (if there are answers, science will find them) but often boldly asserted the categorical claim that science will be able to answer all questions that can be clearly formulated. It is not clear how the virtue of categorical effectiveness so understood would be distinct from that of theoretical comprehensiveness.

This leads to what Rescher identifies as the third virtue: namely, theoretical comprehensiveness. Science will ultimately comprehend reality completely and exhaustively. Rescher reads this not so much as an inflated conception of science as a restricting claim about "reality." The post-Kantian identification of "real" with "ultimately to be known," the rejection of incognizables, puts Peirce in a familiar if not always popular philosophical tradition.

3. *That there are dimensions of our cognitive life properly outside the scope of scientific method.* In spite of his more than occasional flamboyant pronouncements, it goes without saying that Peirce thought that there is more to life than science. And even when we restrict the domain to "our cognitive life" Peirce's view turns out to be more modest and circumspect than might initially appear. Rescher makes the point under the rubric "Peirce was a proponent of science but not of scientism." There are several quite different issues in this neighborhood that I would like to sort out and discuss separately.

First, there are many dimensions to our cognitive life which traditional construals of scientific method would see as extrinsic to science but which Peirce included as part of the fabric of scientific method itself. In contrast to logicist accounts of science, Peirce saw scientific method as intrinsically *social and historical.* His justification of certain abductive strategies bearing on theory preference and certain confirmation techniques presume that scientific explanation emerges from a process that is developing over time and has as its proper logical subject not the individual investigator but the developing community. In addition, *instinct* is seen as playing a crucial and ineliminable role in the abductive phase of inquiry, and *interests* both individual and social are characterized as the driving forces of scientific inquiry. In one of his most striking claims, Peirce maintained that the most vital factors in the development of modern science have been the "moral factors" and that what he had particularly in mind are certain altruistic *virtues* associated with a social sense that virtues enable individual investigators to subordinate their own satisfaction to the long-range goals of the community. Finally, he acknowledged that the scientific enterprise rests on certain common-sense or *metaphysical presuppositions* which, though not in principle beyond criticism, are not themselves under scrutiny but rather guide the process of investigation. In summary, Peirce's account of science included roles for historicity, sociality, interests, virtues, and metaphysical presuppositions, thereby incorporating dimensions of our cognitive life normally outside the ken of scientific method more narrowly construed. But it is important to emphasize that these are not extra-scientific dimensions for Peirce. These diverse features of our cognitive lives are constitutive of scientific methodology.

Second, and more to the point, are there dimensions of belief-formation in human life outside the scope of scientific method understood in this rich Peircean sense? Rescher points to the pre-scientific beliefs of everyday life as instances of such, and Peirce certainly had a view in this neighborhood. He did think that human life in general and science in particular rest on a body of vague indubitable presuppositions about ourselves and our relationship to the world. But I do not think that these beliefs are in principle different from the beliefs over which scientific method normally ranges. They are foundational and indubitable only because they are acritical, that is, for now they are below the threshold of deliberate formation and conscious criticism. They are outside the scope of scientific method *in fact* only because they are outside the scope of all methodological formation. If, however, we encounter experiences that are in tension with these fundamental presuppositions, then doubt intrudes and belief has to be critically realigned. There is a theoretical matter to be settled, and it seems to me that Peirce's view was that when such is the case the matter is within the proper purview of scientific method, not one of the other methods of fixing belief.

Third, it does not follow from the fact that science is the pre-eminent methodology for all theoretical belief-formation that scientific reasoning should function as our basic guide for life. On the contrary, Peirce's view was that when it comes to making important and decisive practical choices instinct is a surer guide than reason. Moreover, he made the point that scientific reason reveals to itself its own limitations. The very theory of scientific reasoning furnishes us with conclusive reasons for not being guided by it in the domain of what he calls "vitally important topics" (CP 1.616-677). A method whose hallmark is long-run correction is not likely to be the best instrument for short-term decisions. It is not that scientific reasoning does not in principle apply to these issues; rather, it is that it is too slow to be helpful. The wait-and-see attitude of science is not naturally suited to practical action. Accordingly, Peirce's suggestion was that it is appropriate in the sphere of practical action with regard to vitally important topics to be guided by hereditary instincts and traditional sentiments. In these areas we should, he said, follow the lead of our humble cousins the lower animals who are guided by instinct and custom in all the important affairs of daily life. Given a benevolent creator and/or a system of efficient evolution, these come as close to infallible guides as we are likely to encounter.

8

Charles S. Peirce, Mathematician

Carolyn Eisele

I

PEIRCEAN SCHOLARS CAN UNDERSTAND the satisfaction I feel that Peirce's considerable mathematical talents are at last being recognized by the prestigious mathematical community in America. I refer, of course, to the August 1988 publication of my essay on his mathematical interest and achievement, "Thomas S. Fiske and Charles S. Peirce"; it is the fourth item in Part I of *A Century of Mathematics in America* (Duren et al. 1988), celebrating at Brown University in 1988 the 100th anniversary of the American Mathematical Society. There are now three volumes devoted to that celebration, and it should be heart-warming to Peircean scholars to find Peirce resting comfortably in Part I, pages 41–56, and again, in Part III, where four full pages of Stephen M. Stigler's "Mathematical Statistics in the Early States" are devoted to his mathematics. Indeed, this recognition is well warranted if only for Peirce's display of a technical scientific and mathematical grounding resulting from his long professional (thirty-one-year) service in the United States Coast and Geodetic Survey. The techniques used in that service were in part associated with the then "advanced mathematics" and had to be skillfully adapted to the many computational problems in hand.

It should cause no surprise, then, to find that after his retirement from the Coast and Geodetic Survey in 1891, Peirce was often to be found on the Columbia University campus in New York City, indeed living in that area for a time, hoping, as I recall, for an appointment in some division of the University. He attended many professional meetings there, especially those of the American Mathematical Society, which had been founded on that campus as the New York Mathematical Society in 1888. Moreover, associated with Peirce's modern interest in the growth and improvement of forms of investigation over the centuries has been his prevailing professional interest in the growth of the logical mechanism underlying acceptable mathematical procedure. Some time ago, in Volume II of my *Historical Perspectives on Peirce's Logic of Science* (Eisele 1985, 955) I pointed to just such a Peircean analysis in a letter he wrote on April 5, 1894, to George A. Plimpton, head of Ginn and Company. Actually, this published letter was but a follow-up to an earlier letter, dated February 1, 1894, which apparently was not sent and has remained unpublished until now. (Both original letters are in the Plimpton Collection, Rare Book and Manuscript Library of Columbia University.)

Arisbe, Milford, Pa.
1894 Feb 1

My dear Sir:
    I write to say that I must and will take advantage of your invitation, but I cannot today say when I should go down. My wife is poorly and everything is at 6's and 7's.
    I have got hold of a copy of the arithmetic of Texeda mentioned by De Morgan (Arith. Books p. 103). It is a very great rarity. Cantor does not mention it. My copy is a splendid one. De Morgan makes two mistakes about it. For one thing he gets the date wrong, owing to his copy having lost the colophon. It is 1546. He took the date from the license to print. The book has many highly interesting features not mentioned by De Morgan.
    Here is the colophon:

> Fue impressa la presente
> obra d'Arithmetica En la muy noble
> y felice villa de Valladolid (Pincia
> otro tiempo llamada) En la offici-
> na de Francisco Fernandez
> de cordoua/junto alas
> escuelas ma
> yores
> Acabose a quatro dias del mes
> de henero deste año del
> señor de mill z quinie
> entos z quaren
> ta z seys
> Años

It has a very pretty wood-cut title page, wh. De Morgan correctly copies. The initial letters are very pretty throughout. It is of course in block letter. Through a large part of the book the examples are marked "en castellanos" that is a sort of modified Roman numerals and "en guarismo" that is in the Arabic figures. One half is written o. The scratch division only is used. Cross multiplication is explained.

Some of the examples are entertaining and will be useful to me.

I will write again in a few days to propose a day for going down.

Yours very truly
C. S. Peircc

Geo. A. Plimpton Esq.
70 Fifth Ave
N. Y.

Although this seems to be only a minor illustration of Peirce's intellectual interest in mathematical episodes of the past, make no mistake—Peirce in his own time was recognized as a professional mathematician, aware of the new currents underlying the field in the late nineteenth century, currents that have stimulated mathematical development to the present time. I am almost ecstatic to have had the support of Max Fisch in the long drawn-out attempt to sustain this point of view.

Indeed, I pause momentarily to pay homage to the sensitive scholarship of Max Fisch in the Peircean field. That is true not only in regard to the substance of Peirce's overall training in mathematics and science as reflected throughout Max's later writings but also in Max's constant professional encouragement of a task that took me a thirty-year period gradually to bring to academic professional notice in the Peirce field. As early as 1971 there were adumbrations in Max's writings of Peirce's leaning in the direction of mathematics and science and their histories. For example, in his paper entitled "Hegel and Peirce" (in Fisch 1986, 269), one finds that

> the most conspicuous constant feature of Peirce's philosophy over the sixty years he devoted to it . . . was his conception of philosophy as research science, intermediate between mathematics and the special sciences in an "ontological line" in which each sci-

ence borrows principles from the sciences above it and data from those below it.

We are most deeply indebted for Max's emphasis on Peirce as a scientist. Indeed, for him, Peirce "was a sort of philosopher who was in the first place a scientist, and . . . he was the sort of scientist who was in the first place a logician of science; . . . no university or college in his time knew what to make of such a philosopher, or such a scientist" (Fisch, 1986, 309). Max continues: "Peirce's most creative students came to him from mathematics and the sciences. Students bent on what then passed for philosophy found little of it in his courses." He tells us that

> John Dewey, shortly after entering as a graduate student, wrote home to his old philosophy teacher: "I am not taking the course in Logic. The course is very mathematical, and by Logic, Mr. Peirce means only an account of the methods of the physical sciences, put in mathematical form as far as possible. It's more of a scientific, than philosophical course. In fact, I think Mr. Peirce don't think there is any philosophy outside the generalization of physical science" [Fisch 1986, 309–10].

At this point sensing the revolutionary stand he was taking, Max then pointed to Peirce's scientific and mathematical connections in Boston, New York, and Washington. Again, "Peirce did not, like Whitehead, have first a career in science and then a career in philosophy" (p. 312). To be sure that Peircean scholars have heard Max, I cite him again: Peirce "had no career in philosophy at all" (p. 312). And he reminds us of Peirce's private practice as a chemical engineer after his resignation from the Coast and Geodetic Survey, for his training had been in the direction of mathematics, physics, and chemistry, which he continued to regard as a study of logic. We learn too that Dewey wrote to William Torrey Harris that "Peirce lecture[d] on Logic, but the lectures appeal more strongly to the mathematical students than to the philosophical" (p. 311). Max tells us that only after another twenty years did Dewey see the value of Peirce's work and only after still another twenty years, when Cohen's *Chance, Love, and Logic* (1923) appeared, did Dewey understand it all (p. 311). This essay becomes in part then a tribute to Max

Fisch, for his courage to portray Peirce as a mathematician and scientist to replace the "now usual portrait of him as architectonic philosopher" (p. 311). And he does just that in the last 150 pages of the 1986 collection of his essays, *Peirce, Semeiotic, and Pragmatism* (1986).

II

It brings me great satisfaction as well to be able to record at this time the gradual improvement over the years in the recognition of Peirce's status as a late nineteenth-century mathematician by some of our top-flight mathematicians. In May 1973, as part of an early celebration of the 200th anniversary of the founding of our country, six mathematical conferences were scheduled to be held in Texas universities under the general title "The American Mathematical Heritage." The theme of the first conference, scheduled for Texas Tech University, was "Men and Institutions in American Mathematics," which was the title of the late Marshall Stone's brilliant survey at those meetings. Considering my own lowly status as a mathematician, I even now recall with some trepidation the prominent academic status of the principal speakers at those sessions. Indeed, so should it be even now. For how could it have happened that I, a fairly good female mathematician, could have such intellectual contact with Marshall Stone and Solomon Bochner and the renowned Garrett Birkhoff as well, the three major speakers at the first of those conferences? This assignment so providential for me was due to the interest of the late Carl Boyer, eminent scholar in the history of mathematics, who had already been prodding me for some time to write a textbook in the field.

Because of Bochner's illness at that time, his paper was read for him; it contained some happy and some unhappy remarks about one Charles S. Peirce. Indeed Bochner, a first-rate mathematician, had tried to change my mind on Peirce in personal correspondence some weeks before the conference took place. To my great surprise, the *Monthly* of the American Mathematical Society published this Congress paper in its October 1974 issue, under the title "Mathematical Reflections," a year and a half after the conference was held. This paper consisted of two parts. Part I contained a paragraph in which Peirce was considered to be a greater intellect than his famous mathematician father, Benjamin. Bochner spoke of Charles as creating the algebra of "relatives" and deemed it Charles's most endurable "achievement of a mathematical turn. . . . But he also tried to create something specifically philosophical of a mathematical hue, which, if successful would have become his greatest feat." Of course, I remind you that it was a very great feat.

Part II of that long paper was specifically labeled "Charles Sanders Peirce" and reflected what was then a lack of easy accessibility to Peirce's mathematical writings other than what was included in the eight volumes of the *Collected Papers* as edited by Hartshorne, Weiss, and Burks. The following is an excerpt from Part II.

> In a very peculiar sense, which I shall try briefly to sketch, the conception of continuity was in the center of a dominant theme of 19th century intellectuality, in all its compartments, in and out of mathematics. And it is a remarkable fact that Charles Sanders Peirce was most peculiarly preoccupied with this theme, overtly and covertly, directly and by contrast. It was an intellectual obsession with him. At any rate, it is possible to view much, or even most, of his philosophical work, in all its complexity, as variations, however diverse, on the theme of continuity. If his work is now so viewed, it is admissable to say, that the preoccupation with this all pervading 19th century theme of continuity made Peirce into the greatest philosopher America has produced thus far, but that it also un-made him, as evidenced by the fact that Peirce was never able to compose a key treatise through which to express himself and in which to summarize himself, as philosophers are wont to do. His was a real American Tragedy. A great philosopher and an even greater failure.

In the discussion of synechism Bochner writes, "But of importance to us is a section in Peirce entitled 'Time' (6.86); the statements are rather intricate and even obscure, even by standards of the writings of C. S. Peirce, in which obscurity is a recurrent phenomenon." It contained the explanation of a paragraph from Bochner's earlier volume *The Role of Mathematics in the Rise of Science* (1966) in which he claimed that while the renowned algebraist Leonard Dickson "was not yet receptive to this kind of explanation, as Charles Sanders Peirce, who was even almost a generation older than Dickson, already had been." Dr. Bochner continued, "I could not off-hand quote a reference in C. S. Peirce to this kind of comprehension mainly because Peirce never wrote any kind of comprehensive treatise himself and because his purely mathematical writings have not been published at all." But by 1974 Dr. Bochner had learned a few pertinent facts and was prompted to say, "But they are being edited, by Carolyn Eisele, in 4 or 5 volumes, and some day I hope to trace this sort of thinking to Peirce who was very advanced in many things of this kind." What a difference even that was from the dictates of a year earlier. It is pertinent to observe that time and a bit of intellectual warfare can wreak changes as the relevant evidence surfaces. It is to be noted that Part II of the original paper was completely omitted in the republication of Bochner's paper in *Men and Institutions in American Mathematics* in October 1976—perhaps because of excessive length in the original or, better still, perhaps because a new point of view was developing by this time. For Max Fisch and I had come to Peirce's rescue in the *American Mathematical Monthly* of May 1975 under a joint title of "Solomon Bochner on Charles S. Peirce."

And further I am pleased to recall in these unique Peircean remembrances the appreciation of Peirce's status on the part of the famous mathematician Garrett Birkhoff. How often, when working on Peirce and his famous father, Benjamin, have I been pleased to recall that Peirce, like Birkhoff, was the gifted mathematician son of a famous father in the field of mathematics. I am referring, of course, to the eminent George D. Birkhoff, who was also affiliated with Harvard.

It is in Volume II of *A Century of Mathematics in America* (Duren et al. 1989) that Peirceans begin to breathe more easily in reading Birkhoff's narration of episodes in Charles Peirce's association with the mathematics field. In the 1976 *Men and Institutions in American Mathematics,* the Birkhoff paper, entitled "Rise of Modern Algebra, 1936 to 1950," noticed him only in the bibliography as "Peirce, C. S. 1880 'On the Algebra of Logic,' (*American Journal of Mathematics*)," and two additional articles in the same journal. The more recent paper reveals a significantly greater appreciation of the role of Peirce in mathematics.

I shall list the points to prove this by references to remarks thereunto in that 55-page essay, which is entitled "Mathematics at Harvard, 1836-1944" (Duren et al. 1989). You can appreciate how they have bolstered my own courage in maintaining my isolated stand in the Peirce field in proclaiming that Peirce's thought is grounded in the basic methodology of mathematical procedure.

After numerous references to the work of Charles's famous mathematician father, Benjamin, Birkhoff takes significant note of the linear associative algebras by father and son that Benjamin published privately in 1870; of the fact that Charles wrote numerous addenda to this in preparing it for republication in Sylvester's newly founded *American Journal of Mathematics* (1881-1884, 97-229). Indeed, Birkhoff writes that "Most important was Appendix III, where Charles proved that the only division algebras of finite order over the Real field are R itself, the complex C field, and the real quaternions." In this context, Birkhoff tells of Charles's working with his father "in improving the scientific instrumentation of the U. S. Coast Survey," which, he says, "by 1880 was surveying the entire United States." He mentions in particular Peirce's publication of "highly original papers on the then new algebra of relatives" and claims that it earned him election in 1877 to the National Academy of Sciences, founded twelve years earlier by the Lazzaroni, a group of eminent American scientists, to promote research. The description of the "zenith" of Charles Peirce's professional career runs as follows: "From 1879-1884 he was a lecturer at the John Hopkins and discovered the fundamental connection between Boolean algebra and what are today called partially ordered sets (*Am. Journ. Math.* 3, 1880, 15-57). He thus foreshadowed the 'Dualgruppen' of Dedekind, 'Verbände' or lattices in today's terminology." There had been an erroneous detail in Peirce's work to which Birkhoff points.

Birkhoff comments on the difficulty of tracing the evolution of a basic idea because each recipient tends to modify it before "passing it on." Two such major ideas in Peirce are identified as his philosophical concept of "pragmatism" and his ideas about the algebra of logic. The latter explanation runs on for four paragraphs. Of particular interest is Birkhoff's awareness of Peirce's connection with the German logician Ernst Schröder. He says that "First in his *Operationskreis des Logikkalkuls*, and then in his three-volume *Algebra der Logik* (1890–95), Schröder made a systematic study of Peirce's papers. In turn, these books stimulated Richard Dedekind to investigate the concept of a Dualgruppe (lattice) in two pioneer papers which were ignored at the time." Later in the essay, a very personal remark by Birkhoff lends deeper significance to the Peirce contribution. For we find Birkhoff saying,

> In retrospect, I think I was very lucky that Emmy Noether Artin, and other leading German algebraists had not taken up Dedekind's "Dualgruppe" concept before 1932. As it was, by 1934 Ore had rediscovered the idea of C. S. Peirce, of defining lattices as *partially ordered sets*, and by 1935 he had done a far more professional job than I in applying them to determine the *structure of algebras*—and especially that of "groups with operators" (e.g. vector spaces, rings, and modules).

A sentence on his famous father, George David Birkhoff, brings mention of the latter's interest in relativity and the philosophy of science. Indeed, we learn that of his father's last five papers one was concerned with quaternions and referred to Benjamin and C. S. Peirce. Moreover, he notes that his father had become intensely interested in natural philosophy much as Simon Newcomb and C. S. Peirce had been.

As regards Marshall Stone, the third of the three featured mathematicians at the meetings in Texas, I believe his appreciation of Peirce had grown over the years. At the Texas Tech University conference, I had encouragement from him to continue my Peirce researches. In the summer of 1988, we had stimulating conversation at his dinner table at the Mathematical Congress celebration, and it is pleasing and heartwarming to remember his continued interest and further encouragement.

This recognition of Peirce's talents grows among mathematicians of stature. There is great need of further investigation in all areas of Peirce's activity as scientist as well as mathematician. My unpopular task among pure philosophers has been to establish a first-class status for him in those areas. He was not a touch-and-go investigator in those fields, merely searching and reaching therein occasionally for material to illustrate his philosophical and logical pronouncements. At those mathematics meetings at Brown University in 1988 I felt it was a great tribute to Peirce that my paper entitled "Thomas S. Fiske and Charles S. Peirce," in which I attempted to strip his portrait of all but mathematical and scientific verities, had been deemed acceptable. It was vital to mention Peirce's production of what became, in my editing and as published by Mouton, a five-volume set of papers in which there is a description of his activities in the field of "pure mathematics," some material representing original research effort on his part, and all illustrating valid logical procedure imbedded in the mathematical methodology he himself constantly acknowledged. The formal story of the thirty-one-year period (1860–1891) of his service in the Coast Survey well reveals the grounding and structure of the intellectual edifice of his later years.

I should like to refer, for example, to Peirce's Quincuncial Projection of the World (1876) which continues to be of current interest in modern geographic representation. His pervasive mathematical approach to problems in political economy has also been well recognized; I instance the volume by W. J. Baumol and S. W. Goldfield, *Precursors in Mathematical Economics* (1968), in which Peirce is called a "precursor." Any investigative process became in time but a mathematical machine involving the four basic steps. I have so often listed it and mention it again here.

(1) The creation of a model that embodies the condition of the premise.
(2) The mental modification of the diagram to obtain auxiliary information.
(3) Mental experimentation on the diagram to bring out a new relation between parts not mentioned in the construction.

(4) Repetition of the experiment to "infer inductively with a degree of probability practically amounting to the certainty that every diagram constructed according to the same percept would present the same relation of parts which has been observed in the diagram experimented upon."

I quote from my article in the *Dictionary of Scientific Biography* (484) Peirce's remark that

> My philosophy may be described as the attempt of a physicist to make such conjecture as to the construction of the universe as the methods of science may permit. . . . the best that can be done is to supply a hypothesis, not devoid of all likelihood in the general line of growth of scientific ideas, and capable of being verified or refuted by future observers. . . .

Peirce held that the observation in a necessary inference is directed to a sort of diagram or image of the facts given in the premises. In mathematics it is possible to observe relations between parts of the diagram that were not noticed in the construction. Part of the business of logic is to construct such diagrams. "In short," he wrote, "logical truth has the same source as mathematical truth which is derived from diagrams" and which, incidentally, may be oral as well as written.

In June of 1988, I was honored by an invitation to speak at Texas A&M University in College Station, in a conference entitled "Frontiers in American Philosophy." My paper was called "The Modern Relevance of the Mathematical Philosophy of Charles S. Peirce." In line with what I have already said, I quote from that paper in the following remarks. Peirce insisted that

> "philosophy requires exact thought, and all exact thought is mathematical thought." By 1894, he announced that his special business was to bring mathematical exactitude into philosophy and to actually apply the ideas of mathematics in philosophy. He meant in part the construction of diagrammatic representation from which consequences of the hypotheses might be deduced intuitionally. . . . His general philosophy, colored by wide scientific experience, requires of necessity a mathematical approach to its conceptual bases. For example, the prevailing element of probabilism in Peirce's epistemology reflects the spirit of fallibilism in

his astronomical gravitational researches for the U.S. Coast and Geodetic Survey. The mathematical groundwork is evident in the rich mathematical allusions of his later writings—in the mathematical terminology, the diagrammatic explication, the very methodology induced by appropriate mathematical symbolism and procedure. Now it is possible to confirm the suspicion of Peirce's essentially mathematical cast of mind that spawned the philosophy he has bequeathed to us. For *The New Elements of Mathematics by Charles S. Peirce* by Carolyn Eisele (Mouton, The Netherlands, 1976) offers at last a knowledge of that mathematical grounding.

Among the examples offered are Peirce's invention of the existential graphs; his philosophical continuum in terms of the mathematical linear continuum; his denumerable set of positive integers and his abnumeral set of real numbers in the logical development of orders of infinity; his need of the infinitesimal in geometric thought; of space as being non-Euclidean; his concept of the Möbius strip; and use of the "barycentric calculus" of Möbius when he explained to William James that "a similar mathematical procedure was applicable in his philosophical demonstrations." In a letter to William James he explained that for a considerable time he "was much too occupied by the question whether or not a notation similar to this (the barycentric model) would not represent the modes in which concepts are, or should be, represented as compounded in definitions, with a leaning to the affirmative."

In a sense, the studies for those meetings and those for the American Mathematical Society have solidified more than ever my conviction that the thought of C. S. Peirce today still has a message for those in the active service of mathematics and science on a world-wide basis. May time bring at last a decisive recognition of this multi-faceted genius whom America can so proudly claim.

9

Peirce at the Intersection of Mathematics and Philosophy: A Response to Eisele

Helena M. Pycior

I

THROUGHOUT HER CAREER, Carolyn Eisele has proven the selfless scholar. She has steered clear of dogmatic historical and philosophical interpretations, and offered her work on Peirce's mathematics not so much as an end in itself but as a foundation for continuing appreciation, study, and analysis. In doing so, she has persisted in the original role she carved in the international community of Peircean scholars—that of the propagandist for or promoter of Charles S. Peirce the mathematician. Thus when addressing the Fifth International Congress for Logic, Methodology, and Philosophy of Science in 1975, she bluntly proclaimed: "I have come to London [Ontario] on the usual mission of propagandizing for an appreciation and celebration of the endlessly fruitful thought of Charles S. Peirce" (Eisele 1979, 245). Distinguishing herself from other major Peircean scholars, Eisele has, of course, promoted "Peirce as primarily a *mathematician*, logician, and philosopher" (Eisele 1979, 295).

Her tripartite description reminds us that she has not studied Peirce's mathematics in isolation but has suggested links between his mathematics and his work in logic, philosophy, the history of science, and even semeiotic. Indeed, she has studied Peirce's mathematics as an essential component of what she describes as his "thoroughly integrated thought" (Eisele 1979, 245). In defense of this approach, she has often quoted Peirce's statement that: "Philosophy requires exact thought, and all exact thought is mathematical thought." Alternately, she has frequently reminded us that in 1894 Peirce described his "special business" as "bring[ing] mathematical exactitude . . . into philosophy, and . . . apply[ing] the ideas of mathematics in philosophy" (Eisele 1979, 276–77).

It is clear that Eisele's recovery of Peirce the *"mathematician, logician, and philosopher"* has deeply affected views of Peirce coming from her fellow Peircean scholars, mathematicians writing history, and professional historians of science. For example, the publication of the four-volumes-in-five-books of *The New Elements of Mathematics by Charles S. Peirce*, which she edited, brought formal recognition of Peirce the mathematician from other major Peircean scholars. Thus, in his address of 1976 at the C. S. Peirce Bicentennial International Congress, Max Fisch proclaimed: "All the time that Peirce was a scientist, he was also a mathematician."

> But until this bicentennial year most of his mathematical writings remained unpublished and so difficult of access that only one of the books on Peirce, that by Murray Murphey, has made any serious attempt to deal with them. With *The New Elements of Mathematics* now in our hands, we can proceed to try out answers to numerous . . . questions [Fisch 1986, 383, 385].

Fisch added: "I like to think of our Congress as a celebration of" the publication of *The New Elements* (Fisch 1986, 397).

But Professor Eisele has promoted Peirce the mathematician among not only Peircean scholars but American mathematicians as well. Because Peirce neither held a permanent mathematical appointment nor left behind a large corpus of mathematical publications, American mathematicians long saw him as primarily the son of Benjamin Peirce. As Eisele has documented, she was therefore obliged to wage a lonely, dogged—but ultimately successful—campaign for Charles Peirce among America's "top-flight mathematicians" of the second half of the twentieth century. Some of the fruits of this campaign have appeared in the three volumes of *A Century of Mathematics in America*, published by the American Mathematical Society.

II

There is still another community of scholars to whom Professor Eisele has addressed her campaign, the professional historians of science and mathematics. It is as an historian of mathematics (and by no means an experienced Peircean scholar or a research mathematician) that I will discuss the potential for collaboration between Peircean scholars and historians of mathematics in the wake of Eisele's pioneering work. My comments on a possible link between symbolical algebra and Peirce's statement of his early pragmatic maxim as well as on his confusion about Augustus De Morgan's philosophy of mathematics are therefore intended as suggestive reflections on the intersection of Peirce's mathematics and philosophy, an aspect of Peirce's thought ripe for such collaboration.

Eisele's pioneering efforts at recovering, editing, publishing, and explaining Peirce's mathematics reached fruition at a favorable moment in the history of mathematics. There are finally major historical studies, either in print or in preparation, that promise a widened context in which Peirce's mathematical corpus can be appreciated and historically evaluated. Of potential interest to Peircean scholars are, for example, histories covering Georg Cantor's mathematics of the infinite, non-Euclidean geometry, the American mathematical community, and modern algebra. As Eisele's own work has shown, such mathematical history offers Peircean scholars the possibility of moving beyond miniature paintings of Peirce the isolated mathematician to broad mathematical landscapes in which Peirce claims his rightful place. At the same time, such history can illumine Peirce's debt to the mathematical traditions of his time, traditions that affected not only his research mathematics but his philosophy, logic, and semeiotic as well. In short, as illustrated by the following examples, to understand the mathematics of the nineteenth and early twentieth centuries is to understand a vital piece of the multidisciplinary framework of Peirce's integrated thought.

III

As the first example highlighting the potential for further collaboration between Peircean scholars and historians of mathematics, I will consider Peirce's debt to the British symbolical algebraists of the early nineteenth century—a mathematical and perhaps philosophical debt as well. It was a reading of Peirce's review of Alexander Campbell Fraser's edition of *The Works of George Berkeley* that suggested to me a firm connection between British symbolical algebra and Peirce's early pragmatism. Indeed, in this review of 1871 (W 2:462–87), Peirce moved directly from a statement about the philosophy of mathematics to what Fisch has called Peirce's "first approximation to the pragmatic maxim: 'A better rule [than Berkeley's] for avoiding the deceits of language is this: Do things fulfil the same function practically? Then let them be signified by the same word. Do they not? Then let them be distinguished'" (Fisch 1986, 122).

The history of modern algebra helps to explain the juxtaposition of Peirce's mathematical reflections and his early approach to the pragmatic maxim. This history suggests that the juxtaposition was no careless act, but rather reveals a possible causal link between Peirce's algebraic ideas and early pragmatism. The paragraph in which the pragmatic maxim is embedded deals with "that argument which is so much used by Berkeley and others, that such and such a thing cannot exist because we cannot so much as frame the idea of such a thing." Peirce initially dismissed the argument as "a mode of reasoning which is to be used with extreme caution," and then wrote:

> But if we ought to infer that it [a thing] exists, if we only could frame the idea of it, why should we allow our mental incapacity to prevent us from adopting the proposition which logic requires? If such arguments had prevailed in mathematics (and Berkeley was equally strenuous in advocating them there), and if everything about negative quantities, the square root of *minus*, and infinitesimals, had been excluded from the subject on the ground that we can form no idea of such things, the science would have been simplified no doubt, simplified by never advancing to the more difficult matters. A better rule for avoiding the deceits of language is this: Do things fulfil the same function practically? Then let them be signified by the same word. Do they not? Then let them be distinguished. If I have learned a formula in gibberish which in any way jogs my memory so as to enable me in each single case to act as though I had a general idea, what possible utility is there in distinguishing between such a gibberish and for-

mula and an idea? Why use the term *a general idea* in such a sense as to separate things which, for all experiential purposes, are the same [W 2:483]?

Encapsulated in this key paragraph was thus a brief history of mathematics. Peirce implied, for example, that some mathematical thinkers had seriously considered restricting mathematical objects to those of which they could frame ideas; he stated, moreover, that Berkeley himself had applied such arguments to mathematics; and he implied finally that mathematicians had ultimately rejected the argument and thus saved the negative numbers, imaginaries, and infinitesimals. But how did this history relate to the pragmatic maxim, which followed immediately? Missing in Peirce's brief history was explicit reference to British symbolical algebra of the early nineteenth century, a movement which, in a nutshell, legitimated the negative and imaginary numbers by replacing traditional definitions of algebraic objects with formulas governing their use. Thus, in his *Treatise of Algebra* of 1830 (the classical statement of the early symbolical approach to algebra), George Peacock defined symbolical algebra as "the science which treats of the combinations of arbitrary signs and symbols by means of defined though arbitrary laws." He offered traditional definitions of neither the negative nor the imaginary numbers; rather, he first gave laws governing their use and only later tried to interpret them. For example, without defining an imaginary, Peacock "assume[d] . . . i to represent the *imaginary* or peculiar sign," such that $i^2 = -1$ (Peacock 1830, 71, 351–52). Peacock's approach can be translated into Peirce's language: after a long, futile search by mathematicians for clear definitions of the negative and imaginary numbers, the symbolical algebraists had decided to accept possible gibberish ("negatives" or "imaginaries") and a formula in place of the illusive ideas (see, for example, Pycior 1981).

The timing of Peirce's "first approximation to the pragmatic maxim," moreover, supports the thesis of a link between symbolical algebra and the maxim. The late 1860s were, after all, a period of intense intellectual interaction between Peirce and his father, Benjamin, as son and father focused on logic and algebra, respectively. Charles presented his memoir on the logic of relatives at the beginning of 1870, and lithographed copies of

Benjamin Peirce's *Linear Associative Algebra* appeared in the same year. Reminiscing on the late 1860s, Peirce himself wrote of "frequent conversations [with his father] on the allied subjects, especially about the algebra" (NEM 3/pt. 1:526). Although Benjamin and Charles Peirce were somewhat careless about acknowledging their intellectual debts (perhaps partially because their American genius seems to have quickly altered foreign ideas), later scholars have associated Benjamin Peirce's linear algebra with British symbolical algebra. Thus in *The Development of Peirce's Philosophy* Murphey described symbolical algebra, although he developed no explicit case for its influence on the Peirces (1961, 183-88). More recent studies, however, have placed *Linear Associative Algebra* firmly in the tradition of symbolical algebra (for instance, Pycior 1979). Moreover, in *Linear Associative Algebra* Benjamin Peirce himself referred to George Boole, Sir William Rowan Hamilton, and Augustus De Morgan (1870b, 98, 103, 105, 107). He cited specifically De Morgan's "Triple Algebra" (1870b, 107)—that is, De Morgan's paper "On the Foundation of Algebra, No. IV., on Triple Algebra," the fourth paper in the series on the "Foundation of Algebra," which De Morgan published between 1842 and 1849 (De Morgan 1842-1849). Furthermore, in the letter he wrote in June 1870 to introduce Charles to De Morgan, Benjamin Peirce reiterated (1870a) his debt to the memoir on "Triple Algebra."

As an algebraist, Benjamin Peirce thus seems to have been influenced especially by De Morgan and Hamilton, and thus it is quite likely that the Peirces' mathematical conversations of the late 1860s—which covered algebra as well as definitions of mathematics—drew on the writings of these two foreign mathematicians. Indeed, in his series on the "Foundation of Algebra," De Morgan had not only developed an early version of linear algebra but explored the philosophy underlying symbolical algebra as well. "Algebra now consists of two parts," De Morgan had explained,

> the technical [De Morgan's term for symbolical algebra], and the logical. Technical algebra is the art of using symbols under regulations which, when this part of the subject is considered independently of the other, are prescribed as the definitions of the symbols. Logical algebra is the science which investigates the

method of giving meaning to the primary symbols, and of interpreting all subsequent symbolic results. It is desirable that the word *definition* should not enter in two distinct senses, and I should propose to retain it as used in the *art* of algebra. . . . Thus a symbol is *defined* when such rules are laid down for its use as will enable us to accept or reject any proposed transformation of it, or by means of it [1842, 173–74].

Thus, the symbolical algebraists' substitution of rules for a more traditional definition of a symbol—proposed by Peacock and elaborated by such second-generation symbolical algebraists as De Morgan—quite possibly helped set the stage for Charles Peirce's acceptance of "a gibberish and formula" in place of an idea.

IV

Peirce used imaginary numbers as an example not only in his review of Berkeley's collected works but throughout his writings. Whereas in the review imaginary numbers illustrated reasoning in the absence of clear ideas, on other occasions these numbers were associated more explicitly with the definition of mathematics offered by his father. For example, in his "Logic of Quantity," chapter 17 of his "Grand Logic" of 1893, Charles Peirce included a wonderful dialogue on the imaginary numbers and the process by which they had been absorbed into mathematics. The dialogue linked the imaginaries, Benjamin Peirce's definition of mathematics, and—at least implicitly—symbolical algebra.

"The algebraist sets out," Peirce began, "with a single continuous quantitative relation. But when he comes to quadratics he finds himself confronted with impossible problems." Because the quadratic formula sometimes leads to solutions of the form $a + b\sqrt{-1}$, the algebraist "says: 'I want a square root of negative unity. Now there is no such thing in the universe: clearly, then, I must import it from abroad.'" Here Peirce asked exactly how the mathematician knows—that is, can prove—that "there is no such thing." He argued: the mathematician is obliged to reason indirectly: he lets i stand for the root of negative unity "if there be one," and then squares *i*. But since the square of any number, either negative or positive, is positive, the mathematician next observes that the square of *i* must be positive, and proclaims that he has reached a contradiction. "Then," Peirce summarized,

> the whole impossibility depends upon this, that every quantity is supposed to be positive or negative. Suppose we make *i* neither positive nor negative. "But there is no such thing," some rule-of-thumb man says. Really? In that respect it is just like all the other objects the mathematician deals with. They are one and all mere figments of the brain.

Still the rule-of-thumb mathematician objects; he argues that it "*means nothing*" to say that *i* is neither positive nor negative (CP 4.132). In retort, Peirce appealed to a version of the definition of mathematics that his father had offered in his *Linear Associative Algebra* (1870b, 97). Mathematics "is merely tracing out the consequences of hypotheses," he reminded the mathematician, and, thus, "to say a thing has no meaning is to say it is not included in our hypothesis." Furthermore, "we are dealing with algebra in the abstract. The only hypothesis we make is that our letters obey the laws of algebra." To solve the problem of the imaginaries, then, the mathematician must re-examine the laws of algebra and delete the law that maintains that "either $x > y$, or $x = y$, or $y > x$" (which Peirce called law 16 of algebra and which is essential to the proof that the square of every number is positive). "The quantity $i \ldots$," Peirce concluded, thus "becomes perfectly possible, and perfectly *conceivable*, in the only clear sense of that word, namely, that we can write down $i^2 + 1 = 0$ without conflict with any formula" (CP 4.132).

The lesson of the dialogue was clear: rule-of-thumb mathematicians (who formed the majority of textbook authors at that time, according to Peirce) erred when they stated that an imaginary number "means nothing." Peirce emphasized that better mathematicians understood "meaning" quite differently from the "thumbists." Indeed, the better mathematicians followed the symbolical approach—or, we can say, followed a mathematical version of Peirce's pragmatic maxim. "Men are anxious to learn what the square root of negative unity *means*," he explained.

It just means

$$i^2 + 1 = 0;$$

precisely as −1 means

$$1 + (-1) = 0.$$

... To say that algebra means anything else than just its own forms is to mistake an *application* of algebra for the *meaning* of it [CP 4.133].

V

In addition to suggesting this link between symbolical algebra and the early pragmatic maxim, recent history of mathematics exposes Peirce's failings as an historian of mathematical philosophy, a role he often assumed. Indeed, in his review of Fraser's edition of Berkeley's works, Peirce (like some later commentators) misstated the Irish bishop's position on algebra, while on two other occasions he erroneously characterized De Morgan as a follower of William Rowan Hamilton's Kantian philosophy of mathematics. Although Berkeley rejected infinitesimals as objects of the calculus, which as a subdiscipline of geometry was supposed to deal with perceptible extension, he nevertheless accepted imaginary numbers. Indeed, Berkeley saw arithmetic and algebra as sciences of signs, and his mathematical reflections helped inspire some of the early British symbolical algebraists, most prominently Robert Woodhouse (see Pycior 1984, 434–35; 1987, 277–86). In *Alciphron*, for example, Berkeley explained that language does not aim solely at "the imparting or acquiring of ideas" but sometimes at "something of an active operative nature, tending to a conceived good." Such a good, he continued,

> may sometimes be obtained, not only although the ideas marked are not offered to the mind, but even although there should be no possibility of offering or exhibiting any such idea to the mind: for instance, the algebraic mark, which denotes the root of a negative square, hath its use in logistic operations, although it be impossi-

ble to form an idea of any such quantity. And what is true of algebraic signs is also true of words or language, modern algebra being in fact a more short, apposite, and artificial sort of language ... [Berkeley 1948-1957, 3:307].

In short, on the issue of the imaginaries, Berkeley and Peirce had more in common than Peirce's review of 1871 let on. As Fisch has noted, moreover, in later years Peirce characterized "the principle of pragmatism . . . [as] but a formulation of Berkeley's practice" (Fisch 1986, 122). "In 1871, in a Metaphysical Club in Cambridge, Massachusetts," Peirce wrote, "I used to preach this principle as a sort of logical gospel, representing the unformulated method followed by Berkeley, and in conversation about it I called it 'Pragmatism'" (CP 6.482).

VI

Whereas for his review of 1871 Peirce could easily have drawn his mathematical characterization of Berkeley from the *Analyst*, where the bishop (writing primarily about geometry and the calculus) demanded that mathematicians have clear ideas of the objects they reasoned on, it is more difficult to understand why Peirce sometimes misrepresented De Morgan's philosophy of algebra. Indeed, renewed scholarly interest in De Morgan makes the present time ripe not only for a comparison of Peirce's and De Morgan's philosophies of mathematics, including an analysis of Peirce's critique of De Morgan's philosophy, but also for a general examination of Peirce's intellectual debt to De Morgan.

Peircean scholars have, of course, already considered the relationship between Peirce's "Description of a Notation for the Logic of Relatives" (DNLR) of 1870 and De Morgan's earlier paper, "On the Syllogism, No. IV, and on the Logic of Relations" of 1864. "We may conclude," Daniel Merrill has summarized, "that while Peirce probably knew of De Morgan's memoir on relations when he was working out the full notation of DNLR, his own Boolean orientation meant that he was working on these topics in his own way" (1982, xlv).

Through his father's work on linear associative algebras—

and subsequently his own (see, for example, Peirce 1881)—
Peirce, however, knew De Morgan as an algebraist and philosopher of algebra as well as a logician. Although a case may be made for an intellectual affiliation between De Morgan's reflections on the nature of algebra and Benjamin Peirce's definition of mathematics (perhaps with De Morgan's philosophy as an intermediate step between more traditional philosophies and Peirce's definition), in at least two separate instances Charles Peirce misstated and then attacked De Morgan's philosophy of mathematics. In both cases, the younger Peirce claimed that Sir William Rowan Hamilton and De Morgan considered mathematics as the science of pure time and space. For example, in his *Elements of Mathematics*, written around 1895, Peirce wrote:

> Hamilton, with the concurrence of the eminent mathematical logician, De Morgan, and of others, then proposed to define mathematics as the science of time and space, being influenced in this by the philosophy of Kant. But Hamilton's definition is, by far, the most objectionable of all that have been widely in vogue. For it implicitly denies the main characteristic of mathematics, namely that this alone among the sciences makes no researches into facts, but attends solely to ideas, without seeking to establish their truth [NEM 2:8].

Hamilton's (and supposedly De Morgan's) definition missed the essential point that mathematics deals with hypotheses alone, not with real time and real space, and not even with mental truths about Kantian time and space, Peirce continued. Furthermore, "the most remarkable characteristic of time, namely, that the passage from the past to the future is qualitatively different from the passage from the future to the past is not represented in algebra. The chief study of the algebraists is a two-dimensional continuum, strikingly unlike time" (NEM 2:9).

> In his "Logic of Mathematics in Relation to Education" of a few years later, Peirce returned to the definition of mathematics as the science of pure time and space. He first wrote that Hamilton and De Morgan had "a superficial acquaintance with Kant, [and] were just enough influenced by the *Critique* to be led, when they found reason for rejecting the definition as the science of quantity, to conclude that mathematics was the science of pure time

and pure space." Dismissing the latter definition as "extremely objectionable" and chiding the two men for not having "attentively read what Kant himself has to say about number," Peirce then tried to penetrate the motives of Hamilton and De Morgan. He speculated that "Hamilton's intention probably was, by means of this definition, to throw a slur upon the introduction of imaginaries into geometry, as a false science." But he acknowledged that De Morgan's motives were less transparent. "What De Morgan, who was a student of multiple algebra, and whose own formal logic is plainly mathematical, could have had in view, it is hard to comprehend, unless he wished to oppose Boole's theory of logic" (CP 3.557).

The first paper in De Morgan's series on the "Foundation of Algebra," which was the likely source for Peirce's associating De Morgan with Hamilton's definition of mathematics as the science of pure time and space, provides additional grounds for doubts about Peirce's reliability as an historian of mathematical philosophy. Although De Morgan here discussed Hamilton's definition and even referred to the "Essay on Algebra as the Science of Pure Time" (Hamilton 1837) as a "very original and methodical memoir," he did not embrace Hamilton's philosophy. Rather, he explained:

> I cannot see why the whole paper might not be as easily applied to succession of points in a line, as to succession of epochs in time. Succession, that is to say *continuous* succession, might be made the fundamental conception in both cases; and if such were the author's intention in the use of the word *time*, I should be very glad to maintain after him that *one* of the explanations which suffice to convert technical into logical algebra, has been fully established in his memoir [De Morgan 1842, 175].

There is thus little wonder why Peirce found it difficult to explain—what he erroneously reported as—De Morgan's espousal of Hamilton's definition. In turn, De Morgan's critique of the definition, as well as his association of algebra with "*continuous* succession" (Peirce's later term was "a two-dimensional continuum"), raise new questions concerning Peirce's reliability as a mathematical chronicler and his debt to De Morgan. Had Peirce learned of De Morgan's paper of 1842 from conversations with his father (and without actually reading it), or had he possibly read it early in life and forgotten some of its finer points by the 1890s?

These are important questions. In this paper De Morgan not only distinguished between technical (symbolical) and logical algebra and criticized Hamilton's definition of mathematics but also reflected on three factors involved in the use of a symbol, factors which, to a certain degree, foreshadowed Peirce's triad of "a sign, its object, and its interpretant" (CP 5.484). "A symbol is not the representation of an external object absolutely," De Morgan explained,

> but of a state of the mind in regard to that object; of a conception formed, for the formation of which the mind knows that it is or was indebted to the presence, bodily or ideal, of the object. Those who do not remember this, the real use of a symbol, are apt to dogmatize, declaring one or another explanation of a symbol, that is, the signification by it of one or another impression produced on their own minds, to be real, true, natural, or necessary: it being neither one nor the other, except with reference to the particular mind in question [De Morgan 1842, 174].

Moreover, even Peirce's characterization of Hamilton as a proponent of mathematics as the science of pure time and space would have benefited from qualification. For example, in his *Lectures on Quaternions* of 1853, Hamilton recounted that in his paper of 1842 De Morgan had "noticed" his "Essay on Algebra as the Science of Pure Time" "in a free but friendly spirit." Because of the influence of Peacock, De Morgan, and other symbolical algebraists, Hamilton indicated here, he was now open to modifications in his philosophy. "I am very willing to believe . . . ," he stated,

> I may have habitually attended too little to the *symbolical* character of Algebra, as a Language, or organized system of *signs*: and too much (in proportion) to what I have been accustomed to consider its *scientific* character, as a Doctrine analogous to Geometry, through the Kantian parallelism between the *intuitions* of Time and Space [1853, 14].

VII

In summary, because of the extraordinary campaign of Carolyn Eisele, Peircean scholars, mathematicians writing history, and historians of science have a deeper appreciation of the "thoroughly integrated thought" of Peirce the *mathematician*, logician, and philosopher; with the publication of her *New Elements of Mathematics*, they also have Peirce's mathematical corpus. Scholarly collaboration on the intersection of Peirce's mathematics and philosophy—on such topics as a link between symbolical algebra and Peirce's pragmatic maxim, his credibility as an historian of mathematical philosophy, and his debt to De Morgan—may be the next order of business. Scholars could offer no clearer sign of the success of Carolyn Eisele's campaign for Charles Peirce.

10

Peirce and History of Science

Joseph W. Dauben

ONE OF THE STORIES Charles Peirce liked to tell about himself also taught a pragmatic lesson. The story was about the theft of a valuable gold watch and the way Peirce went about tracking down the man who had taken it—which in turn involved a conjecture that turned out to be something more than a lucky guess. It was the nature of his conjecture, however, that primarily interested Peirce, although he also delighted in recounting his dramatic hunt for the stolen goods, and his great relief when they were eventually recovered.

The theft occurred during a trip Peirce made from Boston to New York City aboard a coastal steamer, the *Bristol*, where an expensive Tiffany watch and fob, along with his coat, were taken from his stateroom.[1] Peirce later saw the incident as a paradigmatic illustration of an important principle of his pragmatic philosophy, as well as one of his fundamental logical principles, that of abductive reasoning. Abductive reasoning, in turn, is closely related not only to the subject of Peirce and the history of science in general, but to his mathematics in particular.

Recently, several scholars have analyzed Peirce's abduction, comparing it directly with the methods of Arthur Conan Doyle's fictional detective Sherlock Holmes. Thomas and Jean Umiker-Sebeok as well as Umberto Eco have also done so with special reference to the story of Peirce's stolen Tiffany watch. Umberto Eco, for example, in "Horns, Hooves, Insteps; Some Hypotheses on Three Types of Abduction" (both articles are in Eco and Sebeok 1983), draws a direct connection between Holmesian reasoning and Peircean abduction. In addition to the role of intuition, inspired by what often seems to be a "lucky guess," there is another principle at work. This is reflected in a maxim familiar to any Holmes enthusiast, formulated by Conan Doyle in numerous variations, but here given as he formulated it in *The Adventure of the Bruce-Partington Plans*. In the words of Holmes, explaining the "old axiom" to Watson: "When all other contingencies fail, whatever remains, however improbable, must be the truth."[2]

PEIRCE THE ABDUCTIVE DETECTIVE

It was Friday, June 20, 1879, when Peirce boarded the *Bristol* in Boston, bound for New York.[3] The next morning, upon arrival, he felt "a strange fuzzy sensation" in his head, which prompted him to dress quickly and leave the ship in a hurry to get some fresh air. Inadvertently, he left behind both his overcoat and his expensive gold watch. This was no ordinary timepiece, but a prize chronometer in a gold hunting case, designed for Tiffany's by Charles Frodsham. The watch was bought for Peirce by the United States Coast and Geodetic Survey for use in his pendulum research. Suddenly realizing what he had done, Peirce rushed back to the ship, fearing "life long professional disgrace" if he failed to retrieve the watch. Of course, his stateroom was empty, so he insisted on lining up the entire ship's crew in an effort to identify the culprit who had taken the watch. As Peirce vividly described it:

> I went from one end of the row to the other, and talked a little to each one, in as *dégagé* a manner as I could, about whatever he could talk about with interest, but would least expect me to bring forward, hoping that I might seem such a fool that I should be able to detect some symptom of his being the thief. When I had gone through the row, I turned and walked from them, though not away, and said to myself, "Not the least scintilla of light have I got to go upon." But thereupon my other self (for our own communings are always in dialogues,) said to me, "But you simply *must* put your finger on the man. No matter if you have no reason, you must say whom you will think to be the thief." I made a little loop in my walk, which had not taken a minute, and as I turned toward them, all shadow of doubt had vanished [MS 687, 10–11; also in Peirce 1929, 271; Umiker-Sebeok and Sebeok as printed in Eco and Sebeok 1983, 11–12, the transcription is not entirely accurate].

Taking his suspect aside, Peirce offered him $50.00 for the immediate return of the watch, but to no avail. Having failed for the moment, Peirce reported that he then "ran down to the dock, and was driven, as fast as the cabby could, to Pinkerton's," the famous New York detective agency (Peirce 1929, 273).

Peirce gave the General Manager of Pinkerton's, one George Bangs, more than just a general description of his suspect. He not only identified him by name, but also gave Bangs a full description of the watch, along with its serial number, predicting: "He will come off the boat at one o'clock, and will immediately go to pawn the watch, for which he will get $50. I wish you to have him shadowed, and as soon as he has the pawn-ticket, let him be arrested" (Peirce 1929, 273).

Unfortunately, the agent Bangs assigned to the case disregarded Peirce's instructions. Having looked into the backgrounds of all the employees on board the steamboat *Bristol*, he tailed another suspect who did not have the watch. Pinkerton's then sent postcards to all pawnbrokers in New York, Boston, and Fall River (the *Bristol*'s home port) describing the stolen watch and offering a handsome reward of $150.00 for its return. Within twenty-four hours the watch was retrieved from a New York City pawnbroker, who subsequently described Peirce's suspect "so graphically that no doubt was possible that it had been `my man.'"[4]

Peirce insisted on going immediately to the guilty party's home, with every intention of retrieving his still missing overcoat along with the fob chain as well. Pinkerton's detective, who went with him, refused to enter the premises without a warrant, so Peirce proceeded on his own, promising to be back within twelve minutes. Barging into the apartment in question, Peirce found the suspect's wife talking with a friend. It is easy to imagine Peirce rising to the occasion, declaring dramatically: "'Your husband is now on his road to Sing Sing for stealing my watch. I have learned that my chain and overcoat, which he also stole, are here, and I am going to take them.' Thereupon the two women raised a tremendous hullabaloo. . . . I was entirely cool" (Peirce 1929, 275).

Peirce wrote to Superintendent C. P. Patterson of the Coast Survey on June 24, to report that the watch had been stolen but adding the good news that he had successfully recovered it. The following day, Peirce explained in another letter to Patterson: "Everything has been recovered. . . . The thief is the very man I suspected throughout, contrary to the judgement of the detective."[5]

Later, Peirce described the incident in detail to his friend, the Harvard philosopher and psychologist William James (1842–1910).[6] He did so because he had come to regard the story as an excellent example of what he called the logic of abduction. He also described this as the "inclination to entertain an hypothesis," which served to explain "why it is that people so often guess right." In turn, Peirce described the formation of an hypothesis as "an act of *insight*," the "abductive suggestion" coming to us "like a flash" (CP 5.181, 7.39–40, 46, 218–219, 679).

Abduction, or "the first step of scientific reasoning," is also closely linked to Peirce's interests in the history of science, as well as to his thinking about *continuity*, which runs like a unifying thread throughout most of his thought.[7] Continuity, in fact, is also directly linked to his most basic ideas (and his best insights) in mathematics and logic, and is essential to appreciating Peirce's Pragmatism, or later, as he preferred to call it, Pragmaticism.[8]

Working with Peirce Materials: Manuscripts, *Collected Works*, and Recent Editions

Before turning to an examination of Peirce's ideas about abduction, his study of the mathematics of the continuum, and his life's work devoted to fashioning a comprehensive logic of science drawing closely on the history of science, it is necessary to call attention to several basic problems in working with Peirce as an historical subject. The difficulties begin with Peirce himself, but are not entirely his alone.

Bertrand Russell pinpointed one problem when he wrote in 1946 that Peirce "reminds one of a volcano spouting vast masses of rock, of which some, on examination, turn out to be nuggets of pure gold" (1946/1969, xvi). The dilemma, of course, is to spot the gold amid the debris. In surveying the nearly seventy boxes of Peirce's writings in Houghton Library at Harvard University, the magnitude of the problem becomes apparent. Compounding this difficulty is the way in which Peirce worked, for his habit was to write and rewrite, revising continuously through half a dozen or more drafts. Since he kept everything—but rarely bothered to date anything—his papers are a chronological mess.[9]

Another difficulty is that Peirce never managed to produce a general overview—let alone an introduction or summary—for his philosophy as a whole. This means that as he published a review here and a paper there his work came to interested readers in scattered bits and pieces. The Peirce scholar Murray Murphey once described the thousands of manuscript pages of Peirce's writings as "the ruins of a once great structure." He then went on to say, in *The Development of Peirce's Philosophy*:

> But this is an illusion—Peirce's illusion: the grand design was never fulfilled. The reason is that Peirce was never able to find a way to utilize the continuum concept effectively. The magnificent synthesis which the theory of continuity seemed to promise somehow always eluded him, and the shining vision of the great system always remained a castle in the air [Murphey 1961, 407].

Ultimately, however, the greatest obstacle in coming to grips with Peirce's "castle in the air" is the incomplete and unsatisfactory manner in which his voluminous writings, both published and unpublished, have been available for study. Until recently, the most readily available source of Peirce's thought has been the edition of his *Collected Papers* produced by Charles Hartshorne, Paul Weiss, and, later, Arthur Burks.[10] When Hartshorne began organizing the papers in the late 1920s, he "knew almost nothing about Peirce. It was just a job" (Lieb 1970, esp. 149). Later Weiss confessed that "we were ignorant and inexperienced." But in their defense he also noted: "We were young men, who knew nothing about editing, nothing about publishing; but, also, we were given no help [from the Harvard Philosophy Department]. We were not encouraged in our work" (Bernstein 1970, esp. 180).

Unfortunately, as Hartshorne and Weiss set about editing the Peirce papers, many important details of science, and especially of mathematics, were either obscured or left out entirely. A few examples will make clear how seriously misleading the *Collected Papers* can be.

To begin with the positive: readers turning to MS 25 "On Multitude and Number" (CP 4.170–226) will find the following first page in the Houghton Library:

> *Multitude*
> *No. 25*
>
> Multitude and Number. 1579 ¶ 3
>
> Art. 1. Let us consider the relation of a constituent unit to the collective whole of which it forms a part. Suppose A is [to be] such a unit and B is [to be] such a whole. Then [in order] to avoid the circumlocution of saying that A is a constituent unit of B as the collective whole of which it is a unit, I shall simply say A is a unit of B, and shall write "A is a u of B"; or I may reverse the order in which A and B are mentioned by writing "B is u'd by A."
>
> The only logical peculiarities of this relation are as follows:
>
> 1st, whatever is u of anything is u'd by itself and by nothing else. Hence, if anything is u'd by anything not itself, it is not itself u of anything; and consequently nothing that is u'd by anything but itself is u'd by itself.
>
> 2nd, whatever is not u'd by anything does not exist.
>
> Art. 2. By a *collection*, I mean anything which is u'd by whatever has a certain quality, or general description, and by nothing else. That is, if C is a collection, there is some quality, α, such that taking anything whatever, say x, either x possesses the quality α and is a unit of C, or else it neither possesses the quality α nor is a unit of C. On the other hand, if C is not a collection, no matter what quality or general description, β, may be taken, there is either something possessing the quality β without being a unit of C, or there is some unit of C which does not possess the quality β.
>
> ...ill be perceived, therefore, that there is a collection corresponding to ... noun of general description. Corresponding to the common noun 'man' of men; and corresponding to the common noun 'fairy' there

The paper on which Peirce wrote is now brittle with age, and the lower left-hand corner has broken off. In this case the printed transcription, fortunately, has preserved the text in its entirety, despite the fact that part of the original manuscript page is now missing.

But elsewhere there are serious problems to be found with the six volumes of Peirce's *Collected Papers* as edited by Hartshorne and Weiss. Consider MS 25 again, page 5, where lines are drawn through two paragraphs, and in the published version, Peirce's numbering system for "Articles" (including some sentences) was eliminated without ellipsis.

Here the editors simply wrote directly on the manuscript page, and then sent their blue-penciled version out for printing![11] Yet, what was struck from this page is of considerable historical interest. In the first deleted paragraph Peirce explained that "I borrow from Dr. Georg Cantor the following definitions. . . ." Without mentioning Cantor, the founder of transfinite set theory, the *Collected Papers* gives readers the impression that everything Peirce had to say in this passage about infinite multitudes (sets) is the product of his own thinking, there being no indication that he was drawing his definitions directly from Cantor. This is of no small importance when assessing the possible influence Cantor's work may have had on Peirce's own study of "Multitude and Number" and the crucial subject of continuity.

Moreover, due to the way Peirce's papers were edited and printed in the *Collected Papers*, the published edition gives no clues as to the extent of Peirce's revisions and the way in which he developed his ideas. One glance at page 14 of MS 25, for example, shows how his thinking evolved on the subject of the different orders of infinite sets, and how his terminology changed from "number" to "multitude."

Art. 13   discrete
I will now run over the different grades of multitude of collections
of distinct constituent individuals, and point out the most remarkable
properties of those multitudes.
   The first grade of multitude is that of a collection which does not exist,
or the multitude of *none*. A collection of this multitude has obvious
logical peculiarities. Namely, nothing asserted of it can be false. For
of it alone contradictory assertions are true. It is a collection and it is
not a collection. Given that all the X's are black and that all
the X's are pure white, what is the conclusion? Simply that the multitude
of the X's is zero.
Art. 14.
   The least difference by which one multitude can exceed another is by a single unit. By I do not say that the multitude next greater than a
                         given multitude always exceeds it by a single unit.
Art. 15. multitude
   The number of ways of distributing nothing into two abodes is one. This
is the next grade of multitude. This again has certain logical peculiarities. Namely, in order to prove that every individual of it possesses one character,
it suffices to prove that every individual of it does not pos-
sess the negative of that character.
Art. 16. multitude
   The number of ways of distributing a single individual into two
houses is two. This is the next grade of multitude. This again has
certain logical peculiarities which have been noted in Schröder's
Logik.
          multitude of   combinations of two things is four, which
   The number of ways of distributing two individuals into it
is not the next grade of multitude. The multitude of combinations of
four things is 16. The multitude of combinations of 16 things is 65536.

This one change alone is of considerable philosophical interest, for it reveals how Peirce came to see "number" as more restrictive than "multitude," and that the two concepts were not, in fact, synonymous.

Perhaps the most serious omissions occur, however, when the editors of the *Collected Papers*, not being sensitive to (or not being interested in) Peirce's mathematics, excised entire paragraphs that may have seemed too technical, or left out explanations that were essential to making Peirce's meaning comprehensible. For example, what is a reader to make of the following sentence from the transcription of MS 25 in the *Collected Papers*: "The denumerable multitude added to itself gives itself . . . as made plain by zigzagging through two denumerable series . . ." (CP 4.193)?

How many readers are likely to know what Peirce meant by "zigzagging" through two denumerable series? Although this might seem opaque in itself, Peirce provided a diagram that was omitted from the published version in the *Collected Papers*, a diagram that makes all of this transparent. Anyone familiar with the techniques of set theory might guess what Peirce meant by "zigzagging," but readers with only a limited acquaintance (or none at all) with set-theoretical ideas might well be confused.

> *Multitude*
>
> 32.
>
> in seeing what the ~~preferred~~ *supposed* argument would be.
>
> Since the sum of any ~~many~~ *higher* collection of multitudes is formed by first adding two and then successively adding single multitudes to the sum already formed, it follows at once that ~~the~~ sum of any enumerable collection of enumerable multitudes is enumerable.
>
> Art. 27. The sum of an enumerable multitude and the denumerable multitude is denumerable. The proof is excessively simple; for we have only to ~~take~~ *count* the enumerable [*collection in linear*] series first. The count of that has to end; and then the denumerable series may follow in its ordinal order.
>
> Art. 28. That the denumerable multitude added to itself gives itself is made plain by zig-zagging through two denumerable series
>
> \/\/\/\/\/\/\/ etc. etc.
>
> But this comes more properly under the head of multiplication of multitudes, which I propose to consider.
>
> Mathematicians seem to be satisfied to so far generalize the conception of multiplication as to make it the application of one operation to the result of another. But the conception may be still further generalized, and in being further generalized it returns more closely to its primitive type. The more general conception of multiplication to which I allude is ~~as follows~~ *expressed* in the following definition: Multiplication is the pairing of every unit of one quantity with every unit of another quantity so as to make a new unit. Since there are two ~~kinds~~ *acceptions* *of the term pair*, the *un*ordered acception, according to which AB and BA are different pairs, and the ordered acception, there are two varieties of multiplication the non-

Here (MS 25, page 32), thanks to Peirce's simple illustration, it becomes obvious what he meant mathematically by "zigzagging," and how, by zigzagging back and forth between the two infinite series, it is possible to show that there is a one-to-one correspondence between the denumerable set of integers and the members of both of these two sets together:

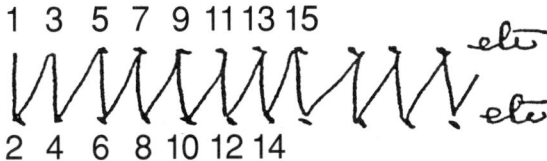

Finally, one last example will suffice to show that even in a case where the editors of the *Collected Papers* did include Peirce's original diagram, they unfortunately took more editorial license than was warranted, going so far as to introduce symbols that were not Peirce's! This is especially disturbing because Peirce, the father of semeiotic, was always very careful about his use of symbols. Worse yet, in the case of MS 25 the editors' intervention was also fundamentally wrong. Not only did they misunderstand Peirce's mathematics, but they conflated his conception of set theory with that of Georg Cantor in a way that could only mislead the unsuspecting reader.

As it appears in the *Collected Papers* (4.196), Peirce is again considering denumerability.

MULTITUDE AND NUMBER [4.196

ing this idea so as to construct the most rigidly formal demonstration. Let $\aleph$ denote the denumerable multitude. Then, I am to show that $\aleph^2 = \aleph$. Let the M's be a denumerable collection. That is, suppose

First: a certain object M_0, is an M;

Second: there is a certain non-identical one-to-one relation, r, such that every M is r'd by an M;

Third. whatever is not necessitated to be an M by the above statements is not an M.

Let A and B constitute a collection of two objects not M's. Let us define the relation ς as follows:

First: the pair of attachments of A to M_0 and B to M_0 is ς'd by nothing;

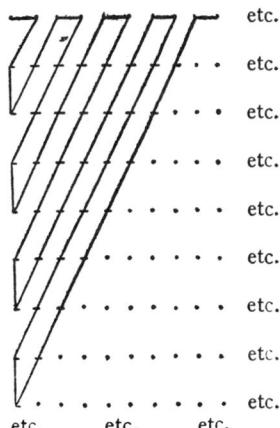

This time he uses another version of zigzagging to show "that the second power of the denumerable multitude is the denumerable multitude." In transcribing the page, the editors rightly included Peirce's diagram, which makes his meaning immediately apparent. But what is *not* to be found in the original manuscript are the Hebrew alephs.

To a mathematician the alephs immediately suggest George Cantor's transfinite cardinal numbers.[12] Instead, where the editors of the *Collected Papers* chose to introduce Cantor's alephs, Peirce used a special symbol of his own devising—⍟.

This is particularly ironic since the editors consciously *omitted* references to Cantor earlier, then introduced an explicitly Cantorial element later.

Even if Peirce had considered using alephs, it must be stressed that his ℵs were not equivalent to Cantor's transfinite cardinal numbers. Peirce introduced ℵ to identify what he called postnumerals, generated by power sets. Thus, given a denumerably infinite set M, Peirce's first postnumeral (he terms it a "primipostnumeral") corresponds to 2^M. All of Peirce's higher postnumerals were generated through the unending sequence of power sets (one of Peirce's fundamental discoveries, discussed in greater detail below). Thus, to interpret ℵ as a transfinite cardinal number in Cantor's sense is to misread Peirce and add a new element of confusion.

To be more exact, beginning from the smallest infinite set, the set of all integers, Peirce concluded that it was always possible to produce increasingly larger sets of greater and greater power. After the denumerable set of integers, the set of all subsets of the integers (equivalent in power to the real numbers), comprised what Peirce called the "first abnumeral" or the "Primipostnumeral" multitude.[13] The set of all subsets of the real numbers in turn produced the "second abnumeral," or the "secundopostnumeral" multitude, and so on. Since one could always form from such sets the set of subsets, Peirce noted that there could be no maximal multitude.[14]

Cantor's alephs, on the other hand, did not arise from the power set principle, as Peirce's postnumerals did. Instead, the transfinite alephs were the result of fundamentally different methods which Cantor called "principles of generation," a much weaker means of defining cardinal numbers than is the case with power sets. Basically, Cantor defined transfinite cardinal numbers in terms of number classes of well-ordered sets. The magnitude of Peirce's own confusion about all this is reflected in a letter he sent to F. W. Frankland in May 1908, in which he said that his power sets "'are really the alephs although differently defined'" (quoted in Murphey 1961, 267).[15]

Readers wishing to avoid the problems and pitfalls described here in reading Peirce through the *Collected Papers* have several options, beginning with the original manuscripts in Houghton Library and the microfiche edition of his complete published works (MF). Carolyn Eisele's five volumes of Peirce's *New Elements of Mathematics* (NEM) have already begun to correct the record regarding Peirce's mathematics, which was, in any event, under-represented in the *Collected Papers*. And it may be that the chronological edition of Peirce's writings (W), now as far as Volume Four (and covering Peirce up to 1884), may also help to redress the editorial deficiencies of the *Collected Papers*, upon which most Peirce scholars until very recently have had to rely.

One point concerning the Peirce Editorial Project (which is producing the chronological edition) should not be overlooked, especially on the subjects of Peirce's mathematics and history of science. In his preface to the second volume, Edward C. Moore, then editor of the series, explains that the chronological edition is necessarily selective (understandably so, since a rough estimate of what it would take to publish *all* Peirce's writings exceeds 100 volumes). Historians of science will be disappointed, however, to learn that in being selective the editors have again given preference to Peirce's philosophical writings at the expense of his scientific, mathematical, and historical writings.[16]

Concerning Peirce's mathematics, it is true that Carolyn Eisele, almost single-handedly, has been the major advocate for its central place in Peirce's thought, as reflected in her five-volume edition of *The New Elements of Mathematics by Charles S. Peirce*.[17] But her prodigious efforts may have served to support the editors of the new chronological edition of Peirce's papers in their decision to de-emphasize mathematics and the technical scientific side of Peirce's life. This seems particularly unfortunate in an edition claiming to honor Peirce's philosophical development; as Moore puts it, "our aim is to show the development of Peirce's thought." The full sentence reads (incredibly): "We rest our case for this procedure on the fact that our aim is to show the development of Peirce's thought, and that development is not shown in his technical scientific papers but in his philosophical papers" (W 2:xv). This, in fact, amounts to an obvious contradiction.

On the assumption that Peirce's understanding of mathematics, logic, and science—including his very deep and abiding interest in the history of science—was crucial to his philosophical development, how can these legitimately be de-emphasized, no matter where else the material may be found, or in what form? To refer readers interested in these subjects of major, even crucial concern for understanding Peirce to the microfiche edition of all the original documents is to confess that the chronological edition will be inadequate for any true appreciation of Peirce's overall development.

There is a lesson to be learned, one might have hoped, from the results of Peirce's so-called *Collected Papers*, where so much of the science (and especially the mathematics) was edited away with such a vengeance that all those who have relied upon these volumes for their understanding of Peirce's philosophical development have come away with a tragically skewed and misinformed view. It would be unhappy indeed if the chronological edition were to suffer a similar fate, for not only would it result in an unbalanced sense of the chronological development of Peirce's thought, but it would also deprive readers of any sense of Peirce's importance as an active figure in the history of American science. To appreciate Peirce as a philosopher, and especially his *originality* as a philosopher of science and the founder of pragmatism, father of semeiotic, and early proponent of mathematical logic (and an innovator in the logic of relations), his interests in mathematics, science, and the history of science must be given the emphasis they deserve.[18]

With all this in mind, can we be surprised that Carolyn Eisele for so long was a voice in the wilderness as she described her plight in such detail as one of the pioneering Peirce scholars in Chapter 8 above? Specifically interested in Peirce's scientific work and working for decades in Houghton Library, she was the leader among the few to have seen the value and extent of his mathematical writing and to have appreciated its historic value.

From what has just been said it might seem that forsaking the published version of Peirce's *Collected Papers* in favor of the original Peirce manuscripts in Houghton Library would put the reader directly in touch with Peirce's thought—including his mathematics. Unfortunately, as anyone who has worked with Peirce manuscripts knows, once one is confronted with the original documents, new problems await. As Christine Ladd-

Franklin, one of Peirce's few students who studied logic with him during the brief period he taught at Johns Hopkins, put it:

> Many of his contributions to the philosophical dictionary were of the purely cabalistic type. The second part of the article on Symbolic Logic, for instance, was finally, against the urgent advice of Professor Couturat, who himself had contributed the admirable first part, sent to the printer, though it is doubtful if any one will ever be able to read it. But it will never be known what reams of closely written matter were excluded [Ladd-Franklin 1916, 721].

On the contrary, anyone with the fortitude to do so can follow Peirce through draft after draft of the multiple versions of his papers as he worked on them over the years. Indeed, our picture of Peirce's mathematics and logic is now much clearer, thanks to the efforts of Carolyn Eisele, above all, who has labored so long to bring these to the attention of Peirce scholars and historians of science alike.

Peirce and History of Science (I):
His Place in the History of Mathematics

Considering Peirce's place in the history of American science, Professor Putnam's contribution in Chapter 1 above provides a very persuasive rational reconstruction of Peirce's analysis of the continuum, drawing upon arguments devised by Abraham Robinson using model theory to characterize a "non-standard" Peircean version of the real line with infinitesimals. But Putnam's rational reconstruction did not consider how Peirce's thinking reached the point where he was confident—despite the judgment of virtually all other nineteenth-century mathematicians against infinitesimals—that it was not only reasonable but *necessary* to assert a radically different view of continuity which logically depended upon infinitesimals. Here, recourse to the history of science—specifically to the history of mathematics—can be of some help.

Viewed historically, Peirce's advocacy of infinitesimals was not predicated on neo-Aristotelian thought, but was in fact based upon the logical consequences of an important result in set theory: the power-set theorem. In appreciating how Peirce came to his understanding of infinitesimals via logic, it is also possible to shed some light on many of the conclusions advanced by Putnam above, who has rightly indicated (by focusing on Peirce's theory of infinitesimals) that continuity was a key to everything Peirce endeavored to do.

Georg Cantor, Richard Dedekind, and C. S. Peirce

Georg Cantor (1845–1918), creator of transfinite set theory, published a theorem in 1872 which brought him to the attention of the mathematical world. It also marked the beginning of his work in set theory.

Cantor's theorem established the uniqueness of representations of functions by trigonometric series over domains from which certain infinite sets of points might be excepted (Cantor 1872/1932). In order to provide a satisfactory foundation for his proof, however, Cantor discovered that he needed to provide a clear—and correspondingly rigorous—theory of real numbers. He did this in terms of equivalence classes of infinite sequences of rational numbers subject to the Cauchy criterion for convergence. In the course of his argument, he was also led to formulate an Axiom of Continuity, which postulated the equivalence of the arithmetic and geometric continua (discussed at greater length in Putnam's paper above). In the same year, 1872, Richard Dedekind (1831–1916) published his own theory of the real numbers in terms of his famous "cuts," acknowledging the similar work Cantor had already done in defining real numbers in his paper on trigonometric series (Dedekind 1872/1930-32, 3).[19]

Cantor's gratifying results and his very general solution of the representation problem using infinite sets of exceptional points seem to have spurred his interest in the properties of continuous domains in general, and late in 1873 he discovered that the set of all real numbers was nondenumerably infinite (Cantor

1874/1932). Several years later, in 1879, he published what at the time was an even more startling proof showing that any continuous space of n-dimensions could be mapped in a one-to-one fashion onto the real line.[20] Cantor was so unprepared for this discovery that it prompted one of his most oft-quoted remarks: "Je le vois, mais je ne le crois pas."[21]

Over the next few decades Cantor developed the basic concepts and techniques of transfinite set theory, including his definition of the transfinite ordinal and cardinal numbers, and struggled to prove his ill-fated Continuum Hypothesis. By the end of the century, the status of Cantor's work was brought dramatically into question by discovery of the paradoxes of set theory. Though Burali-Forti was the first to publish his paradox of the largest ordinal number, Cantor had actually discovered the paradoxes of both a largest ordinal and a largest cardinal number even earlier, probably as early as 1895. He sketched a proof for Dedekind in 1899, in which he concluded that it was a direct consequence of the paradoxical nature of the unending sequence of all cardinals that the continuum must be a set whose cardinality was one of Cantor's transfinite alephs.[22]

Cesare Burali-Forti, however, drew a very different conclusion from his study of the collection of all transfinite ordinal numbers in 1897. Such a collection, he argued, *must* have an ordinal number ß greater than any ordinal in the collection. But if the set contains all ordinal numbers, then it must contain ß, ß being an ordinal number. This forced Burali-Forti to the contradictory conclusion that ß > ß. From this he did not draw comfort, as Cantor did, in believing that this was the key to solving much deeper problems of set theory. Instead, Burali-Forti concluded that mathematicians would have to abandon any hope of strict comparability between transfinite numbers (Burali-Forti 1897). In 1902 Bertrand Russell went a good step further and constructed a strictly logical paradox, famous for having shocked Frege by showing that there were certain antinomies inherently part of logic. Consequently, mathematics as a form of structured reason was also affected.[23]

In considering the paradoxes of set theory, in particular those of the greatest ordinal and cardinal numbers, Peirce agreed with Bertrand Russell that these were, properly speaking, questions of logic. Here it is important to recall that for Peirce, the basic business of mathematics was the formation of hypotheses (see especially CP 4.232-233, 1902). In terms of set theory and the analysis of the continuum, this meant the determination of what grades of multitude between infinite collections were mathematically possible—that is, logically possible on Peirce's view. As we shall see, from the paradox of the largest cardinal number, Peirce drew a positive principle (just as Cantor also viewed the paradox optimistically). Indeed, Peirce believed that the logical implications of the paradox might help to resolve the question of the *true* nature of continuity.

Peirce's Approach to the Infinite and Continuity

Some of Peirce's earliest work relevant to logic and set theory dates from the brief period he spent at Johns Hopkins University (from 1879 to 1884). It was in 1881 that he published one of his most important discoveries in the *American Journal of Mathematics*, "On the Logic of Number." Later he was always proud to emphasize that in this paper he had characterized the difference between finite and infinite sets well before Dedekind had done so in 1888. Peirce even insisted that Dedekind's famous monograph *Was sind und was sollen die Zahlen* had been influenced by his own work, because Peirce had sent a copy to Dedekind.[24] The most noteworthy aspect of Peirce's approach to numbers and continuity, however, is not its similarity to the research then being done in Europe, but how it was different. It is especially instructive to contrast Peirce's approach with Cantor's and Dedekind's, for Peirce's originality—and insight— are most apparent in his treatment of such subjects as continuity and infinity.

Cantor had been led to formulate his theory of real numbers as a result of his early study of the representation theorem for trignometric series. Similarly, Dedekind's characterization of the continuum and his introduction of the famous "Dedekind cut" to define the real numbers was also inspired by analysis. In trying to reach the basic elements of the differential calculus, particularly theorems involving limits, Dedekind realized that geometric intuition, though a guide, was not rigorously satisfactory. And so he was led to produce a purely arithmetical study of continuity and the irrational numbers.

Peirce, on the contrary, took an entirely different approach. Unlike Cantor and Dedekind, whose interests in foundations, irrational numbers, and continuity proceeded from problems arising from within the subject (Cantor from his investigation of trigonometric series and Dedekind from his teaching), Peirce was inspired by his studies in logic. In this distinction lies the key to understanding why Peirce differed so markedly from Cantor and Dedekind in his approach to the problems of continuity and the infinite.

Peirce's first publication describing the difference between finite and infinite classes appeared in 1881, during the brief period he was lecturing on logic at Johns Hopkins. His paper began with the following (but flawed) definition of continuity: "A continuous system is one in which every quantity greater than another is also greater than some intermediate quantity greater than that other."[25]

This is only partly correct; in a continuum no entity should have an immediate predecessor or successor. This means that in the immediate vicinity of any element, however small the neighborhood, there will still be an infinite number of elements of the continuum. But there is more to the concept of continuity than this, for under Peirce's definition the set of rational numbers would be continuous, since no rational has an immediate predecessor or successor. Even so, the rationals do *not* constitute a continuum, and, consequently, Peirce's definition is inadequate. What is lacking is the notion of *completeness*: that the *limit* of any infinite sequence of elements of a continuum must also be an element of the continuum. On this criterion the rationals fail to constitute a continuum because irrational numbers, considered as limits of infinite sequences of rationals, clearly are not contained in the set of rational numbers.

But Peirce was only beginning his study of continuity at the time. The shortcomings of his definition aside, the most interesting feature of his paper of 1881 is found toward the end, where he specified the difference between finite and infinite sets (multitudes). His basic idea had been prompted by the study of a particular logical syllogism. What Peirce discovered was that a set must be finite if no one-to-one correspondence could be found between the set and any proper subset. Otherwise, it must be infinite. Peirce's favorite example of this was a syllogism he liked to give in several variant forms throughout his mathematical and logical writings:

> Every Texan kills a Texan
> No Texan is killed by more than one Texan
> Hence, every Texan is killed by a Texan [CP 3.228].[26]

The syllogism is true only if the set of Texans is finite. The form of the syllogism, Peirce noted, was due to De Morgan, who called it the syllogism of transposed quantity.[27] Thus, Peirce's interest in infinite classes did not stem from *within* mathematics as it had for Cantor and Dedekind. Instead, his interest in the infinite was inspired by logic, specifically the consequences one might draw from the special conditions of the syllogism of transposed quantity.

In keeping with his metaphysical interests related to the continuity of space and time (which were directly related to his study of quantity, both finite and infinite), Peirce decided that a logical definition of continuity was needed. In 1897, when he published "The Logic of Relatives" in *The Monist*, he explained this at length:

> A perfectly satisfactory logical account of the conception of continuity is required. This involves the definition of a certain kind of infinity; and in order to make that quite clear, it is requisite to begin by developing the logical doctrine of infinite multitude. This doctrine still remains, after the works of Cantor, Dedekind, and others, in an inchoate condition. For example, such a question remains unanswered as the following: Is it, or is it not, logically possible for two collections to be so multitudinous that neither can be put into a one-to-one correspondence with a part or the whole of the other? To resolve this problem demands, not a mere *application* of logic, but a further *development* of the conception of logical possibility [CP 3.525].

But what did Peirce mean by the need to define a certain kind of infinity before the concept of continuity could be accounted for logically? What was "inchoate" about the work of Cantor and Dedekind? Why was the comparability of cardinals, in Peirce's view, impossible to establish without developing further the concept of logical possibility? What, in fact, did Peirce mean by logical possibility?

Answers to all these questions hinge on Peirce's view of the infinite and on a very important discovery he apparently made independently of Georg Cantor, one for which he was afterward (and justifiably so) very proud. Peirce proved (although exactly when he did so for the first time is uncertain) that the power of the set of all subsets of a given set is always greater than the power of the original set itself. In other words (in the more familiar version given by Georg Cantor in the 1890s), for any set of elements N, the set of all its subsets $2^N > N$, a result, as Peirce put it, of "prime importance" (NEM 3:51).[28] But what did Peirce see in all this to help solve the mystery of continuity?

Peirce argued that if a continuum did not contain all of the points that it *possibly could*, then there would be gaps or discontinuities, just as there are "gaps" in the set of rationals, where irrationals assume their place in the continuum (see NEM 3:880-881). Thus, it was a problem of the utmost importance to determine what the *maximum* possible multitude was in order to determine the power of continua. But Peirce had already shown that there could be *no* such greatest possible multitude. What he had demonstrated was that the process of forming power sets was unending. Consequently, it was a process that remained potential, and as such, indefinite. Thus, if any continuum were going to contain the maximum possible number of points, it could not stop at any definite number, because to stop at some definite number, even a transfinite number, would mean that there were more points it might yet contain, but did not. This would result in gaps. Peirce's continuum, therefore, had to be correspondingly potential, indefinite.

Ultimately, this sort of argument led Peirce to reject Cantor's view that the geometric continuum was somehow made up of a multitude of points. His reasons for believing so were straightforward. Since the line must contain all points *possible*, Cantor's determination that $R = 2^{\aleph_0}$ meant that R was determinate. To Peirce's mind this meant that it must be discrete, definite, and therefore could not contain *all* possible points—namely those associated with any collections greater in power than $2^{\aleph_0}$. Assuming there were entities greater in magnitude than $2^{\aleph_0}$, $2^{\aleph_0}$ points could never exhaust the continuum. No completed multitude, so far as Peirce was concerned, could ever account for the nature of continuity.

To illustrate his own idea of continuity, Peirce outlined a procedure which he called "interpolation" on the unit interval. This involved decimal representations using only the digits 0 and 1. At step (I), there was only one interpolation: .1; at step (II) there were two: .01 and .11; at step three there were four: .001, .011, .010 and .111; in general, at step (N) there would be 2^{N-1} interpolations. Schematically:

Step 0____.01_____.1_____
    (I):.1
    (II): .01 .11
    (III): .001 .011 .101 .111
    (IV): .0001 .0011 .0101 .0111 .1001 .1011 .1101 .1111

Here Peirce found, as he put it, a "premonition of continuity" (NEM 3:87-88).

In a letter to Ferdinand C. S. Schiller in 1906, Peirce explained what he meant by a "Leibnizian" infinitesimal of the first order: namely, a quantity smaller than any finite positive quantity (NEM 3:989). It was, he said, the first quantity after the sequence:

$$.1, .01, .001, .0001, \ldots$$

But Peirce did not establish that there was any mathematically consistent meaning to be attached to this. On the other hand, he believed that it was impossible to prove that there were no such quantities.[29] As he said, "such supermultitudinous collections stick together by logical necessity. Its constituent individuals are no longer distinct, or independent. They are not subjects but phases expressive of the properties of the continuum" (NEM 3:95). He went so far as to argue that his infinitesimals were given an imprimatur of sorts by nature, since he took their existence to be necessary for physics. This is clear from letters, among others, that he sent to C. J. Keyser in 1908 and to Josiah Royce in 1902.[30]

Above all, Peirce was persuaded of both the reasonableness and the necessity of infinitesimals as a result of his analysis of continuity based upon his own special approach from logic. Logic, in terms of the syllogism of transposed quantity, also gave him a different avenue to the infinite than the one taken by Cantor and Dedekind, which reflected their preoccupations with applications in mathematical analysis. Moreover, the unending "possibilities" provided (literally, in fact) by his power-set theorem convinced Peirce that if the continuum were to comprise "all the points possible," it must be "glued" together by a truly countless number of infinitesimals—at least as many as the number of "possibilities" embodied in the unending series of power sets.[31]

In the history of science in the nineteenth century, specifically with respect to his work on logic, continuity, and infinitesimals, Peirce was clearly one of the pioneers. He was especially remarkable in being one of the first to apply logic to mathematics to achieve positive mathematical results, rather than use logic simply as a critical means of examining foundational questions. As a champion of infinitesimals, as Putnam makes plain, he advanced a view of continuity that was not standard in his own day. And yet Peirce's "metaphysical speculations" involving infinitesimals were "characterized by enormous originality and profundity in conception combined with precision in technical detail" (see above, p. 2).

More generally, as Caroline Eisele has said of Peirce's place among scientists of the nineteenth century, "there is ample evidence that he earned for himself a place of honor" (Eisele 1959/1979, 132)). Peter Skagestad goes even further and suggests that "in almost all areas of his thought, Peirce was what one calls 'ahead of his times,' a thinker more properly belonging to the mid-twentieth than to the late nineteenth century" (Skagestad 1979).

Peirce and History of Science (II):
The Abductive Scientific Method and Creative Genius

From the time Peirce was first aware of having any interest in science, he seems also to have realized the importance of its history. As early as the 1860s (he was then in his early twenties), Peirce had begun to collect old and rare scientific books, and was especially pleased with a number of editions he had acquired of the medieval theologian and philosopher Duns Scotus. On January 1, 1868, he actually compiled a list of books on medieval logic that were available in the Cambridge area—the majority of which proved to be from his own library (W 2:xxiv).

If Peirce was first drawn to the history of science through the history of logic, his interest was further stimulated by an invitation to deliver nine lectures at Harvard on the subject. These Peirce gave in November and December of 1869. Concentrating on British logicians, he clearly valued the important lessons which the history of science could teach. As he said in his first lecture: "So far as the logic of an age adequately represents the methods of thought of that age, its history is a history of the human mind in its most essential relation,—that is to say with reference to its power of investigating truth" (MS 158, in W 2:310).

But at this point, just at the beginning of his career, Peirce regarded such historical study as valuable primarily because "it disciplines the mind to regard philosophy in a cold and scientific eye and not with a passion as though philosophers were contestants" (W 2:310). Among the figures who assumed a prominent place in Peirce's Harvard lectures on British logicians was a philosopher of science who had made an especially great impression on the young Peirce.

Peirce and William Whewell

One of the most important lectures in the British logic series was delivered by Peirce on Christmas Eve, 1869. His subject was then master of Trinity College, Cambridge, William Whewell, who impressed Peirce in part by his devotion to the history of science (W 2:536). Of course, Peirce took Whewell's views seriously as being those of a "truly scientific man," but he also appreciated the fact that Whewell had been led by years of study to what Peirce regarded as a true understanding of the nature of science:

> A theory of science founded on its history in a truly inductive way and not merely using history to make out preconceived opinions as Mill does (for his opinions are quite medieval) must get the larger facts right but may not duly represent what concerns the individual and is not published. A metaphysician would be apt to think this latter was of chief import but that is a mistake [MS 586 (1869), NEM 2:852].[32]

Although it is clear that Peirce had thoroughly studied Whewell's philosophy of science by at least 1869, there is no evidence (if the recent chronological edition is accurate) to suggest that Peirce had interested himself as yet in the history of science (apart from buying books) in any systematic way. Nevertheless, he fully appreciated what Whewell had accomplished: "I am inclined to think that a historical theory of science like that of Whewell is likely to contain the most representative conditions of the success of scientific thought. And I think that Whewell's theory in fact does so" (W 2:339).[33]

Despite Peirce's admiration for the historical details Whewell had amassed and for the method he employed, Peirce felt that Whewell's approach nevertheless lacked concern for the "individual investigator" (NEM 2:856). This was an aspect of the history of science that especially interested Peirce. In his wide-ranging writings, the problem of individual creative genius was a recurrent subject. Peirce himself never tried to account for genius *per se*, but he had no difficulty in rejecting, often contemptuously, the theories of others.

He was especially critical of Cesare Lombroso, who accounted for János Bolyai's discovery of non-Euclidean geometry as the result of insanity.[34] In reading G. B. Halsted's detailed biographical notes accompanying the English translation of Bolyai's "Absolute Science of Space," Peirce said he found nothing to suggest that Bolyai's "genius" was in any way the product of "insanity," unless, Peirce quipped, "it be the circumstance of his fighting thirteen duels in the same day with as many cavalry officers, playing on the violin between every two successive duels, and getting cashiered for the performance" (NEM 1:465-66).

Halsted, believe it or not, went on in his account to surmise that there must have been some psychological connection between Bolyai's dexterity as a fencer and violinist and his mathematical precision! "Even in this day of hardy psychological classifications [Peirce was writing in 1896 for *The Nation*] such a guess startles us" (NEM 1:466). Indeed it does.

Peirce and the History of Astronomy

In the same year as Peirce delivered his Harvard lectures on British logic, he was also working as an assistant to Joseph Winlock at the Harvard College Observatory. There, once again, he came into contact with the history of science, this time in a very practical and direct way. Assigned to a project involving the preparation of a catalogue of latitude stars, Peirce was led to photometric studies and later to ascertaining as best he could the comparative brightness (or magnitudes) of major stars. He continued to pursue these studies even after his appointment to the Coast Survey in 1871. Eventually this early work begun at Harvard resulted in a book-length publication, Peirce's *Photometric Researches* of 1878.[35]

In undertaking this research Peirce made his own photometric observations with a Zöllner Astrophotometer. He then compared his readings with historic observations made by former and often famous astronomers, and found that this historical side of his photometric work was of considerable interest. He consulted, for example, copies of six different editions of Ptolemy, several of which he examined in the Bibliothèque Nationale when he happened to be in Paris in 1876-1877. He also drew heavily on the work of Al-Sufi, the tenth-century Persian astronomer whose work Peirce regarded "of inestimable value because of the almost modern accuracy of the estimations of magnitudes" (NEM 2:664). Al-Sufi's *Book on the Constellations of the Fixed Stars* was an exacting revision of Ptolemy's star catalogue based upon Al-Sufi's own observations. Subsequently, it became a classic of Islamic astronomy. Peirce also examined Ulug Beg's catalogue of 1437, two of Tycho Brahe's catalogues (one presented in the *Stella Nova*, the other in Kepler's *Rudolphine Tables*), and an edition of Hevelius's *Prodromus astronomiae*.

Peirce and Petrus Peregrinus

Peirce's interest in history of science was not limited to critical comparisons of star catalogues. Several years after he had examined the various editions of Ptolemy in the Bibliothèque Nationale, Peirce found himself again in Paris, where he happened upon another rare work in the history of science. This time it was an almost illegible manuscript, of which Peirce later complained, "I succeeded in making out every word, at the expense of my eyesight."[36] What Peirce meant is self-evident from the pages of MS 7474 Latin 7378 A, reproduced in Volume 1 of Carolyn Eisele's *Historical Perspectives on Peirce's Logic of Science*:

① *Bib. Nat. Paris:* 7474 MS Latin 7378 A fol. 67

This manuscript was written by Petrus Peregrinus as an "Epistola . . . de Magnete," on the subject of the lodestone. Peregrinus was the teacher of Roger Bacon, who praised him in his *Opus Tertium* (1267) as "'the only Latin writer to realize that experience rather than argument is the basis of certainty in science'" (quoted in Grant 1974, 537). What impressed Peirce about Peregrinus was his cautious advance from hypothesis to deduction and inference based upon experiments to new hypotheses about magnets. That they could attract and repel iron was known in antiquity. The North–South orientation of the compass needle was known from an early date in China (and since the twelfth century in the Latin West). But Peregrinus was the first to leave a detailed account of magnetic polarities, including precise methods for determining the poles—a term he seems to have invented with respect to magnets. As Edward Grant (1974, 537) has said of the "Letter on the Magnet," it is "one of the most impressive scientific treatises of the Middle Ages."

Peirce especially valued the Peregrinus manuscript because it reflected considerable experimental research underway in the thirteenth century. Even so, Peirce was rightly critical of one claim Peregrinus made for "a wonderful machine which is kept in perpetual motion." This mistake was based upon a presumed sympathetic motion by which the magnet was thought to move in synchrony with the heavens.[37]

Peirce and the Logic of Science

In 1891 Peirce was forced out of the United States Coast and Geodetic Survey, which he had served for more than thirty years, following his appointment as an aide in 1861. There had been considerable friction between him and his various superiors toward the end of his career, in part due to the untimely way in which his work was usually submitted. But the final break came as a result of the rejection (by two out of three reviewers, one of the negative reviews coming from Simon Newcomb) of Peirce's "Report on Gravity at the Smithsonian, Ann Arbor, Madison and Cornell."

Peirce had submitted his "Report" to the Superintendent of the Coast and Geodetic Survey on November 20, 1889, and he expected his massive survey of pendulum experiments to be a major contribution when published.[38] Instead, its rejection led Peirce to resign from the Survey, and beginning in 1891, he was for the first time in his life entirely on his own. Unfortunately, he was now compelled to eke out a livelihood as best he could through consulting, lectures, and writing. As these proved to be only minimally remunerative, he became more and more reclusive, living in near seclusion with his second wife in Milford, Pennsylvania.

No longer burdened with work of the Survey, Peirce hoped to produce a monumental study of the logic of science. With this in mind, he turned the full measure of his attention to the history of science. In 1892 he was invited to Boston, where he gave a series of Lowell lectures on the subject. He envisioned writing a comprehensive history of science, and discussed the details of this project at length over lunches in New York and in a series of letters with James Cattell (editor of a new science series at G. P. Putnam's and Sons). William James apparently agreed, informally at least, to use the text in his classes at Harvard. Although Peirce signed a contract with Putnam's in March 1898, he never completed a publishable manuscript.

The drafts, however, of much of the historical material for this grand scheme have recently been published by Carolyn Eisele in her two-volume *Historical Perspectives on Peirce's Logic of Science*. These make it clear that, above all, what Peirce sought in the history of science were examples, or "hypotheses," with which to test his basic theory about the logic of science, namely, the relative significance and interaction of abduction, deduction, and induction.

Thanks to his explicit concern for the *logic* of science, any example of scientific reasoning was of interest to Peirce. His earlier studies of Ptolemy, Al-Sufi, Duns Scotus, and Petrus Peregrinus had already given him valuable experience in dealing with historical materials and evaluating their testimony. Now he began to branch out and consider the full range of the history of science from the ancient astronomy of the Egyptians and Babylonians, to the latest work in the physical and life sciences, where the accomplishments of Faraday, Mendeleev, and Pasteur especially suited his intentions.

On the subject of Egyptian science, for example, Peirce denounced the Egyptians' almost exclusive use of unit fractions as "absurd." Likewise, he took their value for π (approximately 3.16 as given in the famous Rhind Papyrus), to be "the worst evaluation of π known to the history of mathematics."[39]

In a similar vein, Peirce held special contempt for anyone who thought the great pyramid at Giza gave any evidence that the Egyptians knew the value of π (Peirce showed that it was just as easy to explain how the Egyptians must have known the Naperian base of natural logarithms, 2.7182816 . . . , or any other number one might wish to pull out of a hat[40]).

Peirce was no more sympathetic to John Herschel's suggestion that the entrance gallery to the great pyramid was cut in the middle of the pyramid's northern face at an angle of about 26°31.4', presumably so that it would be in alignment with the pole star.[41] Instead, believing that the Egyptians were essentially *practical*, Peirce suggested that the 26°31' slope (approximately a rise-to-run ratio of 1:2), was just the slope one might expect, since "a heavy stone sarcophagus had to be carried through the long and narrow passage." In this case a slope of 1:2 was the perfect solution (NEM 1:322). As Peirce summed it up, "more learned foolishness has been written of late years about the great pyramid than upon all other subjects" (NEM 1:152).

As for Greek science, Peirce was fascinated by the treacherous difficulty of accurately evaluating and using historical testimony. Applying the methods of his logic to such interesting questions as whether or not Pythagoras was an actual historical figure who could really have had a golden thigh, he sought to determine the true facts and chronology of the life of Pythagoras despite conflicting documentary evidence.[42]

With respect to the history of medieval logic, Peirce's interests have already been mentioned, including his great admiration for Duns Scotus and his studies of Petrus Peregrinus and Roger Bacon. Equally important to him was the sudden rebirth of science in the Renaissance, and his detailed studies of Kepler and Galileo served as paradigmatic exemplars for Peirce in his lifelong study of the logic of science.

Among nineteenth-century figures, Peirce held special admiration for Thomas Young, not only for his theory of light, but also for his lesser-known work on the decipherment of hieroglyphs. Michael Faraday was another favorite, of whom Peirce once said that he "had the greatest power of drawing ideas straight out of his experiments and making his physical apparatus do his thinking" (Peirce 1901, in NEM 2:494).

Mendeleev, too, impressed Peirce for his wonderful capacity for "catching on" to the ideas of nature. He believed that Mendeleev's mental processes were largely "sub-conscious," and that, consequently, they must "indicate an absorption of the man's whole being in his devotion to the reason in facts" (NEM 2:495).

Any of these, in fact, could serve as a case-study to show how each served Peirce in different ways to illustrate his logic of science—the importance of the well-informed guess, the deduction of consequences to predict the position of Mars or the properties of new chemical elements like Gallium, Scandium, and Germanium, to give but a few prominent examples. Instead of any of these, however, there is one especially notable example that Peirce used with extraordinary insight to illustrate both his views on scientific genius and the true spirit of the scientific mind at work in its most creative moments.

Peirce on the History of Biology: The Case of Louis Pasteur

Peirce did not limit his historical research to mathematicians or even to subjects concerned primarily with the physical sciences. Among his earliest forays into biology, for example, was his study of the classification of fishes with Louis Agassiz at Harvard in the early 1860s, which prompted a special admiration for Linnaeus. It was with Linnaeus in mind that Peirce described what it took to be a successful naturalist:

> A great naturalist, as well as I can make out, is a man whose capacious skull allows of his being on the alert to a hundred different things at once, the same alertness being connected with a power of seeing the relations between different complicated sets of phenomena when they are presented in their entirety [Peirce 1901, in NEM 1:495].

In fact, Peirce expected that he could draw important lessons for his logic of science from the work of Cuvier, Agassiz, Bichat, and Méller, among others known primarily for their contributions to biology. But of these, Peirce drew some of his best lessons, especially for the logic of science, from one of the nineteenth-century's most profound researchers—a man whom Peirce had met personally and who had impressed him immensely: Louis Pasteur. Pasteur's "strength in research," Peirce once said, "cracked every nut, however redoubtable, with such surprising promptitude that one really cannot think that it was ever fully tested. When we wish to remind ourselves what scientific logic really is, we may think of Pasteur." (N 3:62).[43]

Of all Pasteur's well-known successes, the one that impressed Peirce most was his discovery of right-handed and left-handed forms of tartaric acid, the implications of which Peirce believed were "destined to lead to the conquest of the most dreadful diseases!" (NEM 1:533). The steps by which Pasteur was led to this discovery, beginning with Herschel's recognition of the polarization of light in 1822, followed by the detailed observations of many chemists over the next few decades, before Pasteur made his own decisive experiments, was to Peirce's mind a perfect example of a great man standing on the shoulders of giants:[44]

> Upon how many men's backs was Pasteur mounted when he attained to the making of this memorable experiment which marks the opening of a scientific era to the close of which our great-grandchildren may not be able to look forward! The novelty of the discovery may, for aught one can clearly discern, be attributable to Pasteur's good fortune rather than to his merit. Yet it certainly illustrates his mysterious faculty of rightly guessing at Nature's ways (a privilege upon which he never presumed); and what at any rate was a property of the man alone, and is truly surprising, was his prompt recognition of all the importance of the thing, even to its remoter consequences. We are told that the moment he first got the fact solidly in his grasp, he sprang up quite wild, and ran out, embracing the janitor in the corridor, and, though no man ever more economized minutes, betook himself to the garden of the Luxembourg, where he occupied the rest of that day in setting his disordered ideas to rights [NEM 1:533].

Particularly illustrative of Pasteur's style, especially in dealing with professional controversies, was an episode Peirce described in 1902 in one of his reviews for *The Nation*. It seems that during a lecture at the Academy of Medicine in Paris, Pasteur once made the offhand remark that chickens were not subject to anthrax. A Parisian physician, Gabriel Colin, happening to be in the audience and professing to know more about anthrax than Pasteur, objected. Colin claimed that nothing was easier than to give chickens anthrax. If so, Pasteur countered, then Colin should produce one, which he agreed to do. But after months had passed with no result, Pasteur's unfortunate critic had to admit before the Academy of Medicine that he had spoken too soon. Despite repeated attempts he finally admitted that it was *impossible* to inoculate a hen with anthrax.

Pasteur, however, anticipating this response, promptly rejoined that this was going too far, for he had only said that hens "do not *take* anthrax." On the contrary, Pasteur insisted that it was possible to *give* it to them, whereupon he promised a demonstration by experiment. The following week he delivered on this promise to the Academy by producing three chickens: one dead, one dying, and the third recovering from anthrax. As Peirce then explained:

> The secret of the matter was that Pasteur had ascertained by experiment what temperature was the highest at which the bacillus of anthrax could live; and, since this had been found to be two or three degrees below the blood of fowls, they could not under ordinary circumstances contract the fever, and he was confident that Colin, looking at the matter from quite another point of view, would never light upon the proper way of giving chickens anthrax, which was simply to immerse them in a cold bath until the disease was developed [NEM 1:535; see also Vallery-Radot 1902/1933, 267-70].

In all Pasteur's work—from his improvements in the manufacture of wine and beer, his cures for silkworm disease, chicken cholera, swine fever, diphtheria, hydrophobia, and anthrax—it was the constant interchange between hypothesis and experiment that made Pasteur the perfect exemplar for Peirce.

As for hypotheses, Pasteur once said that "we fetch them into our laboratories by the armful" (NEM 1:533). This, of course, was just the sort of thing Peirce was looking for. As he reflected on Pasteur: "And what would he do with his armful of hypotheses, when it was fetched? He would begin by sorting them over, with unwearied industry, as he had done his right-handed and left-handed crystals" (NEM 1:534).

First, Pasteur eliminated any hypotheses in direct conflict with known facts. Then, through "a skillful alternation of excogitation and experimentation," as Peirce put it, the others would be successively eliminated ("bisected" is the term Peirce used, which refers to a special method he had for eliminating false hypotheses), "until all but one were discredited, while that one was made gradually luminous with apparent truth" (NEM 1:534).

In the last analysis, Peirce was impressed with Pasteur's "mysterious faculty of rightly guessing at Nature's ways" (NEM 1:533). Of course, guessing, for Peirce was nothing more than abduction.

Peirce and the History of Mathematics

Not long ago Michael Crowe advanced the proposition that "Revolutions *never* occur in the history of mathematics" (Crowe 1975, 161–66, esp. 165). This was actually the last of ten "laws of mathematics" that Crowe promulgated, and though it is clearly an emphatic statement, reflecting a view of mathematics shared by many, it was not one that Peirce would accept. On the contrary, he was an early proponent of the fact that revolutions do occur in mathematics, despite the doubts of most of his contemporaries.[45]

In reviewing Florian Cajori's *A History of Mathematics* for *The Nation* in 1894 (NEM 1:443), Peirce was especially critical of Cajori's old-fashioned view that the history of mathematics was *continuous*, without major upheavals:

> We meet reiterated here for the thousandth time that tasteless objection to Pope's monumental couplet on Newton, to the effect that the important steps of discovery do not take the world by surprise, but were led up to so gradually as to be made almost unawares. It is the worst of German taste to criticise such a couplet because it does not accord with profound historical researches, so long as it expressed what seemed to ninety-nine out a hundred of Newton's contemporaries to be the truth. Moreover, the theory of intellectual development on which the objection proceeds is in silliest conflict with psychology and with history.

Peirce objected strongly to Cajori's traditional view: "He who attempts to expound the history of science, and *a fortiori* the history of mathematics, without recognizing that great, startling, and revolutionary discoveries from time to time get made, will have but a wrenched, unjointed, and enfeebled account of it to offer to his readers" (NEM 1:443-44).

Convinced that revolutions indeed *do* occur in mathematics, Peirce was also concerned with the more difficult question—and the more important problem from an epistemological point of view—*why* should mathematics "work" in science at all? How is it that the abstract, rarefied world of mathematics finds such extraordinarily fertile applications in accounting for—and predicting—phenomena in the physical world? As a working mathematician, logician, scientist, and historian of science, Peirce fully appreciated this problem. In a note on the "Earliest Work of Experimental Science," he considered the example of Faraday:

> It is true that Faraday was a half-educated man, not very well "up" even in his own specialty: but he none the less was a typical scientific man for that. Starting, then, from experimental physics, we find in the most intimate connection with it the science of mathematics. Faraday, himself, though a pure experimentalist, utterly ignorant of mathematics, was, unconsciously, pushing investigation into one of the highest and most difficult branches of mathematics, as Maxwell clearly showed. Now, mathematics, which thus occupies a position near the very centre of science, is not an inductive science . . . [MS 1332, in NEM 1:395].

This seemed to pose a special problem. What, Peirce wondered, might link the two? If, epistemologically, the status of mathematics is so different from the physical sciences, why should its use be so efficacious? Why does it *work*?

These are fundamental philosophical questions. The issue of the connection between mathematics and physics is relevant here, in speaking of Peirce and history of science, because his answer was itself drawn from history of science. The answer, Peirce said, was evolution. "There can, I think, be no reasonable doubt that man's mind, having been developed under the influence of the laws of nature, for that reason naturally thinks somewhat after nature's pattern."[46]

Thus, there was no difficulty for Peirce in understanding

why mathematics, as worked out by the mind, should correspond to the mind's perceptions of the world. As we work out our mathematical physics through the interaction of abduction, deduction, and induction, the abstract precepts of the mind's mathematics and the physical reality of the objective world have, thanks to evolution, forged a kind of one-to-one correspondence.

ABDUCTION AND GUESSING: PEIRCE'S TIFFANY WATCH

In closing, it is appropriate to consider Peirce's history of science along with a series of interconnected issues related to Peirce's overall logic of science, his method of abduction, and the problem of why it is that we so often "guess right." As for abduction and guessing, Peirce believed that "it is a primary hypothesis underlying all abduction that the human mind is akin to the truth in the sense that in a finite number of guesses it will light upon the correct hypothesis."[47]

For Peirce, this was exactly what the history of science demonstrated:

> The history of science proves that when the phenomena were properly analyzed, upon fundamental points, at least, it has seldom been necessary to try more than two or three hypotheses made by clear genius before the right one was found. . . . For the existence of a natural instinct for truth is, after all, the sheet-anchor of science. From the instinctive, we pass to reasoned, marks of truth in the hypothesis [NEM 2:754–755; compare CP 7.162–255].

Peirce found a certain reassurance in the fact that, at least from his vantage point in the nineteenth century, the laws of nature were not "far-fetched" but appeared reasonable and simple: "This feature of the laws of nature is evidence that whatever power it be that is behind them is behind the constitution of human reason, which has such a surprising facility in finding them out."[48]

Was this Peirce hinting that God was ultimately behind the intelligibility of the universe? Was this a sort of Cartesian parallelism with God creating the human mind in conformity with the operation of the material world? Peirce went on to explain that:

> Nature is conformed to general formulae, which really determine how future events shall turn; and these formulae are of such a character that human reason is closely allied to them. Add to this that Nature was not made a long time ago but is even now in the process of being brought about, and is every day growing more wonderfully admirable for human reason. There is enough here, without entering upon other considerations, to make the present tendency toward a more theological and religious conception of the universe tolerably intelligible [NEM 2:888–89].

Whatever God's role might be, Peirce believed that all knowledge was the product of an "inward power of knowing." In a discussion of Hume's arguments against miracles and the problem of natural law, he surmised: "The mind of man has been formed under the action of the laws of nature, and therefore it is not so very surprising to find that its constitution is such that, when we can get rid of caprices, idiosyncrasies, and other perturbations, its thoughts naturally show a tendency to agree with the laws of nature." [49]

Peirce added that the human mind had a "magnetic turning toward the truth" (NEM 2:890–904, esp. 901), but this was honed by the experience of scientific minds over lifetimes, generations, centuries. It did not mean, he said, that the first guess of any Tom, Dick, or Harry had any greater chance of being true than false. It was, in essence, a variant of Pasteur's favorite dictum, "chance favors only the prepared mind." [50]

This is exactly the point Peirce took the case of his stolen Tiffany watch to illustrate, something he thought was typical of all scientific reasoning (and of abductive inferences in particular): namely, the efficacy of guided, carefully intuited guessing—not lucky guessing but *informed* guessing.

Kepler, for Peirce, was the best example of his pragmatic maxim where mathematics, successfully applied to nature, had triumphed. Peirce often brought up the years Kepler spent—the long and tortuous path he took before realizing that the points of Mars's orbit were best approximated by an ellipse. Despite his early rejection of this solution, Kepler's eventual acceptance of the only possibility after exhausting all others was, for Peirce, a perfect example of the maxim Sherlock Holmes always advocated: "when you have eliminated all which is impossible, then whatever remains, however improbable, must be the truth."

Conclusion

Like Peirce, one of Harvard's earliest historians of science, George Sarton, began his academic studies with chemistry and mathematics, graduating with a D.Sc. in 1911 from the University of Ghent. Also like Peirce, Sarton saw the history of science as a *living* history. As he noted in his diary (1910): ". . . living history, the passionate history of the physical and mathematical sciences is still to be written. Isn't that really what history is, the evolution of human *greatness*, as well as its weakness?"[51]

And again, like Peirce's, Sarton's interest in the history of science was "dominated by a philosophical conception"; but rather than the logic of science Sarton sought something else. As he wrote in a letter of 1927: "I am anxious to prove inductively the *unity* of knowledge and the unity of mankind" (Thackery and Merton 1975, 109).

Unlike Peirce, however, Sarton was supported generously by the Carnegie Institution in Washington, the same institution that failed to support Peirce when he applied for a grant in 1902. Peirce's Carnegie application was rejected, so the official reason goes, because logic was outside the scope of the fund, not being a natural science (Weiss 1934, 403)! And again, unlike Peirce, although his financing was perhaps unorthodox at first, Sarton did find a home at Harvard.

Sarton was primarily a European figure working in America, and indeed the great names of the last century that come to mind among historians of science—Tannery, Heiberg, Zeuthen, Cantor, Loria, Poggendorf, and Pearson, to name but a few—are Europeans. Americans like Smith, Cajori, Halsted, or Henderson were primarily specialists, lacking the broad vision of a Sarton or a Peirce. Among his nineteenth-century contemporaries (or near-contemporaries), Peirce perhaps bears closest resemblance to William Whewell, already discussed, or to Émil du Bois Reymond, who even sought to provide a history of mankind through the natural sciences.[52] But in America, Peirce was virtually alone in seeing the history of science as more than biographies, éloges, or stories of human interest.

At the beginning of his "Plea for Pragmatism," Part I of his "Essays on the Reasoning of Science," Peirce was emphatic: "What a magnificent book yet remains to be written unrolling before us the history of the practice of reasoning! How fascinating, stimulating, nourishing! What an opportunity here lies open to the young Gibbon, who in seizing it shall earn the gratitude of generations!" (MS S 77: 1–2).

Alas, just as Randall Dipert has said of Peirce's work in logic, his history of science too remained largely a rubble heap, never systematically worked out or presented in any unified way (see above, p. 51).

Through the history of science Peirce expected to reach the ultimate source of all human knowledge. It was not systematic science of the sort George Sarton tried to elucidate, but living science. Peirce had lived it as a scientist himself; as a child he had grown up surrounded by the active life of scientists from every part of the world:

> The word *science* was one often in those men's mouths,[53] and I am quite sure they did not mean by it "systematized knowledge", as former ages had defined it, nor anything set down in a book, but, on the contrary, a mode of life; not knowledge, but the devoted, well-considered life-pursuit of knowledge; devotion to Truth [Hammond 1980, see also Guerlac 1978].[54]

Truth with a capital T—this brings us back to Peirce, to the history of science and, appropriately, to Harvard in a number of ways.

No one needs to be reminded that the Harvard motto—at least its best-known version—is "Veritas." This is derived from the works of a Puritan divine, one William Ames, whose posthumously printed *Philosophemata* (1643) bore the aphorism "Amicus Plato, amicus Aristoteles; sed magis amica Veritas." Variations of this motto have been attributed to a diverse range of thinkers, including Martin Luther, Roger Bacon, Lactantius, Aristotle, and Plato. Isaac Newton even placed the motto in one of his notebooks in 1664, but probably with no thought of Harvard in mind (Hammond 1955; Guerlac 1976)!

But easily the most prominent Latin motto in Sanders Theatre (where this paper was originally delivered in September 1989), is one painted in red on the Western wall above the balcony, beginning "Hic in siluestribus . . ."—a reference to bygone days when Harvard was indeed surrounded by woods and trees in rural Cambridge. Mason Hammond calls this the "Queen" of Harvard's Latin inscriptions (it was composed by George Martin Lane in 1846). Just below it is another suggested by James Russell Lowell from the Old Testament (Dan. 12:3):

> Qui autem docti fuerint fulgebunt quasi splendor firmamenti et qui ad iustitiam erudiunt multos quasi stellae in perpetuas aeternitates [Hammond 1970, 322–23].

Roughly translated: "Moreover, they who have been learned shall shine like the splendor of the firmament, and they who educate many to justice shall shine as stars for perpetual eternities." In celebrating the sesquicentennial International Congress (of which this volume provides a partial record), there can be little doubt that Harvard is at last doing full justice to Peirce. Both the Congress and this volume attest to the fact that, indeed, Peirce's star continues to shine like a splendor of the heavens.

NOTES

I am grateful to the Department of Philosophy at Harvard University for permission to publish the Peirce manuscripts.

1. The version presented here is derived from Peirce's own manuscript account, "Guessing," MS 687. This manuscript actually contains two different versions of the story, separately paginated, the earlier in a clearer hand, the other (presumably later) in a less steady hand, but with more detail. The story was first published (as his papers were being readied for publication) in a Harvard University magazine (Peirce 1929). It is also mentioned briefly in CP 7.36–48. Recently, another account of the story was given by Thomas A. Sebeok and Jean Umiker-Sebeok (1979). This article has been reprinted in Sebeok 1981 and in Eco and Sebeok 1983.

2. This remarkable story, involving stolen plans for the Bruce-Partington submarine, top-secret at the turn of the century, first appeared in Conan Doyle 1908, and was reproduced in Baring-Gould 1967, 2:432–52; see esp. 446.

3. MS 687 gives two conflicting accounts of what happened, the first saying that the trip was on the Fall River boat from Boston to New York (p. 9); the second says that he took the night boat from Newport to New York (p. 6).

4. MS 687, 18b (there are two pages numbered 18); Peirce 1929, 275; Sebeok and Umiker-Sebeok 1979, as printed in Eco and Sebeok 1983, 13. Initially, Peirce's reaction to the suggestion of a reward for the watch was one of dismay: "A reward! I dare say you mean something approaching a hundred dollars!" Pinkerton's persuaded him that nothing less than $150.00 would do; see MS 687, 18.

5. Sebeok and Umiker-Sebeok 1979, as quoted in Eco and Sebeok 1983, 16. See also Peirce's letters to C. P. Patterson (June 24 and 25, 1879), quoted in notes 4 and 5, respectively, in Sebeok and Umiker-Sebeok 1979, as found in Eco and Sebeok 1983, 48.

6. James encouraged Peirce to submit an account of this episode for publication in the *Atlantic Monthly*. He did so, but the piece was rejected by Bliss Perry, the *Monthly*'s editor. The story was not printed until it was given to *The Hound and Horn* in 1929. See Sebeok and Umiker-Sebeok 1979, in Eco and Sebeok 1983, 48, note 3.

7. Peirce, rarely consistent in his use of terminology, at various times referred to abduction as an "hypothesis," "hypothetic inference," "retroduction," or "presumption." For details, and a general introduction to the subject, see Fann 1970, 5.

8. In the words of K. T. Fann (1970, 44), "From one point of view, pragmatism is simply the 'logic of abduction.'"

9. As Charles Hartshorne and Paul Weiss discovered in the 1920s when they began to work on the Peirce materials at Harvard for the *Collected Papers*, "[Peirce's] manuscripts represent all states of incompleteness. Frequently there is no date or title, and many leaves are out of place or altogether missing. Some of them were rewritten as many as a dozen times: it is often evident that Peirce himself was not able to select a final form" (CP 1:iv).

10. The first six volumes of the *Collected Papers* were produced between 1931 and 1935 by Hartshorne and Weiss. Burks produced volumes 7 and 8 in 1958. When they began working on the Peirce papers, Hartshorne was an instructor and Weiss a graduate student in philosophy at Harvard.

11. Hartshorne does not remember having done so; when asked how he and Weiss worked, he recalled that "we didn't—if my recollection is cor-

rect—mark the handwritten manuscripts at all. . . . " But Weiss, who handled most of the works on mathematics and logic, may have worked differently. In any case, the pages of MS 25 clearly show editorial markings that were followed by the printer in going from manuscript to printed page. For Hartshorne's recollections, see Lieb 1970, 155.

12. Peirce may have misled the editors on this point, since he does say that the proof he gives is "substantially that of Cantor."

13. This, in fact, tacitly assumes as true the validity of what has come to be known as Cantor's Continuum Hypothesis. Peirce discussed the "Primipostnumeral" in his essay "On Multitude and Number," CP 4.200–212; for the "Secundopostnumeral and Larger Collections," see CP 4.213–218.

14. But he also commented that as for the second abnumeral, mathematics could offer no example of such a multitude. This comment reveals that Peirce was apparently unfamiliar with the paper Cantor had published in 1891, in which he showed by his famous method of diagonalization that the set of all continuous functions on [0,1]—the unit interval—was indeed of a power, or cardinality, greater than the set of all real numbers. For details, see Dauben 1979/1990, 165–68.

Peirce also maintained that mathematics never had occasion to consider multitudes as great as secundopostnumeral multitudes, a comment that is especially puzzling in light of his construction of infinitesimals and his assertion that continua were greater in power than any postnumeral multitude.

15. As Murphey says of Peirce's reading of Cantor: "There is good reason to believe, however, that Peirce read selectively and skipped over a good deal of the content of these papers [Cantor's *Grundlagen einer allgemeinen Mannigfaltigkeitslehre*, 1883, and his "Beiträge zur Begründung der transfiniten Mengenlehre" 1895–1897, among others], for . . . he either did not know about some of Cantor's discoveries which are described in those papers or else he very badly misunderstood what he read" (1961, 241).

For a more detailed discussion of Peirce's postnumerals and comparison of his work with Cantor, see Dauben 1977, 1981, and 1982.

16. Moore admits giving "fewer selections from [Peirce's] technical scientific, mathematical and historical writings." For more details of what has been omitted and why, see Moore, "Preface," W 2:xiv. Considering that Max Fisch, in his introduction to this same volume (xxi–xxxvi), places considerable emphasis on Peirce's long association with the practical, scientific interests of the Coast Survey, as well as his purely scientific investigations and extremely important work in logic, especially the logic of relatives, this would seem very wrong-headed.

17. Eisele has also been an indefatigable champion of the significance

of Peirce's mathematics and logic in her many essays on Peirce collected in a volume edited by Richard M. Martin (1979), and in her own recent edition of HP (1985).

18. See my review of W 2 (Dauben 1986). It is encouraging to note that in their preface to W 3, the editors (in an unsigned introduction) have retreated somewhat from the views expressed in Moore's preface for W 2.

19. Dedekind 1872, 3, reprinted in Fricke et al. 1930-32. Dedekind did note certain differences between his work and Cantor's. For details, see Dauben 1979/1990, 37-45, esp. 44.

20. Although not continuously. For details, see Dauben 1974, 105-34, and Dauben 1979/1990, 54-76.

21. "I see it, but I don't believe it," Georg Cantor in a letter to Richard Dedekind, June 29, 1877; in Noether and Cavaillès 1937, 34.

22. See Cantor's exchange of letters with Dedekind on the subject of the paradoxes of set theory in the summer of 1899. These were first edited (rather poorly) by Zermelo, and appear in Cantor 1932, 445-50. For general discussion of the Cantor-Dedekind correspondence, the original copies of which were rediscovered in 1972, see Kimberling 1972 and Grattan-Guinness 1974, esp. 126-31. Dugac 1976 is also worth consulting on the subject of Dedekind and the character of his approach to the foundations of mathematics.

23. See Frege's discussion of the impact that Russell's letter had upon his *Grundgesetze* (and Frege's attempt to repair the damage), in Appendix II to Frege's *Grundgesetze der Arithmetik, begriffsschriftlich abgeleitet,* 1903/1962, 127-43. Russell's letter to Frege is given in van Heijenoort, ed., 1967b, 124-25. Russell's discussion of his paradox and its logical consequences may be found in Russell 1907, 29-53, esp. 31-32.

Further discussion of the implications of Russell's paradox for mathematics in general may be found in Crossley 1973, 70-71. See also Garciadiego 1985, 337-51.

24. Peirce explained this in a letter to the English mathematician and historian of mathematics, P. E. B. Jourdain, December 5, 1908 (see NEM 3:883). See also Peirce's essay on "Multitude," NEM 3:1117. He also mentioned Dedekind in a letter to the Editor of *Science*, 2 (March 16, 1900): 430-33, which appears as "Infinitesimals" in CP 3.563-570, esp. 564.

25. Peirce 1881b, 85-95, esp. 86; reprinted in CP 3.252-288, esp. 3.256. This same number of the *American Journal of Mathematics* also contained Peirce's edition of his father's famous "Linear Associative Algebra," described by the editors as "the *Principia* of the philosophical study of the laws of algebraical operation"; see B. Peirce, Jr.,. 1881.

26. CP 3.288. In a letter to Georg Cantor, December 23, 1900, Peirce substituted "Hottentots" for "Texans," See NEM 3:772. In yet another ver-

sion of the syllogism, Peirce even drew from Balzac's introduction to the *Physiologie du mariage*, and recast the syllogism in terms of the seduction of French women! See Murphey 1961, 259, and CP 6.114.

27. De Morgan 1864, 331–58. This paper was read on April 23, 1860, and was Part IV in De Morgan's ongoing series of articles "On the Syllogism." Basically, De Morgan considered the subject of relation to be a branch of logic. The "Appendix" to this article was devoted solely to "Syllogisms of Transposed Quantity," by which he meant "the syllogism in which the whole quantity of one concluding term, or its contrary, is applied in a premise to the other concluding term, or to its contrary." As an example, De Morgan gave the following: Some Xs are not Ys; for *every* X there is a Y which is Z: from which it follows, to those who can see it, that some Zs (the *some* of the first premise) are not Xs. The appendix is dated March 15, 1860, in *Cambridge Philosophical Transactions* 10 (1864): 355–58.

De Morgan had also taken up examples of the "Syllogism of Transposed Quantity" in his *Formal Logic* of 1847/1926. See also De Morgan's *Syllabus* of 1860.

28. NEM 3:51. See as well Peirce's letters to Georg Cantor (December 23, 1900), and to F. W. Frankland (May 8, 1906), NEM 3: 777, 785. Peirce also discusses transfinite exponentiation and power sets in MS 25, which may have been the draft for a lecture on "Multitude and Number." See in particular the section on "The Primipostnumeral," in CP 4.200–212.

29. Here see the detailed rational reconstruction of infinitesimals discussed in this volume by Hilary Putnam. For a brief introduction to the historical and philosophical significance of non-standard analysis, see Dauben 1987, 177–200.

30. NEM 3:898 and 857, respectively. Georg Cantor did much the same thing in using transfinite set theory to draw certain distinctions between physical matter and the aether. For brief discussion of Cantor's "World Hypotheses" (which he introduced to suggest a set-theoretic approach to mathematical physics), see Dauben 1979/1990, 291–94.

31. For detailed discussion of the subject sketched here concerning Peirce's infinitesimals, in addition to Putnam's essay in this volume, see also Dauben 1977, 123–35; and Dauben 1982, 311–25.

32. Peirce may also have warmed to Whewell because he was "a man who made enemies." It was said of him that "knowledge was his forte, but omniscience was his faith" (NEM 2:855).

33. W 2:339. Peirce was writing about Whewell's *Novum Organon Renovatum*, a "truly scientific work: which he believed to capture the essence of "real Scientific Induction."

34. Peirce went so far as to suggest that Bolyai had inherited a valuable "imaginative element" from his mother, but he rejected any suggestion that

he was insane; see NEM 1:465-66. Lombroso's views were published in *The Man of Genius* (1891).
On the subject of scientific creativity in general, see articles by Bronowski and Stent in Gingerich 1987, 3-9, 95-104.

35. C. S. Peirce, *Photometric Researches* (Leipzig: W. Engelmann, 1878) (P 118 in *CB*). These covered observations made in the years 1872_1875, and were also issued as volume 9 of the *Annals of the Astronomical Observatory of Harvard College*.

36. Peirce's Lecture IX: "Post-Hellenic to the Fifteenth Century," in the 1892-1893 series of Lowell Lectures he gave on history of science, reproduced in NEM 1:239-57, esp. 255.

37. See Peirce's remarks in his Lowell Lecture, "Post-Hellenic to the Fifteenth Century," in NEM 1:256. For background on the Lowell Institute Lectures, see Eisele, "Peirce and the History of Science," in Eisele 1979, 35-40, as well as Peirce's correspondence with August Lowell on the subject in NEM 1 141-42. Peirce apparently planned to use "lantern slides" to illustrate his lectures, as well as various diagrams. See his letter to Lowell of January 13, 1892, in NEM 1:142.

38. Houser, "Introduction" to W 4:xli. Not long ago, Peirce's actual report, presumed lost, was rediscovered in a package marked "save for history." It was among other forgotten papers when the Survey moved from its former home in Washington, D.C., to new offices in Rockville, Maryland; see Lenzen 1969. For an appreciation of Peirce's pendulum research, consult Lenzen and Multhauf 1965.

39. Except for "that of the sage King Solomon (i.e. $\pi = 3$, which seems to have the sanction of holy writ (I Kings vii, 23)." See MS 1269, a draft of Chapter 1 of Peirce's projected grand work on History of Science, in NEM 1:346.

40. "The reason is that you can always find some relation between any two numbers" ("General Review of the History of Science," MS 1287, constituting a draft of Peirce's introduction to the Lowell Institute Lectures, in NEM 1:149-56; see esp. 152-53.

41. "General Review of the History of Science," MS 1287, constituting a draft of Peirce's introduction to the Lowell Institute Lectures, in *NEM* 1: 149-56, esp. 155. Similar material is covered in greater detail in Peirce's "Egypt and Science" (MS 1269), a draft of Chapter 1 of his projected grand work on History of Science, see NEM 1:310-47.

42. Peirce discussed Pythagoras at length in his manuscript "On the Logic of Drawing History from Ancient Documents, especially from Testimonies," in NEM 2:705-800, esp. 791-800. He also discussed the historical Pythagoras in detail in a long letter to F. H. Giddings at Columbia University, June 11, 1910, in NEM 2:996-1004. See also the Eighth of his

Lowell Lectures for 1903, on abduction, the second part of which was devoted to "Pythagoras," in NEM 2:1011–21.

43. C. S. Peirce, review of René Vallery-Radot's *The Life of Pasteur* in N 3:62–67 (1902). Concerning Pasteur's "strength in research," Peirce said in that review (p. 62), that he "cracked every nut, however redoubtable, with such surprising promptitude that one really cannot think that it was ever fully tested. When we wish to remind ourselves what scientific logic really is, we may think of Pasteur. . . ."

44. Robert K. Merton traces the history of this expression in *On the Shoulders of Giants* (1965). Merton mentions Peirce as having given "a truly acrobatic twist to the figure" (263–64).

45. For more detailed discussion of the question of revolutions in mathematics, see Dauben 1984, 81–103. This was the subject of an "International Symposium on `Structures in Mathematical Theories'" held in San Sebastián, Spain, in September 1990. See Gillies 1992.

46. "Guessing," MS 687, 6–7. For a detailed study of Peirce's thoughts about evolution, see Skagestad 1979, 85–114.

47. "On the Logic of Drawing History from Ancient Documents especially from Testimonies,' MS 690, in NEM 2:754, and, in part, in CP 7.162–255.

48. Peirce, "The Idea of a Law of Nature among the Contemporaries of David Hume and among Advanced Thinkers of the Present Day," MS 872; quoted from NEM 2:880–89, esp. 888.

49. "The Proper Treatment of Hypotheses (A Preliminary Chapter, Toward an Examination of Hume's Argument Against Miracles, in its Logic and in its History)," MS 692; and "Hume's Arguments Against Miracles, and the Idea of Natural Law," MS 873, transcribed in NEM 2:890–904, esp. 901.

50. Pasteur first used the phrase in his inaugural address at Lille in 1854. He also used it in another lecture given at Lyons in 1871, and referred to it yet again in discussing his Pouilly-le-Fort experiments on anthrax vaccination. See Pasteur 1933, 6:348, and 1939, 7:131 and 215.

51. Thackray and Merton 1975, 107–14, esp. 108. Sarton founded the journal *Isis* in 1912 to help promote the history of science internationally. The History of Science Society was established soon thereafter, in 1924, and similarly helped to establish the subject as a professional academic discipline not only at Harvard, but also in the United States in general, and abroad as well. For more on Sarton, see the Sarton Centennial Issue of *Isis* (1984: 7–32).

52. Du Bois-Reymond outlined his ideas on the subject in a lecture at the Verein für Wissenschaftliche Vorlesungen in Cologne in 1877, published as *Culturgeschichte und Naturwissenschaft*, 1878.

53. Peirce was referring to the men of science of Darwin's generation, "most of the leaders of which at home I knew intimately, and some very well in almost every country of Europe." See his article on "The Century's Great Men in Science," in NEM 1 489–96, esp. 490.

54. NEM 1:491. Here "Truth" with a capital T meant, for Peirce, "not `devotion to truth as one sees it,' for that is no devotion to truth at all, but only to party—no, far from that, devotion to the truth that the man is not yet able to see but is striving to obtain." Among the best examples of the scientific mind, Peirce suggested, were Sir Humphrey Davy, willing to investigate seriously "the liquefaction of the blood of St. Januarius," John Tyndall, "with scientific ingeniousness proposing that prayer-test to which no clerical Elijah has yet been found with the faith and good faith to respond," and William Crookes, "devoting years of his magnificent powers to examining the supposed evidences of the direct action of mind upon matter, in the face of the world's scorn." On the other hand, Peirce had only scorn for scientists like Laplace and Biot who "refused to believe that stones fall from heaven (evidence proving that they do so daily), simply because their prepossessions were the other way."

11
Discussion: Peirce and the History of Science

Peter Skagestad

AMONG THE PROPOSED MAJOR WORKS Peirce left unfinished at his death was a treatise on the history of science, fragments of which were later published in the *Collected Papers* under the title "Lessons From the History of Science." Of special interest for present purposes is the fragment titled "Evolution," which is exclusively devoted to the evolution of science. In the 1890s, when Peirce was writing, the Darwinian theory had not yet acquired a monopoly on the subject of evolution, but was still in competition with the Lamarckian theory of the inheritability of acquired traits and the cataclysmic theory originating from Cuvier and later defended by Clarence King. After listing the three rival theories, Peirce proceeded to note that all three modes of evolution are in evidence in the history of science.

Peirce described the Darwinian mode of evolution in science in the following words:

> We are studying over phenomena of which we have been unable to acquire any satisfactory account. Various tentative explanations recur to our minds from time to time, and at each occurrence are modified by omission, insertion or change in point of view, in an almost fortuitous way. Finally, one of these takes on such an aspect that we are led to dismiss it as impossible. Then, all the energy of thought which had previously gone into consideration of that becomes distributed among the other explanations, until finally one of them becomes greatly strengthened in our minds [CP 1.107].

Later, in his unfinished "Minute Logic," Peirce made the same point:

> All our knowledge of the laws of nature is analogous to our knowledge of the future inasmuch as there is no direct way in which the laws can become known to us. We here proceed by

experimentation. That is to say, we guess out the laws bit by bit. We ask, what if we were to vary our procedure a little? We try it. If we are on the wrong track, an emphatic negative soon gets put upon the guess, and so our conceptions get nearer and nearer right. The improvements of our inventions are made in the same manner. The theory of natural selection is that nature proceeds by similar experimentation to adapt a stock of animals or plants precisely to its environment, and to keep it in adaptation to the slowly changing environment [CP 2.86].

It is neither far-fetched nor very original to discern here a proto-Popperian account of the history of science as a progressive process of conjectures and refutations. Theories are generated wildly and speculatively—albeit not quite at random—and are then eliminated methodically through the selective mechanisms of deduction and experimentation. The proto-Popperian elements of Peirce's account are magnified in his frequently used example of retroductive inference: namely, Kepler's calculation of the orbit of the planet Mars, which Professor Dauben has already mentioned.

I shall not labor the Popperian analogy, which has been amply documented by Eugene Freeman, Nicholas Rescher, and Sir Karl Popper himself, among others. Also, Ilkka Niiniluoto has drawn attention to Popper's and Peirce's common indebtedness to William Whewell, a point Dauben also brought out. I want to focus rather on the quite different import of the two other modes of evolution Peirce noted: to wit, the Lamarckian and the cataclysmic modes. Regarding the former, Peirce said: "Lamarckian evolution might, for example, take the form of perpetually modifying our opinion in the effort to make that opinion represent the known facts as more and more observations came to be collected" (CP 1.108). Though Peirce did not think that this type of modification plays a prominent part in the evolution of science and even opined that "the average effect of the ordinary research may be said to be insignificant" (CP 1.108), he nonetheless allowed that the cumulative effect of the gradual modification of opinion could on occasion produce significant advances even in the absence of dramatic discoveries, as in the evolution of chemistry in the decades leading up to Mendeleev's formulation of the periodic law.

It is a moot question whether Peirce was expressing here an awareness of what Thomas Kuhn was later to label "normal science," or whether he is simply giving a cursory, obligatory nod to the inductivist picture of scientific progress, which was sufficiently widespread in the nineteenth century to constitute something near the orthodox view of the history of science. But there can be little doubt that in his description of the third mode of scientific evolution, the cataclysmic mode, Peirce is spelling out *some* of the central features of what Kuhn was to label "revolutionary science." (To the best of my knowledge, this observation was originally and independently arrived at by Thomas L. Short and me a decade ago.) Science, to quote Peirce,

> advances by leaps; and the impulse for each leap is either some new observational resource or some novel way of reasoning about the observations. *Such novel way of reasoning might, perhaps, be considered as a new observational means*, since it draws attention to relations between facts which would previously have been passed by unperceived [CP 1.109; emphasis added].

That new observational resources, including new modes of reasoning, create an incommensurability between old and new theories is made especially clear by Peirce in the fragment titled "Observation" (CP 1.99–102). "The men who pursue a given branch [of science] herd together," Peirce noted here; "they understand one another; they live in the same world, while those who pursue another branch are for them foreigners." In the same vein, "The man who is continually making chemical analyses lives in a different region of nature from other men. The same thing is even more true of men who are constantly using a microscope." Finally: "So too the great landmarks in the history of science are to be placed at the points where new instruments, or other means of observation, are introduced. Astronomy before the telescope and astronomy after the telescope. Prephotographic astronomy and photographic astronomy. Chemistry before the exact analytic balance and after." Given Peirce's almost ubiquitous insistence on the epistemically progressive character of science, one might be tempted either to try to explain away this apparent avowal of incommensurability, or to dismiss these statements as uncharacteristic, off-the-cuff remarks, not to be taken too seriously. Either course would seriously impede our understanding of the place of the history of science within Peirce's thinking as a whole.

Peirce's pragmatic maxim equates the meaning of a term with a set of conditionals in which each antecedent describes a possible experiment and the consequent predicts an observable outcome of the experiment. The meaning of a term, such as "electricity," will therefore vary with both the theoretical and the experimental resources the scientific community has at its disposal. As Peirce noted, the wider the range of relevant experiments we are able to perform, the more we are able to mean by the word "electricity" (CP 5.313, 7.587). So, the meaning of a scientific term is at any time a function of the current state of (relevant) knowledge. This important corollary of pragmatism was already noted by W. B. Gallie in 1952, and later explicitly thematized by Hjalmar Wennerberg. In 1961 Wennerberg rightly attributed to Peirce the view that "we can analyze a proposition better if we increase our knowledge of the laws of nature" (1961, 147), and he proceeded to censure Peirce for thus blurring the distinction between logical analysis and empirical research. That Peirce was not so much blurring the distinction as denying its validity becomes clear when we place the pragmatic maxim in the context of the doctrine of signs Peirce elaborated in his classic anti-Cartesian articles from 1868 (P 26, 27, 41). By a "sign" Peirce meant, broadly speaking, anything capable of standing to somebody for something in some respect (CP 2.228). To stand in this relation *to somebody* is to be subject to interpretation in this person's mind; and this process of interpretation, Peirce insisted, is the creation, in the interpreter's mind, of a new sign, which Peirce labeled the "interpretant" of the original sign.

For instance, if a particular sensation leads me to infer that a given object is red, the sensation will have served as a sign to me of the object with respect to color. To say that it has served as a sign to me is to say that I have interpreted it; that is, it has been replaced, in my mind, by a different sign of its object: to wit, by the perceptual judgment "This object is red." This judgment is in turn a sign, capable of further interpretation by me, or, should I choose to utter it, by other minds. The capacity to be thus transformed into a new sign is an essential attribute of signhood. The present-day British novelist David Lodge is thus absolutely right, in his witty academic novel *Small World*, to attribute to Peirce the idea that "every decoding is another encoding"—although Lodge himself must be credited with the pithiness of the formulation.

The concept of incommensurability, then, is seen to be deeply rooted in Peirce's thinking—deeply enough to make his proto-Popperian progressivism now seem to be the anomalous element. The gulf between the two is bridged—surprising as it may seem—by the concept of vagueness inherent in the doctrine of signs. If Newton had had a perfectly precise, definite concept of "mass," and Einstein had a perfectly precise, different concept of "mass," then there could in no meaningful sense be any progress from Newton to Einstein. But all concepts are signs, and all signs are inherently capable of further interpretation; that is, they are inherently vague. Signs become more precise through the process of interpretation; hence, there can be scientific progress across conceptual change insofar as this change is in the direction of increased precision.

In Peirce's view, this was the direction by which subject–predicate statements, containing binary or otherwise discrete variables, were replaced by laws incorporating continuity, laws having the form of differential equations (CP 1.62). In this respect, Peirce appears to have been at one with his contemporary Heinrich Hertz, who stipulated that the form of a first-order differential equation is a formal condition for something to be able to count as a law of nature. Truth, as Peirce understood it, is the limit toward which scientific inquiry will converge in the long run. We do not know what it would mean for a statement like "light is electro-magnetic vibration" to have a limit toward which to converge. As Quine has emphasized, the concept of a limit is not defined for theories. And, as Peirce concluded two generations before Quine, we do not know what it would mean for the statement "light is electro-magnetic vibration" to be true, because we can never know precisely what we mean by "electro-magnetic vibration" or any other descriptive phrase (CP 7.119). By contrast, we know fairly precisely what it means for one determination of a physical constant to be nearer the truth than another determination. Hence, the progression from qualitative theories toward quantitative ones represents progress toward increased precision. This type of progress, in Peirce's view, is amply in evidence in the evolution of modern science. This judgment, finally, is not a philosopher's answer to the meta-question of whether science progresses, but a scientist's answer to the question of the place of the history of science within science itself.

III

Peirce and Semeiosis

12

Unlimited Semeiosis and Drift: Pragmaticism vs. "Pragmatism"

Umberto Eco

MY PURPOSE HERE is rather modest. I shall not try to say something new about Peirce. Rather, I shall point out the fundamental difference between Peirce's notion of unlimited semeiosis and other theories or practices of textual interpretation—in spite of many superficial analogies.

All along the course of history we are confronted with two ideas of interpretation. On one side, it is assumed that to interpret a text means to find out the meaning intended by its original author or—in any case—its objective nature or essence, an essence which, as such, is independent of our interpretation. On the other, it is assumed that texts can be interpreted in infinite ways.

Such an attitude toward texts mirrors a corresponding attitude toward the external world. To interpret means to react to the text of the world or to the world of a text by producing other texts. Both explaining how the solar system works by uttering Newton's laws and uttering a series of sentences to say that a given text means so and so are forms of interpretation. The problem is not to challenge the old idea that the world is a text that can be interpreted (and vice versa), but rather to decide whether it has a fixed meaning, many possible meanings, or none at all.

The two options I mentioned are both instances of epistemological fanaticism. The first option is instantiated by various kinds of fundamentalism and various forms of metaphysical realism (let us say, the one advocated by Thomas Aquinas or by Lenin in *Materialism and Empiriocriticism*). Knowledge is *adaequatio rei et intellectus*. The most outrageous example of the alternative option is certainly the one that in my previous studies (see Eco 1990) I have called *hermetic semeiosis*.

The Hermetic Drift

Hermetic drift is the name I shall give the interpretative habit that dominated Renaissance Hermetism and is based on the principles of universal analogy and sympathy, according to which every item of the furniture of the world is linked to every other element (or to many) of this sublunar world and to every other element (or to many) of the superior world by means of similitudes or resemblances. It is through similitudes that the otherwise occult parenthood between things is manifested, and every sublunar body bears the traces of that parenthood impressed upon it as a *signature*. The basic principle is not only that the similar can be known through the similar but also that from similarity to similarity everything can be connected with everything else so that everything can be seen as a sign standing for something else and every thing is the sign of another.

Since "any two things resemble one another just as strongly as any two others, if recondite resemblances are admitted" (CP 2.634), if the Renaissance Magus wanted to find an occult parenthood between the various items of the furniture of the world, he had to assume a very flexible notion of resemblance.

To show examples of flexible criteria of resemblance let me quote some instances of the semeiotic technique recommended by the authors of the arts of memory. Those authors were neither cabalists nor sorcerers summoning spirits. They simply wanted to build up systems for remembering a series of ideas, objects, or names through another series of *loci*, that is, of architectural places containing objects, or images of objects taken as the interpretants of the previous ones (see Rossi 1961; Yates 1972). But these mnemotechnic devices were something more than practical tools for remembering notions: the systems of *loci* frequently took the form of a Theater of the World and emulated cosmological models. They aimed at representing an organic *imago mundi*, an image of the world as a divine textual strategy.

Cosma Rosselli's *Thesaurus artificiosae memoriae* (1579) lists for instance (and among others) the following correlations:

- by a sample: a quantity of iron in order to recall iron;
- by similarity, which in turn is subdivided into similarity of substance (the human being as the microcosmic image of the

macrocosm) and similarity of quantity (ten fingers for the ten commandments);
- by metonymy and autonomasia: Atlas for the astronomers or for astronomy, a bear for the angry man, the lion for pride, Cicero for rhetoric;
- by homonymy: the animal dog for the dog star;
- by irony and contrast: the fool for the wise man;
- by vestigial traces: the track for the wolf, the mirror in which Titus admired himself for Titus;
- by a word of different pronunciation: *sanguine* for *sane*;
- by similarity of name: Arista for Aristotle;
- by pagan symbol: the eagle for Jove;
- by peoples: the Parthians for arrows, the Phoenicians for the alphabet;
- by common attribute: the crow for Ethiopia;
- by hieroglyphic: the ant for prudence.

The main feature of the hermetic drift seems to be the uncontrolled ability to shift from meaning to meaning, from similarity to similarity, from one connection to another.

Contrary to contemporary theories of drift, the hermetic semeiosis does not assert the absence of any univocal universal and transcendental meaning. It assumes that everything can send back to everything else—provided we can isolate the right rhetorical connection—because there is a strong transcendent subject, the Neoplatonic One Who (or Which), being the principle of the universal contradiction, the place of the Coincidentia Oppositorum, and standing outside of every possible determination, being thus All and None and the Unspeakable Source of Everything at the same moment, permits everything to connect with everything else by a labyrinthine web of mutual referrals. It seems thus that the hermetic semeiosis identifies in every text, as well as in the Great Text of the World, the Fullness of Meaning, not its absence. Nevertheless, this world perfused with signatures, ruled, as it pretends, by the principle of universal significance, resulted in producing a perennial shift and deferral of any possible meaning. The meaning of a given word or of a given thing being another word or another thing, everything that had been said was in fact nothing else but an ambiguous allusion to something else. Thus, the meaning of a text was always postponed, and the final meaning could not be but an unattainable secret.

HERMETIC DRIFT AND UNLIMITED SEMEIOSIS

The hermetic drift can evoke the Peircean idea of Unlimited Semeiosis. At first glance certain quotations from Peirce seem to support the principle of an infinite interpretative drift:

> The meaning of a representation can be nothing but a representation. In fact it is nothing but the representation itself conceived as stripped of irrelevant clothing. But this clothing never can be completely stripped off: it is only changed for something more diaphanous. So there is an infinite regression here [CP 1.339].

Can we really speak of unlimited semeiosis apropos of the hermetic ability to shift from term to term, or from thing to thing? Can we speak of unlimited semeiosis when we recognize the same technique implemented by contemporary readers who wander through texts in order to find in them secret puns, unheard-of etymologies, unconscious links, dances of "Slipping Beauties," ambiguous images that the clever reader can guess through the transparencies of the verbal texture even when no public agreement could support such an adventurous misreading?

There was a fundamental principle in Peirce's semeiotic: "A sign is something by knowing which we know something more" (CP 8.332). On the contrary, the norm of hermetic semeiosis seems to be: "a sign is something by knowing which we know something *else*." To know more (in Peirce's sense) means that, from interpretant to interpretant, the sign is more and more determined both in its breadth and in its depth. In the course of unlimited semeiosis the interpretation approximates even though asymptotically the final logical interpretant, and at a certain stage of the process of interpretation we know more about the content of the representamen which started the interpretative chain.

But we can effectively know more of a sign because we interpret it "in some respect or capacity" (CP 2.228). Indeed, a sign contains or suggests the whole of its remote illative consequences: but to know them all is a mere semieosic possibility that can be actualized only within a given context or under a certain profile. Semeiosis is potentially unlimited, but our cognitive purpose organizes, frames, and reduces such an undetermined and infinite series of possibilities. In the course of a semeiosic process we want to know only what is relevant according to a given *universe of discourse*: "There is no greater nor more frequent mistake in practical logic than to suppose that things which resemble one another strongly in some respects are any the more likely for that to be alike in others" (CP 2.634).

The hermetic drift could, on the contrary, be defined as an instance of connotative neoplasm. I would not like to discuss at this moment whether connotation is a systematic phenomenon of contextual effect (compare Bonfantini 1986). In both cases, however, the phenomenon of connotation can still be represented by the diagram suggested by Hjelmslev (1943) and made popular by Barthes (1964):

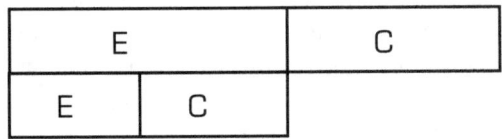

There is a phenomenon of connotation when a sign-function (Expression plus Content) becomes in its turn the expression of a further content. But, in order to have connotation, that is, a second meaning of a sign, the whole underlying first sign is requested, expression plus content. *Pig* connotes "filthy person" because the first literal meaning of this word contains negative semantic markers such as "stinky" and "dirty." The first sense of the word has to be kept in mind (or at least socially recorded by a dictionary) in order to make the second sense acceptable. If the meaning of *pig* were "gentle horse-like white animal with a horn in its front," the word could not connote "filthy person."

Moreover, even when a connotation becomes culturally recorded (like *pig* for "filthy person"), the connotative use must always be legitimated by the context. In a Walt Disney context the three little pigs are neither filthy nor unpleasant. Instead, in cases of neoplasic growth no contextual stricture holds any longer. The following diagram aims at suggesting an idea of neoplasic connotative growth

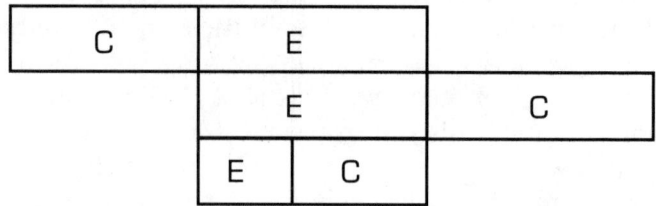

where at a certain point a mere phonetic association (Expression to Expression) opens a new pseudo-connotative chain where the Content of the new sign is no longer depending on the Content of the first one.

Thus, one faces a drift-phenomenon that is analogous to what happens in a chain of family resemblances (compare Bambrough 1961). Consider a series of things A, B, C, D, E, analyzable in terms of component properties a, b, c, d, e, f, g, h, so that every thing can possess some of the properties of the other, but not all of them. It is clear that, even with a short series, we can find a parenthood between two things that have nothing in common, provided they belong to a universal chain of uninterrupted relationships of similarity:

At the end no common property will unite A with E, but one: They belong to the same network of family resemblances. But in such a chain, at the moment we know E, any notion about A has vanished. Connotations proliferate like a cancer, and at every step the previous sign is forgotten, obliterated, because the pleasure of the drift is given by the process of shifting from sign to sign and there is no purpose outside the enjoyment of travel through the labyrinth of signs or of things.

If, on the contrary, we had to represent the ideal process of unlimited semeiosis, we should probably outline something like

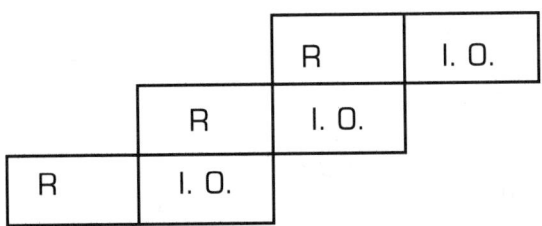

where every Immediate Object of a Representamen is interpreted by another sign (Representamen with its corresponding Immediate Object), and so on potentially ad infinitum. But there is a sort of growth of the global meaning of the first representation, a sum of determinations, since every new interpretant explains on a different ground the object of the previous one and at the end one knows more about the origin of the chain as well as about the chain itself.

A sign is indeed something by knowing which we know something more, but "that I could do something more does not mean that I have not finished this" (Boler 1964, 394).

Unlimited Semeiosis and Deconstruction

If unlimited semeiosis has nothing to do with hermetic drift, it has nonetheless been frequently quoted in order to characterize another form of drift: namely, that extolled by deconstruction.

According to Derrida, a written text is a machine that produces an indefinite deferral. Being by nature of a "testamentary essence," a text enjoys, or suffers from, the absence of the subject of writing and of the designated thing or the referent (1976, 69).

To affirm that a sign suffers from the absence of its author and of its referent does not necessarily mean that this sign has no literal meaning. But Derrida wants to initiate a practice (which is philosophical more than critical) for challenging those texts that look as though they are dominated by the idea of a definite, final, and authorized meaning. He wants to challenge, more than the sense of a text, that metaphysics of presence born from an interpretation based on the idea of a final meaning. He wants to show the power of language and its ability to say more than it literally pretends to say.

Once the text has been deprived of a subjective intention behind it, its readers no longer have the duty, or the possibility, to remain faithful to such an absent intention. It is thus possible to conclude that language is caught in a play of multiple signifying games, that a text cannot incorporate any absolute univocal meaning, that there is no transcendental signified, that the signifier is never co-present with a signified that is continually deferred and delayed; and that every signifier is related to another signifier so that there is nothing outside the significant chain which goes on ad infinitum.

I have purposely used the expression 'ad infinitum' because it reminds us of a similar expression Peirce used (CP 2.303) to define the process of unlimited semeiosis. Can we say that the infinite drift of deconstruction is a form of unlimited semeiosis in Peirce's sense? Such a suspicion can be encouraged by the fact that Rorty (1982), dealing with deconstruction and other forms of so-called 'textualism,' has labeled them as instances of 'pragmatism.'

> The intuitive realist thinks that there is such a thing as Philosophical Truth because he thinks that, deep down beneath all the texts, there is something which is not just one more text but that to which various texts are trying to be "adequate." The pragmatist does not think that there is anything like that. He does not even think that there is anything isolable as "the purposes which we construct vocabularies and cultures to fulfill" against which to test vocabularies and cultures. But he does think that in the process of playing vocabularies and cultures off against each other, we produce new and better ways of talking and acting—no better by reference to a previous known standard, but just better in the sense that they come to *seem* clearly better than their predecessors [1982, xxxvii].

The pragmatism of which Rorty speaks is not the pragmaticism of Peirce. Rorty knows that Peirce only invented the word pragmatism but remained "the most Kantian of thinkers" (1982, 161). But even though Rorty prudently puts Peirce at the margins of such kinds of pragmatism, he puts deconstruction and Derrida within its boundaries. And it is precisely Derrida who summons Peirce.

DERRIDA ON PEIRCE

In the second chapter of his *Of Grammatology* Derrida (1976, 48ff.) looks for authorities able to legitimize his attempt to outline a semeiosis of infinite play, of difference of the infinite whirl of interpretation. Among the authors he quotes after Saussure and Jakobson, there is also Peirce. After having cited Peirce's statements that "symbols grow" and that "omne symbolum de symbolo" (CP 2.302), Derrida writes:

> Peirce goes very far in the direction that I have called the de-construction of the transcendental signified, which, at one time or another, would place a reassuring end to the reference from sign to sign. I have identified logocentrism and the metaphysics of presence as the exigent, powerful, systematic, and irrepressible desire for such a signified. Now Peirce considers the indefiniteness of reference as the criterion that allows us to recognize that we are indeed dealing with a system of signs. *What broaches the movement of signification is what makes its interruption impossible. The thing itself is a sign.* An unacceptable proposition for Husserl, whose phenomenology remains therefore—in its "principle of principles"—the most radical and most critical restoration of the metaphysics of presence. The difference between Husserl's and Peirce's phenomenologies is fundamental since it concerns the concept of the sign and of the manifestation of presence, the relationship between the re-presentation and the originary presentation of the thing itself (truth). On this point Peirce is undoubtedly closer to the inventor of the word *phenomenology*: Lambert proposed in fact to "reduce *the theory of things* to the *theory of signs.*" According to the "phaneoroscopy" or "phenomenology" of Peirce, *manifestation* itself does not reveal a presence, it makes a sign. One may read in the *Principle of Phenomenology* that "the idea of

manifestation is the idea of a sign." There is thus no phenomenality reducing the sign or the representer so that the thing signified may be allowed to glow finally in the luminosity of its presence. The so-called "thing itself" is always already a *representamen* shielded from the simplicity of intuitive evidence. The *representamen* functions only by giving rise to an *interpretant* that itself becomes a sign and so on to infinity. The self-identity of the signified conceals itself unceasingly and is always on the move. The property of the *representamen* is to be itself and another, to be produced as a structure of reference, to be separated from itself. The property of the *representamen* is not to be *proper* [*propre*], that is to say absolutely *proximate* to itself (*prope*, *proprius*). The *represented* is always already a *representamen*. . . .

From the moment that there is meaning there are nothing but signs. We *think only in signs* [1976, 49-50].

Thus, it seems that the whole Peircean theory of unlimited semeiosis supports the position of Derrida by which

if reading must not be content with doubling the text, it cannot legitimately transgress the text toward something other than it, toward a referent (a reality that is metaphysical, historical, psychobiographical, etc.) or toward a signified outside the text whose content could take place, could have taken place outside of language. . . . *There is nothing outside of the text* [there is no outside-text; *il n'y a pas de hors-texte*] [1976, 158].

Is this interpretation of Peirce philologically, and philosophically, correct? I understand how ironical my question can sound. If Derrida assumed that his interpretation is the good one, he should also assume that Peirce's text had a *privileged meaning* to be isolated, recognized as such, and spelled out unambiguously. Derrida would be the first to say that his reading makes Peirce's text move forward, beyond the alleged intentions of his author. But if we are not entitled, from the Derridian point of view, to ask if Derrida read Peirce well, we are fully entitled to ask, from the point of view of Peirce, if he would have been satisfied with Derrida's interpretation.

Certainly Peirce supports the idea of unlimited semeiosis: a sign is

Anything which determines something else (its interpretant) to refer to an object to which it itself refers (its object) in the same way, the interpretant becoming in turn a sign, and so on *ad infinitum*. . . . If the series of successive interpretants comes to an end, the sign is thereby rendered imperfect, at least [CP 2.303].

Peirce could not do differently, since he was assuming (as he did in "Questions Concerning Certain Faculties Claimed for Man" [CP 5.213–263]) that we have no power of introspection and all knowledge of the internal world is derived by hypothetical reasoning; that we have no power of intuition and every cognition is determined by previous cognitions; that we have no power of thinking without signs; that we have no conception of the absolutely incognizable. But in spite of this, deconstructive drift and unlimited semeiosis cannot be equivalent concepts.

I do not agree with Searle when he says (1979, 203) that "Derrida has a distressing penchant for saying things that are obviously false." On the contrary, Derrida has a fascinating penchant for saying things that are non-obviously true, or true in a non-obvious way. When he says that the concept of communication cannot be reduced to the idea of transport of a unified meaning, that the notion of literal meaning is problematic, that the current concept of context risks being inadequated, when he stresses, in a text, the absence of the sender, of the addressee, and of the referent and explores all the possibilities of a non-univocal interpretability of it; when he reminds us that every sign can be *cited* and, in so doing, it can break with every given context, engendering an infinity of new contexts in a manner that is absolutely illimitable (1976, 185)—in these and in many other cases he says things that no semiotician can disregard. But frequently Derrida—in order to stress non-obvious truths—takes too many obvious truths for granted.

Derrida is the first to assert that there are criteria for verifying the reasonableness of a textual interpretation. In *Of Grammatology* he reminds his readers that "[without] all the instruments of traditional criticism . . . critical production would risk developing in any direction at all and authorize itself to say almost anything." But he adds that "this indispensable guardrail has always only *protected*, it has never *opened*, a reading" (1976, 158).

Let us for a while protect the reading of Peirce, instead of opening it too much.

PEIRCE ALONE

For Peirce infinite interpretation is possible because reality appears to us under the form of a continuum where there are not absolute individuals, and this is the principle of Synechism: "A true continuum is something whose possibilities of determination no multitude of individuals can exhaust" (CP 6.170). Reality is a continuum that swims in indeterminacy, and just because of this the principle of continuity is "fallibilism objectified" (CP 1.171). If the possibility of error is always present, therefore, semeiosis is potentially unlimited. This indeterminacy of our knowledge involves vagueness: "A subject is determinate in respect to any character which inheres in it or is (universally and affirmatively) predicated of it. . . . In all other respects it is *indeterminate*" (CP 5.447). In this sense Peirce is affirming a principle of contextuality: something can be truly asserted within a given universe of discourse and under a given description, but this assertion does not exhaust all the other, and potentially infinite, determinations of that object. Every judgment is conjectural, and in this universe "perfused with signs" it is understandable (though strange) that "a sign should leave its interpreter to supply a part of its meaning" (CP 5.449, note).[1]

But there are other ideas in Peirce that seem to undermine Derrida's reading. If the theory of unlimited semeiosis can appear, in Rorty's terms, as an instance of textualism, that is to say, of idealism, we cannot disregard the realistic overtones of Peirce's idealism.[2]

In spite of fallibilism, synechism, vagueness, for Peirce the idea of meaning is such as to involve some reference to a purpose (CP 5.166). The idea of a purpose, pretty natural for a pragmaticist, is pretty embarrassing for a 'pragmatist' (in Rorty's sense). Maybe a purpose has nothing to do with a transcendental subject, but it has to do with the idea of interpreting according to a given extra-semeiosic end. When Peirce provides his famous definition of lithium as a packet of instructions aimed at permitting not only the identification but also the production of a specimen of lithium, he remarked: "The peculiarity of this definition is that it tells you what the word *lithium* denotes by prescribing what you are to *do* in order to gain a perceptive acquaintance with the object of the word" (CP 2.330).

Every semeiosic act is determined by a Dynamical Object—as such still external to the circle of semeiosis—which "is the Reality which by some means contrives to determine the Sign to its Representamen" (CP 4.536). As far as my argument is concerned, we can also speak of Dynamical Objects apropos of texts, since the Dynamical Object can be not only a piece of the furniture of the physical world but also a thought, an emotion, a motion, a feeling, a belief. Prima facie, it seems reasonable to say that, in interpreting ordinary utterances—such as the command "*Ground arms!*"—the Object to look for could be the "universe of the things desired by the Commanding Captain at that moment" (CP 5.178), that is, the intention of the utterer. But I agree with Derrida that any sign is "readable even if the moment of its production is irrevocably lost and even if I do not know what its alleged author-scriptor consciously intended to say at the moment he wrote it, i.e. abandoned it to its essential drift" (1972, 182). Once a complex representamen such as a text has been written, it acquires a sort of semeiosic independence, and the intention of its utterer can become irrelevant in the face of a textual object that we are supposed to interpret according to culturally established semeiotic laws.

Peirce encouraged a stronger assumption, however; since the Textual Object is there under the eyes of its interpreter, the text itself becomes the Dynamical Object of which any further interpretation furnishes the corresponding Immediate Object. When interpreting a text, we are speaking of something that comes before our interpretation, and the addressees of our interpretation are supposed to agree, in some way, on the relationship between our interpretation and the object that has determined it.

It is true that nothing "objective" could be said of a text as Dynamical Object, because it would be known only through an

Immediate Object: when the interpretation is produced, the Dynamical Object is no more *there* (and before the interpretation was produced, there was only an array of Representamina). But the presence of the Representamen, as well as the presence (in the Mind or elsewhere) of the Immediate Object, means that in some way the Dynamical Object, which is not there, *was* somewhere. Being not present, or not-being-there, the Object of an act of interpretation *has been*.

Moreover, that Dynamical Object that *was*, and which is absent in the ghost of the Immediate One, to be translated into the potentially infinite chain of its interpretants, *will be* or *ought to be*. The quasi-Heideggerian sound of this statement should not mislead us: I am simply repeating with Peirce that "an endless series of representations, each representing the one behind it [and until this point Derrida could not but agree with this formula], may be conceived to have an absolute object as its limit" (CP 1.339). Here it appears as something that cannot find a place within the deconstructive framework: outside the immediate interpretant, the emotional, the energetic, and the logical one—all internal to the course of semeiosis—there is the final logical interpretant, that is, the Habit.

The rise of the habit, as a disposition to behave, stops (at least transitorily) the unlimited process of interpretation: the habit, "though it may be a sign in some other ways, is not a sign in that way in which that sign of which it is the logical interpretant is the sign" (CP 5.491). If for the pragmatic maxim the meaning of any proposition is nothing more than the conceivable practical effects which the assertion would imply if the proposition were true, then the process of interpretation must step—at least for some time—out of the semeiosic chain in process. It is true that even the practical effect must then be spelled out by and through signs, and that the very agreement among the members of the community cannot but take the form of a new chain of signs: nevertheless the agreement concerns something that, even though still concerned with semeiosis, stands at the source of the semeiosic process.

In textual terms, to tell what a text is about means to make a coherent decision in order to deal with it in the course of our further readings of it. Such a decision is a "conditional habit" (CP 5.517, note).

To recognize a habit as a Law requires something that is very close to a transcendental instance, that is, a community as an intersubjective guarantee of a non-intuitive, non-naïvely realistic, but rather conjectural notion of truth. Otherwise, we could not understand why, given an infinite series of representations, the interpretant is "another representation to which the torch of truth is handled along" (CP 1.339).

There is a real perfection of knowledge by which "reality is constituted," and it must belong to a community (CP 5.356). Beyond any individual intention of the interpreter, the idea of a community works as a "transcendental" principle. This principle is not transcendental in the Kantian sense, because it does not come before but *after* the semeiosic process; it is not the structure of human mind that produces the interpretation but the reality that the semeiosis builds up. Anyway, from the moment in which the community is pulled to agree with a given interpretation, there is, if not an objective, at least an *intersubjective* meaning that acquires a privilege over any other possible interpretation spelled out without the agreement of the community. The result of the universal inquiry points toward a common core of ideas (CP 5.407): "The fact that diverse thinkers agree in a common result is not to be taken simply as a brute fact" (Smith 1983, 59).

The thought or opinion that defines reality must, therefore, belong to a community of knowers, and this community must be structured and disciplined in accordance with supra-individual principles.

> The real, then, is what, sooner or later, information and reasoning would finally result in, and which is therefore independent of the vagaries of me and you. . . . Thus, the very origin of the conception of reality shows that this conception essentially involves the notion of a community [CP 5.311].
>
> In storming the stronghold of truth one mounts upon the shoulders of another who has to ordinary apprehension failed, but has in truth succeeded by virtue of the lesson of his failure [CP 7.51].

There is community because there is not intuition in the Cartesian sense. The transcendental meaning is not there and cannot be grasped by an eidetic intuition: Derrida was correct in saying that the phenomenology of Peirce does not—like that of Husserl—reveal a presence. But if the sign does not reveal the thing itself, the process of semeiosis produces in the long run a socially shared notion of what the community is engaged to take as if it were in itself true. The transcendental meaning is not at the origins of the process, but it must be postulated as a possible and transitory end of every process.

CONCLUSIONS

This does not mean that for Peirce every text must undergo a unique and privileged interpretation. Peirce's principle of fallibilism is—textually speaking—also a principle of multi-interpretability. Moreover, "no exact conformity is required by the mental law," which resembles "non conservative" forces of physics "such as viscosity and the like" (CP 6.23).

In spite of this, any community of interpreters of a given text (in order to be the *community* of the interpreters of *that* text) must in some way reach (even though non-definitively, and in a fallible way) an agreement about the kind of (semeiosic) object they are speaking about. Thus, even though using a text as playground for implementing unlimited semeiosis, the community can agree that at certain moments the "play of musement" must stop for a while by producing a consensual (even though transitory) judgment. Indeed, symbols grow, but they never remain empty.

I have insisted on the differences between Peirce's positions and various forms of drift, because in many recent studies I have remarked a general tendency to take unlimited semeiosis in the sense of a free reading in which the will of the interpreters, to use Rorty's metaphor, beats the texts into a shape that will serve their own purposes. My own purpose in beating (respectfully) Peirce was simply to stress that things are not that simple. If it is difficult to decide if a given interpretation is a good one, it is easier to recognize the bad ones. Thus, my purpose was not so much to say what unlimited semeiosis is as to say at least what it is not and cannot be.

NOTES

1. "Since no object in the universe can ever be fully determinate with respect to its having or not having every known property, it follows that any proposition about the universe is vague in the sense that it cannot hope to fully specify a determinate set of properties" (Almeder 1983, 331). "Vagueness hence represents a sort of relationship between absolute, final determination, which in fact is not attained (the condition of an ideal, therefore) and actual determination of meaning (again as sense, meaning, signification) in concrete semioses" (Nadin 1983, 163).

2. "The current attempts at a theory of reality are to a great extent characterized by the insight that the problem of reality is now freed from the controversy between idealism and realism which had long been unfruitful, and must be treated on another level. The first and decisive step in the new direction was taken by Peirce. . . . This misleading phenomenon explains why, in his writings, he sometimes calls his own position 'idealistic' and sometimes 'realistic,' without essentially changing it" (Oehler 1979b, 70).

13

Indexicality

Thomas A. Sebeok

THE POET Joseph Brodsky recently remarked that a study in genealogy "normally is owing to either pride in one's ancestry or uncertainty about it" (1989, 44). Indeed, most contemporary American workers in semiotics proudly trace their lineage, or try to, as growing numbers abroad do, to Peirce, whom Max Fisch once justly characterized as "the most original and versatile intellect that the Americas have so far produced" (1980, 7). In this, he perhaps echoed Joseph Jastrow (1930, 135), Peirce's student and sometime collaborator in the early 1880s, who called his teacher "one of the most exceptional minds that America has produced" and "a mathematician of first rank."

Of course, intimations of Western semiotics—sometimes under the distinctly indexical *nom de guerre* "sem(e)iotic"—which, in a sense, culminated with Peirce, gradually sprouted out of the haze of millennia before him. And the doctrine of signs, to which Peirce imparted so critical a spin, today clearly continues to flourish almost everywhere. His reflection that "human inquiries,—human reasoning and observation,—tend toward the settlement of disputes and ultimate agreement in definite conclusions which are independent of the particular stand-points from which the different inquirers may have set out . . ." (CP 8.41, 1885) holds surely no less for semiotics than it applies in other domains of study and research.

In 1975 The Johns Hopkins University hosted The Charles Peirce Symposium on Semiotics and the Arts. The symposium featured invited lectures by Eco, Jakobson, Geertz, and others, and the papers were delivered in the presence of many distinguished discussants. My particular assignment was to give the opening address, on a topic of my choice. Having had in mind at the time to prepare an interlinked trio of papers—one on "Iconicity," another on "Indexicality," a third on the symbol—in brief, to review the overall question "How do different categories of signs signify their objects?" I opted, because the time seemed ripe for this in Baltimore, to explore the mysteries of "Iconicity" (Sebeok 1976; cf. Bouissac 1986). Here, I should like to present some thoughts concerning the second category, "Indexicality." (The third subject has, at least for the nonce, been pre-empted by Eco's detailed analysis [1984, chap. 4]).

It should go without saying that this Peircean category, like every other, cannot be well understood piecemeal, without taking into account, at much the same time, the veritable cascade of other irreducible triadic relational structures that make up the armature of Peirce's semeiotic—indeed, without coming to terms with his philosophy in its entirety. But this ideal procedure would be mandatory only were I bent on exegesis rather than engaged—taking Peirce's ideas as a kind of beacon—in a quest of my own. I should nonetheless give at least one example of the dilemma of selectivity, and do so by noting how Peirce tied together his notions of deduction and indexicality:

> An Obsistent Argument, or *Deduction*, is an argument representing facts in the Premiss, such that when we come to represent them in a Diagram we find ourselves compelled to represent the fact stated in the Conclusion; so that the Conclusion is drawn to recognize that, quite independently of whether it be recognized or not, the facts stated in the premisses are such as could not be if the fact stated in the conclusion were not there; that is to say, the Conclusion is drawn in acknowledgment that the facts stated in the premisses constitute an Index of the fact which it is thus compelled to acknowledge . . . [CP 2.96, ca. 1902].

It was Rulon Wells who, in an article that even today amply rewards close study for its extraordinary fecundity, argued the following three interesting claims (1967, 104):

(1) that Peirce's notion of the icon is as old as Plato's (namely, that the sign *imitates* the signified);
(2) that Peirce's notion of the symbol is original but fruitless; and
(3) that it is "with his notion of index that Peirce is at once novel and fruitful."

I discussed some implications of the first of these statements in 1975; this is not the place to debate the second.

The third assertion is, I enthusiastically concur with Wells, doubtless true. Peirce's views on the index may in truth have been historically rooted in his interest in the realism of Scotus; "*hic et nunc*," he once observed, "is the phrase perpetually in the mouth of Duns Scotus" (CP 1.458, 1896). "The index," he later amplified, "has the being of present experience" (CP 4.447, ca. 1903). Whatever the attested sources of his ideas on this topic may have been, his innovativeness with respect to the index is, as Wells noted (1967, 104), due to the fact that Peirce saw, as no one before him had, "that indication (pointing, ostension, deixis) is a mode of signification as indispensable as it is irreducible."

Peirce contended that *no* matter of fact can be stated without the use of some sign serving as an index, the reason for this being the inclusion of *designators* as one of the main classes of indexes. He regarded designations as "absolutely indispensable both to communication and to thought. No assertion has any meaning unless there is some designation to show whether the universe of reality or what universe of fiction is referred to" (CP 8.368, note 23, from the undated "Notes on Topical Geometry"). Deictics of various sorts, including tenses, constitute perhaps the most clear-cut examples of designations. Peirce identified universal and existential quantifiers with selective pronouns, which he classified with designations as well (CP 2.289, ca. 1893).

He called his other main class of indexes *reagents*. Because reagents may be used to ascertain facts, no wonder they became the staple of detectival fiction, as was dazzlingly demonstrated in the famous Sherlock and Mycroft Holmes duet in "The Greek Interpreter," and thereafter replayed by Conan Doyle's countless copycats.

Space permits but a single cited exemplification here of how this detectival method of abduction (alias "deduction") (cf. Eco and Sebeok, 1983) works in some detail. The *rei signum* of my choice (Quintilian 8.6.22) involves (as it turns out) a bay mare, or yet another horse, an animal which, for obscure reasons, has been favored in this context by dozens of novelists from the 1747 episode of the king's horse in Voltaire's *Zadig*, via the chronicle of Silver Blaze, John Straker's racehorse and the many ensuing racehorses of Dick Francis, to Baskerville's incident of the abbot's horse, by Eco. My parodic pick comes from the Dorothy L. Sayers novel *Have His Carcase* (1932, 209–10).

In Chapter 16, Harriet Vane hands over to Lord Peter Wimsey a shoe she has just found on the beach. He then proceeds to reconstruct—*ex alio aliud etiam intellegitur* (Quintilian 8.6.22)—a horse from this synecdoche:

> He ran his fingers gently round the hoop of metal, clearing the sand away.
>
> "It's a new shoe—and it hasn't been here very long. Perhaps a week, perhaps a little more. Belongs to a nice little cob, about fourteen hands. Pretty little animal, fairly well-bred, rather given to kicking her shoes off, pecks a little with the off-fore."
>
> "Holmes, this is wonderful! How do you do it?"
>
> "Perfectly simple, my dear Watson. The shoe hasn't been worn thin by the 'ammer, 'ammer on the 'ard 'igh road, therefore it's reasonably new. It's a little rusty from lying in the water, but hardly at all rubbed by sand and stones, and not at all corroded, which suggests that it hasn't been here long. The size of the shoe gives the size of the nag, and the shape suggests a nice little round, well-bred hoof. Though newish, the shoe isn't fire-new, and it is worn down a little on the inner front edge, which shows that the wearer was disposed to peck a little; while the way the nails are placed and clinched indicates that the smith wanted to make the shoe extra secure—which is why I said that a lost shoe was a fairly common accident with this particular gee. Still, we needn't blame him or her too much. With all these stones about, a slight trip or knock might easily wrench a shoe away."
>
> "Him or her. Can't you go on and tell the sex and colour while you're about it?"
>
> "I am afraid even I have my limitations, my dear Watson."
>
> . . .
>
> "Well, that's quite a pretty piece of deduction. . . ."

Peirce pointed out that "A scream for help is not only intended to force upon the mind the knowledge that help is wanted, but also to force the will to accord it" (CP 2.289, 1893). Perhaps Peirce's best-known example of a reagent—although a disconcerting one, for it seems exempt from his general rule that an index would lose its character as a sign if it had no interpretant (Ayer 1968, 153)—involved "a piece of mould with a bullet-hole in it as a sign of a shot; for without a shot there would have been no hole; but there is a hole there, whether anybody has the sense to attribute it to a shot or not" (CP 2.304, ca. 1901).

Here belong motor signs as well, when, as is commonly the case, they serve to indicate the state of mind of the utterer; but if a gesture serves merely to call attention to its utterer, it is merely a designation.

An index, as Peirce spelled this out further, "is a sign which refers to the Object that it denotes by virtue of being really affected by that Object" (CP 2.248, ca. 1903)—where the word "really" resonates to Scotus's doctrine of *realitas et realitas*, postulating a real world in which universals exist and general principles manifest themselves in the sort of cosmos that scientists try to decipher.

Peirce specified that, "in so far as the Index is affected by the Object, it necessarily has some Quality in common with the Object, and it is in respect to these that it refers to the Object" (CP 2.305, ca. 1901). He further noted that

> A sign, or representation, refers to its object not so much because of any similarity or analogy with it, nor because it is associated with general characters which that object happens to possess, as because it is in dynamical (including spatial) connection both with the individual object, on the one hand, and with the senses or memory of the person whom it serves as a sign, on the other hand.

(Let it be recalled that all objects, on the one hand, and the memory, being a reservoir of interpretants, on the other, are also kinds of signs or systems of signs.)

Thus, indexicality hinges upon association by contiguity (a technical expression Peirce understandably disliked [CP 3.419, 1892]), and not, as iconicity does, by likeness; nor does it rest, in the manner of a symbol, on "intellectual operations." Indexes, "whose relation to their objects consists in a correspondence in fact, . . . direct the attention to their objects by blind compulsion" (CP 1.558, 1867).

A grisly instance (only recently laid to rest) of association by contiguity was the right arm of the Mexican General Alvaro Obregón. Lost at the elbow during a battle in 1915, the limb had until the summer of 1989 been on display in a jar of formaldehyde at a large marble monument in Mexico City for the last 54 years, where it acquired talismanic qualities referring to the ruthless former President. When the novelist Gabriel García Márquez suggested (Rohter 1989) that "they should just replace [the decaying appendage] with another arm," he was effectively advocating that the limb be transfigured from an index with a mystical aura into a symbol with historical significance.

Iconicity *vs.* indexicality was often, although never by Peirce, polarized with the same or a comparable label in the most various fields, as if the two categories were antagonistic rather than complementary (Sebeok 1985, 77, 132). So, for instance,

- James G. Frazer contrasted homeopathic with contagious magic, "the magical sympathy which is supposed to exist between a man and any severed portion of his person . . .";
- the Gestalt psychologist Max Wertheimer set apart a "factor of similarity" from a "factor of proximity";
- the neuropsychologist Alexander Luria distinguished similarity disorders from contiguity disorders in aphasic patients; and
- linguists in the Saussurean tradition differentiated the paradigmatic from the syntagmatic axis, opposition from contrast, etc.

Contiguity is actualized in rhetoric, among other devices, by the trope of metonymy: the replacement of an entity by one of its indexes. The possessive relation between an entity and its index is often realized in grammar by the genitive case (Thom 1973, 95–98), as in these two Shakespearean couplets, the first with, and the second without, a preposition: "Eye of newt, and toe of frog / Wool of bat, and tongue of dog" (*Macbeth*), or "O tiger's heart wrapp'd in a woman's hide" (*King Henry VI*). The *pars pro toto* proportion is also at the core of the anthropological and, in particular, psychosexual semiotic category known as "fetish" (Sebeok 1989). In poetics, entire genres have sometimes been professed, as lyric verse, to be imbued with iconicity, and, contrastively, epics with indexicality.

The closely related notion of ostension, launched by Russell in 1948, and later developed by Quine, in the sense of "ostensive definition," should be alluded to here at least in passing. The Czech theater semiotician Ivo Osolsobe extensively analyzed this concept in the somewhat different context of "ostensive communication" (for example, in 1979). This is sometimes also called "presentation" or "showing." Osolsobe wanted to distinguish ostension sharply from indexicality, deixis, natural signs, communication by objects, and the like. But I find his paradoxical assertion that "ostension is the cognitive use of non-signs," and his elaboration of a theory of ostension as a theory of non-signs, muddled and perplexing.

Temporal succession, relations of a cause to its effect or, vice versa, of an effect to its cause, or else some space/time vinculum between an index and its dynamic object, as Berkeley and Hume had already discovered but as Peirce went much further to elaborate, lurks at the heart of indexicality. Thus, epidemiologists, responsible for investigating the outbreak of a disease (that is, an effect) impinging upon a large number of people in a given locality, seek for a source carrier (that is, a causative agent) whom they call, in the root purport of their professional jargon, an "index case," who, and only who, had been exposed, say, to an unknown viral stockpile. It is in this sense that a Canadian airline steward, Gaetan Dugas, a.k.a. the infamous Patient Zero, was supposedly identified as *the* index case for AIDS infection in North America.

A given object can, depending on the circumstance in which it is displayed, momentarily function, to a degree, in the role of an icon, an index, or a symbol. Witness the Stars and Stripes:

- iconicity comes to the fore when the interpreter's attention fastens on the seven red horizontal stripes of the flag alternating with six white ones (together identical with the number of founding colonies), or the number of white stars clustered in a single blue canton (in all, identical to the number of actual States in the Union);
- in a cavalry charge, say, our flag was commonly employed to point imperatively, in an indexical fashion, to a target;
- and the debates pursuant to the recent Supreme Court decision on the issue of flag burning behold our banner as an emotionally surcharged emblem, being a subspecies of symbol.

Peirce once stated uncommonly loosely that a sign "is either an *icon*, an *index*, or a *symbol*" (CP 2.304, ca. 1901). But this plainly cannot be so. Once Peirce realized that the utility of his trichotomy is greatly enhanced when, in order to allow for the recognition of differences in degree, not signs, but rather *aspects* of signs are being classified, he emended his statement thus: "it would be difficult if not impossible, to instance an absolutely pure index, or to find any sign absolutely devoid of the indexical quality" (CP 2.306, ca. 1901) (although he did allow demonstrative and relative pronouns to be "nearly pure indices," on the ground that they denote things but do not describe them [CP 3.361, 1885]). Ransdell rightly emphasized that one and the same sign can—and, I would insist, must—"function at once as an icon and symbol as well as an index" (1986, 1:341); in other words, that all signs necessarily partake of Secondness, although this aspect is prominently upgraded only in certain contexts.

Peirce, who fully recognized that an utterer and/or an interpreter of a sign "need not be persons" at all (MS 318, 205, ca. 1907), would not in the least have been shocked to learn that semeiosis, in the indexical relationship or Secondness—along with its elder and younger siblings, Firstness and Thirdness—appeared in terrestrial evolution about 3.6×10^9 years ago. Too, in human ontogenesis, Secondness is a universal of infant prespeech communicative behavior (Trevarthen 1990). The reason for this is that the prime reciprocal implication between *ego*, a distinct sign maker, and *alter*, a distinguishable sign interpreter—neither of which, I repeat, need be an integrated organism—is innate in the very fabric of the emergent, intersubjective, dialogic mind (Braten 1988).

Signs, inclusive of indexes, occur at their most primitive, on the single-cell level, as a physical or chemical entity, external or internal with respect to the embedding organism as a reference frame, which they may "point" to, read, or microsemiosically parse—in brief, can issue functional instructions for in the manner of an index. Such an index, which may be as simple as a change in magnitude, a mere shape, a geometric change in surface area, or some singularity, can be significant to a cell because it evokes memories, that is, exposes previously masked stored information.

The following striking example, from the life of the ubiquitous prokaryotic bacterium *E. coli*, was provided by Berg (1976), here paraphrased after an interpretation by Eugene Yates (in press). This single-celled creature has multiple flagellae that it can rotate either clockwise or counterclockwise. When its flagellae rotate clockwise, they fly apart, causing this organism to tumble. When they rotate counterclockwise, they are drawn together into a bundle that acts as a propeller to produce smooth, directed swimming. Roaming about in your gut, the bacterium explores a chemical field for nutrients by alternating—its context serving as operator—between tumbling and directed swimming until it finds an optimally appropriate concentration of chemical attractant, such as sugar or an amino acid, for its replication. In doing so, it relies on a memory lasting approximately 4 seconds, allowing it to compare deictically, over short times and distances, where it *was* with where it *is*. On that basis, it "decides," with seeming intentionality, whether to tumble (stay in place) or swim, searching for another indexical match somewhere else.

It may be pertinent to note that, with respect to their rhythmic movements, the *hic et nunc* that we humans perceive has a duration of 3 seconds. Poets and composers appear to have been intuitively aware of this fact (proved by Ernst Pöppel) in providing proper "pauses" in their texts. Recent ethological work in societies the world over on ostensive and other body posture movements of an indexical character has revealed that there are no cultural differences in the duration of these kinds of behaviors, and that the time intervals last an average of 2 seconds for repeated gestures and 2.9 seconds for non-repeated gestures. According to the researchers, the 3-second "time window" appears to be fully used up in these circumstances.

The brilliant neo-Kantian theoretical and experimental biologist Jakob von Uexküll (1864–1944), laboring in Hamburg in a very different scientific tradition and employing a discrepant but readily reconcilable technical jargon, was laying down the foundations of biosemiotics and setting forth the principles of phytosemiosis and zoosemiosis at roughly the same time as Peirce was elaborating general semeiotic in the solitude of Milford. Unfortunately, neither knew of the other.

It fell to a contemporary German semiotician, Martin Krampen, in collaboration with Uexküll's elder son, Thure, to show in detail why and precisely how the Peircean distinctions apply to plants. Krampen wrote in part:

> If one wants to extend this trichotomy to plants on the one hand,

versus animals and humans on the other, the absence of the function cycle [which, in animals, connects receptor organs via a nervous system to effector organs] would suggest that, in plants, indexicality certainly predominates over iconicity. . . . Indexicality, on the vegetative level, corresponds to the sensing and regulating, in a feedback cycle, of meaningful stimulation directly contiguous to the form of the plant [1981, 195-96].

After all, as Peirce once mused, "even plants make their living . . . by uttering signs . . . " (MS 318, 205, ca. 1907).

Indexical behavior is found in abundance in animals too. Here, I must restrict myself to citing just a single avian example (one which I described in detail elsewhere). The bird I speak of was presciently named *Indicator indicator* by its ornithologist taxonomer; its English name is "black-throated honey guide." The honey guide's singular habit of beckoning and pointing various large mammals, including men, toward nests of wild bees was first noted in Southeast Mozambique in 1569. When the bird discovers a hive, it may seek out a human partner, whom it then pilots to the hive by means of an elaborate audio-visual display.

The display proceeds in the roughly following manner. The normally inconspicuous honey guide calls out, emitting a continuous sequence of churring notes. Then it flies, in stages, to the nearest tree, lingering motionless on an easily seen branch until the pursuit recommences. When embarking on a flight—which may last from two to twenty minutes, and extend from 20 to 750 meters—the bird soars with an initial downward dip, its white tail-feathers saliently outspread. Its agitated ostensive comportment continues until the vicinity of the objective, a bees' nest, is reached. Avian escorts and their human followers are also capable of reversing their roles in this indexical *pas de deux*: people can summon a honey guide by mimicking the sonancy of a tree being felled, thereby triggering the behavior sequence described.

Such words as "symptom," "cue," "clue," "track," "trail," and so forth are among the high number of English quasi-synonyms of "index." Peirce's telling example of Secondness—that the footprint Robinson Crusoe found in the sand, "and which has been stamped in the granite of fame, was an Index to him that some creature was on his island" (CP 4.531, ca. 1906)—implies, in such a typical case, a key attribute of indexicality: to wit, that the operation Jakobson dubbed *renvoi*, or referral, directs Robinson Crusoe back to some day, presumably prior to Friday, in the past. The index, as it were, inverts causality. In Friday's case, the vector of the index points to a bygone day in that a signans, the imprint of some foot in the sand, temporally rebounds to a signatum, the highly probable presence of some other creature on the island. Renée Thom (1980) has analyzed some fascinating ramifications of parallels, or the lack of them, between semiotic transfers of this sort and physical causality, and the genesis of symbols—that footprint which, Peirce noted (CP 4.531, ca. 1906), at the same time "as a Symbol, called up the idea of a man."

At least twice in his career, Peirce became entangled in true-life encounters with multitudes of indexical signs: once, in the company of his father, in 1867, in the Case of the Witch of Wall Street, for which the world is not yet prepared; and in 1879, in the singular adventure of the Tiffany lever watch. Alas, time does not now allow me to dwell on these fascinating experiences. But I intend to return elsewhere soon to the earlier episode; and I previously used the latter, a real detective story— a genre which, by the way, Caprettini (in Eco and Sebeok 1983, 136) aptly defined as "a tale which consists of the *production of symptoms*"—as a springboard to provide a modest entry into Peirce's semeiotic (Sebeok and Umiker-Sebeok, 1980).

The historian Carlo Ginzburg (1983) has exposed commonalities among art historians who study features of paintings by means of the so-called "Morelli method," medical diagnosticians and psychoanalysts bent on eliciting symptoms, and detectives in pursuit of clues. Ginzburg invokes a canonical trio of physicians—Dr. Morelli, Dr. Freud, and Dr. Conan Doyle—to make out a very convincing case for their and their colleagues' parallel dependence on indexical signs. He shows that, as to their historical provenance, features, symptoms, clues, and the like, all are based on the same ancient semiotic paradigm: the medical.

That model was, of course, implicit in the Hippocratic writings, as in the marvelous depiction of the *facies Hippocratica*, with its perhaps gruesome catalogue of indicial symptoms—in all, sure signs of our mortality; and in this classic, everlasting, well-nigh exhaustive inventory of iatrical indexes, which I cannot refrain from quoting at length (from *Epidemics* I, after Heidel 1941, 129):

> The following were the circumstances attending the diseases, from which I formed my judgments, learning from the common nature of all and the particular nature of the individual, from the disease, the patient, the regimen prescribed and the prescriber—for these make a diagnosis more favorable or less; from the constitution, both as a whole and with respect to the parts, of the weather of each region; from the customs, mode of life, practices and age of each patient; from talk, manner, silence, thoughts, sleep or absence of sleep, the nature and time of dreams, pluckings, scratchings, tears; from the exacerbations, stools, urine, sputa, vomit, the antecedents of consequents of each member in the succession of diseases, and the abessions to a fatal issue or a crisis, sweat, rigor, chill, cough, sneezes, hiccoughs, breathing, belchings, flatulence, silent or noisy, hemorrhages, and hemorrhoids. From these things we must consider what their consequents also will be.

The same model was later made amply explicit by Galen (ca. A.D. 130–201), who not only systematized semiotics in one of his treatises as one of the six principal branches of medicine, but also showed in the same chapter how the formulation of a clinical diagnosis, with an eventual prognostic extrapolation therefrom, based on subjective symptoms and objective "signs" yoked together into coherent syndromes, mandates strict causal thinking by means of indexical signs.

Indexes included for Peirce "all natural signs and physical symptoms . . . a pointing finger being the type of the class" (CP 3.361, 1885). The "signs which become such by virtue of being really connected with their objects" comprehended for him "the letters attached to parts of a diagram" as much as "a symptom of disease" (CP 8.119, ca. 1902). Writing to Lady Welby, he contrasted "the occurrence of a symptom of a disease, . . . a legisign, a general type of a definite character," with its "occurrence in a particular case [which is] a sinsign" (CP 8.335, 1904). This surely means that a symptom is a type, or an indexical legisign, apart from its individual expression, but that it becomes a token, or indexical sinsign when displayed in an actual, particular patient. (See also Short 1982.)

Ginzburg adroitly traced back the origins of this medical model based upon the decipherment and interpretation of clues, clinical and otherwise, to two coupled sources:

(*a*) early man's hunting practices, as he retrogressed from the effects, an animal's tracks and other leavings—"prints in soft ground, snapped twigs, droppings, snagged hairs or feathers, smells, puddles, threads of saliva"—to their actual cause, a yet unseen quarry; and

(*b*) Mesopotamian divinatory techniques, progressing magically from an actual present cause to a prognosticated future effect—"animals' innards, drops of oil in water, stars, involuntary movements" (1983, 88–89).

Ginzburg's subtle arguments, which make learned use of the overarching medieval and modern comparison between the world—metaphorically, the Book of Nature—and the book, both assumed to lie open ready to be read once one knows how to interpret indexical signs, draws comprehensively upon Old World sources. But he could as easily have cited nineteenth-century American fiction, such as James Fenimore Cooper's Leatherstocking saga or other mythic accounts of Noble Savages, to illustrate their dependence on sequences of indexical cues, available to immediate perception, which enabled the art of pathfinding through the wilderness landscape. Thus alone Uncas, the last of the Mohicans, is able to read a language, namely, the Book of Nature, "that would prove too much for the wisest" of the white men, Hawkeye; so also Uncas's crucial discovery of a footprint, in one of Cooper's novels, makes it possible for Hawkeye to assert confidently, "I can now read the whole of it." (Cf. Sebeok 1990.)

So also Robert Baden-Powell, in his military manual *Reconnaissance and Scouting* (1884), adapted Sherlock Holmes's technique of "deduction," that is, inferring important conclusions from seemingly insignificant clues, when teaching his young troopers how to interpret enemy locations and intentions by studying indexic topographical signs, including footprints.

For the farmer, forester, and professional gardener, it is essential, if only for reasons of economy, to be able to sort out animal tracks (for details, see Bang and Dahlstrom 1972). We know from contemporary field naturalists' accounts that Nature continually provides a record of the previous night's activities printed in the ground for anyone who cares to follow it. Thus, Tinbergen used to spend many an hour "in 'countryside detection', reading these stories written in footprint code, revelling in the patterns of light and shade in the stillness of early morning" (Ennion and Tinbergen 1967).

The body of any vertebrate, including human, is composed of a veritable armamentarium of more or less palpable indexical markers of unique selfhood. Certain mantic practices, like haruspication from patterns of liver flukes, and palmistry, but also some highly consequential pseudo-sciences—graphology today (Furnham 1988), phrenology in the past—hinge pivotally on Secondness, as when, according to Kevles's awesome account (1985, 6), the chief of the London Phrenological Institution told Francis Galton, himself to become no mean biometrician, that men of his head type—his skull measured 22 inches around— "possessed a sanguine temperament, with considerable 'self-will, self-regard, and no small share of obstinacy,'" and that "there is much enduring power in such a mind as this—much that qualifies a man for 'roughing it' in colonising."

Some forms of entertainment, such as stage conjury and circus animal acts, rely crucially on the manipulation of indexical signs. So do certain crafts, such as handwriting authentication (à la Benjamin and Charles Peirce); and, of course, identification, criminal or otherwise, by fingerprinting (Moenssens 1971), mentioned no fewer than seven times by Sherlock Holmes, according to a phenotypic system devised by Galton in the 1890s. In 1894, Mark Twain's fictional character Pudd'nhead Wilson became the first lawyer in the world to use fingerprints in a criminal case, antedating Scotland Yard by eight years. Such indexes are called in the business "professional signs"; the distinguished sociologist Erving Goffman called them "positive marks" or "identity pegs" (1963, 56). Donald Preziosi (1989, 94–95) further connects the methods of Morelli, Voltaire's Zadig, Sherlock

Holmes, and Freud with Hyppolyte Taine's *petits faits*, or his system of cultural and artistic indexes, and with Peirce.

All such devices likewise richly hinge on Secondness, as was already evident in proto-semiotic works like Alphonse Bertillon's *Service de signalements* (1888) and *Instructions signalétiques* (1893). He dubbed his system of measurements of parts of the body "anthropometry." On the genotypic plane, so-called "DNA fingerprinting" can (if properly used) in fact now identify with a discrimination far beyond anything available heretofore, in fact with absolute certainty, every individual (excepting an identical twin), even by a single hair root on a small piece of film displaying his or her unique sequence of indexical DNA molecules.

Natural sciences in general work empirically by decoding indexes, then interpreting them. The crystallographer Alan Mackay (1984) in particular has shown how his field shares with divination "a belief that nature can be made to speak to us in some metalanguage about itself, a feeling that nature is written in a kind of code," and how augurers decode nature's indexical messages by magic, scientists by logic. Crystallographers are strongly and consciously influenced by techniques of decryption, and they have heavily borrowed from the semiotic vocabulary of the cryptographers; for example, they speak of x-ray diffraction photographs as message texts.

The study of the distinctive pheromonal function (cf. Toller and Dodd, 1989), nowadays subsumed under a newly designated scientific rubric, "semiochemistry," of human chemical signatures has in fact been compared with individual fingerprints. Patrick Süskind based his beautifully researched novel *Das Parfum* entirely on the indexical facets of human semiochemistry, with its devastating repercussions. This field encompasses the study of odors,[1] of which Peirce wrote in an amazingly lyrical yet seldom remembered passage that these "are signs in more than one way," which "have a remarkable tendency to *presentmentate* themselves . . . namely, by contiguous association, in which odors are particularly apt to act as signs." He continued in this personal vein:

> A lady's favorite perfume seems to me somehow to agree with that of her spiritual being. If she uses none at all her nature will

lack perfume. If she wears violet she herself will have the very same delicate finesse. Of the only two I have known to use rose, one was an artistic old virgin, a *grande dame*; the other a noisy young matron and very ignorant; but they were strangely alike. As for those who use heliotrope, frangipanni, etc., I know them as well as I desire to know them. Surely there must be some subtle resemblance between the odor and the impression I get of this or that woman's nature [CP 1.313, ca. 1905].

Our immune system utilizes approximately as large a number of cells dispersed throughout our body as the number of cells that compose a human brain. These endosymbiotic—or, as I would prefer, endo*semiotic*—aggregations of spirochetal remnants, functioning, as the Nobel Laureate Niels Jerne has shown (1985), in the open-ended manner of a finely tuned generative grammar, constitute an extremely sensitive, sophisticated repertory of indexical signs, circumscribing, under normal conditions, our unique biological selfhood. Sadly, Secondness can go awry under pathological conditions, when, for instance, one is afflicted with certain types of carcinoma, an autoimmune disease, or ultimately even when administered immuno-suppressors after an organ transplant.

Most of the huge literature on indexicality has been played out either in the verbal arena or in the visual (for one recent discussion of the latter, see Sonesson 1989, 38–65). Peirce was right as usual in arguing for the predominance of indexicality over iconicity, with respect to the mode of production, in photographs: "they belong to the second class of signs, those by physical connection" (CP 2.281, ca. 1895). This has now been documented in Philippe Dubois's outstanding study *L'acte photographique* (1988). And it has long been obvious that metonymy—especially the indexical method of *pars pro toto*—far outweighs the uses of metaphor in films.

In the verbal domain, indexicality has chiefly preoccupied, although with rather differing emphases, philosophers of language and professional linguists. Surveying, by one who is not, the contributions of the philosophers—say, Hilary Putnam's insight that lexemes (beyond such obvious deictics as personal or demonstrative pronouns) tend to have an "unnoticed" indexical component, especially as this led to Putnam's startling convergence with Saul Kripke's doctrine concerning natural-kind words—let alone attempting to assess the writings of classic figures of the stature of Russell, Wittgenstein, Reichenbach, Bar-Hillel, or Strawson, would be an act of supererogation, as well as carrying water, or suchlike rigid designators (alias indexical legisigns), from Twin Earth up to Cambridge.

Suffice it to say that I generally found Bar-Hillel's conspectus (originally published in 1954, later variously developed; see 1970, passim) personally useful. He, of course, knew that it was Peirce who had launched the terms "indexical sign" and "index." He went on to remind his readers that Russell used instead "egocentric particulars" (earlier: "emphatic particulars"), though without resolving whether Russell rediscovered indexicality independently of Peirce or simply relabeled it. He further recalled that "Nelson Goodman coined 'indicator', and Hans Reichenbach `token-reflexive word.'" Gale later (1967) compared and contrasted Peirce's, Russell's, and Reichenbach's approaches. Bar-Hillel himself, in his elegant critical investigation (mainly on the sentence level) stuck—if not with all his claims—with Peirce's terminology, "since it provides an adjective easily combined with 'sign', 'word', 'expression', 'sentence', 'language', 'communication' alike" (1970, 79).

The overall interest of philosophers in indexical expressions is bound up, as I understand it, with their search for an ideal language, consisting of a set of context-free sentences as an instrument to employ for probing the universe *sub specie aeternitatis*.

In Ayer's phrasing (1968, 167), the argument has been about "whether language can be totally freed from dependence upon context." Ayer was unable to decide this for himself, and I believe that the matter is still wide open. But whether or not this indecision has any serious consquences for indexicality in general, or for Peirce's view of this matter in particular, seems to me quite doubtful. For, as Ayer thought as well (1968, 167), "although a reference to context within the language may not be necessary for the purposes of communication, there will still be occasions, in practice, when we shall need to rely upon the clues which are provided by the actual circumstances in which the communications are produced."

Peirce once insisted that an index is quite essential to speech (CP 4.58, 1893). So what do linguists mean by an index? For many of us, this term simply and broadly refers to membership-identifying characteristics of a group, such as regional, social, or occupational markers; for others, more narrowly, to such physiological, psychological, or social features of speech or writing that reveal personal characteristics as the voice quality or handwriting in a producing source. Indexicals of these sorts, sometimes also called expressive features, have been analyzed for many languages and in a wide range of theoretical contributions.

In addition, there is a vast, separate literature not as a rule subsumed by linguists under indexicality, devoted to different types of deixis. By this, linguists refer to a whole range of commonly grammaticalized roles in everyday language behavior, that is, to the way in which interlocutors anchor what they talk about to the spatio-temporal context of their utterance. Person deixis, social deixis, place deixis, time deixis, discourse deixis are the major types distinguished in the literature (Levelt 1989, 44-58). Karl Bühler (1934, 149) called the relevant context of the utterance *Zeigfeld*, or indexical field, and the anchoring point of this *hic et nunc* field its *Origo*, or origin (1934, 107; on Bühler's role in the study of deictics, cf. Jarvella and Klein 1982).

Deictics can vary considerably from language to language, and can often be—as, for example, in Wolof (Wills 1990)—very knotty in structure. One examination of the typological and universal characteristics of personal pronouns in general, over a sample of 71 natural languages, claimed the existence of systems ranging from 4 to 15 persons (Ingram 1978). In this array, the English five-person system is highly atypical, which, if true, would lead to fundamental questions about Peirce's and other philosophers' seemingly natural "I-It-Thou" tripartition.

Only a native speaker of Hungarian can appreciate, if not always articulate, the richly differentiated set of terms of address which speakers must control to produce utterances appropriate to various roles and other contextual variables. For instance, to simplify, but not much: two academics of the same sex and approximate rank and age are unable to converse at ease in Hungarian without knowing each other's exact date of birth, because seniority, even if by one day, strictly determines the terms of address to be used in that dialogue. (John Lyons reviewed matters of this sort in his useful 1977 compendium on semantics.)

Otto Jespersen casually coined the term "shifter" in 1923 to refer to grammatical units that cannot be defined without a reference to the message. In 1957, Jakobson reassigned shifters to the Peircean syncretic category of indexical symbols, which are, in fact, complex syncategorematic terms, where code and message intersect (1971, 132).

In a remarkable study of a single four-word sentence consisting of a modal auxiliary, a person-deictic pronoun, a verb and its complement, Charles Fillmore (1973) has hinted at the incredible intricacy demanded of a linguistic theory if it is to capture adequately the conceptual richness of even the simplest sentences. Such a theory must incorporate principles for deriving at least the complete syntactic, semantic, and pragmatic description of a sentence, a theory of speech acts, a theory of discourse, and a theory of natural logic. Although all these are foci of considerable amount of research activity today, I know of no overarching theory that meets all these demanding conditions.

Barwise and Perry (1983, 32–39) coined the expression "efficiency of language" for locutions—even though these retain the same linguistic meaning—which different speakers use in different space-time locations, with different anchoring in their surroundings, capable of different interpretations. To put it in another way: the productivity of language depends decisively on indexicality, which is therefore "extremely important to the information-carrying capacity of language" (Barwise and Perry 1983, 34). These authors convincingly argued that philosophical engrossment with context freedom, that is, with mathematics and the eternal nature of its sentences, "was a critical blunder, for efficiency lies at the very heart of meaning" (32). However this may be, linguists at present have no inkling of, let alone a comprehensive theory to account in general for, how this commonplace, global human enterprise is carried out.

In my pessimistic conclusion, I return briefly to Jakob von Uexküll's *Umweltlehre* (Thure von Uexküll 1989). Reality, according to this neo-Kantian biologist, reveals itself in *Umwelten*, those parts of the environment—*die Natur*—which each organism selects with its species-specific sense organs, each according to its biological needs. Everything in this phenomenal world, or self-world, is labeled with the subject's perceptual cues and effector cues, which operate via a feedback loop that Uexküll called the functional cycle. Nature (the world, the universe, the cosmos, true reality, etc.) discloses itself through sign processes, or semioses. These, according to him, are of three distinct types:

(a) semioses of information, emanating from the inanimate environment;
(b) semioses of symptomatization, where the source is alive (this is equivalent to George Herbert Mead's "unintelligent gestures"); and
(c) semioses of communication (Mead's "intelligent gestures").

The first and second form indispensable, complementary steps in each biosemiosis. The observer reconstructs the exterior sign processes of the observed from the perceived stream of indexes, but never their interior structures, which necessarily remain private. The transmutations of such sign processes into verbal signs are meta-interpretations which constitute objective connecting structures that remain outside the subjective self-world of the observed living entity; these are "involved in its sign processes only as an inducing agency for its perceptual sign and as a connecting link to its operational sign" (Thure von Uexküll 1989, 151).

How reference—the index-driven circuit between the semiosphere and the world—is managed by sign users and sign interpreters remains, despite the best efforts of Peirce and of his many followers, a profound enigma. What then of anchoring? "The forms of things unknown, the poet's pen / Turns them to shapes, and gives to airy nothings / A local habitation and a name" (*A Midsummer-Night's Dream*).

Theories of mapping and modeling have not progressed beyond disciplined speculation. Notwithstanding that I remain intuitively attracted to John Archibald Wheeler's closed loop of the world viewed as a self-synthesizing system of existences (for example, 1988), his teacher, Niels Bohr, considered, rightly in my opinion, such questions as how concepts are related to reality as ultimately sterile. Bohr once replied to this very question: "We are suspended in language in such a way that we cannot say what is up and what is down. The word 'reality' is also a word, a word which we must learn to use correctly" (French and Kennedy 1985, 302).

NOTE

1. Cf. this surprising passage in a letter by Guillaume Mallarmé (1989) to his friend Henri Cazalis: "'Gracious me! Madame Ramaniet ate asparagus yesterday.' 'How can you tell?' 'From the pot she put outside her window.' . . . that ability to see clues in the most meaningless things—and such things, great gods!"

14

Peirce and Communication

Jürgen Habermas

FROM EDWARD C. MOORE, one of the editors of the *Writings of Charles S. Peirce*, we learn that if the publishable works of Charles Sanders Peirce were collected, the set would run to something like 104 volumes. I am no expert even in what has been published and is easily accessible. But, happily, Peirce was of the opinion that *all* signs are fragments of a larger, still undeciphered text—and, just the same, await their interpretation here and now. In this I detect some slight encouragement.

A second reservation I have is related to the topic that has been posed to me: as the subject index in editions of his work reveals, Peirce did not often speak of communication. That is surprising in the case of an author who was convinced of the semeiotic structure of thought (CP 5.421) and who asserted "that every logical evolution of thought should be dialogic" (CP 4.551). But, even in this last passage, Peirce was not talking about the relation between a speaker who uses an expression and an addressee who understands the expression. Rather, what he said there is that every sign requires two quasi-minds—a "Quasi-utterer and a Quasi-interpreter; and although these two are one (i.e. are one mind) in the sign itself, they must nevertheless be distinct. In the sign they are, so to say, welded." Peirce spoke of quasi-minds here, because he wanted to conceptualize the interpretation of signs abstractly, detached from the model of linguistic communication between a speaker and a hearer, detached even from the basis of the human brain. Today this makes us think of the operations of artificial intelligence, or of the mode of functioning of the genetic code; Peirce had crystals and the work of bees in mind.

Peirce wished to conceptualize the process of communication so abstractly that the intersubjective relationship between speaker and hearer is able to disappear, and the relationship between sign and interpreter can be absorbed without a trace into the so-called interpretant-relation. The "interpretant" is at first understood as the picture or impression that the sign calls forth in the mind of an interpreter. This intention explains the heavy sigh with which Peirce accompanied his definition of the sign in a letter to Lady Welby (from December 23, 1908), since this definition might well suggest a concretistic fallacy:

> I define a sign as anything which is so determined by something else, called its Object, and so determines an effect upon a person, which effect I call its Interpretant, that the latter thereby is mediately determined by the former. My insertion of "upon a person" is a sop to Cerberus, because I despair of making my own broader conception understood [PW 80–81].

In another letter (from March 14, 1909), Peirce cautioned against limiting the analysis to the repertoire of signs and the grammar of human language or, worse, to *one* language. The title "Speculative Grammar" announces the ambitious project of a *universal* semeiotic ranging over the universe of all signs. The concept of the sign ought to be so conceived that it is equally appropriate for natural and conventional signs, for pre-linguistic and linguistic symbols, for sentences and texts, as well as for speech acts and dialogues.

A semeiotic of this sort begins with the elementary sign. Yet, in the properties, functions, interpretive possibilities, and transformation rules of the single sign, this semeiotic should already bring features to the fore which are also constitutive for a fullfledged language and its use. A linguistic approach (for example, Saussure's structuralism) does not suffice for this. In contrast, the perspective of the logician which Peirce took up has the advantage of examining expressions from the point of view of their possible truth *and*, at the same time, from the point of view of their communicability. Thus, from the perspective of its capacity for truth, an assertoric sentence stands in an epistemic relation to something in the world: it represents a state of affairs. At the same time, from the perspective of its employment in a communicative act, it stands in a relation to a possible interpretation by a language user: it is suitable for the transmission of information. What, at the level of grammatical language, is thus differentiated into the epistemic relation to the world and the communicative relation to the interpreter Peirce already attended to on the level of the elementary sign when he distinguished two relations: "standing for . . ." and "standing to. . . ." He integrated the representative function of the sign (standing for . . .) with its interpretability (standing to . . .) in such a way that the sign determines its interpretant according to the relation in which the sign itself stands to the object it represents. Everything that brings something else (its interpretant) to refer to an object in the way that it itself refers to the object counts as a sign (CP 2.303). A sign is only able to represent an object thanks to this three-placed relation.

What is thereby represented at first remains unspecified; in any event, we cannot assume from the start that the "object" (*Objekt*) will be an identifiable thing (*I*) or even a state of affairs. We must not lose sight of the fact, however, that Peirce did not explicate the representative function of the sign through the two-placed relation of standing for something. In order to fulfill its representative function, the sign must at the same time be interpretable: "A thing cannot stand for something without standing to something for something" (W 1:466). This is already to be found in the seventh Lowell Lecture of 1866. The sign cannot establish the epistemic relation to something in the world if it is not at the same time directed toward an interpreting mind— that is, if it *could* not be employed communicatively. Without communicability there is no representation—and vice versa. Even though Peirce was interested in semeiotic problems primarily from an epistemological point of view, he set the fundamental conceptual switches in such a way that the epistemic relation of the sign to something in the world cannot be isolated from the communicative relation to a *possible* interpreter. At the same time, however, Peirce insisted on the anonymization of the interpretative process, from which he eliminated the interpreter. What remains after this abstraction are currents of depersonalized sequences of signs, in which every sign refers as the interpreter to the previous sign, and refers as the interpretandum to the following sign. To be sure, these linkages are established only through the mediation of a mind in which signs are able to call forth interpretations: "intelligent consciousness must enter into the series" (CP 2.303). Still, this *mind* remains anonymous, because it consists of nothing other than that three-placed relation of representation in general; *it* is absorbed by the structure of the sign.

In terms of theoretical strategy, this abstract conceptualization has the merit that it does not restrict semeiosis to linguistic communication from the start, but remains open for further specifications. Nonetheless, the question arises whether Peirce's concept of the sign really does leave open the specifications that are required for the communicative level of propositionally organized language, or whether it does not prejudice them in a certain way. A methodological consideration can help us along here. Peirce pursued something like the logical genesis of sign processes. In doing so, he began with the complex structures of language that are accessible to us, in order to feel his way toward the more elementary forms by means of privative determinations—Peirce speaks of "degeneration." In this procedure, one may abstract only from those aspects of a given higher semeiotic level for which it is not possible to identify more primitive predecessors or lower semeiotic levels. Peirce seemed to regard the intersubjective relationship between a speaker and a hearer, and the corresponding participant perspectives of the first and second person (in contrast to the perspective of an uninvolved third person), as such aspects that may be disregarded. He seemed to believe that the fundamental semeiotic structure can be completely defined without recourse to forms of intersubjectivity, however elementary. In any event, he generally suspended his logical–semeiotic analyses at the point where speaker-hearer perspectives come into play.[1]

Like George Herbert Mead later on, the *young* Peirce was clearly of a different opinion. He attached virtually fundamental importance to the attitudes of the first, second, and third persons. On the one hand, the corresponding perspectives are equally fundamental, that is, none can be reduced to the others; on the other, they can be transformed into one another. The primitive expressions "I," "thou," and "it" thus form a system of relations: "Though they cannot be expressed in terms of each other, yet they have a relation to each other, for 'Thou' is an 'It' in which there is another 'I.' 'I' looks in, 'It' looks out, 'Thou' looks through, out and in again" (W 1:45), noted the twenty-four-year-old Peirce. And two years later Peirce connected his speculations about a future communitarian age, which is supposed to supersede the tendencies to reification of the present materialistic age, with the name "Tuism," thus indicating the importance of attitude toward a second person for purposes of social integration.[2] In 1861 Peirce planned to write a book about "I, It, and Thou" as "Elements of Thought." In the first Harvard Lectures of 1865 he attempted to introduce the concept of the sign in connection with the system of personal pronouns; not unreasonably, the interpretant relation, and thus the power of the sign to influence an interpreting mind, were explicated by means of the attitude of the second person (W 1:174). But after that, if I am not mistaken, the system of personal pronouns completely lost its significance for the foundations of semeiotic.

Now, the question that interests me is: What considerations could have brought Peirce to turn away from the intersubjective aspects of the sign process? I want to defend the thesis that it is impossible to give a satisfactory explanation of the interpretant relation of the sign without having recourse to the conditions for reaching an intersubjective agreement, however rudimentary these may be. This remains impossible as long as sign-mediated representation is conceived, as Peirce conceived it, in terms of truth and reality—for these concepts refer in turn to the regulative idea of a community of investigators that operates under ideal conditions. As long as Peirce stuck to his main intuition, that the pragmatic turn cannot be consistently carried through without accepting these or similar counterfactual presuppositions, he could hardly do without an intersubjectively based semeiotic. I would like to explicate this thesis in four steps.

First I want (1) to sketch the critique of the philosophy of consciousness that Peirce carried out in the 1860s and 1870s, as well as (2) to recall the two resulting problems that emerge from the semeiotic transformation of Kantian epistemology. The solutions Peirce proposed depend on (3) the premise of cumulative learning processes, which admits a weak intersubjectivistic reading. But instead of this interpretation, Peirce preferred a strong, or cosmological, one. He developed this version in terms of (4) a theory of natural evolution which has problematic consequences for semeiotic and leads to a Platonistic concept of the person which cannot be brought into harmony with our best intuitions.

(1) A third world of symbolic forms which mediates between the inner and the outer worlds (W 1:168) disclosed itself to the young Peirce along the dual path of religious experience and logical investigation: "Religion . . . is neither something within us nor yet altogether without us—but bears rather a third relation to us, namely, that of existing in our communion with another being" (W 1:108). Whereas for Peirce the Transcendentalist the forcelessly unifying power of communication stood in the foreground, for Peirce the logician something else provided the decisive factor: namely, the idea that "every thought is an unuttered word" (W 1:169).

Peirce, prior to Frege and Husserl, carried through a devastating critique of psychologism in his first Harvard Lecture. Logic is not a matter of mental processes or facts of unconsciousness. Rather, it analyzes general sign operations and properties that are actualized in the symbolic expressions; logical characters "belong to what is written on the board at least as much as to our thought" (W 1:165). But unlike Frege and Husserl, Peirce did not arrive at the conclusions of some sort of meaning-Platonism. Every symbol of itself refers to possible interpretations, that is, to infinitely many reproductions of its meaning *over time*. Like all signs, symbols are what they mean only in relation to other signs. And these relations can in turn be actualized only with the aid of operations that for their part extend in time. The transformation of symbolic expressions requires time. For this reason the world of symbolic forms stands in an *internal* relation to time. From Hegel, Peirce had learned "that the thought descends into time." In his debate with Kant, however, Peirce did not engage this theme from the perspective of a temporalization of mind. Instead, he was concerned with the way the flowing stream of consciousness is stabilized in the form of a symbolically embodied mind.

Under the heading "On Time and Thought," Peirce considered how the flow of our ideas can take on the continuity and the connectedness of feelings, wishes, and perceptions that are in contact with each other. A mere succession of distinct ideas, each of which is absolutely present at a different time, cannot provide an explanation for the way ideas can be determined by previous ideas—that is, the way one idea can be transformed into the next one according to a rule. Ideas that at one point are past must still be capable of being held fast in the mind, as it were, and of existing together and being linked up with the ideas that come after them. The semeiotic interpretation of consciousness offers the key to explaining this reproduction of ideas which makes their recognition possible.[3] If cognitions are signs, then replicas can be generated from past cognitions and linked up with present and future ones: "thus the intellectual character of beliefs at least is dependent upon the capability of the endless translation of sign into sign" (W 3:77). For their power to grant continuity, signs are indebted to the temporal reference that, with an object relation to the past and an interpretant relation to the future, is inherent in them.

With his semantic transformation of Kantian epistemology (Apel 1981), Peirce cleared the way for a critique of the philosophy of consciousness that brings about a specifically pragmatic turn. The architectonic of the philosophy of consciousness had been defined by the subject–object relation, interpreted as mental representation. Within this traditional paradigm of representative thinking, the objective world is conceived as the totality of mentally representable objects, while the subjective world is conceived as the sphere of our mental representations of possible objects. Access to this internal sphere is gained via the epistemic self-relation of the representing subject (or by self-consciousness), that is, by the mental representation of our representations of objects. Peirce undermined this architectonic by giving a semeiotic reinterpretation to the fundamental concept of "representation": the two-placed relation of mental representation (*Vorstellung*) is made into the three-placed relation of symbolic representation (*Darstellung*).

In explicit form, symbolic representation appears as a proposition representing a state of affairs. This only seems to replace the *psychological* perspective with a *semantic* perspective, as if the place of the subject–object relation were taken by the relation between language and the world. But a first complication already emerges from the propositional structure of what the sentence-sign stands for. A simple predicative sentence does not simply stand for an entity; it indeed refers to a singular object in the world, but it attributes to this object a property that can be expressed only in a predicate or a general concept. And it does this in such a way that it is not immediately clear whether this universal belongs more properly in the world or to language.

Another complication is more interesting. It arises from the fact that the sentence-sign not only has a relation to something in the world, but at the same time refers to an interpretative community. A fact is represented in terms of an assertoric sentence that can be true or false; the act of representation, however, is performed in terms of an assertion with which a speaker raises a contestable truth-claim for an addressee. As early as the Ninth Lowell Lecture of 1866, Peirce emphasized this *pragmatic aspect* of representation: "a symbol may be intended to refer to an interpretant or to have *force*. . . . It is intended . . . to inculcate this statement into the interpretant" (W 1:477). An assertion receives illocutionary force through the fact that a speaker offers—at least implicitly—a reason or an argument by means of which he wants to induce the addressee to give assent. Peirce will later say that every proposition is the rudimentary form of an argument (CP 2.344). According to the paradigm of the philosophy of consciousness, the truth of a judgment is based on the subject's certainty that the mental representation corresponds to the object. After the pragmatic turn, however, the truth of a sentence-sign must be measured both against its object relation and against the reasons that could be accepted for its validity by an interpretative community. Thus, in the new paradigm the role of the subject is assumed not by language *per se*, but by communication among those who demand explanations from each other in order to reach reasonable agreement about something in the world. The place of subjectivity is taken over by an intersubjective practice of reaching initial understanding; this practice emits from itself infinite sequences of signs and interpretations. Peirce developed this conception through a penetrating critique of the paradigm of the philosophy of consciousness. He was guided therein by the following *six* considerations:

- The methodological critique is directed against an *introspection* that relies on the private evidence of so-called facts of con-

sciousness, without being able to present verifiable criteria for discriminating mere appearance from reality. In contrast, symbolic expressions and complexes of signs are generally accessible facts whose interpretation is open to public criticism, so that it is not necessary to appeal to a particular individual in place of the community of investigators as the final arbiter of [correct] judgment.
- The epistemological critique is directed against an *intuitionism* that claims that our judgments are constructed from immediately given and absolutely certain ideas or sense-data. The truth is that no idea, no matter how elementary, comes into contact with its object without semeiotic mediation. In an experiential process which is fundamentally discursive, there is no absolute beginning. Whether consciously or not, all cognitions are determined logically by previous cognitions.
- From the above there emerges the critique of any theory that confers a *foundationalist* distinction on *self-consciousness*. The truth is that we draw only inferences about the inner world of mental states and psychic events from our knowledge of external facts. Only when an opinion that is at first held to be true turns out to be merely "subjective" does the experience of error force the hypothesis of a "self" upon us.
- The critique of Kant's construction of a "thing-in-itself" is directed against a kind of *phenomenalism* that is led astray by the mirror-model of representative thinking: into assuming that reality, lying hidden *behind* appearances, has, like the mirror itself, a rear side that evades reflection. The truth of the matter is that reality does impose restrictions upon our knowledge, but only in such a way that it rejects false opinions as our interpretations founder upon it. Yet, it does not follow from this that reality could fundamentally elude better interpretations. Rather, what is real is everything that can become the content of true representations, and nothing else.
- Further, doubt about Cartesian doubt is directed against the *conception* of a *worldless subject* standing over and against the world as a whole. The individual consciousness does not form a monad encapsulated in itself, which could put into brackets the totality of beings just by distancing itself *from everything* through a supposedly radical doubt. Rather, every subject always finds itself already within the context of a world that is familiar to it. The subject cannot by fiat problematize this massive background of beliefs as a whole. An empty, abstract "paper doubt" cannot undermine life-world certainties; on the

other hand, nothing is in principle immune to real nagging doubt.[4]
- Finally, Peirce was opposed to the *privileging* of the *knowing subject* above the acting subject. All our beliefs are interwoven with our practices: "A belief which will not be acted upon ceases to be a belief" (W 3:77). Thus, mind is situated and finds its embodiment simultaneously in the symbolic media of language and of *practice*. Any thought articulated in an utterance is recoupled with action and experience via the belief held by an interpreting mind. Every link in this chain exhibits the three-placed structure that explains the representative function of signs—and to this extent each is itself something of the same sort as a sign.

(2) Even the semeiotically transformed philosophy of consciousness does not, however, escape the old epistemological queries. How is objectivity of experience supposed to be possible if the semeiotically embodied mind remains caught in the spell of discourses and practices and bound by the chains of signs? How can we do justice to our intuitive understanding of reality as something independent of us if the truth of judgments and statements is mired in the rhetorical pro-and-con of argumentation without end? True, Peirce destroyed two dogmas: the myth of the given, and the illusion of truth as the certainty of our mental representations. But then he found himself confronted with the question whether he had not simply traded the dogmas of received empiricism for a second-order empiricism—an holistically renewed empiricism on the level of sign systems, behind which we are no more able to reach than behind "first principles" or "ultimate facts." Peirce suggested three innovative answers:

(*a*) the theory of pre-symbolic signs;
(*b*) the doctrine of synthetic inferences; and
(*c*) the regulative idea of a final consensus (ultimate agreement or final opinion).

(*a*) How is objectivity of experience supposed to be possible? On the one hand, the contact between signs and reality must be established via experience, just as before; on the other, experience is absorbed within a continuum of sign-mediated processes. Peirce thus had to show how strings of signs, which can be endlessly continued through logical operations of inference, are still able to open themselves up osmotically to reality. He had to demonstrate the possibility of *anchoring* strings of signs in reality. Along the path of a logical genesis of perceptual judgments, Peirce, like the late Husserl in *Experience and Judgment*, had to descend into the realm of pre-predicative experience.

The starting point for this descent is provided by the structure of the simple predicative sentence. The proposition is composed of two elements. One of these, the subject expression, establishes the relation to the object of reference, while the other contains the predicative determination of the object. From this, Peirce developed the distinction between the concept of "existence" and the concept of "reality." The two-placed relation between the referential term and its object is an existential relation which does indeed reflect the "outward clash" of a confrontation with reality, but does not mirror reality itself. For the real state of affairs is represented only by the sentence as a whole, including the predicate expression.

Drawing the well-known distinction between symbol, index, and icon was the first move, then, in the game of a logical genesis of the assertoric sentence. Below the level of complete sentences and propositional structures—that is, those representations that are capable of being true or false—there are simple signs which stand either in a relation of denotation or in a relation of similarity to corresponding aspects of reality. From this, Peirce inferred that the subject and predicate expressions, which must be joined together in sentences in order to fulfill an explicit propositional function, are based upon a genetically more primitive layer of index signs and icons, each of which is of itself—that is, independently of any propositional structure—capable of taking up a relation to an object and finding an interpretant (see Oehler 1979a, 9ff.). While terms, propositions, and arguments count as "symbols," the next lower level consists of non-symbolic but still conventional signs.

After this first step in the archaeology of linguistic symbols, the conventional signs are complemented by three classes of non-conventional or natural signs. Whereas symbols as well as independently appearing indices and iconic representations such as diagrams still stand in conventional relations to their objects, natural symptoms and analogues rely upon a causal nexus or on pre-existing similarities in form.[5] Later on, Peirce further differentiated these classes of signs, but he never arrived at a conclusive system. That fits the overall intention to demonstrate that the roots of the semeiotic family tree of predicative sentences branch off endlessly and extend down to a depth where, for the time being, they finally slip out of the sight of an analysis proceeding to ever more primitive signs. In the same way, then, experiential processes can root in preconscious layers of sense and stimuli and feelings, without losing the discursive character of a sign-mediated inferential process.

(b) Of course, these considerations are able to support a claim to objectivity for experience only if the infinitesimal initial phases of our pre-predicative experience elude conscious control, that is, explicitly discursive processing: in a certain sense the "percepts" force themselves on us. But these elementary information inputs that are vested with sensory evidence are no less fallible than the perceptual judgments that are obtained from them (Hookway 1985, 149ff.). What Peirce called "percepts" cannot take on the role of "first premises." Even they depend upon those limiting cases of abductive inference which strike us in the form of lightning insights, and which for that reason merely conceal their fallibility from us: "If the percept or perceptual judgment were of a nature entirely unrelated to abduction, one would expect that the percept would be entirely free from any characters that are proper interpretations, while it can hardly fail to have such characters" (CP 5.184).

Certainly, such percepts and perceptual judgments, which run again and again through the channels of practice and become habitualized, are capable of gelling together with theoretical background suppositions and moral principles to become an unquestioned context of life-world certainties (commonsense beliefs). But none of these habitualized beliefs is immune to being problematized. That is, only in the case of misfires, or negative experiences, does the contact to reality furnish a good criterion for the evaluation of the opinions that are invested in plans of action.[6]

If, however, the objectivity of experience cannot be made secure with an indubitable source of information, at least the mode of information processing will guarantee the truth. Peirce regarded the rules of inferential reasoning as the core of such a procedural rationality. As is well known, he reconstructed this *logica utens* in the form of a doctrine of synthetic inferences. I cannot pursue that here (see Hookway 1985, 208ff.). One reservation is nonetheless important. The circular process of hypothesis formation, inductive generalization, deduction, and renewed hypothesis formation will promise a self-correcting processing of experiences and a cumulative growth of knowledge only as long as abduction is handled correctly. The abductive form of inference is the real knowledge-amplifying element, but at the same time it is far from yielding *necessary* conclusions. In the case of induction, Peirce believed that probability-theoretical considerations could be used to show that we can rely on it "in the long run." Yet, only the rational formation of hypotheses could close the circle of inductive generalization and deduction. So, the question of how the objectivity of experience is possible gets posed again.

How can we explain the quasi-transcendental fact of universal learning processes? Either the doctrine of synthetic inferences needs an objective foundation in reality, so that it could be shown how nature itself directs our formation of hypotheses; the late Peirce would come back to this alternative. Or the burden of proof, which experience—including the experience of practical failure—and inferential reasoning alone cannot sustain, has to be redistributed and *relocated* upon another link in the chain of the semeiotic process: upon argumentation. Indeed, Peirce had always conceived discussion as the "proofstone of truth" (Kant): "Upon most subjects at least sufficient experience, *discussion* and reasoning will bring men to an agreement" (W 3:8). He did not conceive of discussion as a contest (CP 5.406) in which one side seeks to overpower the other rhetorically; discussion is the cooperative quest for truth by means of the public exchange of arguments. Only thus is it able to serve as a "test of dialectical examination" (CP 5.392).

(c) At first, in "The Fixation of Belief," Peirce gave an *historical* grounding for the thesis that procedural rationality, which is effective in everyday practices and elaborated in science, is able to develop only under the conditions of rational discourse: in modernity, the rational authority of discursive learning guided by experience has asserted itself against the power of habits, against thought control, and against wish-fulfilling *a priori* doctrines. But an explanation going beyond such historical suggestions is needed for the proposition that the inferential processing of information would not succeed without the public and unforced exchange of arguments. Peirce again used the tripartite structure of the sign itself to explain why the sign-mediated cognitive process also requires these conditions of operation.

A sign can fulfill its representative function only if, along with the relation to the objective world of entities, it simultaneously establishes a relation to the intersubjective world of interpreters. The objectivity of experience is not possible without the intersubjectivity involved in coming to initial understanding. This argument can be reconstructed in four stages.

• In a distant analogy to Wittgenstein's private-language argument, Peirce emphasized the internal connection between private experience and public communication. A private aspect is always attached to experience, because everyone has privileged access to his own ideas (*Erlebnissen*). At the same time, the sign character of these ideas points beyond the borders of subjectivity. By representing something, a sign expresses something general; therefore, it could not find an interpretant that would remain the exclusive possession of an individual mind. We all become aware of this supra-subjective partnership in the interpretant at the moment when we confront the opinion of someone else and an error becomes apparent to us in a flash.

• This confrontation of opinions must take on the rational form of argumentation, because this form of communication merely makes explicit what is already implicit in every proposition. That is, the illocutionary force of the act of assertion indicates that the speaker invites the addressee to support his statement with an argument if necessary (Peirce said: to develop an argument from the proposition). So, rational discourse, in which a proponent defends validity claims against the objections of opponents, is just the most reflexively developed form of sign processes.

• Because the rules of synthetic inference cannot of themselves generate compelling results, and thus cannot be reproduced on the semantic level as algorithms, the argumentative processing of information has to assume the form of an intersubjective practice. Certainly, in argumentation the yes-and-no positions of the participants are supposed to be regulated by good reasons. The problem is that what may count as a "good reason" in any case has to be decided within argumentation itself. There is no higher court of appeal than the agreement of others which is brought about within discourse and, in this respect, is rationally motivated.

• To be sure, the objectivity of experience cannot be made dependent upon the agreement—no matter how rational—of a contingent number of participants, that is, contingent agreement within any particular group. Better arguments, which would refute what is here and now held to be true by you and me, might emerge in different contexts or on the basis of further experiences. With the concept of reality, to which every representation necessarily refers, we presuppose something transcendent. As long as we move within a particular linguistic community or form of life, this transcending relation cannot be supplanted by the rational acceptability of an argument. Since we cannot break out of the sphere of language and argumentation altogether, we can establish the reference to reality—which is not equivalent to "existence"—only by projecting a "transcendence from within." This end is served by the counterfactual concept of a "final opinion" or a consensus reached under ideal conditions. Peirce made the rational acceptability of an assertion, and thus its truth as well, depend upon an agreement that could be achieved under the conditions for communication among a community of investigators that is extended to ideal limits in social space and historical time. If we understand reality as the totality of all assertions that are true in this sense, then we are able to do justice to its transcendence without having to surrender the internal connection between the objectivity of experience and the intersubjectivity of reaching initial understanding:

> The real, then, is that which, sooner or later, information and reasoning would finally result in, and which is therefore independent of the vagaries of me and you. Thus, the very origin of the

conception of reality shows that this conception essentially involves the notion of a *Community*, without definite limits, and capable of a definite increase of knowledge [CP 5.311].

(3) Out of this semeiotic model of knowledge there emerges an image of a rationally directed process of interpretation in which "men and words reciprocally educate each other" (W 1:497). The semeiotically constituted world of human beings reproduces itself and develops through the medium of signs. At one pole, experience and purposive action secure a contact with reality that is sign-mediated: "The elements of every concept enter into logical thought at the gate of perception and make their exit at the gate of purposive action" (CP 5.212). At the other pole, the exchange of arguments takes place with regard to and in anticipation of the counterfactually presupposed conditions of an ideal communication. At the former pole, learning processes start as more or less quasi-natural events according to the rules of synthetic inference; at the latter, these processes have become reflexive. They come under the direction of a conscious community of investigators that supervises itself. This community is committed to a logic "whose essential end is to test the truth by reasons" (W 1:329). Experience and argumentation stand to each other in the tension between "private" and "public." Correspondingly, everyday action and argumentation are caught up in the tension between the certainty of common sense and the awareness of radical fallibility.[7]

Both common sense and science operate with the supposition of a reality that is independent of us. In our practices, however, what we take to be unavoidable and indubitable has the status of an acritical certainty, although it is by no means immune *a priori* from objections. In the realm of argumentatively tested knowledge, we are, on the other hand, conscious of the fallibility of every insight. In order to believe that we are capable of the truth nonetheless, we need the compensatory reference point provided by the "final opinion." Only those assertations are true which would always be reaffirmed within the horizon of a community without definite limits (CP 5.311).

From his semeiotic model of knowledge, reality, and truth, consequences emerge for the very concepts of the sign and interpretation. Until now we have proceeded from the position that, in the mind of an interpreter, the sign has the effect of reproducing, as it were, the object that is represented by the sign. Strictly interpreted, this would mean

> that a representation is something which produces another representation of the same object, and in this second or interpreting representation the first representation is represented as representing a certain object. This second representation must itself have an interpreting representation and so on ad infinitum, the whole process of representation never reaches a completion [W 3:64f.].

Yet, such an infinite regress would come about only if the process of interpretation were to circle within itself, as it were, without continual stimulation from outside, and without discursive processing. But this description is adequate only for that initial phase, in which, even before any experience, the interpretant relates to that "immediate object" which inheres, so to speak, in the sign as its meaning. But the actual employment of the sign in a particular situation requires an interpretant which refers in view of collateral experience to the "dynamic object." This object is external to the sign and demands of the interpreter both sensory and practical experience, knowledge of the context, and discursive processing of information. Nor is the interpretation of a sign therein exhausted; because the interpretation aims toward an explicit representation, that is, one that is capable of being true, it anticipates the possibility of a "final interpretant." The latter refers to the object as it would be represented in light of an ideal consensus—that is, to the "final object." Only an orientation toward the truth does justice to the role of symbolic expressions which "represent" something, in the sense that interpreters can make use of them *in order to reach an agreement with one another about something in the world.* Understanding, reaching agreement, and knowledge refer reciprocally to each other (Savan 1977, 179ff.; Ransdell 1977, 157ff.).

The interpretation of signs is interwoven with the representation of reality; for this reason, the stream of interpretation takes on a direction. The original text of nature does not go down in the contingent flows of significants. The telos of a *complete* representation of reality is already inscribed in the structure of the first sign. Nonetheless, one consequence of this disturbed Peirce from the start: because of their semeiotic constitution, learning processes are ultimately unable to break away from the circle of the signs given interpretations by us. In the end, the limits of our language remain the limits of the world.

This semeiotic circle closes itself off all the more inexorably when Peirce's *logical* analysis of language is extended to include *linguistic* aspects. It then becomes apparent that in limiting cases successful abduction also requires an innovative modification of language itself—a modification, that is, in the perpective from which we look at the world. In extreme cases, we run up against the limits of our comprehensions, and intepretations that labor in vain on resilient problems begin to falter. They get moving again only when, in light of a *new* vocabulary, the familiar facts show themselves in a different light, so that well-worn problems can be posed in a completely new and more promising way. This world-disclosing function of the sign was neglected by Peirce.

This function does not at all imply that the universalizing force of learning processes becomes fragmented whenever it runs up against the borders of a particular language or a concrete form of life. All languages are porous, and every newly disclosed aspect to the world remains an empty projection as long as its fruitfulness does not also *prove its worth* in learning processes that are made possible by the changed perspective on the world. But this interplay between linguistic world-constitution and innerworldly problem-solving only highlights the question that disturbed Peirce.

If the limits of semeiosis means the limits of the world, then both the system of signs and the communication among sign-users acquire an almost transcendental status. The structure of reality itself is not what is mirrored in the structure of the language in which subjects give a representation of the world. Peirce stubbornly fought against such nominalistic consequences his entire life; and it seemed to him that they could be avoided if the semeiotic circle were to encompass not merely the world of subjects capable of speaking and acting but nature as a whole—to encompass nature and not just our interpretation of nature. Only then would the topos of the "book of nature" shed its metaphorical character, and every natural phenomenon would be transformed—if not into a letter, then at least into a sign that determines the series of its interpretants. Furthermore, the imaginative generation of hypotheses which is at work in all successful abduction would need to bring to consciousness only what has already been "thought out" or prefigured in natural evolution. The synthetic inferences would obtain a *fundamentum in re*. This semeiotic idealism (McCarthy 1984, 395ff.) requires, of course, a naturalization of semeiosis. The price Peirce had to pay for this is the anonymization and depersonalization of the mind in which signs call forth their interpretants. With this metaphysical baggage, however, Peirce overburdens his semeiotic.

I see the great achievement of Peircean semeiotic in its consistent expansion of the world of symbolic forms beyond the limits of linguistic forms of expression. Peirce contrasted our propositionally differentiated language with signal languages. He analyzed those types of intentionally employed indices and icons which attain independence below the level of linguistic signs. He showed how causal symptoms and spontaneous expressive gestures, as well as pre-existing gestalt similarities, can be interpreted on the model of linguistic signs. He thereby opened new realms to semeiotic analysis: for example, the extraverbal sign world, in the context of which our linguistic communication is embedded; the aesthetic forms of representation, especially the formal repertoire of non-propositional arts; finally, the abductive decoding of a symbolically constructed social world, upon which thrive not only our everyday communicative practices, but also figures like Sherlock Holmes (Sebeok and Umiker-Sebeok 1980) or novels like Eco's *The Name of the Rose*. Our lifeworld, which is semeiotically constructed from the bottom up, forms a network of implicit meaning structures that are sedimented in signs which, though non-linguistic, are nonetheless accessible to interpretation. The situations in which participants to an interaction orient themselves are overflowing with cues, signals, and telltale traces; at the same time, they are marked by stylistic features and expressive characteristics which can be intuitively grasped and reflect the "spirit" of a society, the "tincture" of an age, the "physiognomy" of a city or of a social class. If Peirce's semeiotic is applied to this sphere, produced by human beings but by no means intentionally *controlled*, then it also becomes clear that the deciphering of implicit meaning structures, that is, the understanding of meaning, is a mode of experience. Experience *is* communicative experience. Karl-Otto Apel (1984), in particular, has drawn our attention to this.

When we become aware of this wealth of meaning which is not linguistically articulated, but objectivated in pre-symbolic and even pre-conventional signs, then one fact turns out all the more clearly: even if natural signs lack authors who give them meaning, still they have meaning for interpreters who are in command of a language. How should they find their interpretants where there are no interpreters who are able to argue with reasons about their interpretations? Yet, precisely this is assumed by a semeiotic idealism which projects semeiosis into speechless nature. Semeiotic idealism assumes that the process of habit formation that is steered by the interpretation of signs extends far beyond the human world, to include animal, vegetable, and mineral.

(4) Peirce is convinced "that habit is by no means exclusively a mental fact. Empirically, we find that some plants take habits. The stream of water that wears a bed for itself is forming a habit" (CP 5.492). A nature that has developed by means of a semeiotic learning process opens its eyes and becomes a virtual participant in the conversation conducted among humans. This venerable idea obtains its appeal from an image of ourselves entering into conversation with nature and unbinding the tongues of the creatures so far excluded from redemption. To the naturalization of humans there would then correspond a humanization of nature, as Marx thought. But a completely different result emerges out of Peirce's semeiotic reading of this legacy of Judaic and Protestant mysticism, Romantic philosophy of nature, and Transcendentalism: by being absorbed into an all-encompassing nexus of communication, the conversation among humans loses just what is specific to it. This becomes apparent in Peirce's concept of the person (Muoio 1984, 169ff.), in which everything that makes a person into an individual is defined purely negatively in terms of its difference from what is general—namely, in terms of the distance separating error from the truth, and divid-

ing the egoist from the community. The individual is the merely subjective and egoistic: "The individual man, since his separate existence is manifested only by ignorance and error, so far as he is anything apart from his fellows, and from what he and they are to be, is only a negation" (CP 5.317).

Thus, the bad legacy of Platonism is reproduced even in the work of the anti-Platonist Peirce. A metaphysical realism in regard to universals that has been set in motion turns the evolution of the cosmos into the bearer of an inexorable tendency toward universalization, a tendency to ever more organization, ever more conscious control. But the consequence I am examining is not explained by metaphysical realism per se. Rather, it emerges from the semeiotic conception of the universal only as a sign-mediated representation, together with the interpretation of evolution as a learning process. Both present communication, in which the tendency to universalization asserts itself, only from *one* side: communication is not for the sake of reaching initial understanding between ego and alter-ego about something in the world; rather, interpretation exists only for the sake of the representation and the ever more comprehensive representation of reality. This privileging of the sign's representative relation to the world above the sign's communicative relation to the interpreter causes the interpreter to disappear behind the depersonalized interpretant.

This is made all the more feasible by the fact that the doctrine of synthetic inferences now finds its foundation in the laws of natural evolution. If the learning processes of the human species merely continue, in reflexive form, those of nature, then argumentation, of what one human being has to say to another, and the power of the better argument to convince, both lose the weight and value that are proper to them. The unforced agreement of individuals who hold one another accountable, and who are faced with opinions that differ from person to person, ought to issue from argumentation by virtue of the latter's specific character. But this specific achievement falls victim to the leveling force of a universalism propelling itself inferentially from within reality itself. The multi-vocal character of intersubjectivity becomes an epiphenomenon.

It is interesting that finally Peirce is able to picture one interpreter reaching agreement with another only as an emotional fusion of ego and alter-ego: "When I communicate my thoughts and my sentiments to a friend with whom I am in full sympathy, so that my feelings pass into him and I am conscious of what he feels, do I not live in his brain as well as in my own—most literally?" [W 1:498]. In this view, the generalization of a consensus implies not only the dissolution of contradictions, but also the extinguishing of the individuality of those who are able to contradict one another—their disappearance within a collective representation. Like Durkheim, Peirce conceived of the identity of the individual as the mirror-image of the mechanical solidarity of a group: "Thus every man's soul is a special determination of the generic soul of the family, the class, the nation, the race to which he belongs" (W 1:499). George Herbert Mead, pragmatist of the second generation, was the first to conceive language as the medium that socializes communicative actors only insofar as it individualizes them at the same time. The collective identities of the family, class, and nation stand in a complementary relation to the unique identity of the individual; the one may not be absorbed by the other. Ego and alter-ego can agree in an interpretation and share the same idea only insofar as they do not violate the conditions of linguistic communication, and maintain an intersubjective relationship that requires them to orient themselves toward each other as first person is oriented toward second person. That means, however, that each must distinguish himself from the other in the first-person plural from others as third persons. To the extent that the dimension of possible contradiction and difference would close, linguistic communication would contract into a type of communion that no longer needs language as the means of reaching initial understanding.

Peirce once accused the Hegelians—in just the same sense as Feuerbach had—of neglecting the moment of Secondness, which expresses itself in the external resistance of existing objects (CP 8.39ff.). He himself neglected that moment of Secondness that we encounter in communication as contradiction and difference, as the *other* individual's "mind of his own" (*Eigensinn*). To be sure, when it is a matter of a great philosopher, his individuality may also be expressed in his philosophy. As Peirce said: "Each man has his own peculiar character. It enters into all he does. It is in his consciousness and not a mere mechanical trick, and therefore it is . . . a cognition; but as it enters into all his cognition, it is a cognition of *things in general*. It is therefore the man's philosophy, his way of regarding things . . ." (W 1:501)—that constitutes his individuality."

(Translated by William Hohengarten)

NOTES

1. The irrelevance of the intersubjective relationship pointing beyond the structure of the sign-mediated representation is justified thus: "In every assertion we may distinguish a speaker and a listener. The latter, it is true, need have only a problematical existence, as when during a shipwreck an account of the accident is sealed in a bottle and thrown upon the water. The problematical 'listener' may be within the same person as 'the speaker'; as when we mentally register a judgment independent of any registry . . . [;] we may say that in that case the listener becomes identical with the speaker" (CP 2.334). On the other hand, Peirce doubted that a judgment which, as presupposed in this thought experiment, is not structured through the "register" of an internalized proposition, that is, through a sign, would have any logical significance at all. In regard to that it is clear that even the message in a bottle has an addressee, however anonymous.

2. As late as 1891, Peirce defined Tuism as the doctrine "that all thought is addressed to a second person" (Fisch, in W 1:xxix).

3. For a similar approach, cf. Cassirer 1953–1957, vol. I, Introduction and vol. II, first and second part.

4. "It is idle to tell a man to begin by doubting familiar beliefs, unless you say something which shall cause him to really doubt them. It is false to say that reasoning must rest either on first principles or on ultimate facts. For we cannot go behind what we are unable to doubt, but it would be unphilosophical to suppose that any particular fact will never be brought into doubt" (W 3:14).

5. Cf. the introduction of the ten classes of signs in Pape, ed. 1983: 64ff., esp. 121ff.; also Pape 1989.

6. Peirce was long of the opinion "that there is no definite and fixed collection of opinions that are indubitable, but that criticism gradually pushes back each individual's indubitables, modifying the list, yet still leaving him beliefs indubitable for the time being" (CP 5.509).

7. "*Full belief* is willingness to act upon the proposition in vital crises, *opinion* is willingness to act upon it in relatively insignificant affairs. But pure science has nothing at all to do with action. . . . The scientific man is not in the least wedded to his conclusions. . . . He stands ready to abandon one or all as soon as experience opposes them. Some of them, I grant, he is in the habit of calling *established truths*; but that merely means propositions to which no competent man today demurs" (CP 1.634).

15

A Response to Habermas

Klaus Oehler

HABERMAS'S ESSAY CONTAINS four major claims. His first one is that Peirce, after taking an early interest in the intersubjectivity of the speaker–listener relationship, rapidly turned away from intersubjective aspects of sign processes and invariably broke his logical-semeiotic studies off wherever speaker–listener perspectives come into play. The second claim: Peirce could not define the interpretant relation without reference to the conditions of intersubjective communication. His third claim: Peirce preferred to ground the sign processes in cosmology rather than in an intersubjective framework. His fourth claim: the universal realism on which Peirce's theory of natural evolution rests has negative implications for both semeiotic and ethics. I would like to respond to these four claims as follows.

To the first thesis: Habermas's claim is not supported by the texts and must be rejected on historical and philological grounds. Peirce took a deep and lasting interest in the communicative structure of the speaker–listener relation. The most significant and thorough of his many discussions of this topic dates from 1907. The still unpublished MS 318, which contains this discussion, has attracted special attention in recent years because it provides one of the most consistent of all Peirce's expositions of his theory of signs. In this manuscript Peirce carried out a logical-semeiotic analysis of situative speech as it occurs in dialogue. In reconstructing the speech situation, Peirce succeeded in laying bare both the triadic structures of the sign relation and what he refers to as its "essential ingredients": namely, the sign user, the sign expression, and the sign interpreter. The results of this analysis would prove not uninteresting to the author of the theory of communicative action.

What emerges most clearly from MS 318 is that Peirce did not need to draw on the concept of communicative rationality in order to derive the relationality of the sign. Peirce recognized early in his career that a model based on intersubjective communication was in this respect dispensable, and he abandoned it for two specific reasons: first, from the start his systematic intention was of a scope that transcended the speech situation; and, second, he was skeptical about the degree of generality of the rationality structures embedded in natural languages. Habermas himself cites a passage from a letter of 1909 to Lady Welby, in which Peirce warned of the dangers inherent in restricting semeiotic analysis to the sign mechanisms of language and grammar. Instead, he preferred to anchor his theory of the sign in the doctrine of categories, and it is this anchoring that guarantees its generality. The speech situation and the communicative rationality implicit in it should on no account be made to bear the burden of providing the foundation for semeiotic. They represent merely a peculiarly privileged instance through which the basic structures of the sign can be illustrated.

To the second claim: Habermas's assertion that Peirce could not define the interpretant relation without reference to the conditions of intersubjective communication is correct. But Peirce did not seek these conditions in the counterfactual "final opinion" or in the consensus of the "indefinite community of investigators." These conceptions play a different role in his view. Since the unlimited community of investigators does not exist *in concreto*, it had for Peirce only the status of a regulative idea. Habermas tends to transform this regulative function into a constitutive one and to draw idealistic conclusions from Peirce's "notion of a Community, without definite limits, and capable of a definite increase of knowledge" (CP 5.311), which he endows with a quasi-transcendental character. The texts do not support this reading. We should not forget that in the treatise entitled "Critic of Arguments," Peirce described the transcendental method as occultism (CP 3.422).

The conditions of intersubjective agreement are the three sign relations inherent in the sign itself, "First," "Second," and "Third," or, in the language of the young Peirce, "I," "Thou," and "It." These correspond exactly to Peirce's scheme of categories from which they are derived. The categories Firstness, Secondness, and Thirdness are classes of relations: monadic, dyadic, and triadic. Habermas does not discuss the foundation of the sign process in the doctrine of Categories, and this oversight leads him to ignore the logic of relations, which is fundamental to that determination of the conditions of intersubjective agreement he is seeking. Peirce thought that the three pragmatic functions of representation, expression, and communication can be adequately analyzed only with the tools of relational logic, because they conform to the logical conditions of the sign structure exhibited in every linguistic act. The question of the general conditions of possible agreement cannot be adequately posed and answered without relational logic. Peirce's later conception of the categories is no longer based on the analysis of the proposition, or on transcendental reflection, but on what he called "Phaneroscopy," a method that is indifferent to the limits of language.

As far as the third claim is concerned, Peirce emphasized the limitations of language. Habermas acknowledges the role Peirce played in broadening our understanding of symbolic forms far beyond the boundaries of language. But Peirce's own view, it should be noted, did not need to be broadened in this respect, since his approach to the sign, early and late, was a broad one, and was never confined by the boundaries of language. The rose itself, not just the name of the rose, is a sign.

Peirce did not think that the intentionality of the sign and semeiosis depend exclusively on acts of consciousness. He regarded rational discourse as a special case of semeiosis. Human acts of cognition differ from other self-referential and self-correcting processes by virtue of their greater degree of self-reference and self-correction. Human beings achieve this superiority through the creation of symbols, which represent and control our habits of action. It follows that communicative reason is only a particularly complex case of semeiosis, characterized through goal-oriented production, use, and interpretation of signs. This in no way changes the fact that signs also figure at lower levels of life, as we know from research in animal communication. Peirce's semeiotic accommodates natural as well as cultural signs, and can thus systematically take account of the position of human beings in culture and nature, which is more than a theory of communicative rationality can achieve. Habermas likes to refer to this systematic integration as a "naturalization" of semeiosis or even a "semeiotic pragmatism," in order to avoid misunderstandings. Habermas resists an extension of semeiotic into the natural sphere. He makes intentionality depend on consciousness and reason, and divorces it radically from physical processes. This dualism of mind and nature is not merely foreign to Peirce's thought. Peirce opposed it. He would charge Habermas with Cartesianism, and it is difficult to see how Habermas can survive this criticism. Furthermore, Habermas's dichotomization between an intersubjective and a cosmological foundation of the sign process seems to be basically ill-conceived, since the dynamics of both intersubjectivity and natural information processes depend on and develop according to the same logic of the structure of the sign relation.

In his fourth claim, Habermas thinks that Peirce's position has negative implications for both semeiotic and ethics. For semeiotic, because the absorption of human conversation into an all-encompassing, cosmic sign process robs it of its specificity and individuality. But it is Habermas's linguistic apriorism that forces him to this conclusion. His theory of communicative action is founded in a universal pragmatics, according to which certain general validity claims are raised in every act of linguistic communication, the satisfaction of which constitutes what he calls "communicative rationality." Consensus is a function of these universal pragmatic conditions of communication. Reason, as he sees it, is manifested solely in intersubjective communication. This conception of communicative rationality is rooted in the framework of language. But Peirce doubted that language and the rationality structures which it exhibits can ever yield this justification. Just how far he distanced himself from the linguistic paradigm is apparent from his reflections on diagrammatic thinking. The form of diagrammatic-graphic understanding and communication which he used to model not only mathematical and scientific inquiry, but also the basic structure of prescientific, everyday thought transcended and relativized the framework of language pragmatics. We do not yet understand the structures on which thought, especially creative thinking, depends. It would be imprudent to make a decision that would prematurely bind us to a linguistic paradigm.

Habermas sees undesirable ethical implications in Peirce's concept of the person. Peirce characterized individuality negatively. Insofar as it lacks universality, the individual is exposed to error and idiosyncracy. This is not, however, Peirce's main conception of the person, but an almost sacred conception bathed in the glowing, quasi-religious light of the "final opinion." Individuality is error, subjectivity, egoism, privacy, heresy, sin, separation from the *summum bonum* represented by the Catholic Consensus. If Peirce used this almost religious conception of the person to portray humanity under the rule of the "final opinion," then he did no better and no worse than our religions when they talk of an afterlife, or Marx when he painted a glowing picture of the realm of freedom. Peirce did a better job than Marx, since his utopia is at least consistent with the laws of logic, whereas Marx had merely a somewhat simple, pre-industrial pastoral scene in mind. Since every increase in knowledge tends to yield increasing universality, Peirce extrapolated that the limit of this process may be characterized in terms of a speculative universal ideal. The philosopher may well regret that the rule of this "final opinion" will put an end to philosophical discussion and debate. That is indeed regrettable, if not indeed as regrettable as the prospect that heaven will put an end to all sin and transgression. But that remains to be seen.

16

Peirce on Language and Reference

Risto Hilpinen

I

IN ONE OF HIS MANUSCRIPTS (MS 620, written in 1909) Peirce said that he was "naturally deficient in aptitude for language." Peirce's alleged "deficiency" did not prevent him from making seminal contributions to the philosophy of language, even though his accomplishments in this field—as in many other fields of philosophy—went unnoticed for a long time.[1] Peirce's writings of the period 1890-1910 are replete with significant new ideas about language and meaning, many of which have been rediscovered by other philosophers of language in the present century. Here we find the beginnings of a theory of speech acts, Peirce's version of the causal-historical theory of proper names, and his pragmatic interpretation or "pragmatic semantics" of complex sentences and propositions. Here I will discuss briefly each of these topics, beginning with Peirce's account of speech acts, and basing my discussion on Peirce's writings of this twenty-year period, which form a relatively coherent text.

II

Peirce drew a clear distinction between a proposition and an *assertion* or affirmation:

> I grant that the normal use of a proposition is to affirm it; and its chief logical properties relate to what would result in reference to its affirmation. It is therefore convenient in logic to express propositions in most cases in the indicative mood. But the proposition in the sentence, 'Socrates est sapiens', strictly expressed, is 'Socrates sapientem esse'. The defence of this position is that in this way we distinguish between a proposition and the assertion

of it, and without such distinction it is impossible to get a distinct notion of the nature of the proposition. One and the same proposition may be affirmed, denied, judged, doubted, inwardly inquired into, put as a question, wished, asked for, effectively commanded, taught, or merely expressed, and does not thereby become a different proposition [MS 517; NEM 4:248].

An assertion is a speech act; a proposition is a possible content of a speech act, something that may be asserted.[2] Peirce adopted here the view that different speech act types can have the same content, that is, contain the same proposition. This distinction between a proposition and a speech act type (for example, an assertion) was later expressed by other authors as the distinction between the content and the force of a sentence, or the sentence radical and the mood of a sentence (see Dummett 1981, chap. 10; Stenius 1964, chap. 9, esp. 157–65). Frege made the distinction between an assertion and a proposition (or a "thought"), but in his "Über Sinn und Bedeutung" he rejected the view that different speech act types can have the same content; he said, for example, that commands or requests are not thoughts, even though "they stand on the same level as thoughts" (Frege 1985, 200–12, esp. 206). Thus, according to Frege, distinct speech act types are distinguished by their content as well as their "force." In his commentary on Frege's philosophy of language Michael Dummett argues that this view is "definitely wrong," thus adopting the Peircean viewpoint (1981, 307).

In his discussion of the nature of assertion Peirce adopted an interesting methodological view: to understand the nature of an assertion, we should study "exaggerated" assertions in which the main features of the assertion are presented or displayed as clearly as possible. Peirce's standard example of such an exaggerated assertion is a legally binding oath:

> What is the nature of assertion? We have no magnifying-glass that can enlarge its features, and render them more discernible; but in default of such an instrument we can select for examination a very formal assertion, the features of which have purposely been rendered very prominent, in order to emphasize its solemnity. If a man desires to assert anything very solemnly, he takes such steps as will enable him to go before a magistrate or notary and take a binding oath to it [CP 5.546].

This method, which may be called "the method of ideal examples" or (to use Peirce's expression) "the method of the logical magnifying-glass," is, without doubt, superior to the attempts to characterize concepts by necessary and sufficient conditions: the latter method has often prompted philosophers to be excessively concerned about "difficult" and borderline cases, which has sometimes hampered fruitful philosophical theorizing.

The treatment of an assertion as analogous to an oath makes it clear that an assertion consists not merely in saying something, but also in *doing* something by means of a proposition. An assertion is an act, characterized by certain social consequences associated with it: "Taking an oath is not mainly an event of the nature of a setting forth, *Vorstellung*, or representing. It is not mere saying, but is doing. The law, I believe, calls it an 'act'" (CP 5.546).

The most significant characteristic of an act of assertion is that it involves the assuming of responsibility for the truth of what is asserted (that is, for the proposition asserted): "An assertion would be followed by very real effects, in case the substance of what is asserted should be proved untrue. This ingredient, the assuming of responsibility, which is so prominent in solemn assertion, must be present in every genuine assertion" (CP 5.546).

In MS 517 Peirce characterized the act of assertion as follows:

> As an aid in dissecting the constitution of affirmation [assertion] I shall employ a certain logical magnifying-glass that I have often found efficient in such business. Imagine, then, that I write a proposition on a piece of paper, perhaps a number of times, simply as a calligraphic exercise. It is not likely to prove dangerous amusement. But suppose I afterward carry the paper before a notary public and make affidavit to its contents. This may prove to be a horse of another color. The reason is that the affidavit may be used to determine an assent to the proposition it contains in the minds of judge and jury;—an effect that the paper would not have had if I had not sworn to it. For certain penalties here and hereafter are attached to swearing to a false proposition; and consequently the fact that I have sworn to it will be taken as a negative index that it is not false [MS 517; NEM 4:249].

As these passages clearly show, the association of penalties with a false assertion is required by the communicative function of an assertion. According to Peirce, every situation in which a proposition is used for the purpose of performing some speech act (every communication situation) involves at least two participants, an *utterer* and an *interpreter* (or a speaker and a hearer) (CP 2.334).[3] The function of an assertion, according to Peirce, is, first, to express the utterer's belief (or beliefs) about something and "to make the person addressed [that is, the interpreter] to think in a certain way" (MS 284, 41–42), that is, to agree with the utterer: "The assertion consists in furnishing of evidence by the speaker to the listener that the speaker believes something, that is, finds a certain idea to be definitively compulsory on a certain occasion" [MS 787; CP 2.335].

> Clearly, every assertion involves an effort to make the intended interpreter believe what is asserted, to which end a reason for believing it must be furnished. But if a lie would not endanger the esteem in which the utterer was held, nor otherwise be apt to entail such real effects as he would avoid, the interpreter would have no reason to believe the assertion. Nobody takes any positive stock in those conventional utterances, such as "I am perfectly delighted to see you," upon whose falsehood no punishment at all is visited [CP 5.546].

In his discussion of Frege's philosophy of language Michael Dummett denies that an assertion (as a speech act type) can be characterized by its consequences: according to Dummett, such a characterization is applicable to commands (imperatives), but not to assertions. But when he tries to characterize assertive speech acts, Dummett unwittingly or implicitly resorts to a Peircean kind of analysis; he notes that "we should utter [assertoric] sentences with the intention of uttering only true ones" (1981, 302). This characterization is a norm requiring that a speaker make (or at least try to make) only true assertions. The meaning of a normative utterance of the form 'a should do F' (or 'a, do F!') is usually explained by saying that if a does not do F, that is, if a fails to comply with the norm, a will be subject to some sanction or punishment; Dummett himself explains the meaning of normative utterances in this way (1981, 301–302). According to this interpretation of normative utterances, the requirement (or norm) that assertions should be true entails the Peircean analysis.

The Peircean analysis of assertions creates the following symmetry between assertions and imperatives (or commands). In the case of an assertion, the speaker is responsible for the agreement or the fit between the content of his utterance and the world (how things are), but in the case of imperatives and commands, the hearer or the addressee is responsible for this agreement. In the latter case the "world" usually consists of the hearer's actions. In this respect commands can be regarded as mirror images of assertions.[4]

III

Peirce analyzed the structure of propositions by explaining how they and their parts function in communication situations involving a speaker and a hearer. He was mainly interested in the assertive use of propositions, apparently because he took logic to be concerned mainly with assertions: "Among all the thoughts that language may be used to express,—such as emotions, commands, etc., logic limits its concerns to *assertions*, to signs of the truth of assertions, and to other signs involved in those" (MS 10, 9).

This observation should not be taken to mean that an assertion is a kind of proposition: an assertion is a certain kind of *utterance* of a proposition. An utterance is an occurrence or an instance of a proposition. A proposition "may be contemplated as a sign capable of being asserted" (CP 2.252), as a potential assertion, and the logical and semantic properties of propositions reflect this possibility. Peirce was mainly concerned with the assertive use of propositions, but he made interesting observations about other speech act types as well. For example, he noted that interrogative speech acts (questions) can be regarded as a special case of imperatives (CP 8.369),[5] a view that underlies much of the contemporary work on the logic of questions (Åqvist 1965 and 1972; Hintikka 1974 and 1976).

IV

Peirce regarded the *sentence* and the *proper name* as the basic grammatical categories, and defined the *predicate* or the *rheme* in the same way as Frege did, that is, as an incomplete expression (or sign) that becomes a sentence upon completion by one or several proper names: "If parts of a proposition be erased so as to leave *blanks* in their places, and if these blanks are of such a nature that if each of them be filled by a proper name the result will be a proposition, then the blank form of proposition which was first produced by the erasures is termed a *rheme* [or a predicate]" (CP 2.272).

Peirce analyzed the structure and the meaning of propositional signs by using his fundamental semeiotic concepts, namely, the concepts of the *object* and the *interpretant* of a sign, and the threefold classification of signs into *icons*, *indices*, and *symbols*. The interpretant of a sign is a sign in terms of which the first sign can be interpreted; the interpretant of a sign expresses its "meaning" or "content," whereas the object of a sign is what the sign represents or that to which it refers. The distinction between the object and the interpretant of a sign bears a superficial resemblance to Frege's distinction between the *Bedeutung* (the referent) and the *Sinn* (the meaning) of an expression, but is actually quite different, and should not be confused with Frege's distinction. Peirce characterized the object and the interpretant of a sign as follows:

> A sign, or *representamen*, is something which stands to somebody for something in some respect or capacity. It addresses somebody, that is, creates in the mind of that person an equivalent sign, or perhaps a more developed sign. That sign which it creates I call the *interpretant* of the first sign. The sign stands for something, its *object* [CP 2.228].

In his theory of signs Peirce distinguished several *kinds* of objects and interpretants; for example, he makes a distinction between the *immediate object* and the *dynamical object* of a sign: "We have to distinguish the Immediate Object, which is the Object as the Sign itself represents it, and whose being is thus dependent upon the representation of it in the Sign, from the

Dynamical Object, which is the reality which by some means contrives to determine the Sign to its Representation" (CP 4.536). Here I shall consistently use the expression "object" in the sense of a dynamical or "external" object of a sign.[6]

In general, we need not assume that the interpretant is "in the mind" of an interpreter; whenever in a process of interpretation a sign is associated with the sign of a given object as another sign of the same object, the second sign is an interpretant of the first. Thus, the object of the interpretant sign is the same as the object of the sign of which it is an interpretant.

A sign can refer to its object (or objects) in different ways or on different grounds: if a sign is related to an object on the basis of similarity or resemblance (in some respect), it is called an *icon*; if the relationship to the object is an existential or a dynamic connection (for example, a causal relation), it is called an *index* of the object, and if something is an object of the sign simply because the latter is interpreted as a sign of the object, the sign is called a *symbol* (CP 2.274–302). All linguistic signs are, of course, symbols; but some symbols can be regarded as symbolic substitutes for iconic signs: they have iconic interpretants and may be called iconic symbols. There are also symbols which "act very much like indices," demonstrative pronouns and proper names, for example; signs of this kind may be termed indexical symbols.[7]

V

Peirce regarded a proposition as "equivalent to a sentence in the indicative mood" (CP 2.315) and assumed that every proposition consists of a subject (or subjects) and a predicate: "A proposition consists of two parts, the *predicate* which excites something like an image or dream in the mind of the interpreter, and the subject, or subjects, each of which serves to identify something which the predicate represents" (MS 280, 32).

In Peirce's classification of signs, the subject of a proposition is either an index or an indexical symbol; its function is to direct the interpreter's attention to a certain object or objects. The predicate of a proposition is what in Peirce's terminology may be called an iconic symbol: it is a sign which is interpreted in terms of an icon—or which has an iconic sign as its interpretant. Thus, a proposition gives information about the object indicated by its subject by representing the icon signified by its predicate as an icon of the object.

> It is remarkable that while neither a pure icon nor a pure index can assert anything, an index which forces something to be an icon, as a weathercock does, or which forces us to regard it as an icon (of something), as the legend under a portrait does, does make an assertion, and forms a proposition. This suggests a true definition of a proposition, which is a question in much dispute at the moment. *A proposition is a sign which separately, or independently, indicates its object* [MS 517; NEM 4:242; emphasis added].

The definition expressed by the last sentence occurs again and again in Peirce's writings; it is his "standard definition" of a proposition.

What is the object of a proposition? In CP 5.474 Peirce gives the following answer to this question: "The interpretant of a proposition is its predicate; its object is the things denoted by its subject or subjects (including its grammatical objects, direct and indirect, etc.)." In the same way, in CP 2.230 Peirce noted that "A sign may have more than one object. Thus, the sentence 'Cain killed Abel', which is a sign, refers at least as much to Abel as to Cain, even if it be not regarded as it should, as having '*a killing*' as a third Object. But the set of objects may be regarded as making up one complex Object."[8] According to the view formulated above, the object of a sentence or of a proposition is whatever is indicated by its subject. It may seem odd to call the predicate of a proposition its interpretant, but this usage is consistent with Peirce's definition of the concepts of sign and interpretant. For example, in his article "Sign" in J. M. Baldwin's *Dictionary of Philosophy and Psychology* Peirce said that a sign is "anything which determines something else (its *interpretant*) to refer to an object to which it itself refers (its *object*) in the same way, the interpretant in turn becoming a sign, and so on *ad infinitum*" (CP 2.303).[9]

As was mentioned earlier, the object of the interpretant of a sign is the same as the object of the sign itself: "The interpretant of a sign can represent no other object than that of the sign itself" (CP 2.310). A proposition represents the object indicated by its subject as the object of its predicate; thus, the predicate can indeed be regarded as an interpretant of the proposition. (It constitutes the "content" of the proposition.) As an interpretant of a sentence or of a proposition, a predicate can have an object which does not in fact comply with the predicate and its iconic interpretants. In this way a proposition can misrepresent its object. This is Peirce's solution to the problem of misrepresentation which has recently vexed philosophers who have attempted to develop causal (in Peirce's terminology, *indexical*) theories of information content (see Dretske 1986; Fodor 1987, chap. 4).

According to Peirce, a sentence or a proposition can be divided into the subject and the predicate in different ways, and the distinction between the object and the interpretant of a sentence is subject to similar indeterminacy. In different contexts Peirce suggested different conventions for resolving this indeterminacy. In CP 5.474 (MS 318, "Pragmatism") he adopted the following proposal:

> Take the proposition "Burnt child shuns fire." Its predicate might be regarded as all that it expressed, or as "has either not been burned or shuns fire," or "has not been burned," or "shuns fire," or "shuns," or "is true"; nor is this enumeration exhaustive. But where shall the line be most truly drawn? I reply that the purpose of this sentence being understood to be to communicate information, anything belongs to the interpretant that describes the quality or character of the fact, anything to the object that, without doing that, distinguishes the fact from others like it . . . [CP 5.474].

No matter how the distinction between the subject and the predicate is made, a proposition (a potential assertion) should be regarded as a complex consisting of two signs, an indexical sign and an iconic sign; otherwise it could not convey information.[10] Moreover, any "ordinary" proposition that purports to assert something about reality or the "real universe" has that universe as its object, but usually a proposition can also be regarded as having as its "special object" some restricted part of the universe:

> All ordinary propositions refer to the real universe, and usually to the nearer environment [CP 2.357].

> In every case the object is accurately the Universe of which the special Object is a member, or part [CP 8.177, note 4].

Peirce drew a distinction between the "Object-at-large" and the "Special Object" of a proposition—the former is the whole universe or the reality the sentence refers to. If a proposition contains a proper name, the object of the name is a "special object" of the proposition. Can quantified sentences be regarded as having "special objects" in addition to the universe they refer to? This question has recently puzzled some philosophers who have tried to apply the *de dicto/de re* distinction to general beliefs (see Dennett 1982). Peirce's example in CP 5.474 (quoted above) shows that the content-object distinction can be drawn for quantified sentences in different ways, just as in the case of other sentences.[11] According to Peirce, however, quantified sentences have the peculiarity that they can be regarded as referring to certain special objects *indeterminately* (CP 5.448 note, MS 283). Peirce's account of this (metaphorical) notion will be discussed below in sections IX–XI.

One of the most important insights of Peirce's theory of the proposition is his observation that the identity of the proposition uttered on a certain occasion often depends on the context of the utterance:

> If somebody rushes into a room and says, "There is a great fire!" we know he is talking about the neighborhood and not about the world of *Arabian Nights' Entertainments*. It is the circumstances under which the proposition is uttered or written which indicate that environment as that which is referred to. But they do so not simply as an index of the environment, but as evidence of an intentional relation of the speech to its object which relation it could not have if it were not intended for a sign [CP 2.357].

Several important characteristics of propositions and their objects are brought out in this passage. In the light of it, Peirce's statement that a proposition is "equivalent to a sentence in the indicative mood" is seen to be somewhat misleading (or an oversimplification), since the index that, according to him, must be found in every proposition, belongs to the utterance (or the occasion of utterance) rather than to the sentence uttered. The context of an utterance serves as an index which identifies the object of the proposition. (This feature of propositions will be discussed further in sections VI-VIII in the case of proper names.) A proposition must always contain an index, because "The real world cannot be distinguished from a fictitious world by any description" (CP 2.337).[12]

According to Peirce, 'real' (in the sense of 'actual') is an indexical term. A proposition must also contain an iconic sign (or iconic signs), because the indices alone cannot convey information.[13] The view that a proposition must contain an index is one of the central doctrines of Peirce's philosophy of language and philosophical logic. It is related to Peirce's willingness to countenance different universes or "possible worlds" as interpretations of one's language.[14] In this respect Peirce disagreed with Frege and Russell, who take all discourse to be discourse about a single all-encompassing world (see Hintikka 1988, 2). (This difference between Peirce and Frege will be discussed further in section XIII.)

VI

The subject of a proposition can be (i) a genuine *index*, "like the environment of the interlocutors (the utterer and the interpreter), or something attracting attention in that environment, as the pointing finger of the speaker," or a simple indexical symbol—for example, a proper name, a personal pronoun, or a demonstrative; or (ii) a complex (indexical) symbol that describes what the speaker and the hearer must do "in order to obtain an index of an individual of which the proposition is meant to be true," and "assigns a designation to that individual" (CP 2.330). Peirce called such symbols *precepts*, and regarded definite descriptions and quantifier phrases as examples of them. I shall discuss first Peirce's account of the semantics of proper names, and in sections IX-XI his analysis of precepts.

The function of an index (or of an indexical symbol) is to draw the interpreter's attention to a certain object or to indicate a certain object for the interpreter. A genuine index functions in this way by virtue of an existential connection between the object and the sign. A proper name is a symbol, a general type, but its instances or *replicas* can be existentially connected with its object, and such replicas can be regarded as genuine indices. Peirce gave the following description of the way in which a name typically acquires its indexical function.

> A proper name, when one meets with it for the first time, is existentially connected with some precept or other equivalent individual knowledge of the individual it names. It is then, and only then, a genuine index. The next time one meets with it, one regards it as an icon of that index. The habitual acquaintance with it having been acquired, it becomes a symbol whose interpretant represents it as an icon of an index of the individual named [CP 2.329].

As Peirce suggested here, a proper name is a symbolic substitute for an index—or an indexical symbol. It is a "remote index" of an object, to be used in situations in which the object is not present and a "proximate index," such as a demonstrative pronoun, is therefore inapplicable (CP 2.287 note 1). Since "attention can only be drawn to what is already in experience," a proper name "can function as such only if the utterer and the interpreter are already more or less familiar with the object it names" (MS 516, 40). Thus, a logically proper name "denotes a single individual well known to exist by the utterer and the interpreter" (MS 517; NEM 4:243). A proper name is a symbolic sign, and it can function as such only if it is *intended* or understood as an indexical sign of its object (CP 2.357).

VII

The requirement of familiarity Peirce accepted here resembles Bertrand Russell's condition of acquaintance for proper names: genuine proper names can refer only to individuals (or objects) the speaker is acquainted with.[15] But as Peirce's expression "more or less familiar" suggests, his interpretation of this requirement is much broader and more flexible than Russell's requirement of acquaintance. According to Peirce, the speaker's and the hearer's experience of the object of a proper name may be "proximate or remote" (CP 2.337). If a speaker (or a hearer) is acquainted with the object of the name, and uses the name with an appropriate intention, the name functions, according to Peirce, as a genuine proper name *for the speaker* (or the hearer).[16]

This formulation suggests an obvious generalization of the requirement of acquaintance: a name functions as a proper name in a certain speech community or linguistic community only if it functions as a proper name (in the sense described above) for *some* members of the community. This is possible only if some members of the community are acquainted with the object of the name.[17]

Peirce suggested in several texts that a person's "familiarity" or "acquaintance" with an object does not necessarily mean perceptual acquaintance, but only an ability to distinguish it from all the other objects that exist in the logical universe (MS 280, 38).

According to Peirce, it is possible to distinguish three different stages in a person's "acquaintance and familiarity" with a name and its object.

> In what may be called the ideally normal course of a person's acquaintance with a logically proper name, it passes successively from being an indefinite singular term to being a definite singular term, and after that to being a definite general term. For on the first hearing of it, one gathers that it is a singular; but since the word is without signification, the hearer to whom it is strange will be able to gather from any [statement] he may hear made of its object only that there exists something having the characters asserted. But as he subsequently meets with the term time and again, he gradually comes to learn enough about its object readily to distinguish it from all the other singulars that exist. The term then first functions for him as a proper name. Finally, when everybody in the community is perfectly familiar with the chief characteristics of the singular object, if one of these should be very prominent, there will be a tendency to use the name predicatively to signify that character [MS 280, 37–38].

An expression can function as a proper name of an object for the interpreter only if he knows enough about the object to be able to distinguish it from all the other existing singulars—that is, if the interpreter knows *who* or *which individual* the object of the name is. This familiarity (or knowledge) need not amount to direct perceptual acquaintance. If the interpreter does not know the object, the name functions (for the interpreter) as an *indefinite singular term*, that is, as an indexical part of an existential quantifier phrase. (Expressions of this kind will be discussed in sections IX–X.) When the interpreter is not yet familiar with the name (and its object), that is, when the name still functions as an indefinite singular term, it may be said to "signify" the icons associated with it, but this is only "accidental and insufficient signification" (MS 280, 42). When the name reaches its "second stage of maturity," it needs no signification, and the icons associated with it serve as information about its object. Peirce used "Gordius" as an example:

> On first hearing the name ["Gordius"], one gathers that he is or was *some man*. Next one may gather that he was some adventurer; next that he was some *Phrygian*, next that he was *some king*, etc. But when the name has become familiar and reaches its second stage of evolution—is, in short, used and accepted as a true proper name,—one places Gordius in his proper place in one's mental chart of ancient history, and those predicates no longer serve as signification, but as information. The name now neither needs nor bears any signification [MS 280, 42–43].

At this stage of its evolution the applicability of a name to a given object "is not contingent upon that object's fulfilling this or that general condition, but depends solely upon the previous establishment of such a wide-spread habit of speech that the word or phrase is reasonably certain of being understood to denote the very singular that was actually intended" (MS 280, 41). According to Peirce, such a "habit of speech" is established and maintained with the help of iconic signs that are used for the purpose of distinguishing the object of the name from other singular objects. A proper name can be introduced with the help of such descriptive signs, but these signs do not, according to Peirce, constitute a definition of the meaning of the name.

The interpreter can recognize an object only by means of certain *marks*, that is, on the basis of the characteristics possessed by the object:

> The object of a proper name, say the name of an acquaintance of the interpreter, can only be recognized by him by means of marks; and when he hears the name mentioned, the image excited in his imagination will be composed of marks (so to say); and any action he may take in consequence will be guided by those marks. Nay more: it may be granted that the name was conferred in the first instance and its use has been maintained ever since with the definite intention that the individual should be recognized in the manner thus described [MS 283, "assorted pages" numbered 143–44 near the end of the manuscript].

Thus the recognition of the object of a proper name is possible with the help of various *iconic* signs associated with the name. But these icons are not essentially associated with the name. They are not part of its "meaning"; a proper name does not "signify" anything.

> Yet it does not follow and could only very rarely be true that the name *signifies* certain defining marks, so as to be applicable to anything that should possess those marks, and to nothing else. For not to speak of the fact that the interpreter only uses the marks as aids in guessing at his acquaintance's identity, and may possibly be mistaken, however extraordinary they may be, there will be no one *definite* set of marks which the name signifies rather than another set of equally conclusive marks. If there were any mark which a proper name could be said *essentially* to signify, it would be the continuity of the history of its object [MS 283, "assorted pages" numbered 144–45 near the end of the manuscript].

Here Peirce in effect distinguished a proper name from a definite description: the latter signifies certain characters *essentially* and is therefore applicable to anything possessing these characteristics, whereas the icons associated with a proper name determine (for the interpreter) its reference without being part of its meaning. They are, in Peirce's words, part of the "collateral experience" (or information) that helps to identify the object of the name (CP 8.178). Such icons are not part of the interpretant of the proposition in which the name occurs. They can be regarded as analogous to the context of utterance of a proposition which helps to determine its object. We might say that the iconic descriptions associated with a name are a way of pointing to the object of the name (see Kaplan 1977). In the above passage Peirce also recognized the possibility that icons in question need not give a completely accurate "picture" of the object of name. (This might be called the "Donnellan point"; see Donnellan 1966.) The distinction between names and definite descriptions which Peirce made in the above passage was later rediscovered by Keith Donnellan, David Kaplan, Saul Kripke, Hilary Putnam, and others, and has become an essential part of the recently celebrated "new theory of reference" or the theory of "direct reference."[18] The view that proper names are "remote indices" has become generally accepted in the contemporary philosophy of language, about seventy years after Peirce formulated this view.[19]

In CP 8.179 Peirce noted that "by collateral observation, I mean previous acquaintance with what the sign denotes." Collateral experience is experience *of* the object of a sign and can thus be regarded as an *indexical* sign of the object. According to this interpretation of "collateral experience," the information that identifies the object of a name must originate in the object and be determined by the object (CP 8.178). Thus, the object of a proper name can be determined not only by the causal history of (the tokens of) the name, but also by the origin of the information (that is, iconic signs) associated with the name.[20]

VIII

It is interesting to compare Peirce's account with Arthur Burks's theory of proper names, as outlined in his paper "A Theory of Proper Names" (1951), which was partly inspired by Peirce's theory of indexical signs and symbols. Burks observed that a correct account of proper names must employ Peirce's notion of the index, but he complemented this view with the Fregean (or perhaps we should say quasi-Fregean) idea that every occurrence (token) of any proper name is synonymous with a description. Burks argued that proper names should be regarded as synonymous with "indexical definite descriptions" (for example, "this young woman"); but different occurrences or tokens of a given name can have different meanings. According to Burks, "a person cannot be said to understand a proper name unless he has in mind some nonindexical properties which (together with the indexical elements of the name) would enable him sometimes to decide whether a given individual is the designatum of the name or not" (1951, 44).

I shall not attempt to evaluate Burks's proposal here, but his remarks on the "understanding" of a proper name come close to Peirce's account of the identification of the object of a name by means of marks (iconic signs). Burks's view that the tokens (occurrences) of a certain proper name may be synonymous with different descriptions can perhaps be regarded as a peculiar way of expressing the Peircean view that names have no "essential" signification.[21] Of course, Peirce would not say that the icons associated with a name are part of its meaning; according to him, the icons serve as "collateral experience" or information (CP 8.178) which helps to identify the object.

David Kaplan has called names that satisfy a condition similar to Peirce's requirement of familiarity (or acquaintance, in the wide sense) *vivid* names. According to Kaplan, vivid names stand for "those persons [individuals] who fill major roles in that *inner story* which consists of all those sentences which [a person] believes" (1969, 229). Peirce expressed this epistemic condition by speaking about the "proper place" of the object in "one's mental chart" of the subject matter under discussion (for example, ancient history).

It is clear that this epistemic condition of familiarity can be satisfied by a name that does not in fact have an object—that is, a "dynamic," external object (Kaplan 1969, 231–33). A putative object may have a well-defined place in "one's mental chart" even though the place in question is not filled by any existing object; this is the case if the tokens of the proper name in question and the information (that is, the icons) attached to the name lack a unique origin. According to Peirce's criteria for proper names, such an expression would not be a genuine proper name; to use Peirce's expression: it would be only an *imitation* name or an expression "simulating" a proper name.[22]

What is the status of *fictional* names? Should they be regarded as imitation names or as genuine names? Peirce seems to adopt the latter view when he says that the proposition "Hamlet was mad" "relates to [that is, has as its object] a great creation more enduring than bronze" (CP 2.342).

It is possible to distinguish two different ways of using fictional names. In an act of telling (or creating) a story, the author of a fictional narrative may be said to use fictional names performatively or *creatively*, but such names can also be used *descriptively* to refer to the characters created by an author.[23] When a fictional name, such as "Hamlet," is used descriptively, it refers to a certain character and can be regarded as a genuine name (as an indexical symbol).[24] In the paragraph quoted above, Peirce appears to be referring to the descriptive use of the name "Hamlet."[25] But when a storyteller is using a fictional name in his story (within fiction), the name is not an index of any particular entity; it can then be regarded as an "imitation name."[26] In the recent discussion of the semantics of fictional discourse several authors have adopted this view; for example, Saul Kripke, David Lewis, and John Searle have argued that the act of telling a story can be regarded as a form of "pretending," and that fictional names (internally used) are merely "pretend names."[27] A person who is telling a story (a fiction) does not really make assertions, but is only pretending to do so; to use Peirce's words, he utters only "imitation propositions."

Peirce sometimes described a sign as being "determined" by its object, which thus, through the mediation of the sign, determines an interpretant in the mind of the interpreter.[28] This characterization is particularly apposite in the case of those indexical signs which are causally affected by, or dependent on, their objects. The relationship between a sign and its object is understood according to this model in some contemporary causal theories of meaning and reference (see Stampe 1979, 82). The cases in which an object is given a name (or "dubbed") by means of a description do not fit the simple causal model (see Kaplan 1989a, 604–609). Peirce seems to have been aware of this possibility when he remarked that a name can be "conferred" on an individual by means of marks, that is, by certain iconic signs (or with the intention that the individual should be recognized by means of certain marks); this suggests that it is possible to baptize an individual through a description, that is, by means of an iconic sign. In this way it might be possible to name objects and individuals with which the members of a linguistic community do not (and perhaps cannot) have any perceptual acquaintance.[29] In such cases a name is conferred on an object with the understanding that the name denotes the individual that in fact satisfies (or will satisfy) the description used as a means of baptizing the object, but according to Peirce the name cannot be regarded as synonymous with the description (or iconic sign) in question.

Peirce's theory of proper names is a "direct reference theory" in David Kaplan's sense: "the relation between the linguistic expression [a name] and the referent is not mediated by the corresponding propositional component, the content or what-is-said" (1989a, 568). In Peirce's terminology, this condition can be expressed by saying that the relation between a name and its object is not mediated by the interpretant of the sentence in which the name is used. This helps one to understand Peirce's view that the interpretant of a sentence or a proposition is its predicate. According to Kaplan's account of direct reference, the object of a name is itself a constituent of a proposition—Kaplan speaks about "loading [an individual] into the proposition" (1989a, 569).[30] Peirce understood the notion of proposition differently. According to Peirce, an object of a proposition can be one of its constituents only in exceptional and abnormal cases;[31] for him, a proposition is a sign, and its constituents include indexical signs that refer to the objects of the proposition.

IX

I shall now turn to cases in which the subject of a proposition is a complex expression involving common nouns. According to Peirce, such complex expressions function in basically the same way as indexical expressions. They can be regarded as indexical symbols. Peirce characterized the use of common names in the subject-position of a sentence as follows: The function of a common noun is the same as that of the Proper Name. That is, it merely draws attention to an object and so puts its interpreter into condition to learn whatever there may be to be learned from such attention. Now attention can only be drawn to what is already in experience. A proper name can only function as such if the utterer and interpreter are already more or less familiar with the object it names. But the peculiarity of a common noun is that it undertakes to draw attention to an object with which the interpreter may have no acquaintance. For this purpose it calls up to his mind such an image as a verb calls up, appeals to his memory that he has seen different objects [as] the subjects of that image, . . . and then of those which might be so recollected or imagined, the noun indefinitely names one [MS 516, 39–40].

What does it mean to say that a common noun, when it occurs in the subject of a sentence, names an object "indefinitely"? A name either is or is not a name of a given object; there is no third possibility. "Indefinite name" and "indefinite naming" are elliptical expressions. One of the most interesting features of Peirce's theory of language is his explanation of how these expressions are to be understood. Bertrand Russell wrestled in Chapter 5 of *The Principles of Mathematics* (1903) with questions about "indeterminate denotation" without much success, but found an answer to these questions in his paper "On Denoting" (1905); the answer was the translation of denoting phrases into quantificational idiom. Peirce's solution was not unlike Russell's, but instead of presenting a translation of quantifier phrases into the language of quantification theory, Peirce gave a semantical account of such phrases.

If the subject of a sentence is not a simple indexical expression, such as a proper name or a pronoun, Peirce called it a *precept* (CP 2.330). A precept does not denote (or indicate) any definite singular object, but shows how the utterer and the interpreter should act in order to find a singular object or an "occasion of experience" to which the predicate may be regarded as being applicable (CP 2.330, 2.336).

Peirce called such expressions indeterminate signs. An indeterminate indexical symbol can be interpreted, or, as Peirce also said, *explicated*, as representing more than one singular object

(MS 283, 139 among the "assorted pages" near the end of the manuscript). I shall extend Peirce's use of the word 'index' slightly and call such signs *indeterminate indices*.

An indeterminate subject consists, not of a common noun alone, but of a common noun and a quantifier or a *selective*, which indicates the type of indeterminacy exemplified by a given proposition. Peirce distinguished two main types of indeterminacy, which he calls *indefiniteness* (or particularity) and *generality* (or universality) (MS 283; CP 5.448 note). Indefiniteness is indicated by an existential quantifier or "selective" (or by a quantifier phrase); generality, by a universal quantifier. Peirce mentioned the English words *any, every, all, no, none, whatever, whoever, everybody, anybody,* and *nobody* as examples of universal selectives, and the expressions *some, something, somebody, a, a certain, some or other, a suitable,* and *one* as examples of particular selectives. He noted that there are a host of other selectives that do not belong to either of the two main types (or classes) mentioned above: for example, *all but one, one or two, a few, nearly all,* or *every other one* (CP 2.289, 2.339). Peirce called the absence of indefiniteness definiteness, and the absence of generality individuality. Every sign is either individual (not general) or definite (not indefinite), and a sign that is both definite and individual is called a *singular* sign (MS 9; MS 515, 20–21).

X

How does a precept, or an indeterminate index, show what the utterer and the interpreter must do in order to find a singular object or an index of a singular object that may be regarded as the subject of the assertion (or proposition)? Peirce's explanation of the meaning of quantifier phrases is based on his account of the use of a proposition in an assertion, and it resembles the modern game-theoretical interpretation of quantifiers.[32]

By asserting a certain proposition, the utterer accepts responsibility for it and subjects himself to certain penalties in case the proposition turns out to be false. Thus, the utterer is essentially a defender of any proposition that he may assert. On the other hand, it is important for the interpreter to detect any falsehood asserted by the utterer, since, as Peirce noted, "the affirmation of a proposition may determine a judgment to the same effect in the mind of the interpreter to his cost" (MS 517; NEM 4:249). Hence, the utterer and the interpreter have opposite interests and attitudes with respect to the verification of any proposition the utterer asserts.

> The utterer is essentially a defender of his own proposition, and wishes to interpret it so that it will be defensible. The interpreter, not being so interested, and being unable to interpret it fully without considering to what extreme it may reach, is relatively in a hostile attitude, and looks for the interpretation least defensible [MS 9, 3-4].

Peirce sometimes called the interpreter of a proposition its "opponent" (for example, in MS 515, 25). Thus, the language game played by the utterer and the interpreter with respect to an indeterminate proposition is, according to Peirce, a zero-sum game.[33]

Given this asymmetry in the roles of the utterer and the interpreter, the meaning of different types of indeterminate indices may be explained as follows: An indeterminate index is indefinite if and only if the utterer of the proposition may select the object that the index should be regarded as representing, that is, if the utterer is free to choose the interpretation of the subject term. An existential quantifier signifies the utterer's choice or "move" in the language-game. In the case of a definite proposition, the utterer has no such latitude on interpretation: "A definite proposition is one the assertor [that is, the utterer] of which leaves himself no loop hole for escape against attack by saying that he did not mean so and so, but something else" (MS 515, 25).

Moreover, not only may the utterer not leave himself any such latitude of interpretation, but he may also, as Peirce says, allow "his opponent [that is, the interpreter] a choice as to what singular object he will instance to refute the proposition, as in 'Any man you please is mortal'" (MS 515, 25). In other words, if the proposition has a general index, the interpreter has the right to choose the singular object the proposition is regarded as representing: a universal quantifier transfers the choice of the singular to the interpreter.

> It seems an odd thing, when one comes to ponder it, that there should be such a mode of signification as the latter [that is, generality], in which the utterer of a sign transfers to its interpreter the office of determining what that sign is to be apprehended as meaning. Its familiarity blinds us to the wonder of it [MS 283, 136 among the "assorted pages" near the end of the manuscript].

If an indeterminate index is a complex quantifier phrase involving several quantifiers, each existential quantifier indicates the utterer's choice of a singular object and each universal quantifier the interpreter's choice. Peirce observed that "whichever of the two makes his choice of the object he is to choose, after the other has made his choice, is supposed to know what that choice was. This is an advantage to the defence or attack, as the case may be" (MS 9, para. 3). Here Peirce assumed that the semantical games he was describing are games with perfect information; this amounts to the assumption that the quantifiers in a complex indeterminate index are always ordered and do not branch.[34] Consequently, every indeterminate index is either individual (not general) or definite (not indefinite), since the choice of an object cannot simultaneously belong to both parties (both the utterer and the interpreter) (cf. MS 9, para. 2).

If the truth of a proposition is defined as the utterer's ability to defend it successfully against the interpreter's attack, this analysis of quantifier phrases gives quantified sentences correct truth-conditions and is essentially similar to the game-theoretical interpretation of quantifiers. Peirce did not possess a well-defined concept of *strategy*, but his concept of *defensibility against attack* comes close to the game-theoretical analysis of truth. (A sentence is true if and only if its utterer has a winning strategy in the game associated with it; cf. Hintikka 1979, 36 and 1988, 29.)

XI

I have discussed above Peirce's analysis of quantified propositions (propositions containing indeterminate indexical symbols). Many other complex sentences and sentence forms can be understood in a similar way. For example, Peirce observed that a necessary proposition is a sort of universally quantified proposition, and a statement of possibility can be regarded as an existential proposition (CP 2.382). Thus, modal expressions can also be understood in terms of the choices made by the utterer and the interpreter in a language-game, but in this case the players make choices, not among the individuals of a given universe, but among possible courses of events or "possible cases." For example, to say that S *may* be P amounts to saying that "P is true of S under *some conceivable* circumstances which I don't know, or don't say, are not those of the present occasion," whereas the statement that S *must* be P means that "P is true of S under such conceivable circumstances as *you choose to specify*" (MS 642, 19). In MS 137 Peirce characterized necessary propositions as follows:[35] "A necessary proposition is one which makes its predication of whatever case the *interpreter* may imagine, as contradistinguished from a universal proposition which allows the interpreter to choose only among existent cases" (NEM 2:516).

Peirce characterized both universal and necessary propositions as propositions to which "the principle of the excluded middle does not apply," and particular propositions and statements of possibility as propositions to which "the principle of contradiction does not apply" (MS 642). The former are *general* propositions; the latter, *vague* propositions. By this characterization Peirce meant that both 'S must be P' and 'S must be not-P' may be false, whereas both 'S may be P' and 'S may be not-P' may be true; and, analogously, both 'All S are P' and 'All S are not-P' may be false, and both 'Some S is P' and 'Some S is not-P' may be true.

The usual truth-functional sentence connectives can of course be given a similar pragmatic or game-theoretical interpretation (see Brock 1980, 61–63). Conjunctive or "copulative" propositions "offer the interpreter a choice of several simple propositions," whereas disjunctive propositions "reserve [to the utterer] the determination of which simple proposition is true" (MS 290, 53). The operation of negation reverses the roles of the advocate and the opponent of a proposition (CP 3.480–482), just as in game-theoretical semantics.

According to Peirce, the conditional propositions of ordinary speech are usually "a particular category of disjunctives," namely, *modal* disjunctive propositions:

> Thus to say, "If it rains I shall want an umbrella" means, for logical purposes . . . , precisely that every prospective state of the weather worth considering will either be a state in which there will be no rain to speak of or will be a state in which I shall need an umbrella. To say that if Napoleon had been in his best trim he would have won the battle of Waterloo, so far as it means anything, means that taking all the different possible courses of events that might reasonably be admitted as such by taking into consideration the variations of power shown by Napoleon during his life, while external circumstances remain substantially as they were, every such possible course of events would either be one in which Napoleon was not in his best trim or would be one in which he would have won the battle of Waterloo [MS 284, 29].

If we take "external circumstances" to mean circumstances which are independent of (or "external" to) the antecedent of the conditional, this account of the meaning of a conditional statement comes close to the characterization of subjunctive (as opposed to "material") conditionals as "variably strict" conditionals (see Lewis 1973).

XII

Peirce did not restrict the use of the word "precept" to indeterminate indices. In his famous analysis of what *lithium* is (CP 2.330), he noted that instead of an ordinary definition, one could give a "precept" which "is more serviceable than a definition [in that] it tells you what the word lithium denotes by prescribing what you are to *do* in order to gain a perceptual acquaintance with the object of the word." Peirce was considering here the question what the word "lithium" denotes and how the object of the word can be determined and distinguished from other substances.

The passage in question suggests that the word "lithium" should be regarded as essentially similar to a proper name (a name of a substance): according to this interpretation, the iconic signs associated with the precept constitute "collateral experience" (or information) necessary for identifying the object of the word (CP 8.178), but they need not be regarded as part of the "essential signification" of the word. (According to this interpretation, the word "lithium" need not have any "essential signification.") In the light of this example, the game-theoretical account of indeterminate indices (or indeterminate indexical symbols) is simply a pragmatic explication of the metaphorical expression "indeterminate reference" (or "indeterminate denotation").

XIII

Perhaps the most striking feature of Peirce's account of the semantics of simple and complex sentences, quantifier phrases, and proper names is its *pragmatic character*. As we have seen, Peirce explained the meanings of indexical symbols, propositional connectives, and modal concepts by conceptual models describing how the speaker and the interpreter use and interpret these expressions. Thus, Charles Morris's famous semantics-pragmatics distinction seems in certain respects quite alien to Peirce's view of language and its interpretation. Pragmatics is defined by Morris as the "study of the relations of signs to interpreters," and semantics as the study of the "relations of the signs to the objects to which the signs are applicable" (see 1938/1971, 6). According to Peirce's semantics, the semantic relationships between expressions and objects are in many cases constituted by the activities of the speaker and the interpreter; in this respect his semantics has a "pragmatic" character. This is especially clear in the case of complex sentences and quantifier phrases, which are explicated by Peirce by means of certain semantical games. In this case the talk about the "object" of the proposition is partly metaphorical, because the object (that is, the "special object") in question is identified only within the semantical game which characterizes the expression in question. For example, in the course of a game which "explicates" an indeterminate subject, the actions of the utterer and the interpreter determine the object to which the predicate is regarded as being applicable (CP 2.330, 2.336).

Jean van Heijenoort (1967) and Jaakko Hintikka (1979, 1988; Hintikka and Hintikka 1986, chap. 1) have drawn attention to a contrast between two intellectual traditions in twentieth-century philosophy of language and logic, described by Hintikka as the conception of language as the universal medium of communication and the conception of language as calculus.[36] According to the former viewpoint, a speaker is, so to speak, a prisoner of his own language; it is impossible to "step outside" one's language to consider different interpretations (and reinterpretations) of it in a systematic way. This "universality" of language makes (according to the representatives of this tradition) a systematic, theoretical, and *formal* analysis of semantical questions impossible; the semantical relations between language and reality are inaccessible or "ineffable." This conception dominated the philosophy of language in the early part of the century; its main representatives were Gottlob Frege, Bertrand Russell, and Ludwig Wittgenstein. Frege's way of dealing with semantical questions by means of "hints and clues" illustrated this way of thinking: in Frege's logical work semantical issues remained "hidden" behind axiomatic and deductive techniques (see van Heijenoort 1967, 326; Hintikka 1979, 720). The second main intellectual tradition identified by Heijenoort and Hintikka, the language as calculus view, is the tradition of formal and model-theoretic semantics, represented by Ernst Schröder, Alfred Tarski, the later Rudolf Carnap, and their followers. As Jaakko Hintikka has pointed out, the central ideas of Peirce's philosophy of language are clearly associated with the latter tradition (1988, 27–29). Peirce tried to develop systematic theories of semantics, and his work contains the germs of many important contemporary developments in this field. The gamma part of Peirce's theory of logical graphs (existential graphs) contains, in a rudimentary form, the basic ideas of the possible worlds semantics of modal logic,[37] and (as was shown above) his pragmatic theory of complex sentences and quantifier phrases contains some of the main elements of game-theoretical semantics. Peirce's philosophy of language offers the beginnings of a comprehensive and fruitful research program, parts of which are being carried out in the contemporary philosophy of language.

NOTES

1. This paper is based on research supported by the Finnish State Council of the Humanities Grant No. 09/053. I am indebted to Jaakko Hintikka and Jarrett Brock for many discussions on the subject matter of this paper. I am particularly grateful to Brock for his comments and advice regarding Peirce's theory of proper names. I also want to thank Mrs. Rita Luoma for her assistance in the preparation of the paper.

2. Peirce's theory of speech acts and its relationship to contemporary theories has been studied by Jarrett Brock; see Brock 1981a and 1981b.

3. Peirce noted that the hearer or interpreter may have "only a problematical existence"; the problematical "listener may be within the same person as the speaker, as when we mentally register a judgement, to be remembered later" (CP 2.334).

4. A semantical theory of imperatives based on this view has been presented in Hilpinen 1986.

5. See also PW 85. Here Peirce distinguished three kinds of "effective" interpretants of signs, namely, Suggestives, Imperatives, and Indicatives. Peirce notes that "the Imperatives include Interrogatives."

6. For different objects and interpretants, see Eco 1981, Short 1981, and Zeman 1988.

7. According to Peirce, a proper name "differs from an index only in that it is a conventional sign" (MS 517; NEM 4:243).

8. It is interesting to observe that Peirce accepted here a "Davidsonian" analysis of action sentences, according to which simple action sentences refer to (individual) actions or act-individuals. Cf. Davidson 1967.

9. See also CP 2.321: "The proposition purports to intend to compel its Interpretant to refer to its real Object."

10. For example, Peirce noted in CP 2.314 that "An icon cannot, of itself, convey information, since its Object is whatever there may be which is like the Icon, and is its Object in the measure in which it is like the Icon"; thus, "Every assertion [and potential assertion, that is, proposition] is an assertion that two different signs have the same object" (CP 2.437).

11. In "Beyond Belief" Dennett asks, "Should we say entirely general beliefs are about anything?" (1982, 66). According to Peirce, such beliefs are at least about the universe to which they refer.

12. Cf. CP 2.295: "Let the sentence, then, be 'Ezekiel loveth Huldah.' Ezekiel and Huldah must, then, be or contain indices; for without indices it is impossible to designate what one is taking about. Any mere description would leave it uncertain whether they were not characters in a mere ballad; but whether they be so or not, indices can designate them." See also CP 2.287 and CP 2.305.

13. Cf. CP 2.278: "The only way of directly communicating an idea is by means of an icon; and every indirect method of communicating an idea must depend for its establishment upon the use of an icon. Hence, every assertion must contain an icon or set of icons, or else must contain signs whose meaning is only explicable by icons."

14. How can one refer to imaginary worlds or to mere "creations of our minds" by means of indices? According to Peirce (CP 2.305), there is a degenerate form of observation which is directed to the creations of our minds—using the word observation in its full sense implying some degree of fixity and quasi-reality in the object to which it endeavors to conform. This form of experience functions as an index of "imaginary universes." It should be noted here that in CP 5.474 Peirce regarded "the manner in which [an] assertion is made," that is, the modal part of a sentence, as part of the subject of a proposition, that is, as an indexical symbol.

15. Cf. Russell 1956, 205: "To understand a name you must be acquainted with the particular of which it is a name, and you must know that it is the name of that particular."

16. The following characterizations fit this model of proper names: "The name, or rather, occurrences of the name, must be existentially connected with the existent person (or object)" (CP 4.500). "[Proper names] should probably be regarded as indices, since the actual connection (as we listen to talk) of instances of the same typical words with the same Objects alone causes them to be interpreted as denoting those Objects" (CP 4.544). "A word is not a true proper name until one has experience of the object" (MS 49, 2).

17. Gareth Evans has suggested that the users of a proper name (in a certain linguistic community) can be divided into "producers" and "consumers"; the former are acquainted with the object of the name, and produce information about the object for the latter (1982, 376-78).

18. See the papers by Keith S. Donnellan, Saul Kripke, Hilary Putnam, and Gareth Evans in Schwartz, ed. 1977; Kaplan 1989a; and Kaplan 1989b.

19. The manuscripts discussed here were written in 1905. As I mentioned earlier, the present discussion concerns Peirce's "mature" view of names. In his recent paper "The Development of Peirce's Thoughts about Proper Names" (unpublished) Jarrett Brock has shown that in some of his early papers (from 1865 onward) Peirce seems to have adopted a some-

what different view of the semantics of proper names; Brock calls this view the "collective" or the "descriptive" view (as opposed to the "indexical" view discussed here).

20. This interpretation of Peirce's concept of "collateral experience" leads to an account of proper names which resembles the theory presented in Evans 1977. According to Evans, we can say that in general a speaker intends to refer to the item that is the dominant source of his associated body of information (208). By the "associated body of information" Evans means the information associated with a given name.

21. Burks's view foreshadows Kaplan's distinction between the character and the content of an indexical expression; cf. Kaplan 1979. According to Kaplan, the character of an expression determines its content in each context of utterance (1979, 403), but Burks's theory of proper names contains no counterpart of the character of a name—which may perhaps be regarded as an expression of the Peircean view that names have no "essential signification."

22. In CP 7.203 Peirce considers propositional expressions (or putative propositions) that contain "empty" names and predicates, and calls them "imitation propositions."

23. This distinction is related to (but is not identical with) Crittenden's distinction between "inside statements" and "outside statements" (1973, esp. 297–300).

24. For a good defense of this view, see Inwagen 1977.

25. See also Peirce's observation about the sentence "Hamlet is insane" in CP 8.178: "The Object of the sentence 'Hamlet was insane' is the Universe of Shakespeare's Creation so far as it is determined by Hamlet being part of it."

26. This is a plausible account of the creative use of fictional names, but it is not clear whether it can be attributed to Peirce; he may have (or might have) held a slightly different view. In CP 5.153 he makes the distinction between the creative and the descriptive use of fictional names as follows: "It is true that when the Arabian romancer tells us that there was a lady named Scheherazade, he does not mean to be understood as speaking of the world of outward realities, and there is a great deal of fiction in what he is talking about. For the fictive is that whose characters depend upon what characters somebody attributes to it; and the story is, of course, the mere creation of the poet's thought. Nevertheless, once he has imagined Scheherazade and made her young, beautiful, and endowed with a gift of spinning stories, it becomes a real fact that so he has imagined her, which fact he cannot destroy by pretending or thinking that he imagined her to be otherwise." But in CP 8.178 Peirce says that "The Object of a Sign may be something to be created by the Sign." This suggests that the creative use

of a name has the character created by an author as its object, just as the descriptive use does, and the difference between the two ways of using a name lies in the direction of determination. A sign may in some cases determine its object, rather than be determined by it. In CP 8.178 Peirce mentions the command "Ground arms!" given to soldiers as another example of this possibility; he says that the object of this command is "the subsequent action of the soldiers."

27. Saul Kripke formulated this view in his 1973 John Locke Lectures, chaps. 1 and 2, and characterized fictional names as "pretend names." See also Lewis (1978) 1983; and Searle 1979, chap. 3.

28. For example, see CP 4.531 and CP 8.177. In the latter paragraph Peirce gives the following definition of a sign: "A Sign is a Cognizable that, on the one hand, is so determined (that is, specialized. *bestimmt*) by something other than itself, called its Object, while, on the other hand, it so determines some actual or potential Mind, the determination whereof I term the Interpretant created by the Sign, that the Interpreting Mind is therein determined mediately by the Object."

29. Peirce also admitted this possibility in CP 2.232: "The objects—for a Sign may have any number of them—may each be a single known existing thing or thing believed formerly to have existed or expected to exist, or a collection of such things."

30. Here Kaplan follows Russell's early (1903) conception of propositions; see Kaplan 1977, 387.

31. These exceptional cases are those in which an object (as a sign or as a part of a sign) represents itself; normally a sign is distinct from its object. Cf. CP 2.230.

32. Peirce's game-theoretical ideas have been studied by Brock 1980, and by Hilpinen 1982. For game-theoretical semantics, see the articles included in Saarinen 1979, especially those by Hintikka at 27–47, 49–79, and 81–117).

33. The games considered in game-theoretical semantics are zero-sum games; cf. Hintikka in Saarinen 1979, 51.

34. If the requirement of perfect information is given up, the quantifiers need not be linearly ordered, but may branch. For the game-theoretical semantics of branching quantifiers, see Hintikka in Saarinen 1979, 59ff. and 88ff.

35. For the following references I am indebted to Professor Brock; see his "Peirce's Anticipation of Game Theoretic Logic and Semantics," 61.

36. The contrast between Peirce's conception of logic and language and the Frege-Peano-Russell(-Wittgenstein)-tradition (in short, FPR-tradition) has also been pointed out and discussed by Zeman in 1986.

37. For a discussion of the relation of Peirce's gamma graphs to the possible worlds semantics, see Zeman 1974, esp. 252–53, and Zeman 1986. According to Zeman, "Peirce fell just short of the contemporary notion of an accessibility relation" between possible universes (1986, 9); the other main elements of the possible worlds semantics are present in Peirce's theory of gamma graphs. See also Hintikka 1988, 28–29, and CP 4.512, where Peirce discusses the gamma graphs in relation to what he calls "alpha" and "beta" graphs (the latter are graphs for propositional logic and quantification theory): ". . . In the gamma part of the subject all the old kinds of signs take new forms. . . . Thus in place of a sheet of assertion, we have a book of separate sheets, tacked together at points, if not otherwise connected. For our alpha sheet, as a whole, represents simply a universe of existent individuals, and the different parts of the sheet represent different facts or true assertions made concerning that universe. At the cuts we pass to other areas, areas of conceived propositions which are not realized. In these areas there may be cuts where we pass into worlds which, in the imaginary worlds of the outer cuts, are themselves represented to be imaginary and false, but which may, for all that, be true, and therefore continuous with the sheet of assertion itself, although this is uncertain." See also the discussion of Peirce's modal logic in Roberts 1973, 80–104, and Thibaud 1975, 151–58.

17

History as Theory: One Linguist's View

Michael Shapiro

OUR EXPERIENCE OF THE UNIVERSE is characterized by variety, uniformity, and the transformation of variety into uniformity (CP 6.97). Habit-taking and the formation ("induration") of habits are the means by which variations take on the stability of uniformity. "The universal tendency of things to take habits" (CP 6.209) is to be understood as one of the chief functions of continuity. Those variations that survive owe their survival to continuity, which "stabilizes new forms, begotten by spontaneity, and develops them into habits" (Reilly 1970, 108). Since continuity for Peirce is the same as generality (CP 6.173), it is continuity that imparts generality to habits and makes them comprehensible or intelligible. Without the generalizing tendency, alias continuity, variety would never turn into uniformity, and we would be lost in a Heraclitean chaos of complete flux. Habits would have no raison d'être.

The ability gradually to convert chance into law is the chief potency of continuity; this has epistemological consequences:

> Once you have embraced the principle of continuity no kind of explanation of things will satisfy you except that they *grew*. . . . If all things are continuous, the universe must be undergoing a continuous growth from non-existence to existence. There is no difficulty in conceiving existence as a matter of degree. The reality of things consists in their persistent forcing themselves upon our recognition. Reality, then, is persistence, is regularity [CP 1.175].

That growth is part and parcel of continuity follows as a matter of course. What is not immediately evident is the character and the direction of growth. For Peirce, there is no hesitation in ascribing what he calls "concrete reasonableness" to the development of the world:

Consider . . . what Reason . . . really is. In the first place, it is something that never can have been completely embodied. The most insignificant of general ideas always involves conditional predictions or requires for its fulfillment that events should come to pass, and all that ever can come to pass must fall short of completely fulfilling its requirements [CP 1.615].

The relationship between empirical fact and the governing force of law led Peirce to the position that

(a) change or becoming is a primary aspect of reality; (b) that the most important form of change is development or growth; (c) that growth cannot be understood in purely mechanical terms; (d) that it is a unidirectional process involving "creativity" or the "emergence of novelty"; and (e) that the facts entitle us to extend the category of evolution, thus conceived, beyond the domain of the biological to the interpretation of physical, social, and historical phenomena [Goudge 1950, 229].

Pragmatism does not make action the ideal, end, or goal of human life. Beyond action lies the *summum bonum* of concrete reasonableness, which can be attained only by a process of growth through time. This is "the very coping stone of Peirce's thought" (Bernstein 1965, 89). Rationality is always a process of becoming, in which the goal is an increase of the "goodness of fit" between laws and the events they govern. "The very being of the General, of Reason, consists in its governing individual events. So, then, the essence of Reason is such that its being can never have been completely perfected. It always must be in a state of incipiency, of growth" (CP 1.615).

It is noteworthy that Peirce made his understanding of the pragmatic maxim as a principle of utility in attaining clarity of thought depend in part on the attainment of concrete reasonableness. In his definition of "Pragmatic and Pragmatism" for Baldwin's (1902) *Dictionary of Philosophy and Psychology*, he put it as follows: "the only ultimate good which the practical facts to which it [the pragmatic maxim] directs attention can subserve is to further the development of concrete reasonableness" (CP 5.3). In the same article Peirce went on to ground his advocacy of reasonableness as the ultimate good in "the evolutionary process," and his doctrine of synechism as "founded on the notion that the coalescence, the becoming continuous, the becoming governed by laws, the becoming instinct with general ideas, are but phases of one and the same process of the growth of reasonableness" (CP 5.4).

There is a running analogy between the laws of nature and the laws of human conduct. Nature has co-opted man, as it were, in the evolutionary process; mind has a distinct role to play and "does influence the course of evolution through deliberate conduct. In effect human rationality becomes one of nature's agents in the process" (Potter 1967, 65).

Continual change and increasing variety seem to mark linguistic development as they do biological evolution. In the case of biology, the causes are twofold. First, there are random variations in genetic inheritance. They are the motor of evolution and continue even when a species is relatively well-adapted. Second, the environment continues to change, and as it does, new variants will have a relatively better adaptivity. Changes in the environment are largely a product of preceding evolutionary developments (of the same or other species). Despite all this, we can say that natural selection continues to explain the survival of some variants. Hence, through all this change and variety, in which it is not and never will be the case that each variant is adaptive, we can still discern the thread of a tendency toward adaptation. Similarly, in linguistic development: there will be randomly occurring, "sporting" variations, and there will also be new developments meeting new conditions. As our world changes, what we want to say changes, and so our language must change. Also, past developments might reverberate through the system, causing further changes elsewhere—on both the expression and the content plane of language. As to the former, even without a change in the world, learning to say new things might inspire us to say even newer things. So, one might claim that the prominence of changes, both sporting and adaptive to new environments, is no surer proof in linguistics that there is no fundamental tendency than it is in biological evolution. On the other hand, there are tendencies in evolution that serve no purpose, that just, for some reason, happen ("genetic drift"). It is possible that there might be some tendencies in linguistic change that are unmotivated and are not forms of diagrammatization. But such non-diagrammatic changes tend in turn to lose their viability over time and to drop out of the language. Or if it remains, the (diagrammatically) unmotivated result will acquire some other form of motivation, such as the symbolic or indexical one.

The overarching telos of linguistic change, I would like to urge, is the establishment of a pattern—not just any pattern, but specifically the semeiotic kind Peirce called a diagram (see Jakobson 1971, 357; Anttila 1989, 181ff.; Andersen 1980b, 203). Since diagrams are panchronic signs, it is not surprising that they subtend both linguistic synchrony and linguistic diachrony. Indeed, it is only through the notion of semeiosis, prominently including diagrammatization, that the conception of change as an aspect of continuity becomes coherent. It is here, in the character of linguistic semeiosis as goal-directed in both structure and development, that the true meaning of teleology as applied to language emerges. Cast in terms of Peirce's whole philosophical outlook, language, like thinking itself, "consist[s] in the living inferential metaboly of symbols whose purport lies in conditional general resolves to act" (CP 5.402 note 3).

Linguistic signs are legisigns that are primarily symbolic. The nature of the symbol has, therefore, clear implications for language's semeiotic status—but also for its historical development, as we have seen. One of Peirce's many definitions of symbol is a sign "which is constituted a sign merely or mainly by the fact that it is used and understood as such, whether the habit is natural or conventional, and without regard to the motives which originally governed its selection" (CP 2.307). Although this definition says nothing explicitly about the future-directedness of symbols, many of Peirce's other definitions do (see CP 2.292-93, 4.447-48; NEM 4:244, 261).

There are two aspects of Peirce's conception that need to be emphasized. First, the idea that the symbol is the kind of sign that tends to make itself more and more definite or determinate articulates a time dimension in which this process is to unfold. Second, "a symbol is an embryonic reality endowed with the power of growth" (NEM 4:262).

Growth presupposes change, and change is thus conceived as the ability of the symbol to determine itself further and further by the production of whole series of interpretants that are increasingly more definite for being "delimited." Indeed, Peirce identified symbol with "entelechy" (NEM 4:229-300), a term explicitly bound up with Aristotle's notion of teleology. And, as is well known, Peirce's concept of final causation is directly related to Aristotle's. As far as language and linguistic change are concerned, then, the ontology of the symbol already has change built into it as a component of linguistic meaning or semeiosis: the structure of meaning is necessarily mutable (see Shapiro 1980, 59)—in a definite direction, the identity of which may not be immediately discernible. Change in language broadly conceived is thus rendered an inalienable part of the sign situation, as an aspect of semeiotic continuity that ensures interpretability across discontinuous generations of language users. The answer to the question "Why do languages change?" is thus fundamentally: because change inheres in the very ontology of the signs of language (see Saussure 1960, 108-109). The necessary goal-directedness of the production of legisigns, together with the teleological nature of their chief subspecies, symbols, makes change a prime in the structure *and* the perpetuation of language.

Expression X means something Y. The use of X to mean Y can be quite arbitrary. But, in fact, there is a tendency to use that X (to mean Y) which also diagrams Y, reducing the conventional aspect of language. More exactly, if A and X are related expressions designating things B and Y, then the relation of B to Y tends to be reflected (diagrammatized) in the relation of A to X. Thus, in Peirce's terms, the immediate objects of A and X as symbols tend to be also the immediate objects of A and X as icons (or: if B and Y are symbolized by A and X, respectively, then the relation < BY > tends to be diagrammatized by the relation < AX >, so that < AX > is the icon of < BY >, though A is not an icon of B nor X of Y).

Why? One might speculate: there is a telos beyond diagrammatization. The telos of language is to express, and diagrammatization contributes to the clarity and efficiency of expression. The opacity of language becomes a transparency. Words show us their objects in their own characters. Whereas there is a movement in linguistic change away from one form of this—onomatopoeia—there is a counter movement toward it in a more profound sense, that of diagramming relations. That the latter is more profound is indicated by the tendency of modern thought from Galileo to Peirce to Whitehead to make relations the primary reality, and to make relata secondary. The telos of linguistic change that is beyond diagrammatization and accounts for it might be something à la Heidegger: namely, the revealing of being.

But the revelation of being is, at bottom, just a more profound variety of diagrammatization. Since the most fundamental relation of being is between form and substance, and all form is diagrammatically related to the substance it encompasses, the telos of structure and of change remains unitary. There is thus no telos "beyond" diagrammatization.

One can still ask whether or not linguistic change in the direction of (greater) diagrammatization is essential to language. It may reveal the essence—viz., the telos of language. When Peirce spoke of symbols as future-directed (NEM 4:261), it is likely that he meant a change in the rules of interpretation (that constitute symbolhood) and not a change in the expression system (the rules of legisign formation) toward iconization of what is already symbolized. (In terms of structural linguistics, it is a change in the content system that is meant and not a change in the expression system toward diagrammatization of an unchanged content system.) For not only did Peirce speak of symbols in this connection but also, in contexts such as his logic of vagueness, there are indications of a view of symbols as essentially incomplete and therefore changing, not in their shape or sound but in their immediate objects. As such a term as "electricity" was originally used, for example, it raised more questions than it answered (and more interesting ones at that), and the answers would be found (and were found) in a more detailed conception of electricity, that is, in additional rules (and sometimes modifications of existing rules) of *interpretation*. (Of course, such changes will also have effects on the expression system, for example, spawning new terms such as "electron" and "charge" and "volt.") In this respect, change is essential to the function of (inevitably incomplete) symbols. If our concepts are not growing (that is, if our symbols are not growing in *meaning*), then they may be fading out (that is, the corresponding symbols are not being used much). In the one case, what the change is toward is the telos of language, and the change *reveals* the telos. In the other, a change (of that type) *is* the telos of language.

The precise definition of the linguistic diagram is in the character of its logical interpretant. Based on illustrative examples and on arguments developed elsewhere (Shapiro 1981, 1983), I wish to urge the conclusion that this character is markedness, the asymmetric evaluation of the term of linguistic categories. There is compelling support for this conclusion in some recent studies of linguistic change carried out by others with an awareness of the semeiotic nature of language (For instance, Andersen 1972, 1980a; Dressler 1980; Plank 1979, with further literature; Battistella 1985; to name just a few). That form diagrammatizes meaning may almost seem like a commonplace after the achievements of Jakobson. But what has still not been sufficiently understood is that this process, both synchronically and diachronically, is defined by the coherence of markedness values on *both* sides of the form/meaning equation. Indeed, with the role of the logical interpretant in mind, it ought now to be obvious that the form of meaning is *markedness*. Without this understanding, linguistic change would have to be viewed as "willful distortions of inherited patterns" (Andersen 1973, 789). The formula "one form, one meaning" can now be restated in more direct semeiotic terms to read: "one diagram, one (set of) logical interpretant(s)."

From this perspective on characterizing the "essence of language" in its panchronic totality, the question whether or not language change is teleological ceases to be debatable. Linguistic semeiosis is teleological by definition, and so—ineluctably—is language change. Traditional antipathy to teleology stems in part from the received idea that it is anti-scientific obscurantism. How could the future influence the present? In this form, teleology sounds like occultism. But as Short's careful study of Peirce's concept of final cause has made clear, *teleology is rather the doctrine of the potency of present possibilities*. There is nothing mysterious or occult in this, once it is coupled with the idea that types bring about results of a general kind. This is just what happens when acts or events (results) conform to law and by that conformity give the law reality. The greatest strength Peirce's unique concept of final causation has, indeed, is its almost humdrum, unmysterious character. All one need do to apply it "to an apparent tendency toward results of a certain general type" is to "find a relevant tautology—i.e., a tautology that would explain why the apparent tendency observed is not merely coincidental but is, under the given conditions, a real tendency" (Short 1981a, 379). On Peirce's view (to repeat), "being governed by a purpose or other final cause is the very essence of the psychic phenomenon, in general" (CP 1.269). We can infer from this that *language and its development are always teleological, because teleology is of their very essence*.

IV

Peirce and Metaphysics

18

Peirce and Idealism

David Savan

IN RECENT YEARS the work of Hilary Putnam, Michael Dummett, and many others has greatly advanced our understanding of the issues centering on Realism and Anti-Realism. The label "Idealism," like the label "Realism," has been attached to a great many differing and embattled positions. Semeiotic Idealism is the name that best identifies the idealism Peirce defended, and in an essay I published in 1952 I argued that he was strongly attracted to what I called there Semeiotic Absolute Idealism, but that he encountered difficulties that prevented a full embrace (Savan in Wiener and Young 1952). In the years since, the ground of Peirce's Idealism and Realism has been well trodden. Most recently, Bruce Altshuler, Robert Almeder, Christopher Hookway, and Peter Skagestad have published some excellent studies. Nevertheless, none of these scholars has recognized that it is Peirce's semeiotic that is the center from which most of Peirce's thought radiates. Not only his philosophical thought but also much of his scientific work grew out of his semeiotic.

I would like to do two things here. One is to show—or begin to show—how his semeiotic clarifies and unites Peirce's particular kinds of idealism and realism. The other is to suggest that his semeiotic idealism and semeiotic realism are the most interesting ways in which his thought can be connected with, and also distinguished from, present-day work in philosophy. I will try not to labor the obvious, and of course I select from among Peirce's many reformulations of his position and its problems those that I think are closest to the main line of his growth.

By *Idealism* I understand the argued thesis that no proposition is true or false unless there is, or will be, some cognitive event from which the truth or falsehood of that proposition can be inferred. I use the broad term *cognitive*, rather than *knowledge*, because I do not want to appear to exclude perceiving, believing, understanding, or kinds of affirmation short of unqualified certainty. When Peirce spoke of inference, his intention was almost always to include non-demonstrative inference—hypothesis and induction—as well as demonstrative inference.

Peirce's convergence theory of truth is clearly idealist. Scientists may work from widely divergent beginnings. They may work with widely different data and hypotheses. Nevertheless, Peirce said, what sustains their research is the hope that inference will ultimately result in convergence upon permanently agreed truths. The objects represented by such scientifically inferred truths are real.

I want to mention three difficulties with this theory. First, convergence is no more than a *hope* for which there can be no evidence. Empirical evidence can support only specific and limited conclusions. The thesis of convergence supposes a universal and unlimited agreement, an agreement that would include unanimity on the methods themselves by which agreement is reached. Peirce's argument here, his reference to our "transcendent and supreme interest" (CP 5.357, 1868), strongly suggests the influence of Kant's Transcendental Dialectic (Kant 1787/1963, 297–305) and Kant's argument concerning the transcendent ideas of pure reason. The hope for scientific convergence expresses a supreme and transcendent practical interest.[1]

A second difficulty, and Peirce was aware of it, is that if convergence should be achieved, it could not be *known* to be achieved. To know that we have achieved universal and permanent concurrence requires that we know now that the future will never confront us with any experience that might reasonably lead us to doubt or even abandon some present belief. If experience teaches us anything, it teaches us that we cannot know that the future will never surprise us in that way.

> Perhaps we may already have attained to perfect knowledge about a number of questions; but we can not have an unshakable opinion that we have attained such perfect knowledge about any given question. That would be not only perfectly to know, but perfectly to know that we do perfectly know, which is what is called *sure knowledge*. . . . [Such] sure knowledge is impossible [CP 4.63, 1893; cf. 6.610].

This is part of Peirce's familiar fallibilism, of course. But it has this curious consequence: it is possible that we do now know many truths, but if we do, our knowledge of these truths is unknowable. But it is an *anti-idealist* thesis that there may be true propositions that cannot be inferred from any evidence. In fact, Peirce wrote, there cannot be even a scintilla of evidence concerning such second-level truths (CP 5.357, 1868; cf. 2.652ff., 1878). So, Peirce's idealist theory of convergence led him to at least a limited anti-idealist thesis.

There is a third difficulty, and again it is one that Peirce appeared to recognize. "If the act of reasoning must be directed to an end, when that end is attained the act naturally becomes impossible" (CP 7.323, 1873). A mind that could not doubt, because it knew that it knew, would be "necessarily destitute of the faculty of reason" (CP 7.323, 1873). But it is the reasoned support provided by scientific investigation, evidence, and inference that turns general *agreement* into *knowledge* or scientific belief. More than that, it is doubt (whether real or feigned) and reasoning that explicate the meaning of scientific beliefs by showing the difference their truth makes in future action and thought. Once more, then, convergence may lead to truth but not to reasoned cognition.

There cannot be a final utopian state of absolute omniscience, and Peirce rejected absolute idealism. Although he conceded that "there may be a question that no amount of [scientific] research can ever answer" (CP 8.156, 1900), and that the real world is in some respects indeterminate (CP 4.61, 1893; cf. 4.79, 1893), his conception of truth as convergence amounts to the *faith* that some of the rationally grounded beliefs scientists now hold will never be rejected as false. It rests further on the *hope* that many of the questions asked now and in the future by scientists will receive similarly permanent answers. And, finally, it rests on the motivating power of the prospect of arriving at general agreement on some of our questions about the ways of the world.

Peirce's conception of science follows the lead of his three categories. Since the categories are integral to his semeiotic and, as I have said, his semeiotic is basic to his idealism, I will take a moment to outline the point. Peirce conceived of science primarily as a process and method of inquiry, not as systematized bodies of theory. Under the first category come the three sentiments on which science rests: the sincere *love* of truth, and the *hope* and *faith* that we may ultimately discover it. Under the second category, science as it actually exists is divided into a variety of specialized research communities (CP 4.9, 1906). Each of the actually existing areas of research is identified and distinguished by two factors. (1) Observational instruments and experimental procedures are shared. Lavoisier's method, Peirce wrote, was to make his laboratory equipment and its manipulation instruments of thought (CP 5.363, 1877). (2) An area of science is a social group, researchers who share a "mode of life" (CP 7.52-57, ca. 1902), and a language of theory. A scientist "naturally converses with and reads the writings of those who, having the same experience, have ideas interpretable into his own. This society develops conceptions of its own" (CP 1.236, 1902; cf. 1.99, 1896).

The third category under which Peirce described science is the self-critical development of methods of research and methods of thinking. I mean here not only the self-corrective method of induction (see the excellent discussions in Lenz 1964 and Skagestad 1981), but also the gradual development of increasingly powerful and precise methods in the special sciences. Peirce's chief interest in the history of science was in the development of methods of research and reasoning. "Each chief step in science has been a lesson in logic" (CP 5.363, 1877), and the study of the critical development of scientific methods is "the highest and most living branch of logic" (CP 3.333, 1895). Peirce's is an idealist conception of science. It put the emphasis, both in the analysis of science and in the history of science, on love of truth, and on theory and experiment as methods of inference in the search for a fallible understanding of the truth.

So much for the convergence theory and a few of its difficulties. But it must not be overlooked that Peirce also made a different kind of statement about truth. Every truth must come to us through experience (CP 1.417, 1896), and experience is "the compulsion, the absolute constraint upon us to think otherwise than we have been thinking" (CP 1.336, 1905). True belief must be "determined by some external permanency . . . upon which our thinking has no effect" (CP 5.384, 1878). It is "overwhelmingly forced upon the mind in experience as the effect of an independent reality" (CP 5.564, 1906).

Experience presents us, apparently, not with an inferred truth, but with something independent of inference, because it acts upon our beliefs directly, through surprise, disappointing expectation, interrupting habit, stimulating doubt. It acts negatively, "gradually, and by a sort of fractionation, to precipitate and filter off the false ideas, eliminating them and letting the truth pour on . . ." (CP 5.50, 1903).

There is a kind of amphibian character of Peirce's position here. On the one hand, an independent reality acts upon the mind to force positive truth upon it. On the other, experience acts negatively, catching the false propositions and allowing the true propositions to filter through. Evidently Peirce considered that the negative role of experience supported a non-idealist position. Inference from past evidence supports one set of conclusions, but experience compels us to deny one or more of those conclusions. Experience is not inferred. It teaches directly. Peirce was well aware—his own work on the pendulum and in astronomy attests to it—that faulty experimental instruments, methods, or observations may account for a conflict between theory and observation. That, of course, is not his point. His was the simpler one that however strong our evidence, however unreserved our expectation, an actual experiential encounter *may* force some change upon us. It may be that we revise our theory and our future expectations in some way, minor or major. It may be that we re-examine our experimental procedures, our instruments, our own eyes. It may be that we repeat an experiment we would otherwise not have repeated. It may be that we decide to throw it into the wastebasket, to forget about it, to go on as if nothing had happened. In any case, a recalcitrant experience *forces* us to do something we would otherwise not have done, or not done in this particular way. It thrusts some difference upon us. And it makes us aware of something that is independent of what we think. In this way, it also makes us aware of ourselves. This, I think, is at the heart of Peirce's reservations about idealism.

However, when we ask Peirce what kind of truth experience can teach us in any positive terms, a clear answer is not forthcoming. Even the simplest description must be couched in terms that make some theoretical commitment. As I will argue in a moment, his semeiotic led him to the view that all true description is based on inference from evidence. His anti-idealism teeters on the verge of idealism, just as his idealism led him to the edge of anti-idealism.

I turn now to Peirce's semeiotic. Frege wrote (1884, sections 60, 62), "It is only in the context of a proposition that words have any meaning." If he had read the *Grundlagen*, Peirce would have added, "Yes, but it is only in the context of inference that propositions have any meaning." If anything is indubitable, he wrote, it is the reality of valid inference (CP 5.276, 1868). In the very papers in which he argued that there is no premiss not itself a conclusion, he began with the existence of valid inference as just such a premiss. Although he did take this as an indubitable, in the concluding paper of the 1868 series he found that the ground of this indubitable is a "transcendent and supreme interest," as I have already remarked.

Peirce's semeiotic is developed on the basis of his discussion of demonstrative and non-demonstrative inference. His familiar definition of a sign—something which stands, in some respect or capacity, for its object to its interpretant—is sometimes criticized on the score that it does not take into account such items as signs in the arts, emblems like the national flag, or signals for action and prohibition of action. Under the more inclusive term *representation* Peirce did indeed mean to include portraits, attorneys, vicars, and members of the House of Representatives. But he was explicit that this interest is in the cognitive function of a sign, a sign "used by a 'scientific' intelligence, that is to say, by an intelligence capable of learning by experience" (CP 2.227, 1897). Signals for action and emblems for emotion must be interpreted to lead beyond themselves; otherwise they are not signs but mechanical changes.[2] Some discussions of Peirce's semeiotic go astray, because they do not take into account the distinction he drew between a sign and a representamen, a distinction he himself seemed to slur at times. It is only certain aspects of a sign that are relevant to its functioning as a sign, and it is this essential structure that can be called the representamen. For example, properties such as the exact height, or weight or age, of the stop sign and of the motorist are not relevant to the proper functioning of a stop sign. It is those aspects of the situation which are strictly essential to that ground, that object, and that interpretant which together constitute that representamen.

The new key conception is that of the interpretant. The individual interpretant is an instantiation of a translation rule. Meaning "is the translation of a sign into another system of signs" (CP 4.127, 1893; cf. 4.132). The interpretant and the sign it translates must be related to the same object and must express nearly the same information concerning that object. The interpreted sign, since it is related to its object as its interpretant is, must itself be an interpretant to some further sign. Every sign is itself an interpretant, translating and being translated, linked by translation rules with an indefinitely large set of signs.

Peirce expressed his conception of the indefinitely expanding linkage of sign-interpretants in a number of different ways. A mind, or a quasi-mind, is such a linkage. "Admitting that connected signs must have a quasi-mind, it may further be declared that there can be no isolated sign" (CP 4.551, 1906). A mind is a society or community of signs and interpretants engaged in a dialogue in which each affects the others. Peirce's dramatic apophthegm "Man is a sign" (CP 5.324, 1868; 8.304, 1909) is short for: a human mind is a society of communicating signs and interpretants, separated from other such societies only by error and ignorance. Subordinate communities, within this larger one, are the iconic community of feeling (that is, perception and emotion), the indexical community of volition and action, and the symbolic community of the development of thought. By the same token, the various communities of investigators, grouped together in special areas of research, are quasi-minds, overlapping with one another, changing, re-grouping. "Every connected series of experiments constitutes a single collective experiment" (CP 5.424, 1905). And, on Peirce's view, experiments, together with the instruments used, are indices or reagents (CP 8.368n, 1908). Just as a connected set of indices constitutes a single index, so, too, a connected set of symbols constitutes a single symbol. "A whole literature is a sign" (NEM 4.239, ca. 1895).

And, finally, the whole universe is a single vast, evolving sign (CP 5.119, 1903; cf. 1.362).

I am not arguing that Peirce anticipated the Quine-Duhem thesis. He did not. I am trying, rather, to show how Peirce's conception of an interpretant as a rule-governed translation leads to the conception of a community of signs, each in a dialogue directly or indirectly with the other members of the community. The convergence theory of truth rests on a theory of the semeiotic community.[3]

But the interpretant is not a simple translation, and Peirce's well-known example of the dictionary translation of a word from one language into another is somewhat misleading. The translation rules for interpretants are in fact inference rules—the rules for hypothesis, induction, and deduction. The best way to see this is to consider the first and most important use to which Peirce put his semeiotic. Richard Rorty wrote a few years ago (1982, 161) that Peirce developed an elaborate semeiotic and then did not know what to do with it. This is a strange thing to say. It is quite clear in so many of Peirce's writings, early and late, that first he applied his semeiotic to the traditional logic and second, and equally important in his eyes, he applied it to what may be called his philosophical anthropology, the theory of man as a sign. Emotion, perception, action, habit, and inquiry are semeiotic processes.

I have dealt elsewhere (1981) with the semeiotic analysis of emotion, and I showed in some detail how an emotion is a sign. First, it is an hypothesis that simplifies and thus explains a confusing multitude of feelings, feelings that are themselves also signs. Second, an emotion is a sign of external objects—for example, the tiger is fearsome, that behavior is outrageous. And third, the interpretant of an emotion socializes it, translating the emotion into a social and public activity. Peirce's treatment of perception is, with some differences, parallel. He argued repeatedly that a sensory quality—the color red, for example—is an hypothesis that acts as a classifier, a "constitutional word" (CP 5.291, 1868; cf. 2.426), grouping together a variety of stimuli as similar to one another and as different in color from other stimuli. Similarity of sensory or emotional quality is not found or discovered. It is organized through a rule of representation. For cognitive purposes, the purely subjective quality of a perceived color is incommunicable and irrelevant. Hence, Peirce denied that we have images before us in actual perception (CP 5.303, 1878). Hence, also, the power of seeing must be inferred from colored objects, and the only way of investigating a psychological question is by inference from external facts (CP 5.248-249, 1878).

For the purposes of this essay, Peirce's semeiotic treatment of human volition as interaction with an independent world is of special importance. A singular thing or event, interpreted as related to some object, is a sinsign. When the action of the object upon the sinsign is interpreted as identifying the object, the sinsign is then also an index. The salient characteristic of an indexical sign is, then, not that it refers to its object, but that its object acts in real space and in real time upon that singularity which is its sign. It is then possible for the interpretant to reverse this action and make it the route of reference. It is clear that it is only through the indexical sinsign that a sign can be interpreted to refer to whatever exists independently of the sign. Without it there may be descriptions, and indeed descriptions of reference. But there cannot be actual reference to independently existing things unless, apart from the interpretant, the object works on the sign. In this way, the index gives us collateral acquaintance with its object (CP 2.231, 1910).

It would be incorrect to describe the action of the object upon the index as causal. Peirce followed Kant in regarding a cause as something that comes under a general rule, whereas an index is *hic et nunc*, unique, anti-general. An index asserts nothing (CP 3.361, 1885). Rather, it directs our attention: "It has to bring the hearer to share the experience of the speaker by *showing* what he is talking about" (CP 4.56, 1893).

How does the interpretant reverse the direction from the externally initiated action of object upon sign to the internally initiated reference *back* from sign to object? Peirce's answer is that just as the immediate interpretant is an instance of an abductive inference rule, the dynamic interpretant is an instance of the inference rule for induction. In other words, the immediate object within the sign is interpreted to be a *sample*, drawn without predesignation, from that larger population of possible samples that constitutes the dynamic externally existing object. The dynamic object, the external and existent object, is not something noumenal underlying experience. It exists at those places where it acts. But it is the unity of which each sign upon which it acts is a sample. That is why Peirce interprets Kant's *Ding an sich* as fully present in the *Vorstellung*. It is the same dynamically active object as each interpretant shares with the sign it interprets, and so what is shown to speaker and hearer may be shared. Any particular sign, together with its many interpretants, must be collaterally connected with the dynamic environment so that what is *shown* to speaker and hearer in a conversation can be public and open to investigation by the scientific community.

This sounds as though Peirce was a metaphysical realist. But he was not. There are at least two reasons why he was not. First, on his analysis, an index cannot describe. It has nothing to do with meanings. All the characteristics attributed to the objects are entirely the work of theory, that is to say, of interpretants. So, a physical dynamic object can only be *interpreted* to have mass, or to be spatially or temporally extended. As an existing object it can compel us to change, to adjust our interpretation one way or another. But on Peirce's semeiotic account, the dynamic object is neither a wave nor a particle, neither here nor there, neither now nor then. Bearing quantum theory in mind, perhaps this is not a weakness but a strength of semeiotic.

Second, Peirce's position is, in its own distinctive way, a thesis concerning what Quine has called "the inscrutability of reference." If I look out the window to read the thermometer, what is the dynamic object? I cannot say that it is the colored and shaped thing I call the thermometer. That is only the interpretant of the immediate object within the sign. I cannot say it is the light, or the air, or the atomic or other elementary structure. As Peirce wrote, "Whether a fact is to be regarded as referring to a single thing or to more is a question of the form of proposition under which it suits our purpose to state the facts" (CP 3.418, 1892).

Another example: Peirce asked, what is the dynamic object of a character in a play—*Hamlet*, for example. His answer is: the universe or world in which Hamlet occurs. But that answer is not satisfactory. Is Hamlet's dynamic world that of the one play, or of the whole of Shakespeare's creation? Or is it the world of the theater—the theater of Shakespeare's day, or the theater of the West from classical Greece to the present day? Or is it this dynamic world which Shakespeare shared with all his contemporaries and with us?

The best that can be said about the dynamic object, I believe, is that it is that active existential factor which forces the community of interpretants to change and, in the long run, to converge on some stable belief, or stable systematically interrelated set of beliefs. And yet, "Blind existential being may possibly not occur at all; since we know nothing with absolute certainty of existent things . . . and above all know extremely little about the ultimate parts of matter . . ." (CP 6.346, ca. 1909).

I turn finally to the symbol. Peirce's conception of the symbol is the aspect of his semeiotic most telling for his idealism and also for his Scotistic Realism. The trichotomy of which the symbol is the third member is relational. That is to say, its members are defined by their relation to their respective objects. An icon is a sign that need only be *possibly* related to its object. An index must *actually* be related to its object. But a symbol is a sign that is related to its object only in virtue of *being interpreted* to be a sign of that object. Without the interpretant the spoken symbol is mere noise, the written symbol mere scribble. Of course, the interpretant is not a single sign-event. Each interpreting sign-event instantiates a rule that translates the earlier interpretants into further interpretants of the same object. There is no symbol unless there are actual interpretant instances. But actual instantiations are not enough. The rule they instantiate must, in principle, generate indefinitely many instances. The subjunctive conditional is essential. So, it is not only the interpretant that is a rule or law. The symbol itself is a rule. To mark the distinction between the rule and the instance Peirce distinguished between what is *real* and what *exists*. The symbol is real, but it does not exist as such. The replicas of the symbol exist, and since they replicate the symbol they may be said to be derivatively real, while the symbol for which they deputize exists vicariously.[4]

What kind of object can a symbol have? By virtue of its included index, it can denote a singular individual, or a collection of individuals. By virtue of its included icon it will signify qualities or characters. But only the symbol can have a *law* as its object. A regularity—habits, whether human or those of physical nature, are Peirce's premier paradigms of regularities—can make itself known only through symbols, and it is only symbols that can identify and represent nomological truths. It follows that without symbols and semeiosis, whether verbal or mathematical, the laws of nature and the general principles which the physical sciences ascribe to the processes of the natural world are not real. They do not exist, not even vicariously. And though natural events occur, without symbols and semeiosis they have no reality, not even derivatively. Semeiosis is essential to causality and to continuity between past, present, and future. The natural world without law is no more than a chaos of unrepeatable and unreportable shocks, *hic et nunc,* without meaning—"sound and fury, signifying nothing," Shakespeare wrote. Peirce's Scotistic Realism and his Semeiotic Idealism come to the same things.

One consequence of this fundamental distinction between the reality of law or habit and the concrete existence of replicas or instances is that exact synonymy cannot exist. No two tokens of a word or phrase can exist in exactly similar circumstances. So each replica differs in random ways from every other instance. Nevertheless, as the statistical laws of Darwinian evolution (and of the diffusion of gases) show, fortuitous distributions exhibit a finious drift toward order, generality, and law. Drift toward order from random happenings, what Peirce called *finious* change, made historical change of central importance to him. It gave a profound resonance to his conception of the history of science. Had he succeeded in writing the kind of history of science he had in mind, it would have followed the triadic division, indicated earlier in this essay, in Peirce's conception of the nature of science.

First, he would have shown the development of a self-subordinative love of truth (see the comment on Erigena and Hellebore at CP 5.406, 1878). Second, there is, on the one side, the history of the tools, instruments, and experiments of research, and, on the other, the history of the theories and the vocabularies of the special sciences. Together these two create the actual historical communities of scientists and of science. Third, and most important, because it embraces the first two, is the history of methods. Each major step in the development of scientific methods is also a major lesson in logic (CP 5.363, 1877). The study of methodeutic is the study of "the highest and most living branch of logic" (CP 2.333, 1895).[5]

Much of Peirce's own scientific research is directly relevant to this account of thirdness as the growth of order out of random distribution. Consider, for example, the psychological work he conducted with the collaboration of Joseph Jastrow. The subjects were exposed to small differences in pressure on a finger. When the difference in physical pressure was so small that the subjects reported that they could not sense any difference, they are nevertheless asked to guess. It turned out that the guesses were correct in a significantly greater proportion than pure chance would have predicted. There was a significant drift toward the correct answer. In his later reflections on these experimental results, Peirce compared the finious drift toward increasing order to the evolution of biological forms and to the evolution of science (CP 7.38, 1907).

In his conception of the history of science, and in his own scientific experimentation, then, Peirce argued that order and law could not be real without semeiosis, the evolution of symbols, the representation of generality, the formulation of order, the semeiosis needed for mathematics and a theory of probabilities. The evolution of symbols reaches maturity in the growth of a self-critical scientific methodology. Without semeiosis, what would exist (if anything) would be blind turmoil. The object of a symbol, then, is something real; but real as law, or habit, or order, is real. The relation between the symbol and its object is not one of correspondence but one of interpretation. It is the growth of inference and semeiosis that enables correlative law and order to evolve out of insubstantial, fugitive, and aleatory existence.

NOTES

1. It would be interesting to inquire what Peirce thought was in fact the practical interest in truth and its real object. Was it the peace and stability that universal and permanent agreement might bring? That cannot be (unless he had a radical change of mind), since his review of Pearson's *Grammar of Science* attacked Pearson for taking just that position (CP 8.135, 1901). Indeed, there is at least an apparent conflict between Peirce's strong defense of the separation of theoretical research from matters of "vital importance" and his defense of the subordination of scientific research to ethics, esthetics, and "transcendental interest."

2. Peirce did have something to say about self-reference, but I will not deal with that here.

3. Many commentators, beginning perhaps with Bertrand Russell (see his Foreword to Feibleman 1946), have referred to Peirce's stress on the sympathy between the human mind and nature's laws. Our abductions are more often correct than we have any right to expect. Once one grasps Peirce's conception of the expanding semeiotic community his explanation falls into place.

4. Some philosophers reject this distinction between *real* and *exist*. The word *real* can be dispensed with. If the existential quantifier can range over classes as well as spatio-temporal individuals, there is no difficulty in saying that laws exist.

5. Inspired by Peirce's conception of the importance of methodeutic, Josiah Royce conducted a famous seminar in the early years of this century devoted to the study of methods. The seminar brought together scholars from widely varying fields. For example, both T. S. Eliot and L. J. Henderson were members.

19

A Response to Savan

Demetra Sfendoni-Mentzou

IN HIS VERY INTERESTING and stimulating paper David Savan has convincingly elaborated his arguments concerning the relation between Peirce's *idealism* and *realism* and the way they can be linked together through semeiotic. Happily, I am in a position to say that I share many of the fundamental ideas on which Savan has chosen to build the whole edifice of his essay. Thus, I find it proper to start with the main points of agreement.

No doubt, Peirce's philosophy deserves a central place in the debate between contemporary *realism* and *anti-realism*, and certainly an acquaintance with his thought could contribute a lot to the resolution of relevant present-day problems. I also find it essential that to appreciate the problem of idealism/realism in Peirce's philosophy one must relate it to his theory of scientific knowledge, inquiry, and truth. Finally, I agree with Savan's major position that in fact there are idealist and realist tendencies in Peirce's conception of truth and that there must be a way that they can live in harmony and be reconciled. Savan has chosen semeiotic for this reconciliation and in his chosen ground has convincingly offered a profound resolution to the problem. I fully appreciate his attempt.

But I would not share his claim that "semeiotic . . . is the center from which most of Peirce's thought radiates" or that semeiotic can offer the best solution to the problem of idealism/realism in Peirce. I thus wish to suggest another key for resolution of the issue, viewed from a quite different perspective. The position that I intend to elaborate is that there is a *peculiar type of idealism* in Peirce's philosophy—namely, "pragmatistic idealism"—which should not be viewed in opposition to his realism, as Savan claims, since it is not an expression, I believe, of the identity of reality with thought. On the contrary, my argument will be that Peirce's idealism is grounded on the idea of *potentiality*, which is also the key concept of his realism. I must make clear that I put my thesis forward as supplementing, not criticizing, Savan's paper, being in this respect faithful to Peirce's spirit in his expressed conviction that science advances "by coöperation, by each researcher's taking advantage of his predecessors' achievements and by joining his work in one continuous piece to that already done" (CP 2.157).

But before I enter upon this project, I wish to indicate some of the points raised by Savan, which, I must say, I cannot endorse. All of them are related to the way he interprets Peirce's conception of truth,[1] which no doubt raises many problems and has been given differing interpretations.

The major assumption I cannot share with Savan is that Peirce's *convergence theory of truth* is *idealistic*. But viewing this as a problem deserving an extended analysis, I shall suspend my response to Savan's position until I have considered two of the related difficulties that he has pointed out.

(1) There cannot be any scientific evidence that we can arrive at any knowledge of a true proposition. Our use of the scientific method rests on sentiment–hope–faith (see CP 5.357). The first objection I should like to mention is that, although there is certainly textual evidence to support such a view, the ideas expressed in the passage Savan refers to belong to the "Grounds of Validity of the Laws of Logic" of 1868, and are in no way consonant with Peirce's explicitly expressed conviction in his review of a book by Royce in 1885 that the intellectual life of our Universe will continue even after the extirpation of the human race (see CP 8.43; cf. 5.407). Moreover, it cannot apply to Peirce's conception of the "long run" Truth. To be more explicit: this objection is based on my assumption, contrary to what Savan seems to believe, that in Peirce's thought there exist two conceptions of truth, a "short run" and a "long run" Truth. The first is connected with true propositions (see CP 5.589), "established truths" (CP 1.635), referring to individual, particular instances, and belonging to the category of Secondness. Accordingly, whenever Peirce referred to single truths or agree-

ment concerning only one question, this should be taken as an instance of a "short run" Truth. But Peirce was concerned mainly with the "long run" Truth connected with the notions of final opinion, ideal limit, and belonging to the category of Thirdness. This latter type of Truth, in my opinion, is for Peirce not only a hope, but a certainty which is expressed in several places. Truth, claimed Peirce, "will infallibly be reached sooner or later, if favorable conditions continue" (CP 7.78). The same conviction had already been expressed in his "Review of Berkeley" of 1871: "On many questions the final agreement is already reached, on all it will be reached if time enough is given" (CP 8.12).

(2) Even if convergence were achieved, claims Savan, we could not know. So, he draws the conclusion that we cannot have what Peirce calls *sure knowledge* (see CP 4.62–63). Here, I am again led to think of the distinction between "short run" and "long run" Truth. What Savan rightly points out cannot apply to Peirce's conception of Truth as final opinion. A direct implication of my position is that any kind of alleged skepticism, an expression of which is Peirce's fallibilism, can be connected only with short run truths, but not with Truth defined in terms of ultimate agreement or consensus.

Now, I would like to remark on one of Savan's major claims which I have difficulty in accepting. It concerns his view that anti-idealism is the thesis that there are at least some truths which *may* never be known. If my reading of Peirce is correct, then one cannot possibly find a real place in Peirce's thought for such a claim, since it stands in direct opposition to his explicitly repeated rejection of the idea of the absolutely incognizable: ". . . for while there is a real so far as a question that will get settled goes, there is none for a question that will never be settled; for an unknowable reality is nonsense" (CP 8.43; cf. 5.257).

This brings us right to the crucial issue concerning the nature of Peirce's idealism and its relation to his realism. I intend now to concentrate on a range of problems connected with Peirce's conception of truth and reality, so I can offer another option for the interpretation of Peirce's thought. I must make clear that I take idealism as the philosophical thesis that reality is identical with thought. This meaning is close not to the definition given by Savan here, but to one given in an earlier essay of his entitled "Toward a Refutation of Semiotic Idealism" (1983).

Thus, the first question I will deal with is: Can Peirce's idealism be taken as an expression of the identity of thought with reality? The reason this question is so very important is that it is intimately related to the notions of *reality, truth, ideal limit, long run, ultimate opinion*. In this context it is of special interest (and has been much discussed) that Peirce appealed in several places to the concept of "thought in general": ". . . reality is independent, not necessarily of thought in general, but only of what you or I or any finite number of men may think about it. . . . though the object of the final opinion depends on what that opinion is, yet what that opinion is does not depend on what you or I or any man thinks" (CP 5.408).

So, one might say that we have here a clear instance of Peirce's idealism. What better proof do we need? But things are not so simple as they might appear. Accordingly, the question is: What precisely does Peirce mean by "thought in general," and how is it connected with reality? To appreciate the meaning of the above passage, I believe that it is essential to consider "thought in general" as a form of the final opinion of an unlimited community of investigators. This demands an analysis of the concepts of "ideal limit" and "long run," which are intimately connected with Peirce's theory of truth as final opinion. What makes the situation even more difficult is the fact that in some cases it appears as if Peirce made reality dependent on final agreement. This is what Peirce maintained: "There is nothing extraordinary therefore in saying that the existence of external realities depends upon the fact, that opinion will finally settle in the belief in them" (CP 7.344).

Among the various questions raised, as far as this passage is concerned, the most important for our purpose is: Are we supposed to conclude that for Peirce the existence of reality depends upon the existence of final opinion, or ultimate agreement? In other words, can we say that things are not real until the ideal end of inquiry is reached?

If my reading of Peirce is at all correct, then an answer must be given in the negative. It should not escape our attention that

Peirce himself, being acutely aware of the consequences of some misunderstandings of his ideas, was on several occasions careful to clarify his position in order to avoid such misleading conclusions. Thus, in his "Logic of 1873" Peirce started by claiming that "The object of the belief exists, it is true, only because the belief exists." This is how he developed his position in the subsequent lines: "but this is not the same as to say that it begins to exist first when the belief begins to exist" (CP 7.340).

This is undoubtedly a genuine realistic and anti-idealistic position. His example of the hardness of the diamond is notorious. Although the hardness of the diamond is wholly constituted by the fact of another material's rubbing against it, "yet we do not conceive of it as beginning to be hard when the other stone is rubbed against it" (CP 7.340). Therefore, I think that there is no essential supporting evidence for the thesis that final opinion is a presupposition for reality in Peirce's thought, or that idealism, as Savan seems to imply, is predominant.

What we need to keep in mind, however, is the fact that final opinion cannot be confined to a finite time and place, and this raises a number of considerable difficulties. Agreement with final opinion may be postponed "indefinitely" (CP 8.43). Accordingly, final opinion has an *esse in futuro*: namely, it remains an open possibility that would be realized "in the long run." In this respect, final opinion, or Truth, plays the role of an "ideal limit" toward which investigation tends; and here the problem of convergence enters.

We are thus led to the central issue of the interpretation of final opinion as the *ideal limit* to be reached in the *long run* by *an unlimited community of investigators*. If it be proved that the above concepts should be connected with an infinite time in the future, and with an indefinite number of investigators, then an answer can be provided to the question as to the idealistic character of final opinion. To achieve this aim I think that it will be extremely illuminating to consider the issue in the light of Peirce's definition of probability.[2]

In 1905 Peirce connected the idea of a *limit* with that of the *long run* in his definition of probability: "when we say that a certain ratio will have a certain value in 'the long run,' we refer to the *probability-limit* of an endless succession of fractional values"

(CP 2.758). And again, in 1910, he claimed, "This long run can be nothing but an endlessly long run" (CP 2.661).

Thus, Peirce gave expression to an extremely interesting and original definition of probability, which displays a marked and useful similarity with his definition of truth as the ideal limit. In referring to the statement that "the *probability*, that if a die be thrown from a dice box it will turn up a number divisible by three, is one-third," Peirce claimed: "The statement means that the die has a certain 'would-be' . . . so to define the die's 'would-be,' it is necessary to say how it would lead the die to behave on an occasion that would bring out the full consequence of the 'would-be'" (CP 2.664). It is essential to remember here that in Peirce's ontological scheme the *would-be* is another expression for *potentiality* and is intimately connected with *generality* and the *law of habit*, which is expressed by a conditional proposition (see CP 8.380). This can also include the "linguistic sign" which Savan finds identical with the law of habit. We must also notice that the notions of "would-be" and habit have an essential character in common: the character of *inexhaustible possibility* which is open in the *indefinite future*. A "would-be," for Peirce, does not consist in actualities or single events, in any multitude finite or infinite (see CP 8.225). "Real habits" are defined as that "which Really *would* produce effects, under circumstances that may not happen to get actualized, and are thus Real generals" (CP 6.485).

Thus, as Savan points out, in case of habit, would-be, or symbol, "actual instantiations are not enough. The rule they instantiate must, in principle, generate indefinitely many instances." He, therefore, draws the conclusion that if there are truths about the world which require for their expression the symbols of science, then such symbols are integral to the real world. Thus far I agree. But he then continues: "order and law could not be real without semeiosis, the evolution of symbols, the representations of generality, the formulation of order, the semeiosis needed for mathematics and a theory of probabilities." I cannot share this claim with Savan. I believe that the situation with Peirce is the other way around: namely, the basic element on which everything must be considered as grounded in his scheme is reality, mainly in the form of Thirdness. Accordingly, the basic thing here is Peirce's commitment to Aristotelian-Scholastic realism, with the central concept of generality as inexhaustible possibility characterizing the real world. "For the real world," according to Peirce, "is the world of insistent generalized precepts" (CP 8.148), and in this respect the endless future means "to have a mode of being consisting in the truth of a general law" (CP 8.208). And here we are faced with another difficulty springing from a text of the same period. In referring to his *Monist* article, Vol. VII, 3526ff., Peirce noted that there "it [was] shown that an endless series of experiences, each entirely consistent with those that precede it, cannot itself be experienced (*as* such endless series), but involves a first dose of ideality, or generality" (CP 5.528).

The issue here is how ideality is to be taken in this context. Is it to be taken as an expression of the thought-like character of reality? In my opinion, we must be very careful to notice that the prominent feature in the above-mentioned passage (CP 5.528) is the connection of ideality, not with thought, but rather with generality and consequently with *generality-law-potentiality*. In this respect the idea of Secondness or actuality is not entirely excluded from this scheme. In other words, it is my contention that Peirce's "pragmatistic idealism" cannot be separated either from the real process of nature or from the actual procedure of scientific inquiry. I must say that Savan has not omitted reference to the element of Secondness, but I think that he has not given due attention to the idea of reality consisting both in *actuality* and in *potentiality* in Peirce's scheme.

Further light may be thrown on the issue if we take a close look at what Peirce has to say about his idealism in comparison to Hegel's philosophy. "My philosophy," claimed Peirce, "resuscitates Hegel, though in a strange costume" (CP 1.42). And in the third of his Lowell Lectures of 1903, he pointed out the essential differences between his philosophy and Hegel's. One of them is the fact that "the element of Secondness, of *hard fact*, is not accorded its due place in his [Hegel's] system; and in a lesser degree the same is true of Firstness" (CP 1.524).

Therefore, I believe that Peirce's idealism cannot be read as a type of Hegelian idealism, since Secondness as well as Firstness has to be taken into consideration for a full account of reality in Peirce's scheme. We must not forget that science, for Peirce, is connected with concrete scientists and their work, as Savan has already pointed out. It is characterized by Peirce as a living enterprise, and "therefore not as knowledge already acquired but as the concrete life of the men who are working to find out the truth" (CP 7.50). The pursuit of truth goes on indefinitely in the open future. In this respect I wish to refer to one of Peirce's definitions of the nature of thought in relation to the "ideal state of complete information" which deserves special attention: "thought is what it is, only by virtue of its addressing a future thought which is in its value as thought identical with it, though more developed. In this way, the existence of thought now depends on what is to be thereafter; so that it has only a potential existence, dependent on the future thought of the community" (CP 5.316).

This, I think, is one of the best comments for giving an insight into the peculiar type of idealism Peirce propounded—namely, "pragmatistic idealism"—the central idea being that "reality consists," not in thought, but "in the future."

On September 28, 1904, in a letter to William James, Peirce introduces the term "mellonization," from the Greek term "μέλλων," to define his special meaning of ideality:

> the true idealism, the pragmatistic idealism, is that reality consists in the *future*. By mellonization (Gr. μέλλων the being about to do, to be, or to suffer) I mean that operation of logic by which what is conceived as having been (which I call conceived as *parelelythose*) is conceived as repeated or extended indefinitely into what always will be . . . [CP 8.284].

I wish to draw attention to one extremely significant feature here—namely, the character of open-endedness, or reference to the future—which Savan has particularly stressed in connection to semeiotic. But I must say that this open-endedness can be seen only as an expression of generality, continuity, law. Thus, the idea of classical idealism to which Savan seems to lean in his interpretation of Peirce must be restricted. If all things are continuous (and thus general), "the Universe must be undergoing a continuous growth from non-existence to existence" (CP

1.175), which in Peirce's terminology could also be described as growth from potentiality to actuality. Accordingly, Peirce himself drew an extremely illuminating conclusion as far as the connection of thought with reality is concerned. "Therefore, to say that it is the world of thought that is real is, when properly understood, to assert emphatically the reality of the public world of the indefinite future as against our past opinions of what it was to be" (CP 8.284). This was the main idea expressed in Peirce's saying "the existence of thought now depends on what is to be thereafter." Hence, Peirce claimed, "thought has only a potential existence."

In concluding, I wish to draw, according to my reading of Peirce, a picture of the connection of thought with reality and Truth which is Peirce's version of the classic triadic relation of subject-object-reality. Thus, in Peirce's scheme, as reality is continuously unfolding itself without ever exhausting its possibilities, the collective knowing subject of the unlimited community of investigators tends to its everlasting pursuit toward Truth, which stands as the ideal limit. It is precisely the character of open-endedness based on potentiality that offers the ground for a connection of *reality* with the concepts of *Truth* and *community*. The unlimited community of investigators tends towards catholic consensus, which is extended in an indefinite future, not because of any lack of knowing abilities of the collective knowing subject, or because of reality's being unknowable, but merely because of the fact that reality is "undergoing a continuous growth" from potentiality to actuality.

If this reading is accepted, then Peirce's *peculiar type of idealism* should not be considered in opposition to his *realism*; rather, they can be combined into an integral unit, since both are grounded, as I hope I have shown, on the Aristotelian idea of potentiality.

Notes

1. My account of Peirce's theory of truth, as well as a more detailed discussion of some central issues raised here are to be found in Sfendoni-Mentzou 1991.

2. For a detailed analysis of probability and its intimate connection with the concepts of potentiality and "would-be" in Peirce, see Sfendoni-Mentzou 1980; cf. Sfendoni-Mentzou 1993.

20

Peirce's Philosophy on Religion: Between Two Forms of Religious Belief

Charles Hartshorne

I SHALL BE COMPARING HERE three doctrines, Peirce's theism, classical theism, and my neoclassical or somewhat revised Whiteheadian theism.

In a gloomy poem about the state of religion in his time and place, Matthew Arnold wrote the eloquent words: "Wandering between two worlds, one dead / The other powerless to be born." While thinking about Peirce's remarkably various characterizations of his belief in God, I recalled Arnold's words. With slight alterations they seem to fit Peirce's case: "Between two worlds, one dying, the other struggling to be born." I recalled also Nietzsche's criticisms of Christianity as he knew it, especially as expounded by Karl Jaspers, who seems to delight in presenting the doctrine as a tissue of contradictions. Finally I recalled Heidegger's puzzles about Being and about God, not as Being, but as "infinite temporality," rather than as timeless or "pure" actuality (Thomas Aquinas).

Arnold wrote his poem ("Stanzas from the Grande Chartreuse") twelve decades ago; Peirce wrote between thirteen and eight decades ago; Nietzsche's short writing career was chronologically contained in Peirce's; Heidegger's long one ended about two decades ago. None of the other writers named, to my knowledge, was aware of Peirce or his work. It happens that I have long been aware of all five of them. I heard Heidegger speak many times. As a Haverford sophomore I roomed for seven months with a sophisticated senior who was one of a small group of students who took Nietzsche seriously. They were not theists. Many friends of mine have been theologians, but others have been more or less far from that. For some seventy years I have been thinking with care about the ways in which this topic has been viewed in widely different times and parts of the world.

The faith that Arnold saw as dead can be found alive and, if not well, at least vigorously proclaimed in the city in which I live. Various forms of theism many centuries old are, for better or for worse, actively promoted in the Near East. As Peirce impressively put it, "Only the geologic ages" exceed in endurance some stubbornly held religious beliefs employing "the method of tenacity." Although I rejected this method, even before knowing about any philosopher other than Emerson, I still think it reasonable to take seriously the question "Can any view other than theism in some form adequately meet the human need to interpret the cosmic background to our living and dying—the latter of which, as Peirce reminded us, is (in principle though not in detail) `fated' to occur?" Peirce held that, although it is difficult, perhaps impossible, to state in wholly definite terms the religious meaning of "God" (Allah, Isvara, or whatever word is used for the all-surpassing reality), there is a fundamental "instinct" or intuition that calls for some such idea. As a thoroughgoing evolutionist, he took instincts seriously. I think here also of Bergson's "intuition" and his explanation, in his *Two Sources of Morality and Religion*, of the fact that our species, in all its branches or groups, shows religious tendencies. He saw this as a species-specific biological necessity. I recall also Goethe's saying that, whether or not he could demonstrate that God exists, he "felt" God. According to Whitehead—and I agree— every actual entity feels God. To feel is not necessarily to think or know. I find sense and truth in Peirce's notion of "musement," contemplating the cosmos as besouled so that confronting it is pragmatically analogous to confronting a person. But, then, how can God be disembodied? I agree with Peirce that all our science implies analogy between our thinking and what is there in nature. "Anthropomorphism," even "Zoomorphism," in some form is, he said, inevitable.

Analogy means likeness *and* difference. In theism, both the likeness *and* the difference must be *in principle*, not merely in degree. The epistemological religious problem is not that of avoiding all analogy between ourselves and the Eminent-and-Cosmic Reality. The entire problem is to find the right analogy or analogies. Hume saw this truth better than Kant. It was Hume, not Kant, who (via *Cleanthes*) pointed out that, taken seriously, medieval theism destroyed even the analogical import of terms like love, knowledge, or purpose as applied to deity. The notion of an immutable, timeless, yet wholly active, or solely actual, form of thinking, knowing, feeling, willing, purposing is mere contradiction or nonsense. As Peirce suggested, there must in the divine reality be growth, development, also chance, contingency, potentiality, and relatedness to others.

As we all know, there are absurd, even vicious forms of religious anthropomorphism. How are theists to avoid these? Everyone of philosophical pretensions has seen the danger of false analogies here, but all too many have supposed that the very idea of analogy must be dropped. We then have simply Herbert Spencer's proposal that we should worship the unknowable. As F. H. Bradley put it, we should worship it "because we know not what in the devil it may be." The solution, to repeat, can only be found in the appropriate analogy or analogies. The Scholastics knew this. But they (and under their influence sometimes even Peirce) overstated the difference and insofar nullified the analogy. This was the flaw of the famous "Negative Theology." God is *not* changeable, *not* capable of growth in any sense, in *no* way open to influence or enrichment by the creatures, is wholly self-sufficient and therefore *un*influenced by and *un*responsive to others, hence wholly *non*-social and *non*-loving! How can this be the God of religion?

What, then, did Peirce do with this problem? He suggested that, although God is conceived of as "disembodied spirit" and as the "necessary being," yet there is "more truth than falsity" in attributing change and growth to God. He also said that God perhaps does not know everything (since the future is partly a matter of chance and does not consist in advance, still less eternally, of definite particulars). He worried about the idea of other possible worlds; does God limit creation to just one possible world? Peirce also said that talking about the operation of God's mind is "mere gabble."

In the context of nineteenth-century science, comparative

religion, and metaphysics as Peirce knew these subjects, his difficulties in articulating his faith are intelligible. He knew the medieval doctrines sufficiently to appreciate their power (and even today they still convince some trained minds); he knew Hume and Kant, enough of Hegel and perhaps Schelling to know that they did not meet the problem with clear logic. He knew Royce and was impressed by him, but not by his logic as exhibited in his reasoning about the "absolute." He ended up with a strange mixture of appeal to the importance of not "overpreciding" the vague idea of God, suspicion of "the latest patent absolute," and some fragments of the not so new but very definite medieval absolute, the "pure actuality" of Thomism or Scotism.

What did Peirce not know that we can now know? He did not know quantum theory, though he already had its idea of real *chance* rather than strict classical determinism. He knew and largely accepted Darwinian evolution, though without Mendelian genetics. He knew enough about Buddhism to describe his own religious view, correctly in my opinion, as "Buddhisto-Christian," that is, between Christian and Buddhist traditions on some essential points. He did not know the very relevant Socinian theology of the seventeenth century, which dealt incisively with human freedom and its implication of the changeability of deity; or Jules Lequier's similar anticipation of Whitehead's notion of the "self-creative creature" influencing, and giving new content to, the divine awareness. He did not know Fechner's remarkably similar idea, his concept of divine excellence as in principle surpassing all others but surpassing also *itself* esthetically with each new creature. Like Socinus, Lequier, and Fechner, Peirce, with James, believed in freedom in the sense of partial causal indeterminacy.

Since Peirce believed in real, piecemeal contingency, with new examples every moment in all nature (his Tychism), why did he not more definitely see that merely having contingent qualities is not the deficiency of creatures as compared to God? The deficiency is, rather, in having *only* such qualities, and also and above all in what I call *fragmentariness* (being only part of the contingent whole). With Whitehead, and Plato as some interpret him, and with quite a few others between Plato and

Whitehead, I believe that God ideally well and completely embraces all things, both the necessary *and* the contingent. Jaspers's term *Encompassing* is relevant here. God is neither "pure actuality" nor pure potentiality, for both lack coherent sense, but rather inclusive potentiality *and* actuality, always possessing ideally well whatever is so far actualized. I call this the "dual transcendence" of deity, unrivaled in actuality *and* potentiality, in relativity as well as absoluteness, finitude as well as infinity, in manner of changing as well as in aspects of fixity or permanence. This concept was far from fully articulated before Whitehead almost did so, but it was, I hold, implicit in the religious ideals of several religions. With his work before me, as well as Peirce's and a good many others, I have tried to work it out systematically and rationally, taking much of a long adult lifetime to do so. No such genius as Peirce and Whitehead had was required for this task, so far as I have accomplished it. Many factors were more favorable to the undertaking in my time and place than in the times and places of those others. Intellectual change has been great since Peirce and even since Whitehead, and in theology and philosophy as well as in physics and biology.

Peirce did see, or almost see, the intellectual idolatry of substituting one-sided negative abstractions, like *non*-relative, *non*-finite, *un*changing, *in*dependent, *non*-contingent, for the God of religion—as though all relativity, all finitude, all chance, all dependence, all contingency were bad, inferior, or unreal. Others, a few before and more since Peirce, have seen this more clearly than he did. Peirce knew little of this tradition. With his genius he tried to make shift with what he did know. He knew something of Buddhism, and what he valued in this tradition is, I think, what should be valued in it, including its relativizing of self-identity in order to relativize the non-identity among individuals and mitigate the lack of community, the excessive individualism, of much common sense, and some uncommon sense as well. For Peirce, the rationality of altruism was not, as it was not for Hume, in the appeal to enlightened self-interest. Enlightened *interest*, with self-interest a special case, *is* the principle. Hence, "love your neighbor as (at your best) you love yourself" has a literal validity. This is not quite clear in ancient Greek thought, and is nearest to clarity in Plato. Leibniz (following—or rather, grossly exaggerating—Aristotle on "substance") is in this respect a *poor* Platonist, but Whitehead is in this respect a good Platonist—indeed improves upon Plato. One should love or value what is valuable (and therefore is cherished by God), including oneself as special case. This *is* rationality. As Hume saw, practical reason is the generalization of sympathy. Peirce's model, in one passage, of an ethical person, is a normally good mother of five children. Long before them came Buddha and the Bodhisattva ideal of universal compassion. Not for Peirce "the glorious gospel of greed," even if it is a greed for heaven!

Concerning conventional ideas of human immortality, reading Peirce can help one to see two points. One of them is that evidence of individual survival of bodily death would still not prove strict immortality, so far as that means surviving for infinite time. Between finite and infinite there is an infinite gap. Hence, no empirical evidence of mental persistence of the individual could ever show that one's posthumous career lasts forever. If there could be supernatural prolongations of careers, there could also be supernatural terminations of them. Bergson took a similar position. My own view is that there is no argument of any cogency for attributing that kind of infinity to any individual other than God.

Peirce's second point about our mortality seems to me extremely precious and scandalously neglected in philosophy and theology. At the age of twenty-six he wrote as follows: "The doctrine of immortality which makes man last forever is not so ennobling as its contrary which must make man's interest outrun himself in time as well as in space. Do you say that man lives in all time? I will match all your arguments by others to show that he lives in all space" (W 1:338).

The current fashion of emphasizing our human "finitude," that we are mortal, not immortal, subtly fails to capture the real point. I accept Brightman's formula, the finite–infinite God. I hold, and take Plato to have held, that even the World Soul (called by some scholars "Plato's real God") is finite in a genuine sense, and is not timeless, though its becoming is a "moving image of eternity." For Plato, the cosmos of creatures is, analogically speaking, the in some sense finite divine body. The entire tradition made a definite linguistic mistake in choosing finitude as the mark that distinguishes us from God. Our deficiency as not divine is much more drastic than finitude—and indeed finitude as such is no more a deficiency than infinity is. Either by itself is a mere empty abstraction. Divine finitude, however, fully includes *all* the finite actuality there is; your finitude or mine has no such inclusiveness.

If God were merely infinite, divine knowledge could not distinguish between actualized and unactualized possibilities, or between one finite entity and another. (Aristotle saw this, and so denied divine knowledge of or love for individuals.) The neoclassical view is that what God actually knows or loves includes all that is possible as possible, as well as all that is actual as actual. Neither inclusion applies to us. Peirce, like nearly everyone else of his time, was more or less unclear about these matters. Since Whitehead, the dual transcendence of God, as finite *and* infinite, both in ways surpassing in principle our ways of being either finite or infinite, has been easier to conceive. The divine all-surpassing excellence is not to be so simply identified in words as many have assumed. Why *should* the truth be supposed so simple? The history of human ideas is a long, long story of seeking simplicity and finding ourselves being forced to distrust the ultra-simple that we at first hit upon.

As Dewey pointed out, each of our actions influences *all* the future, beyond any limit we can set. But this does not make our influence infinite as God's influence is. Each of us is both cause and effect; so is God, but in ways surpassing equally both our ability to influence and our ability to respond to influence. We are fragmentary effects and fragmentary causes; God is cosmic effect and cosmic cause. God is universal interactor; you and I are extremely localized interactors. God is the quantitatively and qualitatively all-excelling interactor. The divine responses measure and render permanent the significance of our momentary experiences. "Social immortality," with God as supreme *socius*, is indeed the meaning of our lives and the lives of the other creatures. *Our* privilege is that we can understand this as the nonhuman earthly animals cannot. We can consciously grasp our value to God. We can love God as loving us in principle better than we can love ourselves or our friends. I acquired this belief from many sources, including the Bible.

Peirce believed, as did both my pious parents, that love is the basic principle. So did Whitehead. Peirce had several technical words, in addition to the word "love," in this connection: agapism, agapasm, for example. Whitehead's words are prehension, sympathy, love, even Eros. Prehension is explicated as (where the felt object is concrete) the same as "feeling *of* feeling." In one respect Peirce perhaps excelled Whitehead in this matter. He argued that to think rationally is to think in terms of probability; but because the improbable can also happen, there is no guarantee that what happens to each of us will make us as happy as we are good. Hence, rational action must be motivated by concern for the community, by love for self and others on the same universal principle. Love for the Encompassing, the all-cherishing "poet" of the whole, gives the meaning, not calculation of one's own future advantage. This seems akin to what Peirce meant by "concrete reasonableness."

An example of Peirce's hesitation between "two worlds" in philosophy of religion is his saying, on the one hand, that God should not be said to "exist," because that could only mean to "react to other like things," but, on the other, that God *before* all creation is First, *with* all creation is Second, and *after* the completion of creation is Third. So, the categories of phaneroscopy both have, and yet do not have, transcendental application; they do not, and yet do, apply also to God. We have here, before Tillich, the proposition that God is "not *a* being" (even though the in-principle-all-surpassing being). We have also in Peirce more than a hint of Berdyaev's and Tillich's admission that the creatures "enrich the divine life." We have, by implication, decades before Whitehead his distinction between Primordial and Consequent Natures of deity, both the assertion and the denial of the consequent nature.

God, the necessary being, cannot, I agree, depend for existence upon any particular world or set of worlds rather than any other, but, for all that, there may be in God a necessity that there must, and an infallible power to bring about that there shall, always be some world or set of worlds or other, and that, in addition to the essential "defining traits" of deity, there shall always be in God some contingent qualities appropriate to the particularities of what world or worlds there are. I call the abstraction of

God's necessary reality (as embodied in some world or other) the divine *existence*, and God's concretely and contingently having what worlds there are, God's *actuality*. To exist is to have an essence that is *somehow* actualized; concrete actuality is *how*, or *in just what*, the essence is actualized.

Whitehead's Primordial and Consequent divine *Natures* are, I hold, not enough; we must add the notion of consequent *states*, which are instances of the Consequent Nature. A nature, an essence, is an abstraction; abstractions are actualized only by contingent instances. But the class of contingent instances of *metaphysical*, that is, strictly universal, abstractions *could not be empty*. These abstractions are basically two: God as such, and world or universe as such. But only God is one self-identical individual through all possible variations. The world is God's body but not God, somewhat as your body or mine is not you or me. As usual, dyadic analysis is deficient; Peirce taught me that.

The necessary being is one whose defining traits are three abstractions: (1) the divine *essence* simply as that, an abstraction; (2) the divine *existence*, which is that abstraction as, without possible failure, *somehow* or in *some* concrete instance or instances realized; and (3) the concrete divine actuality, which is the *how*, the *in what*, the *de facto* concrete fullness, of the realization. That Whitehead and his followers have had as much trouble as they have had in clarifying this shows that Peirce did not do badly with the theistic problem, considering that his primary specialties were in formal logic and the philosophy of science rather than the philosophy of religion. Yet I think that Fechner and Lequier in some ways did somewhat better in the philosophy of religion before, and Whitehead and Bergson did better after, Peirce.

Long before almost everybody, Plato did rather well, but, as he anticipated, he could not communicate the full subtlety and complexity of his insight to his early followers. Some ineffective hints of the early Church Fathers notwithstanding, the next to escape from the Aristotelian and Neoplatonic trap were definitely the tragically unlucky Socinians. As Spinoza, himself in a different trap, said, "All things excellent are as difficult as they are rare." Lequier too was unlucky indeed in his brief career, and Fechner was thought of chiefly as a specialist in psychology. We stumble into truth by trial and error, and in theology and philosophy, error dies hard.

As Peirce well knew, his special greatness was in his mathematical or "exact" logic, as embraced in his general theory of signs, this as anchored in his three phenomenological or phaneroscopic categories. Even so, I hold that only a genius could have so far anticipated the characteristics of the philosophy of religion in the mid and late twentieth century. Peirce was wonderfully free from the concept of an "immortal soul" for human beings (here, as he probably knew, at one with the Buddhist "no soul" doctrine), and also free from taking seriously ideas of eternal salvation in heaven (or eternal punishment in hell). He was at one with Buddhism, Whitehead, and some recent physicists and biologists in the "mind only" doctrine, that is, the rejection of dualism as well as materialism. Because of his Tychism, or admission of the reality and pervasiveness of chance, he was free from the extreme theory of omnipotence which assigns the details of events to divine decisions, thus eliminating any distinctive meaning for creaturely freedom or responsibility for good or evil! He fully accepted the essentiality of death for all non-divine life. He needed no Heidegger to tell him about that. He implied, but did not quite state, Whitehead's "objective immortality" or everlastingness for our earthly experiences in God as consequent. He implied it by his metaphor (which is common to him and Whitehead) of the creation as a divine poem. Surely the all-surpassing poet does not lose or dismiss from awareness each portion of the poem once created by the joint divine and creaturely "spontaneity" (to use Peirce's word).

Peirce did not quite definitely anticipate Montague's, McIntosh's, or my modernized but Platonic doctrine of the creatures as members of the divine body. All things considered, however, Peirce was great even in his efforts toward a philosophical theology. I find also in his expressed attitude toward the superstitious aspects of popular religion a certain deep charitableness toward the limitations of the disadvantaged, ill-educated, or mediocre in intelligence. We cannot, he thought, expect everyone to keep abreast of the more gifted or fortunate in such matters.

I have not exhausted the ways in which Peirce showed his creativity even as philosopher of religion. Another instance of this is his treatment of the classical theistic arguments. He did not, like so many, just reiterate Kant (for Peirce, "the king of modern thought") or Hume. He did not reiterate as decisive the standard charges against the ontological argument, without which the other arguments are supposed to collapse. No, he said something more subtle and complicated than any of these. He reported that he had examined the arguments (thirteen of them) and found that "They all prove something" but do not always "have much to do with the religious meaning of the idea of God." I do not find this remark wholly satisfactory, but it shows a genuine rethinking of the topic. Peirce also made some favorable remarks about Anselm's argument. Up to that time, no one had come close to anticipating what I am somewhat widely known to have done, and Norman Malcolm almost did, with Anselm's famous argument. My point has been that the argument (or rather, and here I agree with Malcolm, the best of Anselm's two ontological arguments) does not by itself establish the existence of the God of the high religions, but it does show that *either* God exists, and theism in this sense is a necessary truth, *or* the religious idea of God is not self-consistent or coherent and no existence corresponding to it is logically possible (in a broad sense of "logically"). Moreover, the other classical arguments, revised to fit the requirements of dual transcendence and to remove other mistakes in classical theisms and pantheisms, have elements of strength that support the ontological argument just where it is weakest, which is in its assumption that the concept of God as explicated in religion at its best is not inconsistent or incoherent. All this fits what Peirce said about as well as anything I know in American or British writings of Peirce's time.

By contrast, all Whitehead did with the ontological argument is to say that a mere "verbal definition" cannot prove existence. Of course, but since Descartes, no important philosopher has defended the argument as a proof from a mere verbal definition. Rather, one premise of the argument is the explicit *assumption* (Anselm and Leibniz clearly made it) that the definition is neither nonsense nor self-inconsistent but has positive, coherent meaning. No mere words can establish this, as we learned (if we needed to) from "class of all classes" and other paradoxes. This is why further arguments are required to make a rational case. I say, with Peirce, "all the arguments prove *something*," but only taken together can they make a cogent case for theism.

It seems also clear that transparently valid formal logic cannot suffice to justify the complete premises of any of the arguments. Nor can observation of contingent empirical facts suffice. Conceptual intuition, understanding of ideas too ultimate to lack application, must come in. But formal argument *can* show exactly how *many* theoretical options there are among which some one, and only one, *must* be true. Mere logic, for instance, can show that with paired terms like necessary, absolute, infinite, immutable—in contrast to contingent, relative, finite, mutable—and some other similarly ultimate contrasting pairs, each such pair, by mathematical (meaning transparently logical) necessity, yields exactly sixteen ways of applying the concepts (including the zero or negative cases of inapplication) to God and the world (or God and what is not God). For example, the four notions, divine necessity, N, divine contingency, C, worldly necessity, n, worldly contingency, c, yield sixteen combinations. I am the first, I think, to have shown this and to have explored all sixteen cases in relation to historic theistic and atheistic cosmologies. Nothing like this analysis is to be found, so far as I know, except in my writings. So, it is false that the possible metaphysical procedures have been exhausted long ago, or in the time of Hume, Kant, Russell, Dewey, or Heidegger.

Whitehead's best predecessor in ancient times was Plato; Epicurus added an important insight with his recognition of chance and freedom even on the atomic level. Only the Stoics (including their last great representative, Spinoza) tried to reconcile freedom with the denial of chance or piecemeal contingency.

Besides his Tychism or contingentism, Peirce had two other great convictions: his continuitism or Synechism, and his Agapism or the pervasive reality of love or sympathy (feeling of others' feelings). In the Tychism, Peirce agreed with Bergson and Whitehead; in the Agapism, he was not far from Bergson and closer still to Whitehead. As for Synechism, however, all three thinkers disagreed somewhat. Peirce said that in a finite time one has an infinity of successive experiences; Whitehead, that one has a finite number; and Bergson, that number does not apply because the states interpenetrate one another. Peirce's Tychism and Agapism I take to be correct, but the Synechism to be subtly incorrect. Only abstractions, which are possibilities, can be strictly continuous, not concrete actualities. However, Peirce's application of continuity to relations between enduring individuals, including persons, is a happy one; their realities "merge" with one another. Whitehead had a similar idea of the personally ordered societies that correspond to enduring single individuals, but for him the successive states of individuals, or actual entities, are not infinitely many in a finite time. We, for instance, have only a finite number of experiences in a second, not an infinite number, as Peirce thought. And in a single experience only a finite number of qualities of color, for instance, are given. That introspection (really short-term memory) fails to detect distinctly the discreteness in these cases is perfectly compatible with the limitations of human introspection that force psychologists to be extremely cautious in resting any doctrine solely on such evidence.

Peirce made a real blunder, I think, when he said that only people's faults or defects distinguish them from one another. He failed in this to achieve a sufficiently positive understanding of value, whether ethical or esthetic. He failed to realize the importance, for actual positive value, of discreteness, definiteness, contrast, finitude. It is from God that our defects do distinguish us all, and this not because we are finite, but because we are fragmentarily and fallibly finite.

Another difficulty is that Peirce, like many scientists, would have liked to define reality positivistically as what is knowable by our rational-animal type of knowing. My impression is that this stance of Peirce's was superseded in his thinking during the 1890s and thereafter by the idea that much of reality is more than our mode of knowing can distinctly and fully know. Here I say he was right, and so was William James when he asked himself, Could I know just what a tiger, or any other non-human animal, is feeling? and gave the negative reply. Peirce himself took feeling, with its spontaneity or freedom, as the very stuff of reality, and he ought to have seen that there must be qualities of feeling that we cannot imagine. Indeed, he can be quoted indirectly, I think, in support of this. Peirce had no basis for rejecting Whitehead's phrase "ocean of feelings" as descriptive of nature, but he lacked Whitehead's definite theory of Prehension as feeling of (*others'*) feelings. With such a theory, he might have argued, as I do, that it is God "to whom all hearts are open," not human beings. Only divine prehension is the measure of truth! To this extent at least our knowledge of God must indeed, as Peirce thought, be incurably vague. It remains true that love affirms, does not depreciate, the positive value of concrete particulars. Beyond or more beautiful than love there is only a nobler love, not the night in which all cows are black (Hegel), or the eternal "white light" (Shelley) in which all contrast of colors is lost. My deepest conviction has always been that the social structure of experience is *the* structure. Just about every other theoretical possibility has been tried. That primitive animism vaguely implies it I take to be in its favor. Peirce can be cited as indirectly supporting this.

Peirce's stress on the incurable vagueness of the religious idea of "God" needs to be balanced by his statement that, with care, we can arrive at an explication of the word that is "true so far as definite," and open to further "preciding" in the future. I think that is what Whitehead came close to doing, *except* when he took the definite concept of *single actual entity* as covering God both as primordial and as consequent and "in flux." This, I hold, cannot be correct. It is *wrongly* definite. And it is Whitehead who said, "It is as true that the world is one and God is many as that the world is many and God is one." Similarly, it is as true that God is contingent (in some qualities) as that God is necessary (as existing somehow, with some world(s) or other). Peirce was right in holding that we must be both definite and indefinite about God. Above all, we must take love and the good as primary, not hatred, indifference, or the bad. We must also take spontaneity, freedom, or creativity (Plato's self-movement—to which Peirce referred) as primary, and as, in each instance, limited in its scope and made possible only by the freedom of others, not by any stuff that "cannot move itself," or by an all-determining tyrant deity. Quite a host of thinkers might come close to agreement on these requirements. They fit recent science even better than the science Peirce knew.

BIBLIOGRAPHICAL COMMENTS

I

For Peirce's religious views in his first writing period (1857–1866, aged 17–27) I have looked to W 1. For Peirce then it was obvious that the topic of God is metaphysical, since an "Ideal of God is required to bring our general conceptions into unity" (p. 448). (A Kantian influence shows itself here.) Peirce also defended what I call the Anselmian Principle, that (p. 67) the divine existence or reality must be "self-dependent or necessary" (if it is logically possible at all). Metaphysics is not concerned with contingent truths or facts but is "analysis of concepts" (p. 79). This analysis gives knowledge; but knowledge, here and everywhere, is also faith (p. 78). (Elsewhere in his writings Peirce implied that life itself is faith, and that mere pessimism contradicts the will to live, reminding me in this of Albert Schweizer.) Knowledge also involves "unconscious ideas" (in the Lockean, Berkeleyan sense of ideas, meaning data of, or influences upon, consciousness), and these ideas need not be perceived or detected as such. God does influence our consciousness, and in this sense is a given. Peirce here came close to Whitehead's notion of prehension. For neither thinker do we have God only by conceiving God.

In various places in this volume (pp. 44, 62, 67, 68, 83, 447f.) the connotation of deity is seemingly identified with various "abstractions," including "infinity," "perfection," "self-dependent" or "necessary being." Like his medieval predecessors, Peirce seems insufficiently aware that these terms are not so much vague as definitely ambiguous, with two principal meanings, according to whether transcendence is polar and dual, or nondual.

On immortality see p. 338. In the Lowell Lectures (pp.

493–502) Peirce toyed with some (to me) vague reasonings that to him justify a kind of permanence for persons in terms of his theory of signs and the soul as sign. In similar (to me eccentric) style he arrived at the idea of God, including a Trinitarian aspect. Peirce was not yet a Tychist (the change came about 1879, when he was forty), and so he had not yet found the secret of contingency, which is the "spontaneity" of feeling, or the "self-motion" that Plato took as definitive of mind, as Peirce was aware. He was, however, already virtually a pragmaticist (p. 113) and a believer in love as the supreme principle (p. 114). He declared against materialism (and dualism), saying it neither is nor has a philosophy (and for an "idealism" that recognizes a material or physical aspect of reality) (pp. 111–14), yet he regarded an atom as having an "inward existence," for which "God loves it." All this is translatable into neoclassical philosophy.

II

For Peirce's mature religious views arrived at during the last thirty years of his writing life, 1879–1909, the primary source is CP 6, dealing with metaphysics. This discipline is termed an "observational science," because it deals with the most general ideas, those referring to "kinds of phenomena with which every man's experience is so saturated that he usually pays no attention to them." See 6.2, 6.5. There are analogies to Husserl and, closer, to Whitehead's calling metaphysics "a descriptive science." Problems of metaphysics (6.6) include the question of continuity *vs.* an atomic structure. "Tychistic idealism" is "indispensable"; "chance is but the outward aspect of that which in itself is feeling" (6.265); see also 6.35–65, "The Doctrine of Necessity Examined." The gist of Peirce's philosophy of religion is in 6.428–587. See also 6.502, note: what a pragmaticist means by "God."

III

CP 5, *Pragmatism and Pragmaticism*, contains some relevant items: 5.47, note: Why an anthropomorphic conception is better than "the latest patent absolute"; 5.119: the universe as divine poem; 5.536: God as "vaguely like a man"; 5.588: laws of nature are real but not absolutely precise or all-determining (unknowingly anticipates and rejects Einstein's scorn for a "dice-throwing God"); 5.496: "an incomprehensible but personal God"; 5.402, note: some religious implications of Pragmaticism.

IV

CP 8 also has some relevant passages: 8.262: an argument against a finite God (with William James in mind?)—that it implies God would "exist," that is, react with others in the same genus, which would be polytheism. Yet "infinite" is "vague and becomes contradictory if we attempt to make it precise"; 8.277: "The Absolute (of Royce) is God only in a Pickwickian sense, that is, a sense that has no effect" (is a merely infinite God any better?); 8.108: "One-sided and extreme opinions" found in the history of metaphysics form "the thin soil that is most easily turned over to bring up the absurdities that lurk beneath the surface of their assumptions." (I could not agree more!) He rightly praised Royce for doing just this with Brahmanic mysticism and many other systems.

21

A Response to Hartshorne

Vincent G. Potter

PROFESSOR HARTSHORNE'S ESSAY is a remarkable summary of his contribution to recent philosophical theology and an illuminating account of the way Peirce has influenced his thinking on the subject. Beyond that, Hartshorne's critical evaluation of Peirce's philosophical approach to God is a valuable contribution to the understanding of pragmaticism.

For my part here I would like to accomplish three goals: first, to react to some selected remarks of Hartshorne's in his evaluation of Peirce's reflections on God (his essay is much too rich for me to deal with all the points it makes); second, to select two aspects of Peirce's thought for further development; and, finally, to offer my own assessment of Peirce's accomplishment in reasoning about God. I hope to achieve these goals *per modum unius*, that is, without breaking them out separately.

In the first place, then, let me say immediately that I agree almost completely with Hartshorne's assessment of Peirce's strengths and weaknesses. I thoroughly agree that Peirce might indeed be characterized as between two worlds—the world of classical theism (from which he moved away) and the world of process theism (at which he had not arrived). Peirce's philosophical theology is neither Aquinas's nor Hartshorne's. This fact will probably endear him to neither of these schools. Whether Peirce's shortcomings in theological reflection are properly remedied in the ways Hartshorne suggests I leave to the reader to decide. That some of Peirce's reflections on God need clarification, if not correction, I think will become evident as we proceed, if it is not already so.

As is well known, for pedagogical reasons Scholastics frequently divided their treatises on God into two parts: namely, into the two questions "*An sit Deus?*" and "*Quid sit Deus?*"

Ultimately, of course, the two questions cannot be kept apart, since the answer to the first depends upon the answer to the second. Still, I shall use that division as a convenient way of lining up some of Hartshorne's important remarks about Peirce. My impression is that Hartshorne would give Peirce rather higher marks for his treatment of the first question, that is, "Is there a God?" than for his treatment of the second, "What is God?" I would like to consider Peirce's proof more closely to show how, in fact, his answer to the question of whether there is a God is connected to his answer to the question of what God is.

Now, to begin with Hartshorne's positive assessment of Peirce, I take it that he thinks that two of Peirce's most important contributions to philosophical theology are (*a*) his emphasis on the fact that human beings have access to God's reality in ways other than conceptualization and ratiocination; and (*b*) his recognition that all traditional proofs for God—ontological and cosmological—contribute something important to the issue (see, for example, CP 6.504)—in the case of the ontological argument, that either God exists necessarily or else the very notion of God is self-contradictory and incoherent; in the case of the cosmological argument, that the experience of the world shows God's existence to be neither self-contradictory nor incoherent. I agree completely with this assessment.

Peirce constantly insisted that religious belief is instinctive (see, for example, CP 6.497–500). It is a matter of sentiment, of the heart rather than the head. He thought that mankind can perceive God directly and, in fact, if mankind cannot so perceive God, God cannot be known at all. It is this instinctive belief that is at the heart of the first of Peirce's "proofs"—from musement or free contemplation. Moreover, it is well known that the pragmatic movement, following Peirce's lead, set out to recover experience from the narrow and arid thing it had been made to be by certain forms of empiricism. For Peirce, experience is so rich that it is the sole source of whatever man knows—including God (see, for example, CP 6.492–493). Hence, for Peirce, some form of religious experience is necessary (although not sufficient) for any *rational* belief in God.

Peirce frequently remarked that all reasoning about religious matters must be unsound and that all study of them must be sordid and narrow. Nonetheless, Peirce did reason about God, and he did undertake a serious study of religious issues. He did so because he considered Reason to be a development and extension of Instinct. One might say he considered Reason to be the specifically human instinct with which evolution equipped mankind to deal with the as-yet-unfamiliar. But instinctive belief in God is indubitable as long as that belief is left sufficiently vague; but once questions arise which call for attempts at precision which in turn open the instinctive belief to doubt, then only Reason can serve the need, albeit in a halting way. For a pragmatist, furthermore, no belief should be fixed merely by tenacity or authority; doubts and questions must be explored by Reason.

For Hartshorne's second major commendatory point—Peirce's proofs for God's reality, I suggest we rely on Peirce's 1908 *Hibbert Journal* article (CP 6.452–491), since it represents his mature thought on this matter. There Peirce offered us three nested arguments for God's reality (not God's existence, since existence for Peirce is the category of contingent matter of fact, of physical objects interacting in space and time—and to apply this category to God would, in Peirce's eyes, be making God simply another object among objects). These arguments are nested, in that the third argument includes within it the second and the first; the second includes within it the first (in just that way in which the categories are related). The first argument is the so-called Humble Argument based on the exercise of musement or free contemplation of the three Universes of Experience (the Possible, the Actual, and the Necessary). The point of this exercise is that our instinctive belief in God will assert itself on the occasion of considering the beauty and coherence of each of the Universes and of their interconnections. Although the Humble Argument issues in the hypothesis of God, the second nested argument, the Neglected Argument, shows that this hypothesis is the *God*-hypothesis, that is, that the reality so postulated is not merely finite and contingent but infinite and necessary. Writing to William James in 1905 Peirce remarked:

> The God of my theism is not finite. That won't do at all. For to begin with, existence is reaction, and therefore no existent can be *clear supreme*. . . . In the next place, anthropomorphism for me implies above all that the true Ideal is a living power, which is a

variation of the ontological proof. . . . That is, the esthetic ideal, that which we *all* love and adore, the altogether admirable, has, *as ideal*, necessarily a mode of being to be called living. Because our ideas of the infinite are necessarily extremely vague and become contradictory the moment we attempt to make them precise. But still they are not utterly unmeaning, though they can only be interpreted in our religious adoration and the consequent effects upon conduct [CP 8.262].

I would point out (1) that this formulation of the ontological argument in terms of a real infinite Ideal might also have been articulated in terms of the moral Ideal of Goodness or the logical Ideal of Truth; (2) that it is a step away from the classical formulation of the argument toward what I would call a pragmatist variation, since it is not merely in the conceptual order but in the conceptual order insofar as it is linked to human conduct. I think Peirce chose the esthetic formulation as more readily seen to be available in musement.

The third nested argument situates the God-hypothesis within the logic of rational inquiry and so puts it immediately in the context of human conduct. Again, I take this to be a move away from the classical formulation of the cosmological argument insofar as it does not move merely from contingency to necessity by effect to cause but rather from human thinking, willing, and feeling to their adequate sufficient reason, which is in turn a living ideal of that sort of human behavior. Completely to appreciate what Peirce understood by this third argument from conduct (hence, from the world to God—the cosmological move with a pragmatist twist!) one would have to know his doctrine concerning the normative sciences, his understanding of scientific method, and the hierarchy of the sciences. In brief, unless God were a reality, a non-fictional ideal, with real living power, all human inquiry would be meaningless. Conversely, once that Ideal is acknowledged, how we behave is affected.

Perhaps now is the time to make our transition to the second question posed by the Scholastics in the philosophy of God: namely, "*Quid sit Deus?*" Far and away Peirce's favorite characterization of God is "creator." Peirce began the *Hibbert Journal* article by defining God as *ens necessarium*, but as Donna Orange pointed out in her book *Peirce's Conception of God* (1984), this is the only place that Peirce explicitly used this attribute of God. She also shrewdly pointed out that the entire set of nested arguments can be read as an attempt to bring the conception of God to the third degree of pragmatic clarity as achieved through the use of the pragmatic maxim. That maxim would take God to be above all creator. Peirce wrote: "God is *the* definable proper name, signifying *ens necessarium*; in my belief Really Creator of all three Universes of Experience" (CP 6.452). Note that he immediately qualified *ens necessarium* in terms of creator. No doubt, Peirce used the term *ens necessarium* to elicit a connection with both the Anselmian and the Aquinate argument from contingency (the third way). I suspect too that he had in mind Royce's Absolute, which he conceded might be an appropriate abstract characterization of God but which was empty since it had no implications for human conduct. If the Absolute as *ens necessarium* is given the pragmatic interpretation of super-order, of which order and uniformity of the created universes are but particular varieties, then Peirce thought he could argue from the predictability that general laws governing matters-of-fact bring, to the need for such a super-order. The growth of the universe from chaos to order is what Peirce meant by the growth of concrete reasonableness and is probably what he meant by the pragmatic import of *ens necessarium*. In effect, if the universe is intelligible, as science assumes that it is, it must exhibit generality, and the source of that generality must be necessary reasonableness.

This brings us to a central unclarity or waffling in Peirce's philosophy of God. The issue comes down to this: Is "God" for Peirce God or Reason? Is the growth of concrete reasonableness in the universe (Peirce's *summum bonum*) what he means by "God," or is this the sign of God? In a word, is God immanent or transcendent? Is he both? If so, in what sense or senses? Donna Orange concluded, in her study of Peirce's conception of God, "these texts . . . confirm my suspicion that Peirce's theism amounted to a belief that certain inescapable beliefs we hold can be expressed in religious language when such expression is appropriate or necessary for worship and the conduct of life" (1984, 81–82).

Hartshorne has astutely pointed out that because of Peirce's insistence on the role of experience in our understanding of God some form of anthropomorphism is to be expected and that the only real issue is to find which analogies are fitting and proper— that is, to find which predicates of God Peirce would characterize as "less false." In this regard Hartshorne is completely correct, in my opinion. Again, he is right in holding that the merely negative attributes alone will not do. They do serve a purpose, however, and cannot simply be dismissed as "abstractions," since they do set certain boundary limits beyond which predicates are unacceptable and perhaps even "vicious," to use Hartshorne's expression. Still, "negative theology," when coupled with "less false" positive attributes, is useful, even necessary, for theological discourse. Peirce seemed to think that the classical predicates—such as infinite, omniscient, omnipotent, creator—fit the bill better than some of those suggested by William James, for example.

Hartshorne approves of Peirce's attributing growth and change in some sense to God. But this is an area of Peirce's thought that needs clarification. It would perhaps be helpful to quote a passage where Peirce made such an assertion to see the extent to which he hesitated in this matter:

> The hypothesis of God is a peculiar one, in that it supposes an infinitely incomprehensible object, although every hypothesis, as such, supposes its object to be truly conceived in the hypothesis. This leaves the hypothesis but one way of understanding itself; namely, as vague yet as true so far as it is definite, and as continually tending to define itself more and more, and without limit. The hypothesis, being thus itself inevitably subject to the law of growth, appears in its vagueness to represent God as so, albeit this is directly contradicted in the hypothesis from its very first phase. But this apparent attribution of growth to God, since it is ineradicable from the hypothesis, cannot, according to the hypothesis, be flatly false. Its implications concerning the Universes will be maintained in the hypothesis, *while its implications concerning God will be partly disavowed*, and yet be held to be less false than their denial would be. Thus the hypothesis will lead to our thinking of features of each Universe as purposed; and this will stand or fall with the hypothesis. Yet a purpose

essentially involves growth, *and so cannot be attributed to God*. Still it will, according to the hypothesis, be less false to speak so than to represent God as purposeless [CP 6.466; emphasis added].

This paragraph deserves careful study and requires some close analysis to determine just what is being maintained and whether it is defensible. In the first place, it is evident that Peirce hesitated about attributing growth to God. He was still enough under the influence of the classical notion of God as immutable because infinitely perfect—that is, as possessing every perfection in a super-eminent way (the classical understanding of "pure act")—that he thought that the hypothesis of God as *ens necessarium* "directly contradicts" the notion of change and growth in God. What I find curious is the argument that because the hypothesis of God is vague but true insofar as it is definite, and because that hypothesis tends to define itself more and more, "it" (the hypothesis? God?) is subject to growth. Certainly, it is true that the hypothesis in its expression and articulation grows. I fail to see, however, that it follows necessarily that what is true of the hypothesis as expressed is true also of what the hypothesis expresses. Such an error would be the same as attributing to what is measured the properties of the measure. It might be urged that Peirce really meant to attribute growth (and so purpose) to the created Universes, and that insofar as those Universes are a sign of God (as a great poem is a sign of the poet), in some sense something like growth can be attributed to God, but not literally—unless, of course, Peirce meant that in the case of God and the Universes, sign and signified are identified. Again, it seems unlikely to me that Peirce would hold *that*, because then the notion of sign becomes vacuous. It is more likely that Peirce held some partial identity of God and the Universes, a point to which I will return shortly.

In very abstract terms one can ask whether God for Peirce is transcendent or immanent. No doubt, Peirce thought that God is not *merely* immanent. God is immanent in the sense that, as creator, he is a living power present to (even if not identical with) the created Universes. But God is, after all, creator of the Universes (or at least of some of them!); he is their source, and so cannot be simply identical with them. The Universes as created depend upon God and so do not exhaust God's reality. Again, in Peirce's version of the ontological argument, God is characterized as the Ideal (esthetic, moral, logical) and so transcends any instance of beauty, goodness, or truth. The question is whether this transcendence means that God is outside and beyond the Universes of experience or whether God is at least partially identified with those Universes. Hartshorne put his finger on the problem when he asked whether or not, for Peirce, the categories apply to God. Hartshorne rightly points out that you will find indications that seem to support each of these views. It seems to me that Peirce should maintain that the categories apply to God (since they are strictly universal) in some way or other. The real question is: How?

The hesitation in this matter can be seen in the *Hibbert Journal* article when Peirce, laying out the Neglected Argument, described the activity of musement as "that course of meditation upon the three Universes which gives birth to the hypothesis and ultimately to the belief that they, *or at any rate two of the three*, have a Creator independent of them . . ." (CP 6.483; emphasis added). It seems clear from the context that Peirce thought God to be creator of, and so other than, the Universes of Possibility and Actuality, since neither of these alone accounts for reality—possibilities are merely what may be, while actuals are contingent matters of physical fact. But is God identical with the third Universe? Is God Reason, Mind, Concrete Reasonableness? Or is God perhaps the totality or wholeness of Reason as penetrating actuals and as source of possibilities? Peirce might argue that the pragmatic conception of "God" is the ideal wholeness of Reason which alone could be fully real and so in that sense could alone be transcendent creator.

Hartshorne also pointed out in his essay what he takes to be a "real blunder" on Peirce's part, in that he held that only our faults or defects distinguish us from one another. This might also account for his difficulty in relating God's transcendence and immanence. If Peirce had no positive account of individual distinctness, he could hardly think of God as a distinct positive individual reality transcending (and so standing outside of) the three Universes. Thus, for example, Peirce spoke of God as Absolute First (Alpha) and Absolute Second (Omega). Must he also have said that God is all the rest in-between—or at least the wholeness of the in-between? Or might he have said that God is also Absolute Third outside the world and continuously creating and conserving it? The analogy here is that of an hyperbola defined by its asymptotes and generated by an algebraic function. This, then, could be read as a distinct individual reality (distinct from the created arguments). I am not at all sure about what I have just suggested. I raise it more as a question. I would like to say, however, that attempts have been made to use Peirce's principles to construct a positive account of the self and of the subject (see Harrison 1979; Colapietro 1989). Hence, I am not sure that this was so much a blunder as simply an omission, although we still might call such an omission a blunder. At any rate, this raises the correlative question of whether Peirce exaggerated the role of continuity in *identifying* (or seeming to identify) it with reality. It is one thing to maintain that nothing can be real without partaking in continuity; it is another to claim that continuity exhausts reality. The latter claim would, of course, eliminate the category of Secondness from reality—a charge often brought against Peirce by his critics, but something which Peirce, at his best at least, would not hold.

The final issue I would like to raise is whether or not for Peirce creation is free. Hartshorne makes a distinction between creation's being free in specification and being necessary in exercise. Hence, this particular world is radically contingent and so it need not have been, but the creation of some world or other is necessary, since, if God is creator at all, he is creator necessarily. I tend to think that Peirce would be in substantial agreement with that, while I would not. I would prefer to say that any particular instantiation of the possible is contingent, but some actual entity must be necessary in order for anything else to be possible at all. Since there is no realm of entities called "possibles" which have ontological status independent of the actual and the necessary being, God creates *freely*, not necessarily, from all eternity. My question is whether such freedom, as Hartshorne allows God in creating, is sufficient to do justice to God's transcendence. Must there not also be with respect to creation freedom of exercise, that is, must not God be free not to create any world, where "any" has both the collective and the distributive sense? Isn't this required in order for God to be completely independent of the created world? Perhaps the difficulty here is a certain ambiguity in the term "necessary." The term is used in several ways: first, in the usual sense of "causal connection," according to which, when the necessary and sufficient conditions for an event are present, the event happens necessarily—more exactly, when those conditions for the event are fulfilled, the event itself is virtually unconditioned (necessary in that sense); second, in the statistical sense of "what is logically inevitable" given an unlimited long run. Each of these senses of "necessary" is *hypothetical*, not absolute. That is, each requires only that there be *in fact*, not that there must be, some actual world or other. There is yet another sense of "necessary"—a reality which simply *is* unconditionally. It simply has no conditions at all. This is the classical notion of God's necessity. Is this Peirce's sense? Again, I think there is hesitation and waffling here in the same way, and for the same reason, that there is hesitation and waffling about how to understand God's transcendence.

I hope that these reflections, prompted by Hartshorne's essay, will encourage interest in Peirce's religious philosophy in such a way as to clarify further what Peirce himself held, and more important, to show how his reflections might help us to a deeper understanding of that Ideal whose living power bears upon human conduct.

22

Transcendential Semiotics and Hypothetical Metaphysics of Evolution: A Peircean or Quasi-Peircean Answer to a Recurrent Problem of Post-Kantian Philosophy

Karl-Otto Apel

I. EXPOSITION

WITH THE TWO KEY TERMS in the title, I want to point to a problem that, on the one hand, is characteristic of the post-Kantian "architectonic" of Peirce's philosophy and, on the other, relates to an architectonic aporia of post-Kantian philosophy in general, especially that of the present era. This problem may be very provisionally put as follows: "Is it possible to answer the transcendental question about the conditions of the possibility of valid knowledge in such a way that, at the same time, the real process of research (and, hence, of striving for and eventually reaching valid knowledge) may be conceived as a continuation of natural evolution?"

In what follows I will first try to point out in a rather summary way why in Kantian and even more so in post-Kantian philosophy from German Idealism through the so-called evolutionist epistemology of our day this problem had to arise repeatedly without finding any satisfactory solution. To this end it will be especially important to show (a) that, many relevant achievements notwithstanding, both the speculative philosophy of German Idealism, that is, that of Schelling and Hegel, and empiricist extrapolations of the biological theory of evolution such as the so-called "evolutionist epistemology" were doomed to miss the solution of our problem for similar reasons; and (b) that both forms of philosophy lead back to a pre-Kantian type of "dogmatic" metaphysics.

Having pointed to this chronic inability of post-Kantian philosophy to solve a recurring problem, I will then try to show that a solution—or at least a promising solution strategy—may be provided by a Peircean or quasi-Peircean approach; I mean a (transcendental-semiotic) transformation of the Kantian type of (mentalistic) Transcendental Philosophy. Such a transformation would preserve the normative-methodological priority of transcendental philosophy with regard to all types of empirical research, and, at the same time, give free space and even guidance to an empirico-hypothetic type of metaphysics which may explain both the ontological difference and the continuity of natural evolution and human history—in particular, that part of human history which consists in valid knowledge about natural evolution and human history.

To this extent, I am following here systematic goals rather than seeking to contribute to Peirce exegesis, although I wish to acknowledge Peircean inspirations as far as possible. But I will take the liberty of reconstructing Peirce's thoughts from afar, so to speak, because I am at present neither as familiar with his work as I was twenty years ago nor as confident now as I was then about the provable coherence of his writings (Apel, ed. 1967–1970 and Apel 1975/1981)

II. HISTORICAL PRELUDE:
THE APORETICS OF A POST-KANTIAN PROBLEM

1. In Kant's philosophy, the critical rejection of so-called "dogmatic metaphysics" is internally connected with the question about the conditions for the possibility of objectively valid knowledge which are supposed to be discoverable (traceable) as the "legislative" functions of the "transcendental subject" of knowledge. In this way the critical thrust of Kant's philosophy remains bound to the paradigmatical installation of the *subject-object relation* of knowledge which had already been established in a still

ontological-metaphysical form by Descartes's distinction between the *res cogitans* and the *res extensa*. From the critical point of view of Kantianism any kind of metaphysical *ontology*, that is, any attempt to comprehend being as a whole (hence, as well, the mind as part of being), without reflecting on the transcendental subject-object relation as a precondition of the possible objectivity of being, had to be rejected as "dogmatic metaphysics."

At the same time, the transcendental subject-object relation underlying Kant's philosophy also grounded a new line of demarcation and division of labor, so to speak, between philosophy and the empirical sciences. For the *Critique of Pure Reason* made clear that henceforward theoretical philosophy had to restrict itself to investigating the conditions of the possibility of experience, hence had to leave the business of experiential research itself to the empirical sciences. In this connection it must be noted that for Kant the relationship of transcendental philosophy to Newtonian physics constituted the paradigmatic application of the demarcating function of the transcendental subject-object relation.

Now, in the era of post-Kantian philosophy, it turned out that as soon as the relationship of man to nature as presupposed in classical Newtonian physics (mechanics) was substituted or transcended by another type of human experience, it was as difficult to ignore the critical, demarcating function of the transcendental subject-object relation set out by Kant as it was to live with it.

The crux of these difficulties had already manifested itself at the center of the architectonic of Kant's system. For, in order to answer his own final question as to "What is man?" Kant had to introduce a threefold distinction in the pertinent concept of the *Self*.

First, he had to distinguish between the "transcendental Self," which belonged to the transcendental function of the "I think" of the "transcendental subject" or "consciousness," and the "empirical Self" ascertainable in introspection, which was to correspond to man as a possible object of empirical science. Here already there was an irreconcilable dualism between the concept of the legislative and teleological function of the transcendental Self and the concept of man as an object of empirical science, hence as causally determined as any object of natural science, that is, of Newtonian physics. How, then, could it be possible to conceive human beings as free subjects of teleological actions as presupposed by the "ought" of Kantian ethics?

At this point, Kant introduced the concept of an "intelligible Self" as the subject of possible autonomous action. In doing this, he exploited—within the framework of his "transcendental dialectic"—his fundamental, critical distinction between knowable objects as "phainomena" and unknowable "things-in-themselves"; and he exploited this distinction in such a special way (as a solution of the "third antinomy") that one may suspect that the whole distinction between "noumena" and "phainomena" was intrinsically motivated by his concern to solve the problem of man's freedom as a prerequisite of morality in the face of the presumed causal determinism of nature.

But Kant's dualistic solution, even if it were tenable according to the criteria set by his own critical philosophy, could not provide the basis for a philosophy or even an empirical science of human history and culture as a product of responsible actions. For such actions simply cannot have any place in the realm of possible experience as it is portrayed in his *Critique of Pure Reason*. In his writings on the philosophy of history and, more systematically, in the *Critique of Judgment*, Kant sought to solve this problem by re-introducing in a way a possible relationship between man and nature different from that of the subject-object relation presupposed in Newtonian physics. He reintroduced nature as structured by purpose—for example, the purposiveness of organic life or of artistic genius—or even, in his writings on the philosophy of history, as subject to developmental strategies that, in the long run, could lead to a convergence of our postulates of moral or, respectively, political progress, with the natural, nomological course of history. Here Kant came closest to a conception of nature in relation to man's history that could be presupposed in a natural philosophy of evolution as this was already suggesting itself in the second half of the eighteenth century.

But Kant had to reintroduce this quasi-Aristotelian conception of nature on the transcendental preconditions of the subject-object relation as this was grounded in the first *Critique*. This meant that he could not concede a teleology of nature as "constitutive" of the possible objectivity of experience but merely as a "regulative principle" of heuristic value for the faculty of "reflective judgment" in ascertaining the possible coherence of natural processes and their specific laws. Compared with the "objective" processes of nature and of human history, all teleological structures of organic life and even of human actions within the frame of historical experience can only have the status of "as if" constructions.

As a consequence of this Kantian device, for all post-Kantian philosophies of natural evolution and/or human history only the following options appeared to be open: either a full-fledged teleological understanding of human actions and history, and possibly even of natural evolution as the prehistory of human history; or the supplementing of Newtonian physics by a causal-mechanical explanation of natural evolution and eventually of human history or even of human actions in history. As is well known, these options have in fact been tried. But, so far as I can see, the paradigmatic conceptions of evolution and history so far have not been able to provide a satisfactory solution of the problem Kant left behind. I will outline in the following only the most famous examples of this aporetic situation.

2. One great paradigm of a post-Kantian answer to our problem was provided by the German Idealists, in particular, by Schelling and Hegel. This idealistic response consequently developed all those concepts and speculative assumptions that one needs to *understand* the genesis of the world of nature and history so to speak *from above*, that is, from the teleological point of view of a finally accomplished self-consciousness of the transcendental Self. Most important in this respect was Schelling's conception of an original spontaneity or even creative freedom of nature qua *natura naturans* as prior and superior to the nomological determination of nature qua *natura naturata*, an idea bound up with that of a genetic development from unconscious or preconscious drives through growing consciousness of feelings and finally self-consciousness and moral self-determination. This latter movement was understood in Hegel's philosophy of

history as a return of the idea from exteriorization and alienation, a dialectical movement that continued on in, and was *aufgehoben* by, human history.

But this entire speculative response of an idealistic-teleological understanding of nature and history *from above* had to presuppose from the outset some kind of ontological *identity* between the objects and the subject of transcendental consciousness. For this reason it was compelled to annul the transcendental subject-object relation that Kant had established as the basis for the critique of dogmatic metaphysics and for the modern demarcation between transcendental philosophy and empirical science. In short, the price paid for the great conceptual achievements of German Idealism, considered as a first "metaphysics of evolution," was a return to dogmatic metaphysics through a disregard of that modern idea of empirical science the conditions of the possibility of which Kant had set out to articulate.

Two particular remarks on Hegel may supplement this very global assessment. In his critique of Kant's distinction between mere phenomena and unknowable things-in-themselves, Hegel came very close to what I would call a *meaning-critical* meta-critique of the unreflected presuppositions of Kant's conception of a *transcendental critique of knowledge*, that is, to a meta-critique of Kant's transcendental critique of knowledge according to which Kant's enterprise is incoherent because it necessarily presupposes, *qua* theoretical activity, that it can obtain knowledge, yet sets up a criterion of what can be known which entails the negation of this presupposition. But with his own claim to an absolute "knowledge of knowledge" as the anticipated result and presupposition of the reconstruction of the social and natural world, Hegel failed to preserve the good sense of the idea of a critical epistemology that leaves the completion of material knowledge to the indefinite progress of the empirical sciences. He tried to anticipate, as it were, the result of the dialogue of an indefinite community of researchers in the monologue of his speculative dialectics of substance as the subject of self-consciousness.

Corresponding to this disregard of the dimension of possible scientific progress is another consequence of Hegel's taking the absolute standpoint of an ex post comprehension of the world's development: he could no longer account for the need of a future-oriented engagement of human praxis and hence for the very notion of an ethical "ought" different from comprehension of the "actual as reasonable" and the "reasonable as actual." It is in opposition to this characteristic feature of Hegel's philosophy that Marxism, pragmatism, and (with regard to personal life) Kierkegaardian existentialism also arose as philosophies of a future-oriented mediation of theory and praxis; and it is this same problem as a problem of the future continuation of the world's evolution that Peirce had in mind when he spoke of Hegel as a thinker who tried to look upon the world as a completed fact, neglecting thereby the crucial dimension of the "*esse in futuro*" (see CP 5.48, 97, and especially CP 8, page 22).

But here it is also important to realize that the projection of the Hegelian idea of a teleological determinism and the corresponding necessity of the course of history into the future, such as is characteristic of orthodox Marxism, only increases and aggravates the ethical aporia of a dogmatic metaphysics of the world's teleological evolution. This point has been made clear by Karl Popper's vigorous denunciation of "ethical futurism" or "historicism" (see Popper 1944 and 1957), and in our day it has become almost a commonplace through the French post-modernists' dismissal of the great meta-narratives of history set up by the *maître-penseurs* of the nineteenth century. Thus, it has become obvious that an adequate conception of the continuity between the world's natural evolution and the autonomy of the Self and its capacity for responsible teleological action cannot be made plausible simply by supplanting the notion of causal mechanism with that of a teleological determination either of the whole process of evolution or of history.

3. But what about the other option suggested by Kant's dualism: supplementing of Newtonian physics by a mechanistic explanation of biological evolution and eventually even of human behavior at the level of cultural evolution? A powerful and now well-known movement in this direction was initiated by Charles Darwin's theory of the descent of humankind and its numerous continuations and socio-cultural extrapolations through the present day, from Spencer's social Darwinism to

sociobiology and *evolutionary epistemology*. Could this approach explain the transition or, more cautiously formulated, the compatibility between the realm of mechanical necessity and the realm of freedom and normative self-determination—a realm we must presuppose as a transcendental precondition of the activities of human science?

Before attempting to answer this question, I must emphasize that I do not wish to deny the explanatory power and fruitfulness of Darwinian and post-Darwinian theories of evolution considered as theories of natural science—as little, by the way, as I wish to deny the persistent heuristic relevance of certain ideas of German idealist philosophy of nature, such as the presupposition of an original spontaneity as prior and superior to causal determination. It even appears to be very suggestive speculatively to identify this metaphysical idea of spontaneity with the Darwinist idea of chance variation and, in particular, the Neo-Darwinist idea of undetermined mutations. (I shall come back to this later.)

But the crucial problem that Darwinist or Neo-Darwinist theories present for a philosophical understanding of coherence, or at least consistency, between the naturalistic theories of evolution and the transcendental-idealistic presuppositions of the Self/ego as a subject of moral and scientific activities concerns the intrinsic claim of the Darwinian and post-Darwinian theories to *reduce* the possible justification of all normative validity claims raised by human subjects of responsible action and of scientific research to one more form of selective adaptation, of struggle for survival of the fittest. It is indeed true that certain features of this Darwinian key-notion are in a sense applicable to the phenomena of cultural evolution, including even scientific inquiry. Thus, processes of trial and error, or of falsification as analyzed by Karl Popper, for example, can be understood as a process of selection of theories or hypotheses; moreover, all creative innovations of cultural evolution might be regarded, in an analogy to biological mutations, as subject to a struggle for life that is decided by a selection of those innovations which are attractive in themselves or as parts of clusters, as Dawkins suggests. Finally, even *categorial schemes* of scientific thinking, which are a priori valid according to Kant and still argued to be such in contemporary transcendental arguments and protophysics—even these a priori presuppositions of our factual cognition may be considered as phylogenetic results of successful adaptation, in principle explainable through the empirical investigations of evolutionary epistemology.

Still, there remains the truth claim or claim to intersubjective validity as a transcendental presupposition of (criticizable) argumentation and thus of all scientific enterprises including evolutionary epistemology. At least this claim and its implications, which do not include any categorial schemes of cognition but only certain rules of rational argumentation, cannot be justified or refuted by reduction to successful or unsuccessful evolutionary adaptation, if these latter terms are to carry any meaning that can be operationalized by an empirical science of evolution. At least, such a reduction of the truth claim cannot be supposed by the arguer without canceling his actual argument by committing a performative self-contradiction. But it cannot be supposed by anybody else either, so long as we suppose the equivalence of truth and universal intersubjective validity, which I think is a transcendental presupposition of serious argumentation that is rooted more deeply, in principle, than any a priori presupposition of a categorial scheme of experience.

But if we agree on this irreducible transcendental presupposition of argumentation, then also, at least, some fundamental ethical norms of an ideal argumentation community are undeniable without our committing a performative self contradiction, and hence these norms also cannot be justified or refuted by recourse to biological selection in the sense of a survival of the fittest. This is particularly interesting in regard to the fact that, after the transition from biological to socio-cultural evolution, and hence on the level of the selection of attractive innovations in Dawkins's sense, we are practically compelled more and more to adapt nature as our environment to those aims of ours that we can justify by an ethics of responsibility. How then should we apply the evolutionary theory of adaptation to those ethical norms we must rely on in determining how we shall adapt nature to our needs? I once put this question to Steven Toulmin, who was advocating a theory of socio-cultural evolution by adaptation. After some pressure, his answer to the problem was the following piece of advice: "Wait for a hundred years, then you will see what has happened!"

Now, this I think is an answer that Hegel could also have given, since he suggested that our appeals to an "ought" always would come too late with regard to the well-understood course of history (see Hegel 1821, "Vorrede"). Yet I would suggest that the structure of the *practical* problem is just the inverse: the answers of an Hegelian historicist and of a theoretician of evolutionary adaptation to the problem of the possible justification of a validity-claim, be it a claim to truth or to ethical rightness, must always come too late, even if it should be possible to prove from an ex post factum perspective that what is true and what is right is also what is vitally useful and hence even somehow successful in the long run. This anti-reductionist argument even applies to the claims of meaningfulness for the statements and arguments that must precede all our validity-claims. For it is not possible, even in principle, within the argumentative discourse of science or philosophy, to explicate satisfactorily problematic meanings in terms of those practical uses which have already been selected within the frame of successful forms of life. (I shall come back to this quasi-Wittgensteinian suggestion when discussing Peirce's "pragmatic maxim" of meaning explication.)

Thus, at this point our comparison of the way speculative idealism and naturalistic empiricist theories of evolution have responded to the problem of dualism inherited from Kant leads to a strange but interesting result. Actually, it is not only *idealist metaphysics of identity* that has overthrown Kant's demarcation between empirical science and the possible justification of their objective validity by (transcendental) philosophy, thereby restoring dogmatic metaphysics, but also, I suggest, wherever the transcendental subject-object relation of Kantian philosophy has been cast overboard by a *scientistic, naturalist reductionism* that has absolutized the side of empiricist objectivity.

(I think, in fact, that in recent times the impact of those types of dogmatic metaphysics which derive from scientistic reductionism is even greater and more impeding for a critical philosophy than the open effusions of speculative idealism. For the latter may have a heuristic value, whereas the former lead to an obscuring or even to an apparent dissolution of the very problems of a philosophical *justification* of scientific and ethically relevant *validity*-claims.)

But how, then, should we deal with the aporetics of the Kantian dualism? Should we retain Kant's *transcendental subject-object relation* as a basis for critically demarcating between (transcendental) philosophy on the one hand and empirical science on the other, hence also between the realm of normatively oriented free actions and the realm of natural processes determined by causal law? Should we give up the attempt to understand natural evolution as prehistory of human history? Should we renounce the whole idea of conceiving our own future-oriented mediation of theory and praxis as a continuation of natural evolution and of history?

I think that with these questions the stage is set for an examination of the Peircean approach to our problem, that is, for a reconstruction from afar of that architectonic constellation of approaches which may be indicated by the terms "transcendental semeiotic" and "metaphysics of evolution."

THE PEIRCEAN CONSTELLATION OF TRANSCENDENTAL SEMEIOTIC
AND METAPHYSICS OF EVOLUTION

1. The promise held out by this constellation of terms may be outlined as follows:

(*a*) The term "transcendental semeiotic" may be taken as connoting the Peircean program of a transformation of Kant's "transcendental logic," a program that, as it were, replaces the Kantian concept of the transcendental subject of knowledge with that of the indefinite community of sign interpretation (see Apel 1972/1974/1980; and 1981, part I). Thus the (pre-linguistic) *subject-object relation* of Kantian epistemology is transformed by the complementary relation of *intersubjective communication and discursive critique* in such a way that the Kantian dimension of the transcendental a priori becomes accessible for the *fallibilism* and *meliorism* of the processes of synthetic inferences and linguistic interpretations; at the same time, the *transcendental* function of *semeiosis*, that is, of sign-mediated world interpretation, is preserved as a normative foundation of the aims and the long-run validity of synthetic inferences by regulative ideas.

(b) Because the long-run validity of synthetic inferences is no longer bound to, or dependent upon, the "constitutive" functions of the categories as a priori principles of the understanding, it is no longer necessary for a transcendental-semeiotic logic of inquiry to presuppose a dualistic-metaphysical distinction between objects of experience as mere "phainomena" the form of which is definitively prescribed by the mind and "things in themselves" which are completely unknowable yet must be postulated in "transcendental logic" as causally affecting the mind. The "real" *qua* final object of sign interpretation may be conceived instead as that which can never be factually "known" as an "immediate object" of representation but nonetheless is "knowable" in the long run. It is that which in every confirmation or falsification of our hypotheses functions as a constant correlate, so to speak, of our synthetic inferences, whose long term validity is warranted by the necessary postulates and regulative principles of the normative semeiotic logic of inquiry. To this extent, the normative-methodological function of transcendental semeiotic remains an a priori precondition for all empirical sciences, even if the factual processes of inference and sign interpretation, whose normative validity conditions are grounded by transcendental semeiotic, can at the same time be regarded as continuations of biological processes of trial and error in the sense of evolution theory.

(c) This last point leads to a Peircean conception of a "metaphysics of evolution" and its relation to "transcendental semeiotic." In contrast to German Idealism, from which it derives its central ideas, the Peircean conception of metaphysics is not a restoration of pre-Kantian "dogmatic metaphysics," because it does not abolish or disregard the line of demarcation between, and complementarity of, transcendental philosophy and empirical science. Unlike the metaphysics of German Idealism, it does not usurp the a priori grounding functions of transcendental philosophy, but, as an empirical discipline of global hypotheses ("coenoscopy"), it subjects itself to the principles of fallibilism and empirical testing grounded by transcendental semeiotic *qua* logic of inquiry. But this methodological subordination to the normative principles of transcendental semeiotic does not prevent the metaphysics of evolution from introducing ontological concepts that allow us both to thematize the processes of natural evolution and those of human inquiry into, and interpretation of, natural evolution, and to conceive of the latter as continuations of the former. And since both the hypothetical status of the metaphysics of evolution and the procedures through which its scientific consequences might be tested are ensured by the normative methodology implied in transcendental semeiotic, the metaphysics of evolution may take the risk of going far beyond the paradigmatical suppositions of "normal science" through speculative designs that are at the same time bold and conceptually vague. This is indeed characteristic of Peirce's cosmogonic and evolutionist speculations particularly in the early 1890s (see CP 6, book I; Apel 1981, 134–57, and Pape 1988).

This much is a first outline of the novel and promising features of the Peircean approach to our problem. Let us now take a closer look at the two conceptions thus introduced and their internal relationship.

2. By "transcendental semeiotic" in its most comprehensive sense I understand the conception or program that was introduced by Peirce in his early Kant studies, which terminated in the "New List of Categories" of the late 1860s and in his "theory of cognition" and "inquiry" of the early 1870s. The famous papers of 1877 and 1878 containing the "belief-doubt theory" and the "pragmatic maxim" for clarifying meaning belong in this context, as do the theory of (the three classes of) inference and the meaning-critical theory of reality. To be included here, too, are all the improvements to the theory of categories achieved with the aid of the logic of relations and the logic of quantifiers, as well as those papers in which the term "semeiotic" is explicitly introduced and the concept divided into three branches, "speculative grammar," "critical logic," and "speculative rhetoric," which were later complemented by a very differentiated classification of signs.

I think that most of these papers can be shown to pursue, more or less closely, the guiding idea of a transformation of

Kant's "transcendental logic" of cognition along the lines of a *transcendental semeiotic* (see especially Murphey 1961 and Apel 1975/1981). There are some problems with this conception, however, if one tries to ground or verify it by an appeal to the entire corpus of Peirce's texts on "semeiotic," especially those of the later period. For according to Peirce's own "classification of the sciences" in the early years of the twentieth century, only that part of his late semeiotic can be classified as "semeiotic logic" which now constitutes the first part of "normative science" (and presupposes the other normative sciences of "ethics" and "aesthetics"). The other parts of Peirce's late semeiotic writings are to be regarded as belonging rather to his new projects of (hypothetic) "Metaphysics" (of evolution) and of "Phenomenology." But even this distribution leads to difficulties, because much of his writing on semeiotic—his many sign classifications, for example, and the pertinent suggestions in his letters to Lady Welby, in particular—seem, rather, to belong to a specific program of a *general semeiotic* that cuts across the rubrics of logic, metaphysics, and phenomenology.

In what follows I shall of course focus on the relationship of *normative semeiotic logic and hypothetical metaphysics*; but precisely in order to characterize this relationship, it is necessary to point to some difficulties in the discussion of Peirce's semeiotic in general. In order to expose and illuminate the *transcendental* aspect of Peirce's semeiotic, one needs to make clear at least the following points:

(*a*) Even Peirce's general definition of the sign function as a triadic relation whose relata are the *sign* itself, the *object for which* it stands, and the *interpreter* (or, respectively, the *interpretant*) *to whom* it stands is oriented toward the cognitive interest of a *semeiotic logic qua epistemology*. It does not appear to pay special attention to those sign functions or functions of *signifying* which cannot be reduced to "standing for" (or "designating" or "denoting") some object of cognition—functions that have been analyzed by Wittgenstein (1958), Charles Morris (1946), and *speech act theorists* (see Searle 1969). Douglas Greenley (1973) in his book on *Peirce's Concept of Sign* has tried to correct this feature from the point of view of a truly *general semeiotic*, but it seems clear that we can disregard this point since we are interested—as was Peirce primarily—in exploring the *conditions of the possibility of sign-mediated cognition*, that is, in *transcendental semeiotic*. This point leads us immediately to other difficulties with Peirce's definition of the sign function.

(b) It has often been noticed and also criticized that Peirce in his triadic definitions of *signhood* or *semeiosis* (see, for example, CP 2.228, 3.360, 6.347 as against 1.339, 2.92, 303 and elsewhere) seemed to waver between a version that speaks of a person, an "interpreter" or a "mind" *to whom* the sign stands and addresses itself, and another—more characteristic—version that uses the term "interpretant" to denote the third relatum of the triadic definition. With this difference seems to go hand in hand the question whether the sign function is definitely *triadic* in the sense that a sign is related to a *real object*, which is not itself a sign, and a *real interpreter*, who is not a sign either; or whether the triadic sign relation implies an *infinite regression*, so to speak, in both directions, since the "immediate object" for which the sign stands is itself a sign standing for another immediate object that is a sign and so on, ad infinitum; and since the "interpretant" to which the sign stands is also a sign that is to be interpreted and so on, ad infinitum. Thus, one could think that the sign functions only in mediating the continuous (temporal) transfer between a previous sign and a subsequent sign.

Here, I can give only a short answer to this intricate problem: both versions of understanding Peirce's definition of the sign function are justified, and this very fact points to the difference and interrelation to be postulated between *transcendental semeiotic* and *empirical semeiotic*, including *metaphysical semeiotic*. On the one hand, the transcendental aspect of semeiotic as a *logic of cognition* implies indeed that there are *real correlates* of the triadic sign relation; for only this definitely triadic relation makes it possible to speak of *sign-mediated cognition*; and it is precisely this conception of sign-mediated cognition, that is, world interpretation, that makes it possible and necessary for the *real*, as much as it is independent of all individual subjective opinions, to be conceived as the "knowable," that is, as the possible object of the "ultimate opinion" of the real sign interpreters as members of an "indefinite community." From this viewpoint of a transcendental semeiotic, the supposition that there are *only signs* as possible relata of the sign relation can only be called *semeioticism* (Apel 1978), a regression to a magical conflation of signhood and reality (Putnam 1981). This position seems to be suggested by Derrida (see 1967a, 72, 227; 1967b, 99) rather than by Peirce.

On the other hand, it is a postulate precisely of the transcendental-*semeiotic* conception of the triadic structure of *sign-mediated interpretation of the real* that the empirical process of *semeiosis* (that is, of sign-mediated reference to the real object as well as of sign interpretation) must be potentially infinite—even though it takes place between really existing interpreters and really existing things which may be encountered by interpreters as "brute facts" resisting their wills (see Peirce's many allusions to the *relation* between the I and the non-I as an illustration of the category "secondness").

Furthermore, even the solitary thinker's understanding of him- or herself must be understood as a triadic relation of sign interpretation: namely, as a process of semeiosis between two "semi-minds" by which man understands himself as a sign that is to be integrated into the infinite process of world interpretation (see the puzzling passages on man as a sign: CP 5.314, 7.583, and others). This motif also has, I suggest, two faces, depending on whether it is considered as part of transcendental semeiotic or as part of metaphysics (or general semeiotic). From the latter perspective Peirce appeared to play down the specific features of human communication in favor of the abstract general structure of semeiosis that "perfuses" the universe. But from the first perspective—which was worked out in great detail in his early theory of cognition and inquiry and later led to his anticipation of the theory of speech acts—the point of this puzzling idea is, rather, that *even* solitary thinking must be conceived of as an *internalized mode* (I would even say a *deficient mode*) of the genuine communication between real members of the community (see, for example, CP 4.551 and especially 5.546: ". . . even in solitary meditation every judgment is an effort to press home, upon the self of the immediate future and of the general future, some truth. It is a genuine assertion . . . and solitary dialectic is still of the nature of dialogue").

(c) Related to this there is in Peirce's semeiotic yet another problem that may be *dissolved*, I suggest, by distinguishing between the *transcendental normative* and the *general empirical aspect* of semeiotic which includes the *metaphysical* one. This problem concerns the question of whether Peirce's semeiotic presupposes the paradigmatic priority of *language* or whether—in contradistinction to analytical philosophy of language—it considers language merely as a very special class of sign functions or, changing the perspective, as a late stage of the sign function in the process of evolution.

The answer to this question would seem to be that if one focuses on his semeiotic logic of cognition and inquiry, it seems fairly clear that for Peirce as well there is a paradigmatic priority of language, because only language can provide that kind of *sign interpretation*—hence, of sign-mediated *cognition of the real*—which is presupposed by science and by philosophical semeiotic itself. The methodological orientation toward language even led Peirce to anticipate *speech act theory* (Brock 1981a)—although it is once again characteristic of his restricted cognitive interest that he did not deal equally with all kinds of speech acts, hence with interpersonal communication of all kinds but focused primarily on *assertive* acts as vehicles of argumentative discourse serving the search for truth.

On the other hand, it is true that Peirce wished to analyze the sign function or semeiosis in such an elementary and generalized way that it might cover all kinds of natural signs and sign functions and even allow an evolutionary explanation of the genesis of language which would disclose this latter to be a continuation of that prelinguistic process of semeiosis which, as he once put it, "perfuses" the entire universe (see CP 5.448 and Sebeok 1977). This program of course posed in particularly sharp form the question about the relationship between *transcendental philosophy* and a *metaphysics of evolution*.

(d) Finally, an adequate handling of our problem demands that we distinguish the *normative* dimension of Peirce's semeiotic from its *descriptive* dimensions. This is especially important with regard to both the dimension of sign *interpretation* and Peirce's differentiation of different types of "interpretants." It seems clear that a transcendental semeiotic *qua* logic of inquiry cannot primarily be interested in finding out what interpretants constitute the factual, or even conventionally normal, effects of our understanding of signs. Though this might be relevant for the psychologist or the linguist, the concern of a semeiotic logician aiming at a normative methodology of science must be to determine what kind of "interpretants" can be regarded as *results* of a *correct* sign interpretation. This is particularly so in those cases in which the conventional rules of interpretation provided by everyday speech are not sufficient for a scientifically relevant explication of the meaning of concepts. This was the case, for example, with Einstein, who looked for a more adequate explication of the meaning of the physically relevant concept of simultaneity and, more generally, of space and time; yet it was also the case with John Rawls, who looked for a deeper explication of the concept of justice.

I think that at this point the "pragmatic maxim" for the clarification of concepts coincides with the semeiotic conception of the "logical interpretant" or, again, the "ultimate logical interpretant." And it seems clear that it is not the description of those factual habits that might coincidentally terminate the process of sign interpretation but rather the postulate of a habit that *would* correspond to that ultimate consensus on truth which alone may figure as the "ultimate logical interpretant" of a given sign in this context (see CP 5.491 and especially 8.315). This normative dimension of Peirce's conception of the "interpretant" distinguishes his idea of meaning remarkably from those of Charles Morris and Ludwig Wittgenstein, despite the fact that all three try to explicate meaning somehow in terms of habits and practices of behavior (see Apel 1973/1981 and 1987). In virtue of this normative dimension, then, the late conception of "Pragmatism"—or, better, alternatively, "Pragmaticism"—as a "normative science" may be considered a reconfirmation and a more precise determination of that program of a semeiotic transformation of Kantian "transcendental logic" which was initiated as early as the "New List of Categories."

There is indeed one serious difficulty with regard to the idea of a Peircean "transcendental semeiotic" that is raised by Peirce's late "classification of the sciences." In this classification, which proceeds according to the Comtean principle that more concrete sciences presuppose the more abstract sciences, Peirce withdrew the task of founding the (three fundamental) categories from semeiotic logic and transferred it—so it appears—to the new, extra-semeiotic discipline of "phenomenology" or "phaneroscopy." This is indeed a hard challenge for those who think, as I myself do, that a *transcendental semeiotic logic* could and should provide a substitute and equivalent for Kant's "metaphysical" (that is, formal logical) and "transcendental deduction" of the categories. Peirce himself suggested this in his papers of the 1860s (see Murphey 1961, part one, esp. 64ff., 85) and reiterated it after the foundation of the logic of relations and the logic of cognition and inquiry in 1870 and later.

On this latter account, Peirce provided the "metaphysical deduction" of the three fundamental categories—"firstness," "secondness," and "thirdness"—in his "logic of relations" which, as he tried to show, involves three irreducible concepts of relation: the "monad," the "dyad," and, as a basis for all further deductions, the "triad" as identical with the structure of "combination" (see Murphey 1961, xv, 304ff.). The "transcendental deduction" of the categories, on the other hand, is provided by the structure of "semeiosis," or, again, "representation," which in a semeiotically transformed "theory of cognition" replaces Kant's reduction of the manifold of impressions to the unity of consciousness through the transcendental "synthesis of apperception": it involves *firstness*, that is, suchness of the world's qualities, through the *iconic* functions of the predicates in perceptual judgments; *secondness*, through the use of demonstrative pronouns as indices which in our perceptual judgments draw the attention of the I to the qualities of the non-I as immediate object of the factual encounter; and finally, *thirdness*, through the judgment itself which as a semeiotic interpretation of the "percept" provides a mediation of the factual givenness, that is, *firstness* and *secondness*, through the conceptual generality of the predicate.

If one considers that for Peirce even the thirdness of a perceptual judgment is the result of an unconscious abductive inference and that the truth of semeiotic world representation can be defined only in terms of the ideal limit of all pertinent processes of inference and sign interpretation, one might even conclude that the "highest point" in Peirce's "transcendental deduction," what corresponds to Kant's "synthesis of apperception," can only be the final synthesis of sign interpretation that would or should be reached by the joint venture of an infinite community of researchers. Thus, the "highest point" of the transcendental deduction within a transcendental semeiotic would only be a "regulative idea" in the Kantian sense. But because this idea of the "ultimate opinion" or consensus of the community is a *necessary postulate of semeiotic logic* without which inquiry into truth as an enterprise of argumentative discourse makes no sense, one may still speak even in this case of a *transcendental deduction* of the categories and of the validity of the three classes of inferences, abduction, induction, and deduction, which correspond to the three fundamental categories. But if we conceive of the categories in this way, what, then, should we say about Peirce's apparent surrender of the task of founding the categories to an extra-semeiotic *phenomenology*?

Jürgen von Kempsky (1952) and Murray Murphey have concluded that this surrender constitutes a breakdown of the "architectonic" of Peirce's semeiotic logic of cognition and inquiry; and von Kempsky has advanced the thesis that Peirce's recourse to a "phenomenology," which is contemporary with Husserl's project of the same name, shows that he, like Husserl, had never understood the function of the "synthesis of apperception" as that of the "highest point" of Kant's transcendental deduction of the categories. This sounds very plausible from the point of view of the *pre-semeiotic* (that is, *pre-linguistic*) paradigm of *transcendental philosophy*, for which the meaning and function of the categories may be grounded in the necessary synthesis of ideas within a transcendental consciousness. But I would suggest, rather, that Peirce has in fact provided an equivalent to the "transcendental deduction" within the framework of a *transcendental semeiotic*. For within this framework the meaning and function of all concepts—and thus of the categories as well—may be transcendentally grounded in the structure of semeiosis, that is, in the necessary postulate of an ultimate synthesis of sign interpretation, that is, of an ultimate consensus of the community of sign interpreters. And this *transcendental* grounding could find its complement and reconfirmation in the *formal logic of relations* which takes the place of Kant's logical "table of judgments." Perhaps in his later years Peirce failed to reflect thoroughly on this suggestive structure of his early transformation of Kant's transcendental logic. At any rate, I would pursue this heuristic strategy as a fruitful philosophical project, even if in view of his later turn to a phenomenological explication of the categories it should turn out to be an over-interpretation of Peirce's early intentions. (This would be my answer to Oehler [1979b] and Pape [1989, 99f. note 42], who cannot find in Peirce's work anything like a *transcendental semeiotic* of the sort I have suggested.

It might even be possible to deal with the problem raised by Peirce's late "classification of the sciences" by making this compatible with the idea of a *transcendental semeiotic.* After all, Peirce's "phenomenology" is not a *cognitive foundational* discipline at all but only an elucidative or illustrative one: a discipline of intuitive evidence regarding the *firstness* of possible (imaginable) structures which is, so to speak, thrust in between the two parts of logic which originally served as the basis for the "metaphysical" and the "transcendental deduction" of the categories, namely, the formal logic of relations and the semeiotic logic of cognition and inquiry respectively. Even in Peirce's late "classification of the sciences" *phenomenology* still *presupposes* the deduction of the categories by the so-called "mathematics of logic," which is nothing other than the former "logic of relations." The late Peirce in his "classification of the sciences" seemed to think that "mathematics of logic" and "phenomenology" could be conceived as *pre-critical* disciplines based on human competences that cannot and need not be grounded (see Hookway 1985, 101ff., 203ff.). But it seems clear that if the formal-abstract results of the "mathematics of logic" and the illustrative results of the "phenomenology" are to be linguistically interpreted as relevant presuppositions of philosophical *knowledge*, they must be subordinated somehow to the *normative prin-*

ciples of true knowledge as these are grounded in the semeiotic logic (of cognition and inquiry). (Here Peirce simply seemed not to reflect on what he himself was doing or, respectively, claiming in his own classification of the sciences. But this deficit in reflection is quite common in philosophy, even in transcendental philosophy, for Kant had displayed it in failing to inquire into the conditions of the possibility of the validity of his own transcendental arguments.)

In any case, most important for our problem is the fact that Peirce even, indeed precisely, in his late classification of the sciences maintained the normative claims of the semeiotic logic of inquiry with regard to all empirical sciences, including the metaphysics of evolution that he had elaborated in the decade before. He even renewed and emphasized these claims in his critique of Dewey's "genetic" conception of logic (CP 8.239f.) and his declaring "pragmatism" to be "the normative science" (CP 5.14-40). It therefore seems to me highly important to interpret carefully the relationship between Peirce's metaphysics (of evolution) and his normative (semeiotic) logic of inquiry from the point of view that he himself developed only in his late classification of the sciences.

As far as I can see, this is usually not done. For those who are interested in Peirce's *metaphysics of evolution* as a speculative anticipation of the problems of our day often do not pay heed to Peirce's earlier transformation of Kant's transcendental logic. Hence, they deal with Peirce's "metaphysics" as if it were meant to cover the whole of Peirce's problems, for example, the whole of his so-called *theory of reality and truth*. I suggest that this architectonic simplification must lead to precisely those aporias of *reductionism* which I have tried to expose in the foregoing discussion. For Peirce, metaphysics of evolution, then, is understood either according to the model of German Idealism or just as a speculative version of the modern theory of evolution. In either case such an interpretation amounts to a reductionist elimination of all *normative* problems concerning the justification of validity-claims and of aims of reasoning for the sake of which Peirce himself introduced his conception of "pragmatism" as "the normative science" or, later, of "pragmaticism."

In the closing part of this essay, I will suggest at least some features of an alternative interpretation, primarily with regard to the theory of reality and truth (and its ethical presuppositions). I must admit from the outset that I will have to rely on determined reconstruction rather than on a close interpretation of the various, sometimes bewildering lines of Peirce's self-interpretation.

I take the following thesis as my point of departure: All those explications or definitions of the meaning of reality or of truth in terms of what *would be* the ultimate opinion or belief of an infinite community of researchers reached in an infinite process of inquiry—that is, of inferences and sign interpretations, under appropriate conditions—all those fundamental determinations which constitute the core of *normative pragmaticism*—do not have the status of *metaphysical hypotheses* and do not presuppose such hypotheses either, because they fulfill the function of *transcendental-logical presuppositions* of all possible metaphysical and scientific hypotheses, in particular, of the abductive and fallible inference character of such hypotheses.

Thus, if it is to make sense for us to enter into argumentative discourse, we *must* presuppose that it is possible in principle, that is, under ideal conditions, to reach an ultimate consensus that would be identical with what we mean by truth. And this we must have already done when discussing, for example, the problem of whether some presuppositions are fallible hypotheses. We cannot understand what this *means* (and rightly postulate that all hypotheses, being synthetic inferences, must be fallible) without presupposing the validity of certain pragmaticist explications of the *meaning of reality and truth* and, for that matter, of the structure of argumentative discourse. Hence, we cannot in fact suppose, as many claim we can, that even these presuppositions are fallible metaphysical hypotheses, for that would mean that it would be possible to falsify them by simultaneously presupposing them.

Of course, I am aware that with these statements I am expressing a radicalized philosophical reflection on those features of Peirce's *pragmaticism* which can be understood as a result of the semeiotic transformation of Kant's transcendental logic. The transcendental character of these features is easily overlooked not only because Peirce himself never realized it clearly but also because it is indeed only a *transformed residuum* of the Kantian transcendentalism. For it no longer implies any *synthetic a priori principles* that would correspond to *categorial schemes* of experience. In so doing, it makes as I have already intimated, the realm of a priori presuppositions of cognition susceptible to empirical correction—something which accords well both with the demands of those holistically minded philosophers of our day who have questioned the idea of "transcendental arguments" by questioning "the very idea of categorial scheme" (Davidson 1973–1974), and with those suggestions from the history of science and evolutionary epistemology to the effect that the Kantian tenets on categorial schemes and a priori forms of intuition are to be explained by restricting their validity to a realm of human adaptation to nature that might be called "mesocosmos" in distinction to the realms of the "macrocosmos" and the "microcosmos" that have become the subject of post-classical physics.

(Peirce's distinction between "instinctual" and indubitable but vague "common sense" concepts, on the one hand, and precise but highly fallible hypotheses of advanced stages of science, on the other, shows him to be one of the first to anticipate these ideas; see Hookway 1985, 229ff., and Pape 1988.)

Nevertheless, Peirce's semeiotic transformation of Kant's transcendental logic consists precisely in his replacing Kant's *constitutive apriorism* with certain *postulates* and *regulative ideas* that ground a priori the aim and long-run validity of those synthetic inferences the finite results of which can only be fallible conclusions. The twist of this grounding is easily overlooked and lies, I suggest, in reflection on those presuppositions which render the whole project of research, nay even of philosophical argument about it, *meaningful*. (This is the reason why in my book on Peirce I tried to interpret his semeiotic transformation of Kant's transcendental logic as a "meaning-critical" transformation of the transcendental critique of cognition which parallels the standards [after the linguistic turn] of present philosophy; see Apel 1981, 19ff.)

I think indeed that a great deal of the notorious difficulties and confusions about Peirce's most fundamental ideas may be dissolved by considering his pertinent suggestions as *meaning-critical versions of transcendental arguments*. This applies, for example, to those versions of his explications of his postulate of the "ultimate opinion" in which he clearly indicated that we cannot avoid making this postulate because any meaningful hypothesis must presuppose it, and no meaningful hypothesis can possibly refute it. Here it is important to appreciate that—certain utterances of Peirce's notwithstanding—the definition of "reality" in terms of what would be the object of the ultimate opinion of the indefinite community of investigators does not mean that the *existence* of the real—or the real as the existing universe—is made dependent on the successful outcome of the process of cognition, or that the existence of the real has to be proved independently because the successful outcome of the cognition process is uncertain (this much against Murphey 1961, 123ff.). For the existence of the real and, for that matter, of a real argumentation community itself belongs to those presuppositions of arguing and of inquiry which cannot be denied in meaningful argument. (The Cartesian dream argument, for example, is self-defeating, as can be shown in various ways.)

Not even the *reality* of the real must be made dependent on the future *fact* of its being completely known as some quasi-nominalistic statements of the early Peirce could suggest (see Apel 1981, 76ff., 134ff.). For there cannot be such a *fact*, as the late Peirce realized when he came to recognize that *counterfactual* postulates are "regulative ideas," that is to say, cases of *thirdness* which cannot, in principle, be reduced to *secondness*. But the reality of the real must indeed be understood a priori as something that is in principle "knowable." Or, rather, its meaning is identical with that of the "knowable (in the long run)," and thus it must indeed be identified with what, according to a *real possibility*, *would be* the object of the ultimate opinion of the indefinite community, because this is what we *must mean* in order to be able to distinguish between the *real* and all possible objects of idiosyncratic opinions of individuals or of finite communities.

(The structure of this problem is partly analogous to the famous one of the "hardness of the diamond." For as Peirce made definitively clear only in his late papers on "Pragmaticism," this property of a real thing cannot be made dependent on the *fact* of its being scratched or not being scratched by somebody, although it cannot be understood without supposing the *real possibility* of its proving resistant if it is scratched. There is, of course, a *difference* between this paradigmatic application of the "pragmatic maxim" and the more fundamental paradigm of understanding the meaning of *reality*. It is constituted by the fact that the *hardness* of the diamond can be counterfactually explicated—although never completely—in terms of the *possible facts* of human actions, manipulations, and subsequent experiences, whereas in the case of the *reality of the real* even this is impossible. Only that almost irrational aspect of the real, its brute external resistance to the will, can be explicated in terms of a possible fact of experience. This is the reason why we cannot identify the real individual object of our true and false hypotheses by means of complete conceptual descriptions, as Leibniz and the Hegelians postulated, but only by using demonstrative pronouns or "indices.")

So much by way of defending my thesis that the most fundamental tenets of Peirce's theory of truth and reality do not have the status of metaphysical hypotheses because they belong to transcendental semeiotic. Nor can I agree with the claim that Peirce's *theory of reality* is a combination of *idealism* and *realism* or even a combination of these two classical metaphysical positions with pragmatism, as some have suggested on the strength of certain early and incoherent statements by Peirce. I think that, properly understood, Peirce's *meaning-critical realism* is not a metaphysical position at all, but rather is of a piece with what he eventually called *normative pragmaticism*.

Nor do I believe that in his theory of cognition and reality the early Peirce defended a kind of "transcendental idealism," which he later, following F. E. Abbot, rejected in favor of a kind of *pre-Kantian metaphysical realism* (Hookway 1985, 113ff.). On my account, it was a necessary consequence of his semeiotic transformation of Kant's "transcendental logic" in the 1860s that

Peirce—his acceptance of Kant's "empirical realism" notwithstanding—had to realize the *nominalistic* character of Kant's "transcendental idealism" in his early theory of reality; and he in fact did so in many places, although he misleadingly called himself a Kantian "phenomenalist" or an "idealist." On the other hand, he was still right in his somewhat confused review of Abbot's *Scientific Theism* of 1886, in insisting on his quasi-Kantian point that the very meaning of reality must be dependent on "thought in general" and to this extent on the idea of the "final upshot of sufficient investigation" (N 1:74). The point of Peirce's transcendental-semeiotic theory of reality—that is, the point of *meaning-critical realism*—in my opinion was from the outset different from, that is to say, systematically prior to, the point of all traditional metaphysical conceptions of idealism and realism, and it was also different from Kant's "transcendental idealism" in that it could do without the notion of an *unknowable thing-in-itself*. On the other hand, Peirce's position of meaning-critical realism, which was the result of his semeiotic transformation of Kant's "transcendental idealism," must also be distinguished, in my opinion, from the metaphysical position of "objective idealism" or the "philosophy of identity (of matter and mind)"; for to suppose the "knowability" (or "explainability") of the real is not necessarily to suppose also that the real is "rational" in the same sense as the normatively guided process of semeiosis *qua* human argumentation is rational. (In his conception of "semeiotic idealism" Pape seems to overlook this difference, thereby appearing to confuse the "normative pragmaticism" of "semeiotic logic" with "metaphysical idealism," positions which are indeed both held by the late Peirce but are distinguished from each other, at least according to the "classification of sciences.")

3. But all this does not mean that the classical ontological positions play no role in Peirce's philosophy or are ruled out as "senseless" as Carnap, for example, has done. For within the frame of his *hypothetical metaphysics*, the question of *materialism* or *(objective) idealism* was indeed a crucial problem for Peirce, as was the question of *determinism* vs. *indeterminism*. It is well known that Peirce adopted a kind of *objective idealism* or Neo-Schellingianism that involves "tychism," that is, spontaneity of

chance variation and feeling or "quasi-consciousness" as the origin and essence of natural evolution, matter being conceived as "effete mind" whose inveterate habits have become physical laws (see CP 6.101, 158, 23, 148, 261, 264ff., 605; Pape 1988 and 1989).

I would indeed suspect that this conception (which involves a certain rehabilitation of teleological thinking through assumption of unconscious trends toward "habit-taking" and thus provides an evolutionist explanation of the genesis of laws) is quite relevant and even plausible as an ontological background hypothesis for what Ilja Prigogine and others nowadays have called the "self-organization of matter." It may indeed provide an understanding of natural evolution (especially of the aspect of "chance-variation" or "mutation" in Darwinism and Neo-Darwinism) which makes it possible to conceive of natural evolution as the prehistory of human history. But this "objective idealism," which is a heuristic global hypothesis that may or may not prove to be fruitful, is not to be confused, I suggest, with the conception of meaning-critical realism that, together with normative pragmaticism, belongs to the framework of transcendental semeiotic. For this latter framework provides the normative conditions of the possibility for the understanding and testing even of global ontological hypotheses.

Finally, I would like at least to point to some consequences of this architectonic distinction for the interpretation of the relationship between the metaphysics of evolution and normative, transcendental semeiotic in Peirce's work.

(a) One good illustration of this relationship is provided by the relationship between the objective *generality of concepts* and *synechism* or *continuity* which, on my interpretation, represent, respectively, the transcendental-semeiotic and the metaphysical aspects of the category *thirdness*. Both the generality of concepts and the *objective validity* of this generality (hence, the *reality of universals*) are transcendental-semeiotic presuppositions of knowledge as *sign-mediated interpretation*. They are not hypotheses, since they are presuppositions of understanding the structure of testable hypotheses. For nomological hypotheses cannot even be falsified without presupposing that if they are valid at all, they must be valid universally, that is, in all cases that can be considered as relevant instances. And even the nominalist critic of the reality of universals must presuppose that his distinction between real individuals and terms or concepts is itself *universally valid*. (I understand this as the crucial Peircean argument against nominalism.) Thus far Peirce's realism with respect to universals is not a metaphysical position but an implication of meaning-critical realism. But the idea of "habit-taking" as a teleological tendency to generalization, which makes it possible to think of real generality and of *continuity* in time, is a metaphysical hypothesis, presumably the most characteristic and important one in Peirce's cosmology and theory of evolution. And of course Peirce's metaphysics of evolution allows one to think of human concept formation and conscious habit-taking as a continuation of natural evolution by normatively guided methods of cognition and of self-controlled action. (Thus it allows one to think of an habitual realization of the maxims that are described as possible laws of nature in Kant's second version of the "categorical imperative.")

(*b*) This leads to a second illustration of the relationship between the metaphysics of evolution and transcendental semeiotic. It is provided by Peirce's interpretation of *perceptual judgment* as something that *mediates*, so to speak, between natural evolution and normatively guided processes of human cognition and inquiry. On the one hand, from the perspective of a normative semeiotic logic of inquiry, a perceptual judgment is a special case of hypothesis, that is, of abductive inference and linguistic world interpretation. As such, it is subject to critique and to the principle of fallibilism to be found in the methodology of both Peirce and Popper. On the other hand, at least the later Peirce shared the Aristotelian conviction that the perceptual judgment is in some sense uncriticizable because all cognition must proceed from it. And he could even support this Aristotelian view through appeal to his insight into the quasi-iconic representation of *firstness*, that is, of qualitative suchness, in the predicates of perceptual judgments—although this does not mean that the perceptual judgment could be, qua judgment, free from *thirdness*, that is, criticizable interpretation of the given "percepts." But the element of firstness or qualitative evidence present in perceptual judgments—hence also in experiential science—cannot be reduced to a mere *external cause* of our accepting "basic propositions," as Popper would have it (see Popper 1957, 95ff., 105; Apel 1984, esp. 202, 221 note 36). On Peirce's account, this interpretation would be based on a category mistake because *firstness* as qualitative evidence (insofar as it cannot be separated from the *thirdness* of interpretation) provides a *reason*, not just an *external cause*, for our accepting a perceptual judgment.

This much can be said at the level of transcendental semeiotic or normative logic of inquiry. But at the level of the metaphysics of evolution, Peirce even offered an explanation of the fact that perceptual judgments are on the one hand, or in one respect, uncriticizable beginnings of human cognition, and, on the other, or in another respect, already the product of abductive inferences and sign interpretations, thus criticizable and fallible. They are, so to speak, joints between natural processes (in our sense organs and nervous system), which are of course not criticizable) and our synthetic inferences and sign interpretations, which are criticizable, at least in principle, even though they are partly unconscious and to this extent not criticizable in fact.

As results of natural processes, the perceptual judgments, or, more precisely, the "percepts" that are interpreted by them, are of course a well-proven outcome of our adaptation to nature—as are presumably the instinctual concepts or pre-conceptions that, on Peirce's account, form the a priori elements of our cognition. This provides evolutionist support for the methodological maxim that we should subject our cognitive hypotheses as thoroughly as possible to critique and improvement, even though we must always take as our point of departure the uncriticizable indubitability of vague common sense conceptions which must even provide the common reference basis for competing theories.

(*c*) A third illustration of the relationship between Peirce's metaphysics of evolution and his transcendental normative semeiotic can be obtained by comparing the "synechistic" and "agapastic" conception of the genesis of laws through habit-taking with the grounding of norms and aims of reasoning and action.

The metaphysical hypothesis about habit taking makes it possible to think of human habits, which may be the result of normatively guided processes of research and of action, as possible continuations of the natural evolution of laws of such a kind that their outcome would at least possibly amount to something like the *rationalization of the universe* if the human continuations of law formation could be supposed to be *rational* in a *normative* sense. But this metaphysical hypothesis cannot *guarantee* that the process of law formation will in fact be continued and successfully carried out by human beings; nor, what is more important, can it provide a *normative foundation* for that mode of continuation which *ought* to be intentionally and purposefully pursued by human beings.

On the other hand, "pragmaticism" as the "normative science" should provide an ultimate foundation for our moral duty to continue the natural evolution of habit taking toward the goal of a rationalization of the universe and to make this enterprise an object of hope, regardless of what the facts of success and failure may turn out to be. With regard to search for truth and the business of understanding the meaning of signs in the light of its possible consequences for this search, Peirce has outlined the best normative methodology I know; apart from this he was aware from his early writings onward that the enterprise of research, necessarily the enterprise of a community, presupposes an ethic (see CP 5.354ff., 402 note).

Unfortunately, Peirce did not exploit this approach to the full by extrapolating from the community of researchers, whose members *idealiter* are required to "surrender" all their personal interests to the common interest of the search for truth, to the *ideal communication community of humankind*. This latter community, which we must presuppose and counterfactually anticipate in every case of serious argumentation, does not consist of persons who are required to surrender their personal interests; but they are required to surrender all egoistic preparedness to achieve their personal interests by strategic means to the discipline of asserting them only by means of arguments acceptable to all affected persons. Such an extrapolation of Peirce's notion of the community would, I think, provide a foundation for a *for-*

mal-deontologic ethics of discourse which would constitute a transcendental-semeiotic transformation of Kant's ethics of the moral law as a possible continuation of the lawfulness of nature.

In his reorganized conception of pragmatism as the "normative science," Peirce went another way in grounding ethics as a presupposition of "good reasoning." He sought a final goal or *summum bonum* that all human beings could and should strive for in the long run, in the end defining this aim in a quasi-Platonic way as something "aesthetical": namely, the "admirable" (CP 5.36). I would not deny that this *teleological* grounding of ethics is a necessary complement to the formal-deontological foundation of a discourse ethics, mentioned above. But I think it is, rather, a guiding standard for an *ethics of the good life* to be realized by individual persons or even collective groups in different forms of life. By contrast, I would think, the formal-deontological principle of a discourse ethics may be grounded as a universally valid and binding principle, namely, as a principle that prescribes the *restrictive conditions* of everybody's realizing his idea of the good life, and the *procedural conditions* of the struggle for agreement by humankind about the common aims of responsible cooperation (Apel 1988).

23

Metaphysics, Science, and Self-Control: A Response to Apel

Christopher Hookway

Peirce and Metaphysics

QUESTIONS ABOUT Peirce's metaphysics can be raised at a number of levels. We could consider the details of his answers to particular metaphysical questions such as:

- Is there any real possibility or impossibility?
- Is Time a real thing, and if not, what is the nature of the reality that it represents?
- What external reality do the qualities of sense represent, in general?
- Are time and space continuous? (see CP 6.6).

But we can also raise the question of how metaphysical knowledge is possible at all. What methods of inquiry are appropriate for answering metaphysical questions? How can Peirce's respectable metaphysics avoid the destiny of the "ontological metaphysics" whose fate is sealed through application of the pragmatist maxim (CP 5.423)?

This question is, in fact, easily answered. Since Peirce espoused a "scientific metaphysics," its methods did not differ in kind from those used in the special sciences—except that the latter make more use of special observations and controlled experiments, while the former normally draws its data from frequently unnoticed features of everyday experience. This characterization invites an investigation of how far Peirce's metaphysical practice conformed to this description. But such an investigation is not our concern here. For a further question that is raised is:

Just what distinguishes metaphysical investigations from those that belong to the special sciences? And why did Peirce believe that he needed a metaphysics at all? What is the role of metaphysics in Peirce's system?

Peirce described the business of metaphysics as being to "study the most general features of reality and real objects," calling metaphysics "the completing department of philosophical science (coenoscopy) which in places welds itself into idioscopy or special science" (CP 6.6). A philosopher like Russell or Quine would be content to allow physics to describe for us "the most general features of reality and real objects." We shall understand why Peirce supposed he needed a scientific discipline that was more general than physics (one of the special sciences) if we attend to its role in his classification of the sciences. As is well known, Peirce's mature classification of the sciences saw mathematics as the "first" science, needing no foundations and supporting the phenomenological elucidation of the categories which succeeds it in his ordering. The three normative sciences follow: Aesthetics, Ethics, and Logic in that order. Metaphysics then falls into place, belonging with the philosophical disciplines and somehow effecting a bridge from them to physics and the rest.

Karl-Otto Apel defends the view that the place occupied by metaphysics is central to the Peircean solution to some fundamental epistemological issues. He claims that it promises a way out of a dilemma that destroyed the system of Kant's first *Critique* and which was ducked by subsequent philosophical movements. My role here is handicapped by the fact that I am in agreement with what I understand as the central theme of his paper. I agree that the role of metaphysics in Peirce's classification of the sciences is central to understanding his mature philosophy; and I agree too that, for example, the theory of reality derived from the pragmatist principle is neither itself a metaphysical thesis nor something the proof of which depends upon the results of metaphysical investigations. So, I shall proceed as follows. The core of my essay restates in rather different terms what I understand Apel to be claiming. Thus, I shall first explain why I think that such a restatement is worth presenting, and then qualify my acceptance of the general point that Peirce's logical writings make no metaphysical assertions.

Peirce often commented on the "deplorably backward condition" of metaphysics (CP 6.2), finding it a "puny, rickety, and scrofulous science" (CP 6.6). Such remarks occur in the context of denying that this relative immaturity results from the fact that metaphysics is more difficult than physics, psychology, and the other special sciences. It is the result, rather, of the fact that "those who pretend to cultivate it carry not the hearts of true men of science in their breast" (CP 6.6). Most were theologians who were unwilling or unable to strive "with might and main to find out what errors they have fallen into." Because they could not exult "joyously at every such discovery, they are scared to look Truth in the face" (CP 6.6). Peirce anticipated that his scientific metaphysics would be "somewhat more difficult than logic, but still on the whole one of the simplest sciences" (CP 6.4). Indeed, because he thought that Logic required metaphysics to be developed earlier than the more concrete special sciences (CP 6.1), its "main principles" being "settled before very much progress can be gained either in psychics or in physics" (CP 6.4), it was important for him that scientific metaphysics not be a difficult field of inquiry. The final section of this essay considers Peirce's reasons for supposing that metaphysics was relatively straightforward.

Peirce and Transcendental Philosophy

Apel has defended a distinctive interpretation of Peirce's writings in logic and semeiotic, and this interpretation is reflected in the argument of the present essay. All would agree that Peirce was much influenced by Kant and that this influence was evident throughout his writings. Apel makes the further claim that Peirce's strategy is Kantian through and through. Peirce is credited with effecting a transformation of the critical philosophy from "transcendental logic" to "transcendental semeiotic," and Apel's exegesis of Peirce's writings in logic and epistemology focuses upon finding correspondences between stages in Peirce's argument and stages of Kant's argument in the first *Critique* (Apel 1980, 1981). Few can doubt that this reading has yielded insight into the structure of Peirce's thought, and it has been valuable in focusing attention upon Peirce's emphasis on the relations between the different sciences. But my aim here is to articulate the points about the role of Peirce's metaphysics without relying upon this framework of interpretation. I shall now explain why it is valuable to restate the points in this way. Since my central concern is with Peirce's metaphysics rather than with the relations of his philosophical approach to Kant's, I shall be brief.

Like Kant, Peirce aimed to explain both the possibility of empirical scientific inquiry and the legitimacy of the rules we use in subjecting our inquiries to rational self-control. And like Kant, he thought it inappropriate to use materials drawn from such self-controlled inquiries into the nature of reality while attempting to vindicate this practice of self-control. In earlier writings, the resemblances go further. Consider the avowed argumentative structure of the "Illustrations of the Logic of Science" (P 107ff. 119-23). In the "Fixation of Belief," we learn that some facts are taken for granted by the very posing of the logical question; and that the most fundamental logical rules are those that can be derived from these presuppositions of logic (W 3:246). The demonstration in that essay that the methods of authority and tenacity and the a priori method cannot be sustained in all circumstances is intended to reveal that the fundamental hypothesis of the method of science—that there are real things whose characters are independent of our beliefs about them, but whose characters can be discovered through empirical investigation (W 3:254)—is itself one of the presuppositions of the logical question.[1]

In several places, Peirce denied that he was a "transcendental philosopher": "I am not one of those transcendental apothecaries, as I call them—they are so skillful in making up a bill—who call for a quantity of big admissions, as indispensable *Voraussetzungen* of logic" (CP 2.113). We might suppose that Peirce was criticizing those who *misuse* the "transcendental" method by identifying far too many "indispensable postulates." But Peirce was making a more substantial point: "I do not admit that indispensability is any ground for belief." Suppose it is established that some proposition is a presupposition of inquiry; this fact does not legitimate my *believing* it to be true, although it does explain why I am warranted in *hoping* that it is true.

> For example, when we discuss a vexed question, we *hope* that there is some ascertainable truth about it, and that the discussion is not to go on forever and to no purpose. A transcendentalist would claim that it is an indispensable "presupposition" that there is an ascertainable true answer to every intelligible question. I used to talk like that, myself; for when I was a babe in philosophy my bottle was filled from the udders of Kant. But by this time I have come to want something more substantial [CP 2.113, 1902].

A passage from the 1903 "Lowell Lectures" shows that he distinguished his logic from Kant's on the grounds that where Kant viewed logical principles as "Constitutive Principles," for Peirce "every principle of logic is a Regulative Principle (viz. a hope) and nothing more. Logic has nothing to do with existence" (NEM 3:371). Peirce and the "transcendentalists" differ on the logical status of the "presuppositions of logic." The Kantian believed that showing that something is a precondition of experience or of inquiry somehow legitimates our assurance of its truth. Peirce denied that *belief* in fundamental commitments can be legitimated in this fashion: at best we are warranted in hoping that they are true.

André De Tienne has recently argued that "anti-transcendentalism" characterized Peirce's writings as early as the 1860s, claiming that Peirce objected to a Kantian demand "for a justification of what the mind does 'normally'" (1988, 25–26). This accords with the suggestion above that what is at issue is the possibility of a legitimation of our practices which is independent of, or prior to, experiential knowledge. For Peirce, all justification and legitimation must occur within consciousness or within experience. It is such considerations that have led Klaus Oehler to denounce any description of Peirce as a "transcendental philosopher" (Oehler 1987); and it is the source of Apel's admission (see chap. 22 above) that Peirce's attempt to vindicate his categories phenomenologically by testing them against *experience* is an embarrassment for his "transcendental" reading.

The fundamental issue involved in evaluating the "transcendental" characterization turns on the relations between the methods employed in philosophical inquiry and those in empirical science. The Kantian terms suggest a methodological dualism: logic and semeiotic make no use of the scientific method, their results being in some sense known a priori. As I shall illustrate, avoidance of various circles requires some sort of distinction between philosophical method and the method of science. We might put this by saying that the materials used in logic must be acquired through investigations that are pre-logical: logical reflection can have no role in the inquiries whose goal is to justify the tools of logical reflection. This is enough to justify the thought that such inquiries possess a kind of priority or a "relative a priority." Whereas this may be enough to give the term "transcendental" some application, its use can conceal the fact that this dualism rests upon a deeper unity. The pre-logical sciences use observation, experiment, deductive and abductive inference, and even a form of inductive reasoning; the knowledge they provide all rests upon experience.

Kant's transcendental framework is a diagram that can be applied to Peirce's philosophy to provide insight into the relations of its parts. Such diagrams are valuable only insofar as we understand the limits of the analogy as well as the positive points of resemblance. Indeed, it is worth noting that Apel admits that the Peircean "transformation" of Kantian transcendental logic turns Kant's constitutive principles into regulative ones and does not permit the deduction of any synthetic principles as knowable a priori: the passage from CP 2.113 need not disturb Apel's interpretation. His sense that the resemblance between Kant's strategies and Peirce's is only partial is evident from his occasional use of the term "*quasi*-transcendental" to describe Peirce's strategy (Apel 1980, 88). Working exhaustively with such a picture or diagram can lead us to raise questions about the relations of the parts of Peirce's philosophy which can encourage us to distort Peirce's intentions. Because Peirce explicitly disavowed the epithet "transcendental," we can take it that he felt that such a representation of his thought could conceal some of his fundamental commitments.[2] But it is compatible with this that those who approach Peirce's thought from a different intellectual background may find that the benefits of the Kantian analogy outweigh these dangers. At the very least, because I think that Apel's chief point is detachable from this transcendental perspective, it is useful to illustrate this by reformulating it in terms closer to those that Peirce favored. This will enable us to sidestep the debates over the permissible use of the term "transcendental."[3]

The Problem

I shall now present some epistemological problems that are (at least) analogous to those confronted in Apel's essay. In the background is the thought that logical reflection must provide confidence that empirical investigation of reality is possible and that we can control our inquiries using normative standards whose legitimacy we can trust. We aspire to a sort of autonomous self-control: we monitor and control our activities; and in order to avoid a skeptical sense of alienation from our practice of evaluation, we need to be sure that the standards we use are accepted because they are right. We are not constrained to use certain standards whether they are correct or not; we actively endorse them rather than, in Pyrrhonist fashion, passively acquiescing in what seems right to us.

There are two problems. The first is a simple difficulty about circularity and justification. If we make use of results obtained through logically monitored empirical (or metaphysical) inquiry in carrying out investigations into the legitimacy of methods of inquiry, then we risk uncorrectable error: we might use an incorrect empirical theory that leads us to adopt mistaken procedures of inquiry which, in turn, confirm our acceptance of that empirical theory. For Peirce at least, the fundamental principles of the method of science must receive a vindication that avoids that danger. If we adopt the method of science, we face no risk that our best efforts at inquiry will ultimately be thwarted.

But, second, the belief that we are capable of such autonomous self-control appears to involve a substantive conception of the self. If we are products of natural selection, equipped with a battery of instincts—inferential practices, standards of plausibility, broad views of the nature of reality, or tendencies to seize on some similarities and ignore others—we may judge that our position is that of the Pyrrhonist alluded to earlier. We are the prisoners of our cognitive apparatus, unable to rise above it to achieve the autonomous self-control that prompts our interest in logic.

The fundamental dilemma is this: The second problem appears to entail that our logical investigations require a distinctive metaphysics of the person, one that shows that we are not just the victims of our natural instincts. But if we do rely upon a metaphysics of the person in carrying out our logical investigations, then we face the circularity posed by the first problem.

This can suggest that logic is impossible. I agree with Apel that the structure of Peirce's mature philosophy—and particularly the role of his metaphysics—provides an ingenious response to this difficulty. The claim that his pre-logical sciences themselves all use the scientific method may make it hard to see how this can be. Therefore, I shall next try to explain the character of pre-logical inquiries which enables him to do this. How can these sciences use techniques of confirmation and observation ultimately analogous to those used in reflective empirical inquiry without themselves requiring legitimation from logic?

The Role of Metaphysics

How can the Peircean logician make use of material that results from applications of the scientific method (in a broad sense) without facing circularity? Space is insufficient for a full answer to this question, but I can indicate the character of Peirce's answer by describing three of the resources employed in logic and semeiotic. Logic attempts to explain the validity of the inferences we use when we carry out investigations, and it guides us in our attempts to exercise self-control in our inquiries. Peirce's claim was that critical self-control, employing standards defended within logic, has a fundamental role in inquiry in the special sciences, in sciences that attempt to describe the laws governing objects and events in the empirical world. Although pre-logical inquiries employ the scientific method, they do not require the kind of critical self-control that makes use of logical principles.

Although mathematics uses observation and experiment to arrive at results, it makes no claims about the nature of *reality*. Its results are hypothetical, and are not answerable to anything independent of the diagrams and structures used in constructing proofs and calculations. There is only limited scope for fallibility in mathematics: we may make slips or blunders in evaluating proofs or carrying out calculations, but we cannot discover that misconceptions about method in mathematics have led us to radical misunderstandings of the referents of mathematical terms. Moreover, in physics, even if we carry out our inquiries as well as possible, current scientific "beliefs" can be false; subsequent experience can refute them. Peirce denies that this is possible in mathematics: the only source of mathematical fallibility is our propensity to make blunders (these claims are documented and defended in Hookway 1985, chap. 6). Phenomenology and the normative sciences similarly make no claims about the nature of reality. Although they rely upon observation, experiment, and mathematical reasoning, they investigate the categorial structure of all possible appearance and ask: What is it *possible* to admire? What is it *possible* to adopt as an ultimate end? What is it *possible* to adopt as an ultimate principle of reasoning? The notion of "possibility" employed here is not limited to what is possible in reality: we are to take into account whether our ultimate aims could be sustained in worlds that conform to laws of nature other than those that obtain in reality. Once again, we are not concerned with the nature of reality, and reflection on whether our methods will take us to the truth about reality has no place (Hookway 1985, 58ff.).

The second component is a broad range of common-sense beliefs about inquiry, inquirers, and the objects of inquiry (CP 5.438ff.). Unlike the first component, these beliefs do concern the nature of empirical reality. They result from experience, but they are not the products of deliberate self-controlled inquiry. When asked what supports them we can only say with the common sense philosophers: "Everything counts for them and nothing counts against them." It does not occur to us that we can question them: their extreme vagueness renders them immune from straightforward falsification. Once again, relying upon them appears not to introduce any immediate circularity into logic. Like the results of mathematics and the normative sciences, these beliefs are acritical: logical assessment has no role in their acquisition and retention.

In later writings, Peirce insisted that some of Kant's constitutive synthetic a priori principles are interpreted by pragmaticists as such common-sense certainties. These are not—like the principles of logic—transformed into regulative hopes. They are *believed,* and this belief has withstood the test of an enormous amount of uncontrolled observation. Hence, such beliefs are not known a priori; but because they are acritical common-sense certainties they do not require legitimation by logical investigations or defense by further metaphysical investigation (CP 5.452).

But these materials are accompanied by a third component: a battery of regulative hopes (CP 2.113; see also the section "Pierce and Transcendental Philosophy" above). We aspire to logical self-control. This is possible only if we can trust our ability to carry out the normative sciences (and thus possess the required autonomy); and it is possible only if our common sense, which gives shape to key terms in inquiry, will continue to be trustworthy; and it is possible only if we can expect our abductive instincts to lead us to the right hypotheses as inquiry develops. We cannot know that these things are true, but because we shall not otherwise achieve rational self-control, Peirce proposed that we should *hope* that they are true. We rely upon a Pascalian practical judgment rather than the product of self-controlled empirical inquiry. But where common sense and mathematics provided an acritical *certainty,* these hopes introduce a tentative *contingent* character to our assurance that empirical science and self-control are possible.

Peirce wrote that metaphysics tells us how the world must be if the regulative hopes that guide our logical investigations are absolutely true (CP 1.487). Our work in logic commits us to the construction of a distinctive metaphysical system, but we need not appeal to the *results* of our metaphysical inquiries when carrying out logical investigations. And here I agree with Apel: unless metaphysics can explain how minds possess the powers required for logical self-control, the results of logic are vitiated; but our logical investigations can be (must be) completed *before* metaphysical investigations begin. The interplay of practically grounded regulative hopes and subsequent metaphysical confirmation enables us to hold that:

1. Logic places certain requirements upon an adequate metaphysical theory.
2. Metaphysical investigations do not need to be carried out before logic can be completed.[4]

If I disagree with Apel, it is in employing as the fundamental distinction here one between beliefs produced by the scientific method in a broad sense which calls for no logical monitoring and self-control and beliefs resulting from reflective investigations of the nature of reality. Apel's talk of the "transcendental" *suggests* a more radical methodological dualism. Although, as indicated in the section "Peirce and Transcendental Philosophy," I am unsure how far this suggestion is correct.

Logic and Metaphysical Neutrality

There may be further limits to my agreement with Apel. In this section, I shall question one of the conclusions that he draws from the argument I have just described. This is that for Peirce no "metaphysical" assertions are made in the course of doing logic. I shall suggest that the preceding argument does not establish that this is so. Clearly, if, within logic, I express the hope that there will be a metaphysics that will explain how I am indeed capable of autonomous self-control, then I *assert* no metaphysical proposition. Equally, my hope that metaphysics will underwrite the objectivity of subjunctive conditionals or my hope that it will explain why we are likely to be good at thinking up plausible hypotheses does not involve the assertion of a metaphysical hypothesis. Equally clearly, an assertion arrived at through reflective metaphysical investigation has (for Peirce) no place in Logic.

The possibility has not yet been excluded that assertions with a metaphysical subject matter (albeit not defended through self-controlled metaphysical inquiry) may yet have a place in logic. For logic does make use of assertions about reality: the vague, acritical certainties that make up common sense. As long as we make every effort to doubt such propositions, Peirce thought that we are not at fault in using them as the basis of self-control.

The relation of such common-sense propositions as have a metaphysical subject matter to metaphysics is different from that of the regulative hopes. Although they call for further investigation in post-logical metaphysical inquiry, they are genuine assertions with a metaphysical subject matter. The task of metaphysics here is to arrive at a precise and testable version of such vague common-sense certainties. So, if some of these common-sense certainties do have a metaphysical subject matter, then the metaphysical neutrality of logic has not been established.

What is required for a belief to be "metaphysical" may be somewhat indeterminate. But suppose that it is part of the common-sense background of logic—linked to Peirce's doctrine of the dynamical object—that we have direct perceptual knowledge of external things. Many of Peirce's remarks suggest that this is his view, and although vague, it would appear to be a metaphysical claim. Indeed, we might suppose that unless some such vague metaphysical commitments are involved in logic, the question whether theories are to be interpreted realistically or, say, instrumentally would be left open. And, on pain of circularity, that question could not be resolved by a "realist" metaphysics which could, in principle, itself be interpreted instrumentally.

I have nothing to say in response to the complaint that these common-sense certainties do *not* have a metaphysical subject matter. "Metaphysics" is a term of art, and the boundaries of its application are not clear. Moreover, I could agree that no metaphysical *hypotheses* are employed in logic. Acritical common-sense certainties are not correctly described as (testable) hypotheses. But that does not contradict the claim that assertions with a metaphysical subject matter are made in the course of logical investigations. Peirce's claims about the structure of the different sciences do not eliminate that possibility.

How Easy Is Metaphysics?

At the beginning of this essay, I noted Peirce's insistence that metaphysics was quite an easy subject: it is more difficult than logic but easier than any of the special sciences. Two distinct points were at issue. The first is that the place of metaphysics in Peirce's classification of the sciences explains why it is fairly easy: Peirce believed that the closer a discipline was to mathematics (the foundational discipline), the easier it would be. And he held that unless metaphysics made progress, the special sciences (especially psychology) would be checked, this being "a great disadvantage to all the other psychical sciences" (CP 6.2). These doctrines follow from a principle announced in 1898:

> Logic requires that the more abstract sciences should be developed earlier than the more concrete ones. For the more concrete sciences require as fundamental principles the results of the more abstract sciences, while the latter only make use of the results of the former as data; and if one fact is wanting, some other will generally serve to support the same generalization [CP 6.1].

Experience of mathematics (the most abstract science) suggested that what logic required was in fact forthcoming: the more abstract a discipline, the less difficult it is (CP 6.2).

Peirce thus claimed both that it was possible to develop metaphysical theories before carrying out investigations in the special sciences and that it was necessary to do so. In concluding this essay, I shall make some comments about both these claims. The analogy with mathematics offers very weak support for the claim that it is possible to develop metaphysics before physics. It appears to equivocate on what is involved in a science's being "abstract," suggesting that the relation of more fundamental to less fundamental sciences is always the same.

Mathematics is abstract because it does not deal with *existing* objects; it is relatively easy because it is an ideal and hypothetical science. It provides tools to be employed in less fundamental sciences but makes no claims about reality. Once we turn to the special sciences, the more "general" ones are expected to explain the laws of those sciences that are subordinate to them. Peirce's suggestion appears to entail (very implausibly) that the relation between logic and metaphysics, say, is analogous to that between physics and chemistry.

Peirce sometimes explained the structure of his classification of the sciences by saying that sciences employ principles from those sciences they are subordinate to and draw data from (or apply those principles to) sciences that are subordinate to them (CP 6.1). It is natural to complain that this explanation finds more uniformity in the relations between sciences than is warranted by experience. The advice that empirical science hopes to receive from logical or methodological investigations seems different in kind from the input that chemists expect from physics. Before qualifying this judgment, however, we should explore some of Peirce's other comments about why metaphysics is supposed to be easier than the special sciences.

The claim that metaphysics draws data from physics (or psychology) might suggest that the special sciences must be developed *before* metaphysical theories can be tested. But when discussing the relations between the metaphysics of mind and scientific psychology, Peirce remarked that it had never been proved that "metaphysical psychology stands in need, in any degree worth consideration, of the scientific results of positive psychology." He continued:

> We must distinguish between results which depend upon the scientific method of psychology—scientific discoveries—and those rough facts about the mind which are open to everyone's observation, and which no sane man dreams of calling into question. As a matter of fact, it is upon these latter facts, and upon a series of similar facts about the outer world, that every man actually and really bases, first, his general metaphysics, and then his metaphysics of the soul. Even modern conceptions of the nature of intelligence, although facts of physiology have aided their devel-

opment, can be more logically defended without resort to anything but those general facts about which nobody ever simulates a doubt, and never did do more than simulate one [N 3:49; and for a useful discussion, see Colapietro 1989, 51ff.].

There are similar remarks about our common-sense physics (CP 8.198; see Hookway 1990). They suggest that metaphysics is easy because it does not use sophisticated experimental techniques. "The data of metaphysics are not less open to observation, but immeasurably more so, than the data of the highly developed science of astronomy, to make any important addition to whose observations requires an expenditure of many tens of thousands of dollars." We fail to see this only because metaphysical observations are of a kind "with which every man's experience is so saturated that he usually pays no particular attention to them" (CP 6.2).

Other passages conflict with this. "The architecture of theories" recommends that our metaphysics should borrow conceptions from the latest and best scientific theories (CP 6.9); and in "Man's Glassy Essence" Peirce found it useful to refer to equations from recent doctoral theses in order to state his conception of the nature of matter (CP 6.238–245). These writings date from the early 1890s, while the passages in the previous paragraph were written at least five years later. But since CP 6.1 (from 1898) retains the claim that metaphysics draws data from the special sciences, we should not conclude simply that the development of Peirce's thought led him to reject his earlier insistence that metaphysics should exploit scientific results. I shall suggest that a more interesting theme in Peirce's thought is involved. To formulate this, we must ask why it was *necessary* for metaphysics to be developed before physics and the other special sciences.

One answer is suggested by the earlier sections of this essay: unless we have some positive reason to suppose that metaphysics will provide the concept of the self (and the view of reality) required to vindicate the regulative hopes we adopt in constructing our logic, those hopes might fade. It accords with this that the current discussion suggests that the materials for constructing this conception of the self and reality are available in everyday experience and common sense. But the source of Peirce's insistence that metaphysics be developed before the special sciences lies elsewhere. If metaphysics were ignored, he believed, progress in physical science and (especially) psychological science would be impeded. Metaphysics is "applied" to physics and psychology in two distinct ways. As a more general science, it is required to explain the obtaining of physical laws: Peirce's evolutionary cosmology explains fundamental physical law by showing how such laws evolved over time. But metaphysical knowledge is applied in physics in a different way as well: just as the approximate truth of our common-sense understanding of dynamics "is assumed by everybody who devises an experiment, and is therefore more certain than the result of any laboratory experiment" (CP 8.198), so our common-sense conception of mind serves as background for all scientific psychology. Reflection on this common-sense conception of nature or mind can prevent our taking seriously theories that conflict with it: it guides us in constructing hypotheses, and in deciding which are interesting enough to be tested experimentally. It is clear that Peirce thought that inattention to our common-sense metaphysics of mind was responsible for the popularity of psychological approaches that are familiar to us from the writings of Hume and other empiricists. Attention to metaphysics would have convinced us that they ignored features of mind which were potentially evident to all.

So understood, Peirce's insistence that psychological research had been "checked" by the backward state of metaphysics (CP 6.2) is of a piece with Wittgenstein's insistence (in the *Philosophical Investigations*) that the "confusion and barrenness of psychology is not to be explained by calling it a 'young science'": rather, "in psychology there are experimental methods and *conceptual confusion*" (1958, 232). Unless a metaphysical theory is developed, the wrong framework of concepts may be used to formulate psychological theories and evaluate their plausibility.

I suggested that an interesting feature of Peirce's thought explains his apparent uncertainty about the role of information from the special sciences in metaphysics. It relates to his insistence that common sense changes, although it does so very slowly (CP 5.444). Since he acknowledged that "modern science with its microscopes and telescopes" (CP 5.513) showed that we inhabit a world which the "old beliefs" do not fit "except in extended senses," our "common-sense" metaphysical view will lose its methodological value as scientific inquiry develops. Physical inquiry in the late twentieth century is guided by a conception of reality which may be enshrined in the "common-sense" and unreflective experience of trained physicists but which is foreign to our everyday common-sense "folk-physics." The common-sense view of the world has developed with the progress of physical inquiry—except that it is now the possession of only a few, and thus not properly described as "common sense." But it is now this scientifically refined conception of reality which is relevant to our attempts to formulate and evaluate hypotheses.

When Peirce was writing (and to this day), physics was a flourishing research program that had already escaped the confines of our everyday conception of the physical world, while psychology was still attempting to forge the concepts that were required for experimental research to be possible at all. In that case, we should expect his investigations of the metaphysics of the self to focus upon elucidating the psychological views implicit in ordinary common sense and everyday experience; but when he turned to the metaphysics of the physical world, we should expect attention to the physical concepts manifested in the beliefs and practices of physicists. It seems to me that this is what we do find. Hence, the uncertainty about whether scientific information is relevant to metaphysics is a reflection of the different states of development of different sciences.

This interpretation does not conflict with Peirce's insistence that metaphysics should be "developed" before physics and psychology. "Developed" need not mean "completed." Peirce may have intended to stress only that progress in physics or psychology (at a particular time) would be checked if we lack a clear understanding of the metaphysical conception of mind and nature which is available at that time. Metaphysical pictures of mind and nature have a role in evaluating hypotheses, so science will suffer if the task of articulating them is postponed.

In this section, I have examined Peirce's reasons for thinking it important to develop a metaphysics sooner rather than later. It turns out that these reasons rest upon a role for metaphysics distinct from the one that Apel has focused on and which was discussed in the earlier sections of this paper. The themes I have just discussed are likely to prompt metaphysical investigations with a different focus from those examined earlier. Of course, that does not diminish the importance of the considerations that concerned Apel; but it helps us to understand the variety of roles that Peirce's metaphysics was intended to fill. Moreover, the arguments discussed in this section help to explain why Peirce needs a metaphysics in addition to the special sciences.

Notes

1. This interpretation of the argumentative structure of "Fixation of Belief" is defended more fully in Hookway 1985, 43ff., Hookway 1990, and in Hookway 1993. The second of these papers suggests that some of these "presuppositions" are transformed into common-sense certainties in Peirce's later thought.

2. Peirce's criticisms of "transcendentalism" have to be interpreted carefully. An attack on "transcendental apothecaries" challenges transcendental approaches to philosophy in general only if *all* transcendental philosophers are guilty of the excesses that Peirce describes. And an attack on "occult transcendentalism" (CP 3.422) may just be directed at a subset of transcendental approaches: the context does not suggest that Peirce believed that all transcendentalism was "occult."

3. I should confess to being more tolerant of "stretching" the use of "transcendental" than some of Apel's critics (see Hookway 1985, 113ff. and Hookway 1988). Varying degrees of tolerance of this may be due to the different roles of Kant (and post-Kantian German philosophy) in both philosophical education and philosophical thought in Britain and on continental Europe.

4. Peirce's use of metaphysics to explain or ground logical principles emerged before he became clear about the "regulative" character of the principles of logic. William Davenport (1981) has traced his evolutionary cosmology to "Design and Chance," a manuscript dated 1884 (W 4:544–54).

BIBLIOGRAPHY

Almeder, Robert. 1980. *The Philosophy of Charles S. Peirce*. Blackwell: Oxford.
———. 1983. "Peirce on Meaning." In *The Relevance of Charles Peirce*. Ed. Eugene Freeman. The Monist Library of Philosophy. La Salle, Ill.: Open Court. Pp. 328–47.
Andersen, Henning. 1972. "Diphthongization." *Language* 48:11–50.
———. 1973. "Abductive and Deductive Change." *Language* 49:765–93.
———. 1980a. "Morphological Change: Towards a Typology." In *Recent Developments in Historical Morphology*. Ed. J. Fisiak. Berlin: Mouton. Pp. 1–50.
———. 1980b. "[Summarizing Discussion:]." Introduction to *Typology and Genetics of Language.*" Ed. T. Thrane et al. Travaux du Cercle linguistique de Copenhague 20. Copenhagen: Linguistic Circle of Copenhagen. Pp. 197–210.
Anttila, Raimo. 1989. *Historical and Comparative Linguistics*. Current Issues in Linguistic Theory 6. Amsterdam: Benjamins.
Apel, Karl-Otto. 1972/1974/1980. *From Kant to Peirce: The Semiotic Transformation of Transcendental Logic*. Proceedings of the Third International Kant Congress 1970. Dordrecht: Reidel. Pp. 90–104. Repr. in *Kant's Theory of Knowledge*. Ed. L. W. Beck. Dordrecht: Reidel. Pp. 23–37. Repr. also in Karl-Otto Apel, *Towards a Transformation of Philosophy*. London: Routledge & Kegan Paul.
———. 1973/1980. *Transformation der Philosophie*. 2 vols. Frankfurt a. M.: Suhrkamp. Select. Engl. trans. *Towards a Transformation of Philosophy*. London: Routledge & Kegan Paul.
———. 1973/1981. "Charles Morris und das Programm einer pragmatisch integrierten Semiotik." Introduction to *Charles W. Morris: Zeichen, Sprache, und Verhalten*. Dusseldorf: Schwann. Pp. 9–66. Repr. in *Zeichen bei Zeichen der Zeichen: 15 Studien bei Charles W. Morris*. Ed. A. Eschbach. Tübingen: Narr.
———. 1975/1981. *Der Denkweg von Charles Sanders Peirce*. Frankfurt a. M.: Suhrkamp. Trans.: *Charles S. Peirce: From Pragmatism to Pragmaticism*. Amherst: University of Massachusetts Press.

———. 1978. "Transcendental Semiotics and the Paradigms of First Philosophy." *Philosophic Exchange* 2(4):3–22.
———. 1980. *Towards a Transformation of Philosophy*. London: Routledge & Kegan Paul.
———. 1981. *Charles S. Peirce: From Pragmatism to Pragmaticism*. Amherst: University of Massachusetts Press.
———. 1984. *Understanding and Explanation: A Transcendental-Pragmatic Perspective*. Trans. Georgia Warnke. Cambridge: The MIT Press.
———. 1987. "C. S. Peirce and Post-Tarskian Truth." In *The Relevance of Charles Peirce*. Ed. Eugene Freeman. The Monist Library of Philosophy. La Salle, Ill.: Open Court. Pp. 89–223.
———. 1988. *Diskurs und Verantwortung*. Frankfurt a. M.: Suhrkamp.
———, ed. 1967–1970. *Charles Sanders Peirce: Schriften*. 2 vols. Frankfurt a. M.: Suhrkamp.
Åqvist, Lennart. 1965. *A New Approach to the Logical Theory of Interrogatives. I. Analysis*. Uppsala: Filosofiska föreningen i Uppsala.
———. 1972. "On the Analysis and Logic of Questions." In *Contemporary Philosophy in Scandinavia*. Ed. R. E. Olson and A. Paul. Baltimore and London: The Johns Hopkins University Press. Pp. 27–39.
Aristotle. 1985. *Nicomachean Ethics*. Trans. T. Irwin. Indianapolis: Hackett.
Ayer, A. J. 1968. *The Origins of Pragmatism: Studies in the Philosophy of Charles Sanders Peirce and William James*. London: Macmillan.
Baldwin, James M., ed. 1901–1905. *Dictionary of Philosophy and Psychology*. 3 vols. New York: Macmillan.
Bambrough, R. 1961. "Universals and Family Resemblances." *Proceedings of the Aristotelian Society* 50.
Bar-Hillel, Yehoshua. 1970. *Aspects of Language: Essays and Lectures on Philosophy of Language, Linguistic Philosophy and Methodology of Linguistics*. Jerusalem: Magnes. Pp. 69–88.
Barthes, Roland. 1964. *Le Degré zéro de l'écriture, suivi de Éléments de sémiologie*. Paris: Gonthier.
Baring-Gould, William S., ed. 1967. *The Annotated Sherlock Holmes*. 2 vols. New York: Porter.
Barwise, Jon, and Perry, John. 1983. *Situations and Attitudes*. Cambridge: The MIT Press.
Battistella, Edwin. 1985. "Markedness Isomorphism as a Goal of Language Change: The Spread of Periphrastic *Do* in English." *Lingua* 65:307–22.
Baumol, W. J., and Goldfield, S. W. 1968. *Precursors in Mathematical Economics*. London: London School of Economics and Political Science.

Berg, H. C. 1976. "Does the Flagellar Rotary Motor Stop?" *Cell Motility, Cold Spring Harbor Conf.* 3:47–56.
Berkeley, George. 1948–1957. *The Works of George Berkeley, Bishop of Cloyne.* Ed. A. A. Luce and T. E. Jessop. 9 vols. London-Edinburgh-Paris: Nelson.
Bernays, P. 1975. Review of Schröder, *Vorlesungen über die Algebra der Logik* I (1890). *Journal of Symbolic Logic* 40:609–14.
Bernstein, B. A. 1914. "A Complete Set of Postulates for the Logic of Classes in Terms of the Operation `Exception' and a Proof of the Independence of a Set of Postulates due to Del Re." *University of California Publications in Mathematics* 1:87–96.
———. 1916. "A Set of Four Independent Postulates for Boolean Algebras." *Transactions of the American Mathematical Society* 17:50–52.
Bernstein, Richard J. 1965. "Action, Conduct, and Self-Control." In *Perspectives on Peirce.* Ed. Richard J. Bernstein. New Haven: Yale University Press. Pp. 66–91.
Black, Max. 1971. "The Elusiveness of Sets." *Review of Metaphysics* 24:614–36.
Bochner, Solomon. 1966. *The Role of Mathematics in the Rise of Science.* Princeton: Princeton University Press.
———. 1970. "Paul Weiss's Recollection of Editing the Peirce Papers." *Transactions of the Charles S. Peirce Society* 6:161–83.
———. 1974."Mathematical Reflections. Part II. Charles Sanders Peirce." *American Mathematical Monthly* 81:838–52.
Boler, John. 1964. "Habits of Thought." In *Studies in the Philosophy of C. S. Peirce.* Ed. E. C. Moore and R. S. Robin. Amherst: University of Massachusetts Press.
Bonfantini, Massimo A. 1987. "Sulla Connotazione." In *La semiosi a l'abduzione.* Milan: Bompiani.
Boole, George. 1847. *An Investigation of the Laws of Thought, on Which are Founded the Mathematical Theory of Logic.* London: Walton & Moberly.
Bouissac, Paul, et al., eds. 1986. *Iconicity: Essays on the Nature of Culture.* Tübingen: Stauffenburg.
Braithwaite, R. B. 1953. *Scientific Explanation.* Cambridge: Cambridge University Press.
Braten, Stein. 1988. "Dialogic Mind: The Infant and the Adult in Protoconversation." In *Nature, Cognition, and System.* I. *Current Systems: Scientific Research on Natural and Cognitive Systems.* Ed. Marc E. Carvallo. Dordrecht: Kluwer. Pp. 187–205.
Brock, Jarrett. 1980. "Peirce's Anticipation of Game Theoretic Logic and Semantics." *Semiotics 1980.* Ed. M. Herzfeld and M. D. Lenhart. New York and London: Plenum. Pp. 55–64.

———. 1981a. "An Introduction to Peirce's Theory of Speech Acts." *Transactions of the Charles S. Peirce Society* 17:319-26.
———.1981b. "Peirce and Searle on Assertion." *Proceedings of the C. S. Peirce Bicentennial International Congress*. Ed. Kenneth L. Ketner et al. Texas Tech University Graduate Studies 23. Lubbock: Texas Tech University Press. Pp. 281-87.
———. Unpublished. "The Development of Peirce's Thoughts About Proper Names."
Brodsky, Joseph. 1989. "Isaiah Berlin at Eighty." *The New York Review of Books* 36:13:44-45 (August 17).
Bronowski, J. 1958/1987. "The Creative Process." *Scientific American* (September 1958). In *Scientific Genius and Creativity*. Ed. Owen Gingerich. New York: Freeman. Pp. 3-9.
Bühler, Karl. 1934. *Sprachtheorie: Die Darstellungfunktion der Sprache*. Stuttgart: Fischer.
Burali-Forti, Cesare. 1897. "Una questione sui numeri transfiniti." *Rendiconti del circolo matematico di Palermo* 11:154-64.
Burks, Arthur. 1951. "A Theory of Proper Names." *Philosophical Studies* 2:36-45.
———. 1972. "Logic, Computers, and Men." *Proceedings of the American Philosophical Association* 46:48ff.
Cantor, Georg. 1872/1932. "Über die Ausdehnung eines Satzes aus der Theorie der trigonometrischen Reihen." *Mathematische Annalen* 5:123-32. Repr. in Georg Cantor, *Gesammelte Abhandlungen mathematischen und philosophischen Inhalts*. Ed. E. Zermelo. Berlin: Springer. Pp. 92-102. Repr. Hildesheim: Olms, 1966. Repr. Berlin: Springer, 1980.
———. 1874/1932. "Über eine Eigenschaft des Inbegriffes aller reellen algebraischen Zahlen." *Journal für die reine und angewandte Mathematik* 77:258-62. Repr. in Georg Cantor. *Gesammelte Abhandlungen mathematischen und philosophischen Inhalts*. Ed. E. Zermelo. Berlin: Springer. Pp. 115-18. Repr. Hildesheim: Olms, 1966. Repr. Berlin: Springer, 1980.
———. 1932. *Gesammelte Abhandlungen mathematischen und philosophischen Inhalts*. Ed. E. Zermelo. Berlin: Springer, 1932. Repr. Hildesheim: Olms, 1966. Repr. Berlin: Springer, 1980.
Carnap, Rudolf. 1950. *Logical Foundations of Probability*. Chicago: The University of Chicago Press.
Cassirer, Ernst. 1953-1957. *The Philosophy of Symbolic Forms*. 3 vols. New Haven: Yale University Press.
Church, Alonzo. 1936. "A Bibliography of Symbolic Logic." *Journal of Symbolic Logic* 1:121-216.
———. 1939. "Schröder's Anticipation of the Simple Theory of Types." *Erkenntnis* 9:149-53.

Cohen, Morris Raphael, ed. 1923. *Chance, Love, and Logic*. London: Routledge & Kegan Paul.
Colapietro, Vincent. 1989. *Peirce's Approach to the Self: A Semiotic Perspective on Human Subjectivity*. Albany: State University of New York Press.
Conan Doyle, Arthur. 1908. "The Adventure of the Bruce-Partington Plans." *Strand Magazine* 36:689-705. Repr. in *The Annotated Sherlock Holmes*. Ed. William S. Baring-Gould. New York: Porter. Pp. 432-52.
Cramer, H. 1945. *Mathematical Methods of Statistics*. Princeton: Princeton University Press.
Crittenden, Charles. 1973. "Thinking about Non-Being." *Inquiry* 16:290-312.
Crossley, J. 1973. "A Note on Cantor's Theorem and Russell's Paradox." *Australian Journal of Philosophy* 51:70-71.
Crowe, M. J. 1975. "Ten `Laws' Concerning Patterns of Change in the History of Mathematics." *Historia Mathematica* 2:161-66.
Dauben, Joseph. 1974. "Denumerability and Dimension: The Origins of Georg Cantor's Theory of Sets." *Rete* 2:105-34. Repr. in Joseph Dauben, *Georg Cantor: His Mathematics and Philosophy of the Infinite*. Cambridge: Harvard University Press, 1979. Pp. 54-76. Repr. Princeton: Princeton University Press, 1990.
——. 1977. "C. S. Peirce's Philosophy of Infinite Sets." *Mathematics Magazine* 50(3):123-35.
——. 1979/1990. *Georg Cantor: His Mathematics and Philosophy of the Infinite*. Cambridge: Harvard University Press. Repr. Princeton: Princeton University Press.
——. 1981. "Peirce's Critique of Cantorian Set Theory." *Proceedings of the C. S. Peirce Bicentennial International Congress*. Ed. Kenneth L. Ketner et al. Texas Tech University Graduate Studies 23. Lubbock: Texas Tech University Press. Pp. 93-98.
——. 1982. "Peirce's Place in Mathematics." *Festschrift in Honor of Carolyn Eisele. Historia Mathematica* 9:311-25.
——. 1984. "Conceptual Revolutions and the History of Mathematics: Two Studies in the Growth of Knowledge." In *Transformation and Tradition in the Sciences*. Ed. E. Mendelsohn. Cambridge: Cambridge University Press. Pp. 81-103.
——. 1986. Review of *W2*, in *Isis* 77:384-86.
——. 1987. "Abraham Robinson and Nonstandard Analysis: History, Philosophy, and Foundations of Mathematics." In *New Perspectives on the History and Philosophy of Mathematics*. Ed. P. Kitcher and W. Aspray. Minneapolis: University of Minnesota Press. Pp. 177-200.
Davenport, H. William. 1981. "Peirce's Evolutionism and His Logic:

Two Connections. *Proceedings of the C. S. Peirce Bicentennial International Congress.* Ed. Kenneth L. Ketner et al. Texas Tech University Graduate Studies 23. Lubbock: Texas Tech University Press. Pp. 307-12.

Davidson, Donald. 1967. "The Logical Form of Action Sentences." In *The Logic of Decision and Action.* Ed. Nicholas Rescher. Pittsburgh: University of Pittsburgh Press. Pp. 81-95.

———. 1973-1974. "On the Very Idea of a Conceptual Scheme." *Proceedings and Addresses of the American Philosophical Association* 47:5-30.

Dawkins, Richard. 1976. *The Selfish Gene.* Oxford: Oxford University Press.

Dedekind, Richard. 1872. *Stetigkeit und irrationale Zahlen.* Braunschweig: Vieweg. Repr. in *Richard Dedekind: Gesammelte mathematische Werke.* Ed. R. Fricke, E. Noether, and O. Ord. 3 vols. Braunschweig: Vieweg, 1930-1932.

———. 1888. *Was sind und was sollen die Zahlen?* Braunschweig: Vieweg. 2nd ed. Trans. W. W. Berman in *Essays on the Theory of Numbers.* Chicago: Open Court, 1901. Repr. New York: Dover, 1963.

De Morgan, Augustus. 1842-1849. "On the Foundation of Algebra." *Transactions of the Cambridge Philosophical Society* 7 (1842):173-87, 287-300; 8 (1849):139-42, 241-53.

———. 1847. *Formal Logic: or, The Calculus of Inference, Necessary and Probable.* London: Taylor and Walton. Repr. ed. A. E. Taylor, London: Open Court, 1926.

———. 1860. *Syllabus of a Proposed System of Logic.* London: Walton & Maberly.

———. 1864. "On the Syllogism, No. IV, and the Logic of Relations." *Cambridge Philosophical Transactions* 10:331-58. Appendix "On Syllogisms of Transposed Quantity." Pp. 355-358.

———. 1966. *On the Syllogism and Other Logical Writings.* Ed. Peter Heath. London: Routledge & Kegan Paul; New Haven: Yale University Press.

Derrida, Jacques. 1967a. *De la grammatologie.* Paris: Minuit.

———. 1967b. *La voix et le phénomène: Introduction au problème du signe dans la phénoménologie de Husserl.* Presses Universitaires de France.

———. 1972. "Signature, événement, contexte." *Marges.* Paris: Minuit.

———. 1976. *Of Grammatology.* Baltimore: The Johns Hopkins University Press.

Dennett, Daniel. 1982. "Beyond Belief." In *Thought and Object: Essays on Intentionality.* Ed. A. Woodfield. Oxford: Clarendon. Pp. 64-76.

De Tienne, André. 1988. "Peirce's Search for a Method of Finding the Categories." *Versus* 49:19–30.
Dipert, Randall R. 1973. "Peirce on Mach and Absolute Space." *Transactions of the Charles S. Peirce Society* 9:79–94.
———. 1977. "Peirce's Theory of the Geometrical Structure of Physical Space." *Isis* 68:404–13.
———. 1978a. "Development and Crisis in Late Boolean Logic: The Deductive Logics of Peirce, Jevons, and Schröder." Ph.D. Diss., Indiana University.
———. 1978b. "Peirce's Theory of the Dimensionality of Physical Space." *Journal of the History of Philosophy* 1:61–70.
———. 1981a. "Ernst Schröder's *Beitrag zur Logik und den Grundlagen der Mathematik.*" *Fredericiana* 27:23–44.
———. 1981b. "Peirce's Propositional Logic." *Review of Metaphysics* 34:569–95.
———. 1982. "Set-Theoretical Representations of Ordered Pairs and Their Adequacy for the Logic of Relations." *Canadian Journal of Philosophy* 12:353–74.
———. 1984. "Peirce, Frege, Church's Theorem and the Logic of Relations." *History and Philosophy of Logic* 5:49–66.
———. 1994. "The Life and Logical Contributions of O. H. Mitchell: Peirce's Gifted Student." *Transactions of the Charles S. Peirce Society*. 30(3):515–42.
Donnellan, Keith. 1966. "Reference and Definite Descriptions." *Philosophical Review* 75:281–304. Repr. in *Naming, Necessity, and Natural Kinds*. Ed. Stephen P. Schwartz. Ithaca and London: Cornell University Press. Pp. 42–65.
Dressler, Wolfgang U. 1980/1982. "A Semiotic Model of Diachronic Process Phonology." *Wiener Linguistische Gazette* 22/23:31–94. *Perspectives on Historical Linguistics*. Ed. Winfrid P. Lehmann and Yakov Malkiel. Amsterdam: Benjamins. Pp. 93–131.
Dretske, Fred. 1986. "Misrepresentation." In *Belief*. Ed. Radu J. Bogdan. Oxford: Clarendon. Pp. 17–36.
Dubois, Philippe. 1988. *L'Acte photographique*. Brussels: Labor.
Du Bois-Reymond E. 1878. *Culturgeschichte und Naturwissenschaft*. Leipzig: Veit.
Dugac, Pierre. 1976. *Richard Dedekind et les fondements des mathématiques*. Paris: Vrin.
Dummett, Michael. 1981. *Frege: Philosophy of Language*. 2nd ed. Cambridge: Harvard University Press.
Duren, Peter, ed. 1988. *A Century of Mathematics in America, Part I*. Providence: American Mathematical Society.
———. 1989. *A Century of Mathematics in America, Part II*. Providence: American Mathematical Society.

Eco, Umberto. 1981. "Peirce's Analysis of Meaning." In *Proceedings of the C. S. Peirce Bicentennial International Congress*. Ed. Kenneth L. Ketner et al. Texas Tech University Graduate Studies 23. Lubbock: Texas Tech Press. Pp. 179–221.
———. 1984. *Semiotics and the Philosophy of Language*. Bloomington: Indiana University Press.
———. 1990. *Limits of Interpretation*. Bloomington: Indiana University Press.
———, and Sebeok, Thomas A., eds. 1983. *The Sign of Three: Dupin, Holmes, Peirce*. Bloomington: Indiana University Press.
Eisele, Carolyn. 1959/1979. "A Nineteenth-Century Man of Science." *Scripta Mathematica* 4:305–24. Repr. in *Studies in the Scientific and Mathematical Philosophy of Charles S. Peirce: Essays by Carolyn Eisele*. Ed. R. M. Martin Studies in Philosophy 29. The Hague: Mouton. Pp. 118–37.
———. 1975. "Solomon Bochner on Charles S. Peirce. I." *American Mathematical Monthly* 82:477–78.
———. 1976. *The New Elements of Mathematics by Charles S. Peirce*. The Hague: Mouton; Rahwey, N.J.: Humanities.
———. 1979. *Studies in the Scientific and Mathematical Philosophy of Charles S. Peirce: Essays by Carolyn Eisele*. Ed. R. M. Martin. Studies in Philosophy 29. The Hague: Mouton.
———.1970. "Peirce, Charles Sanders." *Dictionary of Scientific Biography*. New York: Scribner's, 1970. Pp. 482–88.
———. 1985. *Historical Perspectives on Peirce's Logic of Science: A History of Science*. Ed. C. Eisele. Berlin: Mouton, 1985.
———. 1988. "The Modern Relevance of the Mathematical Philosophy of Charles S. Peirce." *Proceedings of the Conference on Frontiers in American Philosophy*. College Station: Texas A&M University Press.
Ennion, E. A. R., and Tinbergen, N. 1967. *Tracks*. Oxford: Clarendon.
Evans, Gareth. 1977. "The Causal Theory of Names." In *Naming, Necessity, and Natural Kinds*. Ed. Stephen P. Schwartz. Ithaca and London: Cornell University Press. Pp. 192–215.
———. 1982. *The Varieties of Reference*. Ed. J. McDowell. Oxford: Clarendon. Pp. 376–78.
Fann, K. T. 1970. *Peirce's Theory of Abduction*. The Hague: Nijhoff.
Feibleman, J. K. 1946/1969. *An Introduction to the Philosophy of C. S. Peirce*. New York: Harper & Bros. Repr. Cambridge: The MIT Press.
Fillmore, Charles. 1973. "May We Come In?" *Semiotica* 9:97–116.
Fisch, Max Harold. 1975. "Solomon Bochner on Charles S. Peirce II." *American Mathematical Monthly* 82:478–81.

———. 1980. "Foreword." In *You Know My Method*. Ed. Thomas A. Sebeok and Jean Umiker. Bloomington, Ind.: Gaslight Publications.
———. 1984. "The Decisive Year and Its Early Consequences." In *Writings of Charles S. Peirce: A Chronological Edition*. II. 1867–1871. Bloomington: Indiana University Press. Pp. xxi–xxxvi.
———. 1986. *Peirce, Semeiotic, and Pragmatism: Essays by Max H. Fisch*. Ed. K. L. Ketner and C. J. W. Kloesel. Bloomington: Indiana University Press.
Fisher, R. A. 1930. "Inverse Inference." *Proceedings of the Cambridge Philosophical Society* 26:528–35.
Fraenkel, A. 1968. *Abstract Set Theory*. Amsterdam: North Holland.
Fodor, Jerry. 1987. *Psychosemantics*. Cambridge: The MIT Press.
Freeman, Eugene, ed. 1983. *The Relevance of Charles Peirce*. Ed. Eugene Freeman. The Monist Library of Philosophy. La Salle, Ill.: Open Court.
Frege, Gottlob.1896. "Über die Begriffsschrift des Herrn Peano und meine Eigene." In *Kleine Schriften*. Ed. I. Angelelli. Darmstadt: Wissenschaftliche Buchgesellschaft.
———. 1903/1962. *Grundgesetze der Arithmetik, begriffsschriftlich abgeleitet*. Jena: Pohle. Repr. Hildesheim: Olms.
———. 1952. *Translations from the Philosophical Writings of Gottlob Frege*. Ed. P. Geach and M. Black. Oxford: Blackwell.
———. 1964. *Begriffsschrift und andere Aufsätze*. Ed. I. Angelelli. Hildesheim: Olms. Translation:. *Conceptual Notation, and Related Articles*. Trans. T. Bynum. Oxford: Clarendon.
———. 1967. *Kleine Schriften*. Ed. by I. Angelelli. Darmstadt: Wissenschaftliche Buchgesellschaft.
———. 1969. *Nachgelassene Schriften und wissenschaftlicher Briefwechsel*. Ed. H. Hermes, F. Kambartel and F. Kaulbach. Hamburg: Meiner. Translation: *Posthumous Writings*. Trans. P. Long and R. White. Chicago: The University of Chicago Press.
———: 1985. "On Sense and Meaning." Repr. in *The Philosophy of Language*. Ed. A. P. Martinich. New York and Oxford: Oxford University Press. Pp. 200–12.
French, A. P., and Kennedy, P. J., eds. 1985. *Niels Bohr: A Centenary Volume*. Cambridge: Harvard University Press.
Furnham, Adrian. 1988. "Write and Wrong: The Validity of Graphological Analysis." *The Skeptical Inquirer* 13(1):64–69.
Gale, Richard M. 1967. "Indexical Signs, Egocentric Particulars, and Token-Reflexive Words." *The Encyclopedia of Philosophy* 4:151–55.
Gallie, W. B. 1952. *Peirce and Pragmatism*. Harmondsworth, Middlesex: Penguin.

Garciadiego, Alejandro. 1985. "The Emergence of Some of the Nonlogical Paradoxes of the Theory of Sets, 1903-1908." *Historia Mathematica* 12:337-51.
Gillies, David. 1992. *Revolutions in Mathematics*. Oxford: Clarendon; New York: Oxford University Press.
Gingerich, Owen. 1987. *Scientific Genius and Creativity*. New York: Freeman.
Ginzburg, Carlo. 1983. "Morelli, Freud, and Sherlock Holmes." In *The Sign of Three: Dupin, Holmes, Peirce*. Ed. Umberto Eco and Thomas A. Sebeok. Bloomington: Indiana University Press. Pp. 81-118.
Goffman, Erving. 1963. *Stigma: Notes on the Management of Spoiled Identity*. Englewood Cliffs, N.J.: Prentice-Hall.
Goldfarb, Warren. 1979. "Logic in the Twenties: The Nature of the Quantifier." *Journal of Symbolic Logic* 44:351-68.
Good, I. J. 1981. "An Error by Peirce Concerning Weight of Evidence." *Journal of Statistical Computing and Simulation* 13:155-57.
——. 1983a. *Good Thinking*. Minneapolis: University of Minnesota.
——. 1983b. "Weight of Evidence: A Brief Survey. *Second Valencia International Meeting on Bayesian Statistics*.
Goodman, Nelson. 1983. *Fact, Fiction, and Forecast*. 4th ed. Cambridge: Harvard University Press.
Goudge, Thomas A. 1950. *The Thought of C. S. Peirce*. Toronto: University of Toronto Press.
Grant, Edward. 1974. "Peter Peregrinus." *Dictionary of Scientific Biography* 10:533-37.
Grassmann, Hermann. 1878. *Die Ausdehnungslehre von 1844*. 2nd ed. Leipzig: Wigand.
——. 1894-1911. *Gesammelte mathematische und physikalische Werke*. Ed. Friedrich Engel. Leipzig: Teubner.
Grassmann, Robert. 1872. *Die Begriffslehre oder Logik*. Stettin: Grassmann.
——. 1875-1876. *Die Wissenschaftslehre oder Philosophie*. Stettin: Grassmann.
——. 1966. *Die Formenlehre oder Mathematik*. Hildesheim: Olms.
Grattan-Guinness, Ivor. 1974. "The Rediscovery of the Cantor-Dedekind Correspondence." *Jahresbericht der Deutschen Mathematiker-Vereinigung* 76:104-39.
——. 1975. "Wiener on the Logics of Russell and Schröder." *Annals of Science* 32:103-32.
Greenley, Douglas. 1973. *Peirce's Concept of Sign*. Paris and The Hague: Mouton.

Guerlac, Henry. 1978. "Amicus Plato and Other Friends." *Journal of the History of Ideas* 39:627-33.
Hacking, I. 1965. *The Logic of Statistical Inference.* Cambridge: Cambridge University Press.
——. 1980. "The Theory of Probable Inference: Neyman, Peirce, and Braithwaite." In *Science, Belief, and Behaviour: Essays in Honor of R. B. Braithwaite.* Ed. D. H. Mellor. Cambridge: Cambridge University Press.
Hallett, Michael. 1984. *Cantorian Set Theory and Limitation of Size.* Oxford: Clarendon.
Hamilton, Sir William Rowan. 1837. "Theory of Conjugate Functions, or Algebraic Couples; With a Preliminary and Elementary Essay on Algebra as the Science of Pure Time." *Transactions of the Royal Irish Academy* 17:293-422.
——. 1853. *Lectures on Quaternions.* Dublin: Hodges and Smith.
Hammond, Mason. 1980. "Latin, Greek, and Hebrew Inscriptions on and in Harvard Buildings. Part I: Memorial Hall." *Harvard Library Bulletin* 28(3):299-346.
Harrison, Stanley. 1979. "Man's Glassy Essence." Ph.D. Diss. Fordham University.
Hegel, Georg Wilhelm Friedrich. 1821. *Grundlinien der Philosophie des Rechts.* Berlin: Nicolai.
Heidel, William A. 1941. *Hippocratic Medicine: Its Spirit and Method.* New York: Columbia University Press.
Heijenoort, Jean van. 1967. "Logic as Calculus and Logic as Language." *Synthèse* 17:324-30.
——, ed. 1967. *From Frege to Gödel: A Source Book in Mathematical Logic, 1879-1931.* Cambridge: Harvard University Press.
Herbrand, Jacques. 1971. *Logical Writings.* Ed. W. Goldfarb, Cambridge: Harvard University Press.
Hilbert, David. 1899. *Grundlagen der Geometrie.* Leipzig: Teubner.
——. 1932-1935. *Gesammelte Abhandlungen.* Berlin: Springer.
——. 1962. *Grundlagen der Geometrie.* 9th edition. Rev. P. Bernays. Stuttgart: Teubner. Translation: *Foundations of Geometry.* Trans. L. Unger. 2nd ed. La Salle, Ill. : Open Court, 1971.
Hilbert, David, and Ackermann, Wilhelm. 1967. *Grundzüge der theoretischen Logik.* 5th ed. Berlin: Springer. Translation: *Principles of Mathematical Logic.* 2nd ed. Trans. L. Hammond, G. Leckie and F. Steinhardt. New York: Chelsea, 1950.
Hilpinen, Risto. 1982. "Peirce's Theory of the Proposition: Peirce as a Precursor of Game-Theoretical Semantics." *Monist* 65:183-88.
——. 1986. "The Logic of Imperatives and Deontic Logic." In *Mérites et*

limites des méthodes logiques en philosophie. Ed. J. Vuillemin. Paris: Vrin. Pp. 193–206.
Hintikka, Jaakko. 1974. "Questions about Questions." In *Semantics and Philosophy*. Ed. M. K. Munitz and P. K. Unger. New York: New York University Press. Pp. 103–58.
———. 1976. "The Semantics of Questions and the Questions of Semantics." *Acta Philosophica Fennica* 28:4.
———. 1979. "Frege's Hidden Semantics." *Revue Internationale de Philosophie* 33:716–22.
———. 1988. "On the Development of the Model-Theoretic Viewpoint in Logical Theory." *Synthèse* 77:1–36.
Hintikka, Merrill B., and Hintikka, Jaako. 1986. "Wittgenstein and Language as the Universal Medium." In *Investigating Wittgenstein*. Oxford: Blackwell.
Hjelmslev, Louis. 1943. *Prolegomena to a Theory of Language*. Madison: University of Wisconsin.
Hookway, Christopher J. 1985. *Peirce*. London: Routledge & Kegan Paul.
———. 1988. "Pragmaticism and `Kantian Realism.'" *Versus* 49:103–12.
———. 1990. "Critical Common-Sensism and Rational Self-Control. *Nous* 24:397_412.
———. 1993. "Belief, Confidence, and the Method of Science." *Transactions of the Charles S. Peirce Society* 29:1–32.
Houser, Nathan. 1966. "Introduction." *Writings of Charles S. Peirce: A Chronological Edition. IV. 1878–1884*. Bloomington: Indiana University Press. Pp. xxi–xlviii.
Hugly, P., and Sayward, C. 1984. "Do We Need Quantification. *Notre Dame Journal of Formal Logic* 25:289–302.
Ingram, David. 1978. "Typology and Universals of Personal Pronouns." In *Universals of Human Language* III. Ed. Joseph H. Greenberg. Stanford: Stanford University Press. Pp. 213–47.
Inwagen, Peter van. 1977. "Creatures of Fiction." *American Philosophical Quarterly* 14:299–308.
Jakobson, Roman. 1971. *Selected Writings: Word and Language* II. Ed. Winfred P. and Malkiel Lehmann. The Hague: Mouton.
Jastrow, Joseph. 1930. "Joseph Jastrow." *A History of Psychology in Autobiography*. Ed. Carl Murchison. New York: Russell & Russell.
Jerne, Niels K. 1985. "The Generative Grammar of the Immune System." *Science* 229:1057–59.
Johnson-Laird, Philip N. 1983. *Mental Models: Towards a Cognitive Science of Language, Inference, and Consciousness*. Cambridge: Harvard University Press.

Kant, Immanuel. 1787/1963. *Critique of Pure Reason.* Trans. N. K. Smith. London: Macmillan.
Kaplan, David. 1969. "Quantifying In." In *Words and Objections: Essays on the Work of W. V. Quine.* Ed. J. Hintikka and D. Davidson. Dordrecht: Reidel.
———. 1977. "That." In *Contemporary Perspectives in the Philosophy of Language.* Ed. Peter A. French et al. Minneapolis: University of Minnesota Press. Pp. 383–400.
———. 1979. "On the Logic of Demonstratives." In *Contemporary Perspectives in the Philosophy of Language.* Ed. Peter A. French et al. Minneapolis: University of Minnesota Press. Pp. 401–12.
———. 1989a. "Afterthoughts." In *Themes from Kaplan.* Ed. Joseph Almog et al. New York and Oxford: Oxford University Press. Pp. 565–614.
———. 1989b. "Demonstratives." In *Themes from Kaplan.* Ed. Joseph Almog et. al. New York and Oxford: Oxford University Press. Pp. 481–563.
Kempsky, R. Jürgen von. 1952. *Charles S. Peirce und der Pragmatismus.* Stuttgart and Cologne: Kohlhammer.
Kennedy, Hubert C. 1980. *Peano: Life and Works of Giuseppe Peano.* Dordrecht: Reidel.
Ketner, Kenneth Laine, et al., eds. 1981. *Proceedings of the C. S. Peirce Bicentennial International Congress.* Texas Tech University Graduate Studies 23. Lubbock: Texas Tech University Press.
Kevles, Daniel J. 1985. *In the Name of Eugenics: Genetics and the Uses of Human Heredity.* New York: Knopf.
Kimberling, Clark. 1972. "Emmy Noether." *American Mathematical Monthly* 79:136–49.
Kneale, W., and Kneale, M. 1962. *The Development of Logic.* Oxford: Clarendon.
Kolmogorov, A. N. 1950. *Foundations of the Theory of Probability.* New York: Chelsea.
Krampen, Martin. 1981. "Phytosemiotics." *Semiotica* 36:187–209.
———, et al., eds. 1987. *Classics of Semiotics.* Trans. from *Die Welt als Zeichen: Klassiker der modernen Semiotik.* New York and London: Plenum.
Kuhn, S. T. 1983. "An Axiomatization of Predicate Functor Logic." *Notre Dame Journal of Formal Logic* 24.
Ladd-Franklin, Christine. 1916. "Charles S. Peirce at the Johns Hopkins." *Journal of Philosophy* 13:715–22.
Lambroso, Cesare. 1891. *The Man of Genius.* London: Scott.
Lenzen, Victor F. 1969. "An Unpublished Scientific Monograph by C. S. Peirce." *Transactions of the Charles S. Peirce Society* 5(1):5–24.

———, and Multhauf, R. P. 1965. "Development of Gravity Pendulums in the Nineteenth Century," *U.S. National Museum Bulletin* 240:301–48.
Levelt, Willem J. M. 1989. *Speaking: From Intention to Articulation.* Cambridge: The MIT Press.
Levi, I. 1965. "Hacking Salmon on Induction." *Journal of Philosophy* 63:481–87.
———. 1967. *Gambling with Truth.* Cambridge: The MIT Press.
———. 1980a. *The Enterprise of Knowledge.* Cambridge: The MIT Press.
———. 1980b. "Incognizables." *Synthèse* 45:413–26.
———. 1980c. "Induction as Self-Correcting According to Peirce." In *Science, Belief, and Behaviour.* Ed. D. H. Mellor. Cambridge: Cambridge University Press. Pp. 127–40.
———. 1984a. *Decisions and Revisions.* Cambridge: Cambridge University Press.
———. 1984b. "Messianic vs. Myopic Realism." *PSA-1984: Proceedings of the 1984 Biennial Meeting of the Philosophy of Science Association* II. Edd. P. D. Asquith and T. Nickles. East Lansing, Mich.: Philosophy of Science Association [1985]. Pp. 617–36.
Lewis, David. 1973. *Counterfactuals.* Oxford: Blackwell.
———. 1978/1983. "Truth in Fiction." *American Philosophical Quarterly* 15:37–46. Reprinted with Postscripts in David Lewis, *Philosophical Papers* I. Oxford and New York: Oxford University Press. Pp. 261–80.
Lieb, Irwin C. 1970. "Charles Hartshorne's Recollections of Editing the Peirce Papers." *Transactions of the Charles S. Peirce Society*, 6(3–4):149–59.
Lombroso, Cesare. 1891. *The Man of Genius.* London: Scott.
Lyons, John. 1977. *Semantics.* Cambridge: Cambridge University Press.
McCarthy, J. E. 1984. "Semiotic Idealism." *Transactions of the Charles S. Peirce Society* 20:395ff.
Mackay, Alan L. 1984. "The Code Breakers." *The Sciences* 24(3):13–14.
McKinsey, J. C. C. 1940. "Postulates for the Calculus of Binary Relations." *Journal of Symbolic Logic* 5.
Merrill, Daniel D. 1978. "De Morgan, Peirce, and the Logic of Relations." *Transactions of the Charles S. Peirce Society* 14:247–84.
———. 1982. "The 1870 Logic of Relatives Memoir." In W2:xlii–xlviii.
Merton, Robert K. 1965. *On the Shoulders of Giants: A Shandean Postscript.* New York: Free Press.
Miller, G. A. 1903–1904. "On The Definition of Infinite Number." *The Monist* 14.

Mitchell, O. H. 1883. "On a New Algebra of Logic." In *Studies in Logic by Members of the Johns Hopkins University*. Ed. C. S. Peirce. Boston: Little, Brown. Repr. Amsterdam: Benjamins.
Moore, E. C. 1984. Preface. *Writings of Charles S. Peirce: A Chronological Edition*. II. *1867-1876*. Bloomington: Indiana University Press.
——, and Robin, R. S., eds. 1964. *Studies in the Philosophy of C. S. Peirce, Second Series*. Amherst: University of Massachusetts Press.
Moore, G. 1982. *Zermelo's Axiom of Choice: Its Origins, Development, and Influence*. New York: Springer.
Morris, Charles. 1938/1971. "Foundations of the Theory of Signs." *International Encyclopaedia of Unified Science* I, No. 2. Chicago: The University of Chicago Press. Repr. in Charles Morris. *Writings on the General Theory of Signs*. Mouton, The Hague. Pp. 17-71.
——. 1946. *Signs, Language, and Behavior*. New York: Prentice-Hall.
Muoio, P. A. 1984. "Peirce on the Person." *Transactions of the Charles S. Peirce Society* 20:169ff.
Murphey, Murray G. 1961. *The Development of Peirce's Philosophy*. Cambridge: Harvard University Press.
Nadin, Mihai. 1983. "The Logic of Vagueness and the Category of Synechism." In *The Relevance of Charles Peirce*. Ed. Eugene Freeman. The Monist Library of Philosophy. La Salle, Ill.: Open Court. Pp. 154-66.
Niiniluoto, Ilkka. 1978. "Notes on Popper as Follower of Whewell and Peirce." *Ajatus* 37:272-327.
Noether, E. and J. Cavaillès, eds. 1937. *Briefwechsel Cantor-Dedekind*. Paris: Hermann.
Oehler, Klaus. 1979a. "Idee und Grundriss der Peirceschen Semiotik. *Semiotik* 1.
——. 1979b."Peirce's Foundation of a Semiotic Theory of Cognition." In *Studies in Peirce's Semiotics*. Ed. M. Fisch et al. Peirce Studies 1. Lubbock, Tex.: Institute for Studies of Pragmaticism. Pp. 67-76.
——. 1987. "A Transcendental Foundation of Semiotics?" *Transactions of the Charles S. Peirce Society* 23:45-63.
Orange, Donna M. 1984. *Peirce's Conception of God: A Developmental Study*. Lubbock, Tex.: Institute for Studies in Pragmaticism.
——, ed. 1988. "Introduction." *Charles S. Peirce: Naturordnung und Zeichenprozeß—Schriften der Semiotik und Naturphilosophie*. Aachen: Alano.
Osolsobe, Ivo. 1979. "On Ostensive Communication." *Studia Semiotyczne* 9:63-75.
Pape, Helmut. 1988. Introduction. *Charles S. Peirce: Natuordnung und*

Zeichenprozeß — Schriften über Semiotik und Naturphilosophie.
———. 1989. *Erfahrung und Wirklichkeit als Zeichenprozeß.* Frankfurt a. M.: Suhrkamp.
———, ed. 1983. *Phänomen und Logik der Zeichen.* Frankfurt a. M.: Suhrkamp.
Parsons, Charles. 1983. *Mathematics in Philosophy.* Ithaca: Cornell University Press.
Peacock, George. 1830. *A Treatise on Algebra.* Cambridge: J. and J. Deighton.
Peano, Giuseppe. 1888. *Calcolo geometrico secondo l'Ausdehnungslehre di H. Grassmann.* Turin: Bocca.
———. 1890. "Démonstration de l'intégrabilité des équations différentiales ordinaires." *Mathematische Annalen* 37:182–228.
———. 1957. *Opere scelte.* 2 vols. Rome: Edizioni Cremonese.
———. 1973. *Selected Works of Giuseppe Peano.* Toronto: University of Toronto Press.
Peirce, Benjamin Jr. 1870a. "Letter to Augustus De Morgan. 17 June 1870." Stored in *Linear Associative Algebra,* [De Morgan] L.2. [Peirce] fol. Secondary Strong Room, De Morgan Library, University of London Library.
———. 1870b. *Linear Associative Algebra.* Washington, D.C. The original lithographed work was printed, with addenda by B. and C. S. Peirce, in "Linear Associative Algebra," *American Journal of Mathematics* 4 (1881), 97–229.
———. 1881. "Linear Associative Algebra," *American Journal of Mathematics* 4:97–229.
Peirce, Charles Sanders. 1878. *Photometric Researches.* Leipzig: Engelmann.
———. 1881a. "On the Algebras in Which Division Is Unambiguous." *American Journal of Mathematics* 4:225–29.
———. 1881b. "On the Logic of Number." *American Journal of Mathematics* 4:85–95. Repr. in CP 3.252–288.
———. 1883. "The Logic of Relatives." In *Studies in Logic, by Members of The Johns Hopkins University.* Ed. C. S. Peirce, Boston: Little, Brown.
———. 1897. "The Logic of Relatives," *The Monist* 7:161–217. Repr. in CP 3.526.
———. 1929. "Guessing." *The Hound and Horn* 2(3):267–82.
———. 1931–1935. *The Collected Papers of Charles S. Peirce.* 8 vols. Ed. C. Hartshorne, P. Weiss, and A. Burks. Cambridge: Harvard University Press.
———. 1976a. *Complete Published Works, Including Secondary Materials.* Greenwich, Conn.: Johnson. Microfiche.

BIBLIOGRAPHY 433

———. 1976b. *The New Elements of Mathematics by Charles S. Peirce*. Ed. C. Eisele. The Hague: Mouton; Atlantic Highlands, N.J.: Humanities.
———. 1982. *Writings of Charles S. Peirce: A Chronological Edition*. I. 1857–1866. Bloomington: Indiana University Press.
———. 1984. *Writings of Charles S. Peirce: A Chronological Edition*. II. 1867–1871. Bloomington: Indiana University Press.
———. 1986a. *Writings of Charles S. Peirce: A Chronological Edition*. III. 1872–1878. Bloomington: Indiana University Press.
———. 1986b. *Writings of Charles S. Peirce: A Chronological Edition*. IV. 1879–1884. Bloomington: Indiana University Press.
———. 1992. *Reasoning and the Logic of Things: The 1898 Cambridge Conferences Lectures by Charles Sanders Peirce*. Ed. Kenneth Laine Ketner. Cambridge: Harvard University Press.
Plank, Franz. 1979. "Ikonisierung und De-Ikonisierung als Prinzip des Sprachwandels." *Sprachwissenschaft* 4:121–58.
Popper, Karl. 1944. *The Open Society and Its Enemies*. London: Routledge & Kegan Paul.
———. 1957. *The Poverty of Historicism*. London: Routledge & Kegan Paul.
———. 1959. *The Logic of Scientific Discovery*. New York: Basic Books.
Potter, Vincent G., S.J. 1967. *Charles S. Peirce on Norms and Ideals*. Amherst: University of Massachusetts Press.
Preziosi, Donald. 1989. *Rethinking Art History: Meditations on a Coy Science*. New Haven: Yale University Press.
Putnam, Hilary. 1973. "Meaning and Reference." *The Journal of Philosophy* 70(19):699–711.
———. 1975. "Mathematics Without Foundations." In *Mathematics, Matter and Method: Philosophical Papers of Hilary Putnam* I. Cambridge: Cambridge University Press.
———. 1981. *Reason, Truth, and History*. Cambridge: Cambridge University Press.
———. 1982. "Peirce the Logician." *Historia Mathematica* 9:290–301.
Pycior, Helena. 1979. "Benjamin Peirce's Linear Associative Algebra." *Isis* 70:537–51.
———. 1981. "George Peacock and the British Origins of Symbolical Algebra." *Historia Mathematica* 8:23–45.
———. 1984 "Internalism, Externalism, and Beyond: Nineteenth-Century British Algebra. *Historia Mathematica* 11:424–41.
———. 1987. "Mathematics and Philosophy: Wallis, Hobbes, Barrow, and Berkeley." *Journal of the History of Ideas* 48:265–86.
Quine, Willard van Orman. 1931. Rev of CP 2–3. *Mind* 51.
———. 1940. *Mathematical Logic*. Cambridge: Harvard University Press.
———. 1966. *Selected Logic Papers*. New York: Random House.

———. 1986. *Philosophy of Logic*. 2nd ed. Cambridge: Harvard University Press.
Ransdell, Joseph Morton. 1977. "Some Leading Ideas of Peirce's Semiotic." *Semiotica* 19.
———. 1986. Index. *Encyclopedic Dictionary of Semiotics* 1:340–41. Berlin: Mouton de Gruyter.
Reichenbach, Hans. 1938. *Experience and Prediction*. Chicago: The University of Chicago Press.
Reilly, Francis E., s.j. 1970. *Charles Peirce's Theory of Scientific Method*. The Orestes Brownson Series on Contemporary Thought and Affairs 7. New York: Fordham University Press.
Roberts, Don D. 1973. *The Existential Graphs of Charles S. Peirce*. The Hague: Mouton.
Robinson, Abraham. 1966. *Non-Standard Analysis*. Amsterdam: North Holland.
Rorty, Richard. 1982. *Consequences of Pragmatism*. Minneapolis: University of Minnesota Press.
Rosselli, Cosma. 1579. *Thesaurus artificiosae memoriae*. Venice: Paduanius.
Rossi, Paolo. 1961. *Clavis universalis: Arti della memoria e logica combinatoria da Lullo a Leibniz*. Milano: Ricciardi. 2d ed. Bologna: Mulino, 1983.
Russell, Bertrand. 1901. "Recent Work on the Principles of Mathematics." *The International Monthly* 4:83–101.
———. 1903. *The Principles of Mathematics*. Cambridge: Cambridge University Press.
———. 1905. "On Denoting." Repr. in *Bertrand Russell: Logic and Knowledge*. Ed. R. C. Marsh. London: Allen & Unwin, 1956.
———. 1907. "On Some Difficulties in the Theory of Transfinite Numbers and Order Types." *Proceedings of the London Mathematical Society* 4:29–53.
———. 1946/1969. "Foreword." In J. K. Feibleman. *An Introduction to the Philosophy of C. S. Peirce*. Cambridge: The MIT Press.
———. 1956. "The Philosophy of Logical Atomism." Repr. in *Bertrand Russell: Logic and Knowledge*. Ed. R. C. Marsh. New York: Macmillan.
———. 1959. *My Philosophical Development*. New York: Simon & Schuster.
Saarinen, Esa, ed. 1979. *Game-Theoretical Semantics*. Dordrecht: Reidel.
Saussure, Ferdinand de. 1960. *Cours de linguistique generale*. Ed. C. Bally et al. 5th ed. Paris: Payot.
Savan, David. 1977. "Questions Concerning Certain Classifications Claimed for Signs." *Semiotica* 19.
———. 1983. "Toward a Refutation of Semeiotic Idealism." *RS/SI* 3:1–8

Sayers, Dorothy L. 1932. *Have His Carcase*. London: Gollancz.
Schröder, Ernst. 1877. *Der Operationskreis des Logikkalküls*. Leipzig: Teubner.
——. 1880. Review of Frege's *Begriffsschrift*. *Zeitschrift für Mathematik und Physik* 25:81–94. In G. Frege. *Conceptual Notation and Related Articles*. Trans. T. Bynum. Oxford: Clarendon. Pp. 218–32.
——. 1890–1905. *Vorlesungen über die Algebra der Logik*. Vol. I 1890; Vol. II.1 1891; Vol. II.2 1905; Vol. III.1 1895. Leipzig: Teubner.
——. 1892. "Signs and Symbols." *The Open Court* 6:3431–44, 3463–66.
——. 1898. "Über zwei Definitionen der Endlichkeit und G. Cantor'sche Sätze." *Nova Acta Leopoldina* 71:303–36.
Schwartz, Stephen P., ed. 1977. *Naming, Necessity, and Natural Kinds*. Ithaca and London: Cornell University Press.
Searle, John R. 1969. *Speech Acts*. Cambridge: Cambridge University Press.
——. 1979. *Expression and Meaning*. Cambridge: Cambridge University Press.
Sebeok, Thomas A. 1976. "Iconicity." *Modern Language Notes* 91:1427–56.
——. 1977. *A Perfusion of Signs*. Bloomington: Indiana University Press.
——. 1980. *Charles S. Peirce und Sherlock Holmes*. Frankfurt: Suhrkamp.
——. 1981. *The Play of Musement*. Bloomington: Indiana University Press.
——. 1985. *Contributions to the Doctrine of Signs*. Lanham, Md.: University Press of America.
——. 1986. *I Think I Am A Verb*. New York: Plenum.
——. 1989. "Fetish." *American Journal of Semiotics* 6.
——. 1990. *Semiotics in the United States: The View from the Center*. Milano: Bompiani. [In Italian.]
——, and Umiker-Sebeok, Jean. 1979. "'You Know My Method': A Juxtaposition of Charles S. Peirce and Sherlock Holmes." *Semiotica* 26:203–50. Repr.in *The Sign of Three: Dupin, Holmes, Peirce*. Ed. Umberto Eco and Thomas Sebeok. Bloomington: Indiana University Press, 1983. Pp. 11–54.
Seidenfeld, T. 1979. *Philosophical Problems of Statistical Inference*. Dordrecht: Reidel.
Sfendoni-Mentzou, Demetra. 1980. *Probability and Chance in the Philosophy of C. S. Peirce*. Ph.d. Diss. University of Thessaloniki.
——. 1991. "A Potential-Pragmatic Account of C. S. Peirce's Theory of Truth." *Transactions of the Charles S. Peirce Society* 27:27–77.
——. 1993. "The Role of Potentiality in Peirce's Tychism and in Contemporary Discussions in Quantum Mechanics and

Microphysics." In *Charles S. Peirce and the Philosophy of Science.* Ed. E. C. Moore. Tuscaloosa: University of Alabama Press, 1993.
Shapiro, Michael. 1980. "The Structure of Meaning in Semiotic Perspective." In *Papers from the Fourth International Conference on Historical Linguistics.* Ed. E. Traugott et al. Amsterdam: Benjamins. Pp. 53–60.
———. 1981. "Peirce's Interpretant from the Perspective of Linguistic Theory." In *Proceedings of the C. S. Peirce Bicentennial International Congress.* Ed. Kenneth Ketner et al. Texas Tech University Graduate Studies 23. Lubbock: Texas Tech University Press. Pp. 313–18.
———. 1983. *The Sense of Grammar: Language as Semeiotic.* Bloomington: Indiana University Press.
Short, Thomas L. 1981a. "Peirce's Concept of Final Causation." *Transactions of the Charles S. Peirce Society* 17:369–82.
———. 1981b. "Semeiosis and Intentionality." *Transactions of the Charles S. Peirce Society* 17:197–223.
———. 1982. "Life Among the Legisigns." *Transactions of the Charles S. Peirce Society* 18:4:285–310.
Skagestad, Peter. 1979. "C. S. Peirce on Biological Evolution and Scientific Progress." *Synthèse* 41:85–114.
———. 1981. *The Road of Inquiry.* New York: Columbia University Press.
Skolem, Thoralf. 1970. *Selected Works in Logic.* Ed. J. E. Fenstad, Oslo: Universitetsforlaget.
Sluga, Hans. 1980. *Gottlob Frege.* London: Routledge & Kegan Paul.
———. 1987. "Frege Against the Booleans." *Notre Dame Journal of Formal Logic* 28:80–98.
Smith, John E. 1983. "Community and Reality." In *The Relevance of Charles Peirce.* Ed. Eugene Freeman. The Monist Library of Philosophy. La Salle, Ill.: Open Court. Pp. 59–77.
Sommers, Frederic. 1982. *The Logic of Natural Language.* Oxford: Clarendon.
Sonesson, Göran. 1989. *Pictorial Concepts: Inquiries into the Semiotic Heritage and Its Relevance for the Analysis of the Visual World.* Lund: University Press.
Stampe, Dennis W. 1979. "Towards a Causal Theory of Linguistic Representation." In *Contemporary Perspectives in the Philosophy of Language.* Ed. Peter A. French et al. Minneapolis: University of Minnesota Press. Pp. 81–102.
Stenius, Erik. 1964. *Wittgenstein's Tractatus: A Critical Exposition of the Main Lines of Thought.* Oxford: Blackwell.
Stent, G. S. 1972. "Prematurity and Uniqueness in Scientific

Discovery," *Scientific American* (December). Repr. in *Scientific Genius and Creativity*. Ed. Owen Gingerich. New York: Freeman, 1987. Pp. 95–104.

Styazhkin, N. I. 1969. *History of Mathematical Logic from Leibniz to Peano*. Cambridge: The MIT Press.

Tarski, Alfred. 1941. "On the Calculus of Relations." *Journal of Symbolic Logic* 6:73–89.

——, and Givant, S. 1987. *A Formalization of Set Theory Without Variables*. Providence: American Mathematical Society.

Tarwater, J. Dalton, White, J. T., and Miller, J. D., eds. 1976. *Men and Institutions in American Mathematics*. Lubbock: Texas Tech University Press.

Thackray, Arnold, and Merton, Robert K. 1975. "Sarton, George Alfred Léon," *Dictionary of Scientific Biography* 12:107–14.

Thibaud, Pierre. 1975. *La Logique de Charles Sanders Peirce: De l'algèbre aux graphes*. Aix-en-Provence: Éditions de l'Université de Provence.

Thiel, Christian. 1979. "From Leibniz to Frege: Mathematical Logic Between 1679 and 1879." *Proceedings of the Sixth Congress of Logic, Methodology, and Philosophy of Science*. Hannover. Pp. 755–70.

——. 1981. "A Portrait, or, How to Tell Frege from Schroeder." *History and Philosophy of Logic* 2:21–23.

Thom, René. 1973. "De l'icone au symbole." *Cahiers Internationaux de Symbolisme* 22–23:85–106.

——. 1980. "L'espace et les signes." *Semiotica* 29:193–208.

Trevarthen, Colwyn. 1990. "Signs Before Speech." *The Semiotic Web 1989*. Berlin: Mouton de Gruyter.

Uexkull, Thure von. 1989. "Jakob von Uexkull's Umwelt-Theory." *The Semiotic Web 1988*. Ed. Thomas A. Sebeok and Jean Umiker-Sebeok. Berlin and New York: Mouton de Gruyter. Pp. 129–58.

Vallery-Radot, Renée. 1902. *The Life of Pasteur*. Trans. R. L. Devonshire. London: Constable; New York: McClure, Phillips. Repr. New York: Garden City Publishing, 1933.

Venn, John. 1866. *The Logic of Chance: An Essay on the Foundations and Province of the Theory of Probability, with Special Reference to Its Application to Moral and Social Science*. London: Macmillan.

Vickers, John. 1980. "Truth, Consensus, and Probability: On Peirce's Definition of Scientific Truth. *Pacific Philosophical Quarterly* 61:183–203.

Weiss, Paul. 1934. "Peirce, Charles Sanders," *Dictionary of American Biography* 14:398–403.

Wells, Rulon. 1967. "Distinctively Human Semiotic." *Social Science*

Information 6(6):103-24.
Wennerberg, Hjalmar. 1961. *The Pragmatism of C. S. Peirce*. Lund: Gleerup.
Wheeler, John Archibald. 1988. "World as System Self-Synthesized by Quantum Networking." *IBM Journal of Research and Development* 32(1):1-15.
Whitehead, Alfred North. 1898. *A Treatise on Universal Algebra*. Cambridge: Cambridge University Press.
———. 1903. "The Logic of Relations, Logical Substitution Groups, and Cardinal Number." *American Journal of Mathematics* 25:157-78.
———, and Russell, Bertrand. 1910-1913. *Principia mathematica*. Cambridge: Cambridge University Press.
Wiener, Norbert. 1913. "A Comparison Between the Treatment of the Algebra of Relatives by Schroeder and That by Whitehead and Russell." PhD. Diss., Harvard College.
Wiener, P. P., and Young, F. H., eds. 1952. *Studies in the Philosophy of C. S. Peirce*. Cambridge: Harvard University Press.
Williams, Donald C. 1947. *The Ground of Induction*. Cambridge: Harvard University Press.
———. 1966. *Principles of Empirical Realism*. Springfield, Ill.: Thomas.
Wittgenstein, Ludwig Johann Joseph. 1958. *Philosophical Investigations*. 2nd ed. Oxford: Blackwell; New York: Macmillan.
Wright, G. H. von. 1957. *The Logical Problem of Induction*. Oxford: Blackwell.
Yates, F. Eugene. In press. "Microsemiosis." In *Semiotik: Ein Handbuch zu den zeichentheoretischen Grundlagen von Natur und Kultur*. Ed. Roland Posner, Klaus Robering, and Thomas A. Sebeok. Berlin: De Gruyter.
Yates, Frances. 1972. *The Art of Memory*. London: Routledge & Kegan Paul.
Zeman, J. Jay. 1974. "Peirce's Logical Graphs." *Semiotica* 12:239-256.
———. 1986. "Peirce's Philosophy of Logic." *Transactions of the Charles S. Peirce Society* 22:1-22.
———. 1988. "Peirce on the Indeterminate and on the Object: Initial Refections." *Grazer Philosophische Studien* 32:37-49.

LIST OF CONTRIBUTORS

KARL-OTTO APEL, Professor of Philosophy at the Johann Wolfgang Goethe-Universität, Frankfurt, is the author of many books, including *Towards a Transformation of Philosophy* (1980), *Charles Sanders Peirce: From Pragmatism to Pragmaticism* (1981), and *Towards a Transcendental Semiotics* (1994).

JOSEPH W. DAUBEN is Professor of History and History of Science at Herbert H. Lehman College of the City University of New York, and a member of the graduate faculty of the Ph.D. Program in History at the Graduate Center, CUNY, where he directs the Specialization in History of Science. He has served as editor of *Historia Mathematica* (1976-1986) and as Chairman of the International Commission on History of Mathematics (1986-1993). His books include *Georg Cantor: His Mathematics and Philosophy of the Infinite* (1979, 1990) and *Abraham Robinson: The Creation of Nonstandard Analysis, A Personal and Mathematical Odyssey*. In 1991 Professor Dauben was a visiting member of the Institute of History, National Tsing-Hua University, Taiwan, and he is currently at work on a critical, English edition of the *Ten Classics of Ancient Chinese Mathematics* with a team of scholars from Beijing, Singapore, and Taipei.

C. F. DELANEY is Professor of Philosophy at the University of Notre Dame and a past president of the Charles S. Peirce Society. He has been chair of the philosophy department at Notre Dame and is currently director of its Honors Program. His most recent book is *Science, Knowledge, and Mind: A Study in the Philosophy of C. S. Peirce* (1993).

RANDALL R. DIPERT is Professor of Philosophy at the State University of New York at Fredonia and at the United States Military Academy, West Point. He is the author of numerous articles on Peirce, logic, and the history of logic, including "Modern Logic" in the *Encyclopedia Britannica*, as well as on the history of philosophy, artificial intelligence, action theory, and aesthetics. He is co-author of *Logic: A Computer Approach* (1985) and the author of *Artifacts, Agency, and Art Works* (1993).

UMBERTO ECO is Professor of Semiotics at the University of Bologna and President of the Center for Semiotic and Cognitive Studies at the University of San Marino. Among his scholarly works which have been translated into English are *A Theory of Semiotics* (1976), *The Role of the Reader* (1979), *Semiotics and the Philosophy of Language* (1984), *The Limits of Interpretation* (1990), and *Six Walks in the Fictional Woods* (1994).

CAROLYN EISELE is Professor Emeritus of Mathematics at Hunter College in Manhattan. Her editions and essays on Peirce as a mathematician, scientist, and historian of science are widely known and admired. She holds an honorary doctorate of Humanities from Texas Tech University and from Lehigh University.

JÜRGEN HABERMAS is Professor of Philosophy at the University of Frankfurt am Main. From 1971 to 1982 he was Director of the Max Planck Institute.

CHARLES HARTSHORNE, Ashbel Smith Professor Emeritus of Philosophy at the University of Texas, Austin, is a Fellow of the American Academy of Arts and Sciences, and past president of the Charles S. Peirce Society (1950-1951) and the Society for the Philosophy of Religion (1963-1964). The co-editor of the *Collected Papers of Charles S. Peirce* (1931-1935), he has contributed countless articles to symposia and professional journals, and is the author of a number of books, among which are *Creative Synthesis and Philosophic Method* (1972), *A Natural Theology for Our Times* (1967), *Creativity in American Philosophy* (1984), and *The*

Darkness and the Light: A Philosopher Reflects on His Fortunate Career and Those Who Made It Possible (1990).

RISTO HILPINEN is Professor of Philosophy at the University of Turku (Finland) and at the University of Miami (Coral Gables, Florida). He has written articles on philosophical logic, epistemology, philosophy of science, the philosophy of C. S. Peirce, and the theory of norms and the foundations of ethics. He is a former editor of the journal *Synthèse*, and was from 1983 to 1991 the Secretary General of the International Union of History and Philosophy of Science, Division of Logic, Methodology, and Philosophy of Science. He is a member of the Institut International de Philosophie.

CHRISTOPHER HOOKWAY is Professor of Philosophy at the University of Birmingham. He has also taught at the University of Pittsburgh and spent a year as a Fulbright Scholar working on Peirce's manuscripts at Harvard. His publications include *Peirce* (1985), *Quine: Language, Experience, and Reality* (1988), and *Scepticism* (1990).

KENNETH LAINE KETNER is Charles Sanders Peirce Professor of Philosophy and Director of the Institute for Studies in Pragmaticism at Texas Tech University. He is a Fellow (past president) of the Charles S. Peirce Society, and author of a number of works on Peirce and related matters. He has also published several editions of Peirce's works.

ISAAC LEVI is John Dewey Professor of Philosophy at Columbia University. He is author of *Gambling with Truth, The Enterprise of Knowledge, Hard Choices*, and *The Fixation of Belief and Its Undoing*. Some of his essays are collected in *Decisions and Revisions*. The focus of his philosophical work has been on the elaboration of an account of inquiry where changes in point of view are justified by showing that they are optimal in the situation for given ends. The affinity of some of his ideas to the views of Peirce and Dewey explain his interest in their contributions.

KLAUS OEHLER, now Professor Emeritus, was Professor of Philosophy at the University of Hamburg from 1964 to 1990. In 1981 he was president of the Deutsche Gesellschaft für Semiotik; and in 1982, of the Charles S. Peirce Society. The author of books on ancient and medieval philosophy, pramatism, semiotics, and Peirce, he is a former member of the Institute for Advanced Study in Princeton.

VINCENT G. POTTER was Professor of Philosophy at Fordham University. A former president of the Charles S. Peirce Society, he served as consultant to the Peirce Edition at Indiana University. He was the author of *Charles S. Peirce: On Norms and Ideals* (1987) and *On Understanding Understanding* (1994), and the translator of John Pecham's *On the Eternity of the World* (1994) and Thomas Aquinas's *De malo* (forthcoming). From 1985 until his death, he served as editor of *International Philosophical Quarterly*.

HILARY W. PUTNAM is Walter Beverly Pearson Professor of Modern Mathematics and Mathematical Logic in the Department of Philosophy at Harvard University. He is a Fellow of the American Academy of Arts and Sciences and a Corresponding Fellow of the British Academy. His books include three volumes of *Philosophical Papers*; *Reason, Truth, and History*, and three recent volumes: *Renewing Philosophy*, *Realism with a Human Face*, and *Words and Life*.

HELENA M. PYCIOR is a professor of history at the University of Wisconsin-Milwaukee. Her articles on the history of algebra have appeared in *Historia Mathematica*, *Isis*, the *Journal of the History of Ideas*, and *Victorian Studies*. Her recent writing includes a book on the history of British albegra through 1750 (forthcoming).

W. V. QUINE is the Edgar Pierce Professor of Philosophy, Emeritus, at Harvard University. The author of many books on logic, he has held visiting appointments at Oxford, Tokyo, Sao Paolo, and the Institute for Advanced Study at Princeton.

List of Contributors

NICHOLAS RESCHER is University Professor of Philosophy at the University of Pittsburgh, where he has also served as Chairman of the Department of Philosophy and Director of the Center for Philosophy of Science. The author of more than sixty books in various areas of philosophy, for more than three decades he has been editor of the *American Philosophical Quarterly*.

DAVID SAVAN was Professor of Philosophy at the University of Toronto. He contributed numerous chapters and journal articles on Peirce and other topics in linguistics and semiotics.

THOMAS A. SEBEOK is Distinguished Professor of Linguistics and Semiotics, Emeritus, at Indiana University. He has held many visiting appointments in the United States and abroad. He has been the editor or editor-in-chief of several journals in linguistics and semiotics and the author of various books in these fields.

DEMETRA SFENDONI-MENTZOU is Associate Professor of the Philosophy of Science at the University of Thessaloniki. She has also taught at York University in Toronto and has been a Visiting Research Scholar in Philosophy at Oxford University and at Harvard University. Among her publications are *Probability and Chance in the Philosophy of C. S. Peirce* (1980), *The Pragmatic Philosophy of C. S. Peirce: "How to Make Our Ideas Clear"* (1984), and numerous articles.

MICHAEL SHAPIRO, whose main fields are Slavic linguistics and poetics, was a student of Roman Jakobson's at Harvard in the early 1960s. Professor of Slavic Languages at Brown University since 1989, he has also taught at the University of California (Los Angeles and Berkeley) and Princeton and has served as president of both the Charles S. Peirce Society (1991) and the Semiotic Society of America (1992-1993). Professor Shapiro is founder and editor of *The Peirce Seminar Papers: An Annual of Semiotic Analysis*.

PETER SKAGESTAD has taught philosophy at Williams College and at Trinity College, Hartford, and since 1982 has taught logic at the University of Massachusetts-Lowell. His books include *Making Sense of History* (1975) and *The Road of Inquiry: Charles Peirce's Pragmatic Realism* (1981). He is a frequent contributor to the *Journal of Social and Evolutionary Systems*.

JOSEPH S. ULLIAN is Professor of Philosophy at Washington University, where he has been on the faculty since 1965. He has written extensively on logic and linguistic philosophy, and he is co-author, with W. V. Quine, of *The Web of Belief*.